IDENTITY, CONFLICT AND POLITICS IN TURKEY, IRAN AND PAKISTAN

COMPARATIVE POLITICS
AND INTERNATIONAL STUDIES SERIES

Series editors, Christophe Jaffrelot and Alain Dieckhoff
Series managing editor, Miriam Perier

The series consists of original manuscripts and translations of noteworthy manuscripts and publications in the social sciences emanating from the foremost French researchers.

The focus of the series is the transformation of politics and society by transnational and domestic factors—globalisation, migration and religion. States are more permeable to external influence than ever before and this phenomenon is accelerating processes of social and political change the world over. In seeking to understand and interpret these transformations, this series gives priority to social trends from below as much as to the interventions of state and non-state actors.

GILLES DORRONSORO
OLIVIER GROJEAN
(*Editors*)

Identity, Conflict and Politics in Turkey, Iran and Pakistan

HURST & COMPANY, LONDON

First published in English in the United Kingdom in 2018 by
C. Hurst & Co. (Publishers) Ltd.,
41 Great Russell Street, London, WC1B 3PL
© Gilles Dorronsoro, Olivier Grojean and the Contributors, 2018
All rights reserved.
Printed in India

The right of Gilles Dorronsoro, Olivier Grojean and the Contributors to be identified as the authors of this publication is asserted by them in accordance with the Copyright, Designs and Patents Act, 1988.

A Cataloguing-in-Publication data record for this book is available from the British Library.

ISBN: 9781849043724

This book is printed using paper from registered sustainable and managed sources.

www.hurstpublishers.com

CONTENTS

CONTENTS

PART THREE

TRANSITIONS TO VIOLENCE

LIST OF ACRONYMS

AKP	Adalet ve Kalkınma Partisi (Justice and Development Party—Turkey)
BIFT	Bangalore Islamic Foundation Trust
BJP	Bharatiya Janata Party (Idian People's Party)
BLA	Baloch Liberation Army
BLF	Baloch Liberation Front
BLUF	Balochistan Liberation United Front
BNDP	Balochistan National Democratic Party
BNM	Baloch National Movement
BNP	Balochistan National Party
BPLF	Baloch People's Liberation Front
BRA	Baloch Republican Army
BRP	Baloch Republican Party
BSO	Baloch Student Organisation
BUITM	Baloch IT University
BWP	Baloch Women Panel
CHP	Cumhuriyet Halk Partisi (Republican People's Party—Turkey)
CLG	Communities and Local Government
DEHAP	Demokratik Halk Partisi (Democratic People's Party—Turkey)
DEP	Demokrasi Partisi (Democracy Party—Turkey)
DSP	Demokratik Sol Partisi (Democratic Left Party—Turkey)
DTP	Demokratik Toplum Partisi (Democratic Society Party—Turkey)
DYP	Doğru Yol Partisi (True Path Party—Turkey)
FC	Frontiers Corps
HADEP	Halkın Demokrasi Partisi (People's Democracy Party—Turkey)
HEP	Halkın Emek Partisi (People's Labor Party—Turkey)

LIST OF ACRONYMS

HUT	Hizb-ut Tahrir (Party of Liberation)
IT	University see BUITM
JI	Jama'at-i Islami (Islamic Congress party—India, Pakistan, Bangladesh)
JWP	Jamhoori Watan Party (Republican National Party—Balochistan, Pakistan)
KDPI	Partîya Demokrata Kurdistan—Iran (Kurdistan Democratic Party—Iran)
MHP	Milliyetçi Hareket Partisi (Nationalist Action Party—Turkey)
PIB	Punjabi Itehead Balochistan
PJAK	Partiya Jiyana Azad a Kurdistanê (Party of Free Life in Kurdistan)
PKK	Partiya Karkerên Kurdistan (Kurdistan Workers' Party)
SAVAK	Sa-zma-n-e Ettela-'a-t va Amniyat-e Keshvar (Organization of Intelligence and National Security—Iran)
SHP	Sosyaldemokrat Halkçı Partisi (Social Democratic Populist Party—Turkey)
TJ	Tablighi Jamaat (Society for Spreading Faith)

EDITORS AND CONTRIBUTORS

Editors

Gilles Dorronsoro is Professor of Political Science at the University Paris I—Panthéon Sorbonne. A prominent expert on contemporary Afghan politics, he has lectured throughout the world and has been a non-resident scholar at the Carnegie Endowment for International Peace. He is the author of *Revolution Unending: Afghanistan, 1979 to the Present* (London: Hurst, 2005). Co-founder of the *European Journal of Turkish Studies* and the *South Asia Multidisciplinary Academic Journal* (*SAMAJ*).

Olivier Grojean obtained his PhD in sociology from the French École des Hautes Etudes en Sciences Sociales (EHESS, Paris) and is currently Senior lecturer in political science at Université Paris 1—Panthéon Sorbonne, a fellow of CESSP-CRPS. He was previously in charge of the CNRS "International Relations" chair at Aix-Marseille-University (CERIC). He is the author of *La révolution kurde. Le PKK et la fabrique d'une utopie* (Paris: La Découverte, 2017).

Contributors

Luc Bellon is an independent researcher in anthropology, a documentary-maker and Head of Mission at Handicap International.

Amélie Blom is a political scientist at the Center for the Study of India and South Asia (CEIAS-EHESS, Paris). Her PhD research focuses on jihadism in Pakistan. Amélie is the co-editor (with Laetitia Bucaille and Luis Martinez) of *The Enigma of Islamist Violence* (London: Hurst, 2007).

EDITORS AND CONTRIBUTORS

Hamit Bozarslan is a historian and a political scientist at CETOBAC-EHESS, France, specializing in the study of the Middle East—particularly Turkey, Kurds, and violence—through a historical- and political-sociological approach. His recent publications include *Révolution et état de violence. Moyen Orient 2011–2015* (Paris: CNRS Editions).

Christian Bromberger is Emeritus Professor of Anthropology at Aix-Marseille Université, former director of the Institut Français de Recherche in Iran. He is the author of several works on Iran and on football, his other research interest.

Benoît Fliche is an anthropologist and researcher at Aix-Marseille Université (Institut d'Ethnologie Méditerranéenne, Européenne et Comparative). He is the author of *Odyssées Turques: Les migrations d'un village anatolien* (Paris: CNRS Editions, 2007).

Laurent Gayer earned his PhD in political science from Sciences Po in 2004. CNRS Assistant Research Professor with tenure at Sciences Po CERI, Gayer specializes in the Indian sub-continent, and more particularly in the study of urban dynamics and violent mobilisations in India and Pakistan. His recent publications include *Karachi: Ordered Disorder and the Struggle for the City* (London: Hurst, 2014).

Elise Massicard holds degrees in Political Science (Sciences Po), Turkish Studies (INALCO) and Social Sciences (Freie Universität Berlin); she presented her thesis in Political Science to Sciences Po in 2002. CNRS Research Professor, she is currently based at the Center for International Studies (CERI-Sciences Po). She works on the political sociology of Turkey, mobilizations, the politics of identity and political territoriality.

Aminah Mohammad-Arif explores the evolution of Islam in minority and in diaspora among South Asians. She is particularly interested in the individualization process, a fairly significant indicator of the transformation of local societies, the inter-linkage between ethics and emotions, and the relations of "born-again" young Muslims with the Other. Another focus of her current research is on the deconstruction of "South Asia" as a geographic and political category. Her publications include *Salam America: L'islam Indien en Diaspora* (Paris: CNRS Editions, 2000).

Chirine Mohséni is an independent researcher in ethnology.

Christine Moliner is a PhD candidate at the Center for the Study of India and South Asia (EHESS-CEIAS), Paris. Her doctoral research has focused on the production of identity narratives in the British Sikh Diaspora, on the tension between a normative, orthodox definition of Sikh identity (in line with that imposed by the Singh Sabha), and actual practices. In that respect, caste has been her major area of investigation (negation vs. reinvention of caste in the Diaspora).

Gilles Riaux is a specialist on the ethnic issue in Iran and a researcher in political science at the French Ministry of Defence's "Institute for Strategic Studies" (IRSEM) and a Research Associate at CETOBAC. His main publications include *Ethnicité et nationalisme en Iran: La cause azerbaïdjanaise* (Paris: Karthala, 2012).

Clémence Scalbert-Yücel is a senior lecturer in Ethno-politics at the University of Exeter, within the Institute of Arab and Islamic Studies. Her research interests broadly lie in the interplays between ethnicity (ethnogenesis, ethnic mobilisation, ethnic conflict) and the fields of cultural production and development. Her main publications include *Langue, Littérature et engagement: Le champ litteraire kurde en Turquie, 1980–2010* (Paris: Petra, 2014).

INTRODUCTION

IDENTITY, HIERARCHY, AND MOBILIZATION

Gilles Dorronsoro and Olivier Grojean[1]
Translated by Adrian Morfee

Whilst there is always an identity-based dimension to collective action,[2] defining a conflict as "ethnic" or "religious" runs the risk of becoming an unbridled exercise in labeling. The choice of descriptive categories is, in fact, both an "emic" and an "etic" undertaking,[3] involving the development of an explanatory model and the building up of a description of events by the actors. Furthermore, the label "identity-based" is in competition with other interpretive frameworks such as "fanaticism", "terrorism", "cultural backwardness", and "manipulation by foreigners" for instance,[4] and this despite the fact that the actors tend to be motivated by multiple and ambiguous factors. It is worth remembering that the slew of publications on the emergence of "new types of conflicts", mainly in reference to Huntington's "clash of civilisations"[5] turned out to be a somewhat illusory phenomenon caused largely by ideological presuppositions. Even attempts to classify ethnicities have been criticized as reflecting the prejudices and interests of the colonizers (Amselle and M'Bokolo, 1985). Lastly, it is hard to pinpoint any specificity of identity-based conflicts with regard to their duration and eventual resolution

1

(Wucherpfennig, Metternich, Cederman, Gleditsch, 2012). Bruce Gilley, following the lead of others, therefore suggests that we abandon the concept of "ethnic conflict" as being too bound up with non-scientific agendas and as tending to fluctuate between post-modern vagueness and statistical hyper-empiricism (Gilley, 2004). Is an identity-based approach linked to ethnicity or religion simply a bad way to go about apprehending conflict?

Before declaring its irrelevance, we need to understand the centrality of identity in certain societies. Starting from the hypothesis that identity is a specific form of capital, it follows that multi-identity contexts necessarily come with differences, with a hierarchy—, and hence by definition, with a certain degree of hostility. These "differentiation conflicts" are characterized by the construction and the mobilization of cultural, religious or ethnic differences within contentious interactions. Furthermore, the state plays a central role in organizing the differential access to resources, with state institutions often being the main target of demands, rather than other groups. In addition, there are many different forms of conflict other than armed confrontation (Féron and Hastings, 2002). With regard to the widely differing forms of religious and ethnic conflict, we made the methodological decision not to limit the research to violent conflict.[6]

We can now reformulate our initial question as follows: how are "differentiation conflicts" transformed and redefined? We concentrate on certain moments and passages that have given rise to multidimensional reconfigurations: semantic fractures, the emergence of collective actors, and the recourse to violence. The rapid transformation of identity hierarchies is due to political fractures, social economic transformations, and the emergence of new regimes of subjectification. These contexts enable entrepreneurs of collective action to play on those identity differences which serve to help expand the scale of mobilization, and to align local and national conflicts. Lastly, violence does not result from a failed upsurge in mobilization (Tarrow, 1989, p. 70; Della Porta, 1995, pp. 50 and f.), and does not necessarily imply the stigmatization of those having recourse to it. On the contrary, violence can become autonomous in certain contexts, and serve to prime collective action and transform the relations between communities, where it is the victims who undergo stigmatization.

We have tested these hypotheses on three fields: Turkey, Iran, and Pakistan, while also observing the transnational recompositions of the Pakistani fieldwork via the Indo-Pakistani diaspora in the United-Kingdom. The political regimes of Turkey, Pakistan, and Iran are characterized by authoritarian forms in which political participation is historically limited by the weight of the army (Turkey until very recently, Pakistan) or of religious leaders (Iran). Additionally, the experience of foreign domination including colonialism (in Pakistan) and the international support to this or that ethnic or religious group have determined the legitimacy of minority identities. Moreover, the ethnic and religious dimensions of identity compete with class and gender as principles shaping the everyday organization and classification of individuals, both in practical and, frequently, legal terms. Religious and ethnic affiliations thus play a role in numerous social practices ranging from marriage to professional activity. Religious allegiance generally has legal consequences, for instance, being indicated on identity cards (as was the case until recently in Turkey) and establishing different electoral colleges, as well as being a constitutional principle in Iran and Pakistan.[7] The political agenda reflects how important these questions are, and collective action is based partly on defending community interests. Furthermore, identity movements are not the expression of some periphery that has been mobilized during a transitional period before acceding to a class-based social structure (Nagel and Olzak, 1982). Such modes of social perception and organization, far from being some historically regressive form, as might appear to be the case from a Marxist or developmental perspective, are not on the decline, and in Turkey are becoming ever more present. The increasing tension between Sunnis and Shi'ites is indicative of how important such divisions are. Although all the studies are based on non-Western fieldwork, there is no reason to think that a similar logic of communitization is not at work within European societies (Amselle, 2011). A strong institutional structure makes it possible to express differences in multi-community systems without establishing any hierarchy between them. The weakening of class bonds and the undermining of regulatory apparatus—the law and public policy—are therefore tending as a matter of course to align European societies with more community-based models of organization.

In addition, the presence of long-term armed conflicts is something the three areas under study (Iran, Pakistan, and Turkey) have in common. One of the major justifications for the political role of the army in Turkey has been the existence of a Kurdish separatist threat. Conflicts arising from the multi-ethnic nature of Pakistani society lie behind the progressive militarization of the regime and the Islamicization being driven by the state itself, resulting in sectarian violence aimed mainly at non-Sunnis. Ethnic and religious minorities in Iran, particularly the Kurds and the Baloch, are perceived as a threat, and recent events there have shown how there is a very real possibility of violence erupting. Armed confrontations are sometimes only a limited dimension—yet tragic and spectacular—of a much wider disagreement. Other types of conflict coexist alongside armed confrontation (or have no direct links with them) and they do not necessarily affect the same groups. Conflict can take the form of friction, vilification, public protest, and electoral struggle occurring at the local, regional, and sometimes transnational levels, and mobilizing individuals and groups operating both independently or as part of an organization.

Beyond their similarities, these countries differ by the trajectories of their state and by the way they deal with their minorities. Two types of institutional structures are represented here: federal, in Pakistan and strictly unitary in Turkey and Iran. None of these two systems has been able to prevent violence—which is in itself very telling—but the issues at stake during conflicts are partly linked to the forms of administrative organization. The two centralized states manage their territory in an analogous way: integrated and homogeneous, tolerating no subordinate judicial status. The prefect, who represents the central state, is the superior authority of each province (Iran) or department (Turkey). There is therefore no specific representation of localities at the state level. In Turkey, any local interest is rapidly considered *bölgecilik* (a negative term for regionalism), if not separatism. In Pakistan, however, the centralizing politics of the state has been incapable of putting an end to the patchwork of territorial statuses and to the overlapping of competing political authorities: federal capital, provinces, tribal agencies on the Afghan border, disputed territory (Kashmir), confinements, municipalities, governors, and provincial prime ministers. Paramilitary forces monitoring the borders generally include a fixed percentage of the main local group These specific forms of the state contribute to explaining the great variation of policies concerning minorities. Yet the pervasiveness of the administrative apparatus, combined with efforts to create a national feeling, trigger the mobilizations of minority groups.

The Specificities of Identity Capital

It is almost impossible to summarize the literature on identity, and the term has by now become a notion—or a language-game—more than a concept (Brubaker and Cooper, 2000). Following on from work by Barth (Barth, 1969),[8] identity is thought of as a boundary rather than a territory, and a set of differences replaces ticking off some list of criteria. Consequently the idea of "objectively" small gaps is irrelevant when seeking to understand the mechanisms of differentiation. Nevertheless, this constructivist approach does not imply that identity is something that may be freely redefined by elites cynically exploiting a form of rationality shorn of the values and perceptions specific to their group. The emergence of new identities is bound up with contexts of social transformation, especially migration, which severely curtails the scope for the short-term reinventing of identities.[9] Equally, the differentiation criteria—the "content" of identity, such as the color of the skin, the phenotype, the body *hexis*, practices, and beliefs—are of intrinsic importance since they induce the possibility (or not) of dissimulating identity, strict hereditary definitions, or interbreeding, the emergence of a specialized group deciding on who belongs to that group or on the contrary the fluidity of affiliations. All these elements help explain the internal dynamics of construction and the rationales of differentiation.

Certain distinctions are particularly useful for our perspective. Firstly, allegiance to a group—of varying degrees of institutionalization and possibly with a territorial dimension too—is different from the (self-) assignment to an abstract category such as "Muslim" or "Pathan", say. Secondly, assigned identity and subjective identity do not necessarily coincide (Digard, 1988). Alevis and Shi'ites see themselves as Muslims, a view which is not shared by certain Sunnis. What is the identity of a Pathan who does not comply with tribal norms? Furthermore, criteria and markers are sometimes ambiguous, and the importance of what is at stake can explain individual and collective strategies to (re) define their identity or that of the other. From this perspective, the issue of the phenotypes associated to identities is crucial.[10] When it is possible to conceal the fact of belonging to a group, the individual is able to choose (to a relatively large extent) his or her identity strategy. In our areas of study, classification tends not to relate to skin color—the issues of body *hexis* and of language are more ambiguous—and so can be "forgotten" depending upon the context. In Turkey, the Alevis (a heterodox minority of Islam) have strategies to dissimulate their identity, especially in towns. In certain cases, identities can become dormant or disappear as they no longer enable people to mobilize resources or else become too problematic, especially in the event of internal migration if there is no spatial structuring of the newly arrived groups.[11]

Lastly, rather than speaking of a single identity it would be more appropriate to speak of an identity system given that individuals are caught up in a network of different allegiances that only partially overlap and which are related to different spheres (such as religion, macro-ethnicity, tribe, and territory). These levels interact in complex ways, which is the reason why we consider religious and ethnic groups together as these two categories can sometimes be difficult to analyze separately.[12] Another factor making religious allegiance somewhat confusing is that it is in fact hereditary. In certain cases, religious and ethnic differences are mutually reinforcing to the extent where religious allegiance determines membership of the ethnic group. Ethnic minorities in Iran are mainly Sunnis, which reinforces the difference with the Persian-speaking Shi'ites; the Hazara of Baluchistan are Shi'ite by definition. In other cases one category or another may prevail within movements: Alevi Kurds do not play as great a part in collective action as Sunni Kurds do. If there are numerous links between ethnic and religious identity, the most extreme cases of rejection relate to religious identity. For example Shi'ite Pathan tribes are subject to constant pressure from their Sunni neighbours, to such an extent that they would have disappeared without the (partial) protection of the state; the 1984 Blasphemy Laws which passed under the Zia ul-Haq regime openly discriminate against the Ahmadis (a religious sect), a phenomenon also found in Iran for the Bahá'i religion. The current strategy of Pakistani fundamentalist Sunni Ulema is to have Shi'ites declared non-Muslims, leading to their civil death. In these cases the aim is to eliminate a group by obliging it to go into exile or else to convert.

Identity and Hierarchy

What are the relationships between identity and group hierarchy? Identity classification is one of a larger set of processes that attribute individuals in the same class (in the logical sense of the term) with certain characteristics. Whilst there would appear to be certain universal characteristics to the cognitive processes underlying these operations (such as resistance to change, their activation mechanisms, and the fact of occurring subconsciously) (Brubaker, Loveman, Stamatov, 2004; J.Gil-White, 2001), the content of the categories is composed of historical constructs. The functioning of differences between groups and the reproduction of these differences necessarily involve a certain degree of hostility, generally relating to the marriage market, symbolic places, and economic exchange. Cultural traits are promoted to the status of identity markers, thus helping to plot out the boundary between "them" and "us". Matters relating to food preparation, hygiene, and sexuality are generally deployed to denigrate the other as part of a general logic of group classification and hierarchy. Linguistic and physical interaction between members of different groups serves both to mark the boundaries of the group and to build up a mental construct of the other. In the religious sphere differences tend to be harder to ignore than in the case of ethnicity, due simply to the absence of any equivalent of intermarriage (interreligious marriages are rare in the fields we study),[13] and they construct a devaluation of the Other who is, generally, said to be destined to hell. These differences between, say, an Alevi and a Sunni, or a Christian and a Muslim are something that can be put into words—they are intellectual constructs whose principles are fundamentally non-negotiable.[14] The relations of recognition that build up around donations, especially during religious festivals, produce harmony, a necessary condition of which is the strict maintenance of boundaries between groups (Kanafani-Zahar, 2000).

The differences and inequalities, which are built up in this way, are naturalized in a popular anthropology, producing "general statements about the human groups present, their nature, and their behavior" (Centlivres, 1980, p. 29).[15] Stigmatizing visions of the Other are still powerful in Pakistan, where they were inherited from the colonial and pre-colonial periods. Oppositions between the men of the plains and those from the mountains, between a "warrior race" and an "effeminate race" feed into the stereotype of the Balochs (wild and backward), the Pashtuns (warriors, but effeminate), the Kashmiris (pacifists hence cowardly), the Sindhi (unreliable as Hinduized), and the Punjabis (hard-working and cunning). In Iran the stigmatization of the peripheral populations also conforms to a standardized pattern: Azeri Turks (simple-minded and sturdy), Gilanis (effeminate), and Arabs (violent). Lastly in Turkey, the Kurds are "primitive", "less civilized" and often seen as making up the working classes in the large towns in the west of the country. We may observe here the frequently discussed link between class and "race", which is related to a naturalization of social classes. These mental constructs are associated with an internal Orientalism reproducing the East-West relationships as described by Edward Saïd (Saïd, 1978; Pouillon and Vatin, 2011).

Is this naturalized hierarchy of the same order as the symbolic violence performed by states, known to play a key role in the formation of thought patterns (Bourdieu, 2015)? The answer differs from one country to the next, and it is necessary to specify the limits encountered by the states in imposing classificatory categories as well as those that non-state actors run up against in producing alternative frameworks. Firstly, the articles in this volume show that the role of the state in defining the relative value of various capitals, and as a relevant framework for conflicts, is in fact frequently contested. Rather than seeing these differences as being due to some provisional form of incompletion or (illusory) difference related to Islam, we emphasize the conditions that forbid states from monopolizing the definition of categories. In particular, and this is not specific to our areas of study, a state—that is to say a network of institutions—can pursue contradictory policies (partial recognition and discrimination for example). Furthermore, if the society is clearly divided on ethnic or religious grounds, two symbolic systems or local memories at least may be in competition (Todd, 2005). Lastly, migrations and the resources available abroad facilitate the emergence of alternative arenas, one example being the recognition and definition of Kurdish identity. A good illustration of these dynamics is the emergence of a remote form of identification via media such as the Internet between an individual and an abstract community (for example the *umma*) which, without any direct experience of discrimination, can lead on to violent action.

On the other hand, simply perceiving the increasing freedom of expression—and, as an inseparable part of this, the increasing significance of private enterprise—as fundamentally bringing into question dominant representations would amount to falling into the opposite illusion to that of state omnipotence. In a previous collective volume about Turkey we have shown how the discourse of protest frequently draws on state categories (Dorronsoro, 2005, and in particular the chapter by Grojean, pp. 167–182). Although "civil society" is central to the justification of media discourse, the categories it promotes are largely those of state institutions, especially if we distinguish between the principle on which the hierarchy is based and the stereotypes. In fact, the state still plays an important role in the establishment of a hierarchy via the imposition of classifications used in school history and more generally in official history, as well as by dividing up the territory into administrative units, cartography, and population censuses.

Access to Resources

The strong emotional charge that accompanies a (perceived) threat against group identity may be interpreted as following a logic of honor (Bourdieu, 1990, pp. 118 and f.) relating to a larger category than that of the family outside highly integrated societies. Identity therefore has the social properties of capital and may be used in many different ways. Why is identity capital a particularly strategic resource? Identities (be they regional, ethnic, or local) are not merely principles of social and territorial affiliation—not just categories of ethnographic description and popular perception. They are also allegiances signaling a rank in the access to various resources in the context of rivalry or unequal cooperation between groups. How is this differential access to resources organized?

Some processes are based on individuals' or families' micro-decisions. The psychosocial and ethnographic literature on this issue shows that categorization and internal group dynamics automatically give rise to discrimination as, even if there is no open conflict, individuals' decisions are naturally biased towards their allegiance group (Tajfel and Turner, 1985). Robert Bates (Bates, 1983)[16] for instance describes the market process, which leads to discrimination via the attribution of ethnic skills to an entire group. Furthermore, multi-ethnic societies are often organized in accordance with the principle of economic complementarity,[17] though this idea is far from being contrary to that of hierarchy. Indirect and often implicit discrimination fashions the hierarchy between groups, especially due to their capacity to accumulate capitals, and tends as a matter of course to augment initial gaps, which were sometimes minute. Micro-decisions can also be the far more direct expression of informal yet binding norms. For instance affiliation to a group tends to define a marriage market as a matter of course: in Pakistan there are virtually no interethnic marriages, and marriages between Alevis and Sunnis in central Anatolia are rare.

The role of the state is all the more significant as public policy plays a role in producing and reproducing the hierarchy. Among the various resources that the state controls, at least partially, figure infrastructure investment, public sector employment, property deeds in rural areas, and rights of nomads on pastoral land. The level of state investment varies depending upon the regions, depending in particular on the ability of groups to win recognition from the center. In Iran, for example, a hierarchy may be made out running from the Persians of the central plateau, to the Balochs and Kurds, with each group being assigned a position relative to the others (Aghajanian, 1983).[18] The state can settle ethnic groups in certain regions for instance, or manipulate property deeds so as to benefit one particular group. In certain cases the state makes public investment in an Alevi village dependent upon building a mosque. Similarly, state policies in host countries play an essential role in transforming conflicts amongst the diaspora as they establish a hierarchy between different migrants' access to state resources as a function of their community allegiance.

Certain public policies relating to territorial and cultural issues are of greater interest for identity differences.

Thus the division of the territory into administrative units frequently seeks to counter or even override the distribution of populations and groups, making it more difficult for them to conduct collective negotiations with institutions and, as an end result, to gain access to resources. This can extend to place names. In Iran, the prefect, who represents the central state, and Imam Jom'e, representing the locality, are the two superior authorities in each province. Whilst most provinces are named after the main town, some are named on the basis of the majority ethnicity living there (Baluchistan, Kurdistan, Azerbaijan) yet, symptomatically, these divisions never correspond to the territory actually occupied by these populations. In Pakistan the redrawing of administrative boundaries is always a very sensitive issue, often giving rise to riots. Here, however, the boundaries and denomination of administrative entities does accommodate local references, which is never the case in Turkey where changes in place names, which were fairly frequent during the Republican period, display a certain number of recurrent features, such as Turkification, naturalization, and neutralization. The administrative districts do not correspond to any pre-existing economic area or any cultural, linguistic, or religious units. Hence there are virtually no names designating a portion of the territory on the basis of natural, historical, economic, or other criteria, with the districts simply being named after the provincial capital. Equally, the regional level appears arbitrary and does not correspond to any pre-existing reality. Thus the EU alignment process entails the setting up of regional entities so as to benefit from structural funds, but those that have been created have deliberately ignored human and linguistic boundaries. As a matter of principle the majority Kurd region has not been endowed with any territorial form for fear of a shift to federalism.

Certain forms of particularism are tolerated and encouraged even by institutions via a process of "folklorisation", with the USSR still acting as the model here. The Islamic Republic recognizes the cultural diversity of the country in its school textbooks, ethnographic museums, and in its publishing policy, whilst at the same time limiting any expression of this diversity to the most conventional of forms. Numerous associations have been set up over the past few years to promote regional languages, history, and cultures via numerous journals and conferences. In Pakistan, too, whilst the state accepts cultural diversity, it tends to rigidify the representation of ethnic communities as in certain museums where cultural diversity is presented via waxwork dummies with highly typical facial characteristics and old-fashioned clothing. Until recently Turkey forbade the use of any language other than Turkish and it still displays a certain distrust of non-Turkish cultural expression.

Three Ways in which Hierarchies are Transformed

The rapid and even brutal transformation of identity hierarchies, a common feature in the countries studied here, is based on three dynamics: a revolution in which the center redefines the reference identity, socio-economic transformations increasing the level of interaction and competition, and moral shocks or changes to the regimes of subjectification.

The brutal denaturalization of group hierarchies occurs when the state instigates a new relative value of religious or ethnic identities in the aftermath of a revolution. In Iran, for example, the fact of being Sunni or Shi'ite is of different value depending upon the political regimes, as is ethnicity. The identity of the Turks depreciated with the establishment of the Republican regime, when the great Turkish dynasties lost their privileged relationship to the state. The Iranian revolution, on the contrary, brought about an increased freedom for formulating demands, as a different relationship to ethnicity opened up new perspectives for leaders of movements. In Pakistan the policy of shariatization and the outlawing of the Ahmadis is an illustration of this phenomenon. In the 1920s the Republic of Turkey eliminated, in principle, religious reference in favor of Turkish-ness, which devalued the identity of non-Turkish Muslims.

Migrations, rural exodus, and the redefinition (rather than the disappearance) of ethnic skills in industrialized modes of production all transform the value of identities. Rather than diminishing tensions, modernity actually accentuates them due to the greater level of contact in large multi-ethnic cities, as well as the competition on the labor market. There are more frequent interactions due to urbanization and migration, and the model of spatial and economic complementarity is not easily reproduced in towns. Internal migration in particular transforms relationships between groups, with some previously majority groups becoming minority ones. Migrant Kurdish populations in western Turkey, for example, have become an urban working class or a rural working-class for seasonal harvests. These tensions can become explosive, as illustrated by the pressure exerted on the Muhajir by Pashtuns and Punjabis, which caused the bloody revolt that set Karachi alight in the 1990s.

Lastly, the shift from the left-wing "revolutionary idea" to Islamism brings with it new regimes of subjectification, placing religious identities at the center of the political stage and of individuals' identifications, as is the case for example with the figure of the Mudjahid. Equally, exceptional events produce moral shocks, which facilitate mobilization (Jasper, 1997). These can be defining events for a generation, enabling collective actors to build up and continue to operate over time, an example of an "event" becoming a "structure". These events can also constitute unforeseeable hiatuses in normal causality, moments of fluidity in which anodyne causes can have significant consequences (Sewell, 1994; Bessin, Bidard and Grosseti, 2009).[19] For example, the riots in Maraş (in southern Turkey) in late 1978 had a considerable impact on Turkish politics.[20] A few years later, in July 1993, the torching of a hotel in Sivas by an Islamist crowd, in which forty or so intellectuals were burnt alive, had a major impact on Alevist mobilization in the 1990s.

The Emergence of Collective Actors

The context of rapid transformation of identity hierarchies makes it easier for the organizers of social movements to act. Two factors would appear to be decisive here: the degree of integration of elites from the periphery, and the advantages derived by movement leaders from playing on identity issues.

The very existence of elites involved in identity movements is indispensable to their trajectory and degree of integration in the political system. Elites with significant cultural capital tend to be integrated in the political system, whereas those with more "local" capital have been involved in setting up the rights movement. This analysis may also be applied to the Kurds in Turkey, where the local middle classes are more or less integrated. It is, however, those with cultural capital (especially due to their educational attainments) as well as with limited degrees of social or economic capital, who have been active in calling for identity rights.

Let us now turn to the question of the advantages of an ethnic movement from the point of view of its leaders, given that attempts to mobilize people around identity issues run up against institutional mechanisms and state strategies seeking to curb them—both repression and integration. Our hypothesis is that the material and cognitive resources available to leaders of movements (including those outside the national territory) encourage the emergence of movements, which in return gives greater impetus to protests against existing hierarchies.[21] Even the framework itself is perhaps determined by those seemingly usable resources, with the leaders ethnicizing the conflict as a result of them (Brubaker and Laitin, 1998, p. 425). In practice there is a shift from demands in universal terms to group-specific ones, and only exceptionally the other way round. This exploitation of identity issues has an influence on the movements concerned. The objectives and ideology shift, the recruitment of people becomes more homogenous, and it becomes impossible to return to a non-identity movement as a result of the way the group in question is perceived by other groups. It would appear that there are two important elements explaining the comparative advantages of an identity movement: this partially avoids the free rider paradox and gives greater fluidity to the demands being put forward.

Firstly, using identity issues can make it possible to limit the number of defections and acquire a monopoly over representation. Individuals become the targets of the conflict independently of whether or not they were part of the movement beforehand. For example, not all Alevis are left-wing, but the 1970s stereotype which saw them as being so (as well as being atheist) have shaped their political allegiances. The strategic use of violence by the Turkish extreme right has sought, predictably enough, to reinforce community boundaries so as to facilitate movements (Gourisse, 2010). Moreover, any humiliation and/or violence undergone by a member are perceived by the whole group, and this encourages the movement—Oberschall uses here the concept of a "multiplier effect" (Oberschall, 2007). The mechanism of "bounded solidarity" makes it possible to move beyond the free rider paradox via the formation of social capital.[22] The other mechanism is "enforceable trust", which guarantees transactions and thereby diminishes their cost. What is the relationship between closeness of a group and mobilization? The concept of "internal colonialism" (Hechter, 1975) implies that limiting a movement along ethnic lines makes it possible to mobilize the group more easily. To this extent legal discrimination encourages the movement, whilst the absence of any (legal) discrimination acts as a brake on it (Marx, 1998). However, the opposite argument, that contact increases conflicts and hence the scope for mobilization (Hannan, 1979), would appear to hold good in the fields studied here. Lastly, the resources available for ethnic movements in other countries increase with the presence of diasporas, with what John Meyer refers to as the "world polity" acting as a spur to ethnic movements (Meyer, 1987).[23]

Secondly, identity issues have a specific feature useful to the leaders of movements: their plasticity regarding both content and the potential demands formulated. These may be related to the cultural, religious, or political fields either in turn or simultaneously, making it possible to exploit legal constraints and, more fundamentally, mobilize people from different social sectors. Thus depending upon how closed the political system is, cultural or religious associations start putting forward larger demands and they eventually become political movements.

Interrelated Scales

Three mechanisms by which conflicts spread can transform them. Conflicts may spread by cascade,[24] by a local conflict aligning itself on a national conflict or, alternatively, by a local conflict spreading to a greater level (Sahlins, 2005). As a movement is expanding, the local reinterpretation of a more general conflict can draw on the relevant aspects of the collective memory and thus help it spread. For example, as Fredrick Bailey shows (Bailey, 1996), Croat society in 1983 was multicultural. Ethnicity was something people joked about, and there were was a large number of mixed marriages. But the war led to the dissolution of the community, including marriages. It thus overrode the local context. We find this too in our areas of study, for example in the case of Azeri-Kurd conflicts which only make sense within the political context of Iran, and Alevi-Sunni tensions in Turkey against the backdrop of the confrontation between left and right in the 1970s. This alignment of local conflicts on overarching rationales produces a transformation in the meaning of the conflict and, generally, of the forms it takes.

However, if the spread of conflict is often related to interrelating scales, the very complexity of the local in terms of the configuration of actors and identities also acts as a brake to identity movements. The local hierarchies are not necessarily the same as those found at the national level, which can complicate the establishment of an agenda. Firstly, the multiple levels of identification (local, macro-ethnic, and regional solidarities) give rise to various forms of competition.[25] Leaders of the movement cannot always impose an effective framework, especially as demands tend to be fluid, as we have seen, and may be seen as cultural, religious, or political. Secondly, identity demands may be part of more general movements and play on the differences between the local and national.

This interpenetration of the local and national leads on to a larger question: whilst actions are necessarily localized, the actors' thought patterns, the resources mobilized, and the networks are only "local" in the sense that the actors define them as such. The "local", far from being some natural category, may in fact be defined as a configuration where the actors regularly interact with regard to a reference territory acting both as the framework and the issue that is at stake in their interactions. The boundaries of this configuration are defined in a process of differentiation that operates both horizontally (in relation to other territories) and vertically (in relation to overarching levels). The fact that territories and networks do not match up perfectly explains why the local is a fluid category with regard to practice. Consequently, the actors interact at several different levels, sometimes at the same time, and this means that the question of changes of scale is of greater interest than that of the "local" *per se*. These changes of scale enable actors to draw on the fact of belonging to multiple configurations using resources that are wholly specific to them. The local is thus a point of view related to the intentionality of the actors, fundamentally shaping the stakes, rhetoric, and means of action. It would be wholly illusory to refuse to acknowledge the political dimension (in the sense of relationships to the state) of hyper-local confrontations which, in fact, only make sense within the framework of hierarchies objectified by the institutions.[26] The state is always a key actor in conflicts, including when it does not get involved in them, for what is at stake is access to public resources, and the setting up (or application of) legislation. Furthermore, local configurations are based to varying extents on higher-level oppositions, depending also on the degree of ideological proximity to national actors and their ability to redefine conflicts. In other words, the capacity to interpret "local" conflicts transforms them for good. Thus in Pakistan for instance the conflict between radical Sunni and Shi'ite organizations, that has been going on for twenty years now, is overlaid on other oppositions, such as newcomers against long-term residents, or industrialists against landowners (Abou Zahab, 1999).

Violence

There are a certain number of ideas in the abundant literature on the recourse to violence which need to be questioned. Firstly, violence does not correlate to a social movement that has failed to transpire (Wieviorka, 1995). Violence can characterise a movement or a mobilization by causing relations between communities to deteriorate and become entrenched. To this extent violence is a technique to mobilize people, sometimes imported by marginal groups. Secondly, and contrary to what is sometimes supposed, the formation of identity-based parties does not necessarily result in violent conflict nor in a general polarization of politics along identity fault lines (Kanchan, 2005). The way the institutional system responds is crucial here, as illustrated by the emergence of the BJP in India, which has made ethnicity/religion a key element in its political statements yet without provoking any increase in violence.

Violence may act as an instrument to maintain the status quo. And indeed whatever may be done to naturalize domination, community hierarchies are never perfectly accepted and interiorized. Hence competition between groups sometimes results in more direct forms of conflict—such as riots or lynching—which seek to protect the status quo via the brutal reaffirmation of differences, yet without fundamentally bringing into question the state's monopoly on violence. Group violence occurs in particular when something occurs which brings the hierarchy into question, such as marriages that fail to respect group hierarchy, incidents which question the way land or economic roles are attributed, and illegitimate access to symbolic places.[27] This sort of violence is essentially reactive and certain recurrent features may be observed in the procedures and contexts in which they emerge (Bass, 2003).[28] This form of violence is different, initially at least, from that which leads to the elimination of a group (ethnic cleansing or genocide). In these contexts the recourse to violence may arise from a strategic calculation. For example Fredrick Bailey[29] shows that government decisions bring caste hierarchies into question, thus opening up the theoretical possibility that "Untouchables" be allowed to pray in temples. The tensions do not lead to violence as the groups are interdependent and need to calculate costs.[30]

However, far from always resulting in some form of calculation, the emergence of violence as the rule of the game arises from context and largely unforeseeable events, even if the non-involvement of the state would appear to be a necessary condition. This shift to violence thus results from a Clausewitzian dialectic but is also the consequence of the opportunities it offers individuals. But contrary to one of Elias's hypotheses,[31] violence would not appear to be a regression but most of the time an effect of socialization by an institution (a party or the Army) or, more loosely, of conforming to a virile ethos or religious duty. It is thus associated with particular skills, with violence being a resource that young men are socially more inclined to use in comparison to other age and sex groups. In particular, high-intensity violence requires coordination—as well as a monopolistic rationale, especially with regard to territories, as this automatically provides roles (resources) and an extension of the organizations using violence.

Lastly, the repertoire of violent action has specific effects on relations between groups, including those who do not participate directly in it, but who produce the effects of violence. The effects of violence are then co-produced and, contrary to what the standard literature implies, do not lead to the stigmatization of its instigators. We may here note a possible rationale for violence as at one and the same time it is able to mobilize the group, it makes it possible to renegotiate group relations due to the shifts in the balance of power, and it stigmatizes the victims. Violence against a group can act as a *post hoc* justification of pre-existing polarizations and of exclusion mechanisms.

Contributions

The contributions to this volume tackle several of the questions developed in this introduction. It is possible to group them into several themes, each constituting research options on the transformation and the redefinition of differentiation conflicts: the formation of identities, the emergence of mobilizations and the transition to violence.

1) The question of how identities are formed is first of all addressed through three complementary scales: micro, macro and meso-sociological. The perspective of identity as a frontier goes with the evidencing of unconscious logics linked to the "narcissism of the small difference", with the study of how the media produce identities, and lastly by taking into account contexts specifically marked by multiple overlapping and competing identities.

The chapter by Benoît Fliche questions the relations between Sunnis and Alevis in Turkey and shows how small differences are important in the unconscious making of the Other. Of Turkey's two major religious groups, the Alevis and the Sunnis, the Alevis represent a minority corresponding to approximately twenty percent of the population and considered by the Sunnis as heterodox. In order to explain the contentious relationships between Alevis and Sunnis, the author demonstrates the tenuousness of the differences between the two categories before describing the violence suffered by Alevis over the past thirty years. Grounding his analysis in the "narcissism of the small difference" and the concept of "identification", the author contends that unless research in this area takes the unconscious into account, its results are doomed to remain somewhat uninterpretable.

On another scale, Clémence Scalbert-Yücel's chapter deals with the production of identity by the media. Grounding her analysis on how private Turkish television channels deal with the Kurdish population and "problem", the author shows how ethnic categories are used to legitimize, explain or deny cultural difference, thereby conditioning political practices and public perceptions. These televised productions thrive on a common and limited "discursive background" relative to "diversity" and to the "Kurdish issue". This has contributed to creating a double discourse that consolidated during the next

IDENTITY, CONFLICT & POLITICS IN TURKEY, IRAN AND PAKISTAN

decade: the new rhetoric of "cultural diversity" coexists with the older one on the Kurdish issue, defined as a development or civilization issue. The coexistence of these two discourses shows the relative value of identities and their ranking. The chapter explores the hypothesis according to which, recognizing cultural diversity in Turkey—and in particular the existence of Kurds—triggers a change in the definition of the conflict and in the political practices at a certain level while, at another level, allowing to confirm old categories founding the ethnic hierarchies.

Lastly in this first section, focusing on Gilan (Iran) Christian Bomberger exposes how the identity claim is restricted to its cultural dimension. Claims are indeed limited to cultural activism and translate into an editorial and associative fever. This limitation of the identity claim is to be researched in the complexity of the scales that are mobilized, forbidding a dichotomy between the region and the rest of the country.

2) In this section, mobilizations are addressed through the study of how political parties take on the identity dimension, where mobilization entrepreneurs originate from, and, lastly, how identity mobilizations are redefined off shore. Elise Massicard's chapter explores the partial, and at times total, failure of mobilizations via mechanisms aiming to neutralize the political weight of identity within political parties. Christine Moliner discusses the role of the political context (mostly state policies) bringing a transformation of identity rankings in diasporas, while Gilles Riaux sheds light on the central role of entrepreneurs of mobilization. Hamit Bozarslan's contribution insists on the regional ruptures transforming the settings of the 1979 mobilizations and installing the revolutionary idea in the Islamist camp.

As Elise Massicard indicates about Turkish parties: "[t]here is in fact a kind of unavowed representation of identity within the parties, a paradoxical form of transfer of identitary tension into the field of politics; this process takes place without being reflected in the public space, without overt expression of demands, in short, without politicization." In Turkey, identity politics has become a means of claiming and proclaiming particularist rights since the 1980s, although such questions are often settled and regulated outside "legitimate" policies. The article is intended to analyze the way in which the principal actors in the political arena, the political parties, manage the identity dimension both within their constituencies and externally. Demands based on issues of identity, which are illegal, are quasi-taboo for the political parties, which are reluctant to become public relays for these sorts of demands, particularly on the national level. The parties consider the identity dimension as a central param-

18

eter in their relations with voters, however, and they incorporate it for this purpose, particularly in terms of personnel management of candidates and party officials. In order to face this double constraint, they use specific modes of communication that are characterized by connotation and ambiguity.

The study of different routes taken by entrepreneurs of the Azeri cause has proven helpful when attempting to understand the genesis of the cause. These actors play a crucial role in the initiation and development of the movement, restructuring it throughout the revolutionary period and working towards the subversion of ethnic ranking. As Gilles Riaux points out, Azeri elites with significant cultural capital tend to be integrated in the political system, whereas those with more "local" capital have been involved in setting up the Azeri rights movement.

Christine Moliner's chapter looks at the role played over the past 15 years by British state policies in the transformation of relationships between two migrant communities originating from South Asia, Sikhs and Muslims. Each community shares antagonistic representations of the other, based on past conflicts, such as the Partition. What they perceive as a hereditary antagonism is not simply imported but transformed in the diaspora by several local variables. Among these, British integration policy towards ethnic minorities is a key factor. While striving since 2005 to foster "community cohesion", it actually tends to exacerbate the competition between migrants communities related to the allocation of resources, both symbolic and material.

Finally, Hamit Bozarslan shows how important historical breaks are in the transformation of the identity categories that are relevant for mobilizations. In particular, year 1979 is a break-year in the history of the Middle East and opens a new historical cycle. However, the Camp David Accords and the occupation of Afghanistan are perceived as "treason" by the Arab nationalist left and the internationalist left respectively, the Iranian Revolution and the Ka'aba occupation by Islamist activists signal the move from the leftist "revolutionary idea" to Islamism that had until then been omitted because it was considered a "servant of imperialism". Even if these four events—with their own historicity—have no causality links, their contemporaries, through their understanding and subjectivities, put the events in relation. They give the events a new meaning, they transform the events into new markers of new "political realities".

3) The different dimensions of violence are finally addressed from the issue of self-mobilization at a distance, stigmatization of victim communities, empowerment of violence—which loses its instrumental character and rede-

fines configurations—and finally, inter-communal violence as an opportunity to accelerate the state's penetration. Amélie Blom and Aminah Mohammad-Arif's chapters show two opposed cases of transition to violence, by self-mobilization (outside militant structures) through an exacerbation of identity and difference, and on the opposite, by a spontaneous collective mobilization aiming to protect the identity capital of a community.

Luc Bellon and Laurent Gayer's chapters bring two counter-intuitive elements to the analysis of violence. On the one hand, violence cannot be reduced to its instrumental dimension in certain contexts; on the other hand, victims may be more stigmatized than those who perpetrate violence. Finally, Chirine Mosheni's contribution indicates that intercommunity violence stemming from a transformation of identity hierarchy in a revolutionary context can be useful for the state to increase its presence in the periphery.

Aminah Mohammad-Arif's article explores the trajectory of a young Indian jihadist who, together with an accomplice, planted bombs in London 2007 and then tried to ram Glasgow airport with a car. The sources are exceptional: the author interviewed the jihadist before the events, which offers a unique perspective. The varying differences in scale at work are symptomatic of a transformation in conflicts of differentiation. The contribution describes how one goes from a "banal" identity differentiation (an expatriate becoming aware of his or her status as Muslim in a non-Muslim land) to the stage where the feeling of difference appears insurmountable, with violence its only discernible expression.

How can we explain why it is that one image can cause a riot thousands of kilometers away? The riot that took place in Lahore (Pakistan) following the publication of the "Danish cartoons" on February 14, 2006 provides a rich case study to analyze the phenomena of "long distance insulting." Based on interviews with protesters and rioters, Amélie Blom shows the importance of emotions in the transition to violence by focusing on three levels of observation. At the micro (individual) level, we must articulate certain types of emotions (anger, love) to moral sentiments (honor) and specific frameworks of perception (provocation). At the meso level (the riotous crowd), we see that the "emotional work" of the entrepreneurs of mobilization failed to stem the micro-conflicts that were playing in the crowd, and that these entrepreneurs are to be seen in the wider context of everyday urban violence. Finally, at the macro level (the political system), this article highlights the need for a renewed interest in an aspect often neglected in studies on the impact dimension of social movements, namely the politics of emotions produced by the state.

INTRODUCTION

Luc Bellon's article focuses on incidents linked to Baloch nationalism, highlighting what is at play behind this urban armed struggle, with a special focus on the city of Quetta. Quetta is the capital city of Balochistan, Pakistan's most underdeveloped province. Since 2000, and for the first time, violent clashes of very different natures coincided in the city: target killings by Baloch nationalists, suicide attacks from militant Islamist groups, assassinations against the Shiite (primarily Hazara) community, and a growing non-politically motivated criminality perpetuating a number of murders and kidnappings. The contribution shows that the semi-urban social fabric of Quetta—made up of a conglomeration of surrounding villages, each of them partly ruled by tribal logics which work in parallel to the structures of the state—ended up weakening rather than strengthening the stabilizing role of the city as it was developed under colonial rule. Given that the established or pre-established social relationships are, by definition, challenged by a context of violence such as the one prevailing in Quetta today, the article describes the grass root realities on which the Baloch rebellion thrives to expand its popular support, as well as the social repercussions of their violent actions on the urban population. The main hypothesis is that the legitimization of some aspects of this violence by a population witnessing but not producing it enables the reconfiguration of social relationships and/or spaces in the urban context. In particular, Luc Bellon points out that violence, far from bringing about a rejection and delegitimization of groups using it, can on the contrary redefine the relationship between social groups, leading in particular to the marginalization of the groups it targets.

As Laurent Gayer states in his contribution, "violence is not merely the outcome of social, economic, and political changes predating the conflict; it also takes unanticipated courses and tends to reproduce itself by generating its own causalities. What are the mechanisms at play in the shift from one sequence of a conflict to another? What are the technological and organizational contexts in which they operate? How are they related to changes in the social identities of the protagonists and in the maneuvers of the state? These are some of the questions that will be addressed here through an exploration of student violence at the University of Karachi, between 1979 and 1989. During this decade there was a spectacular rise in student violence at the university, from fistfights to gunfights (in 1979), to "political" assassinations (from 1981 onwards), and culminating in a massacre (in 1989). On one occasion, this violence spilled over from the campuses and acquired an international dimension (when a PIA airplane was hijacked in March 1981 by

Salamullah Tipu). During the second half of the 1980s, it also spread through the city of Karachi, fuelling larger social and political conflicts. This case study will therefore consider two different aspects of the dynamics of conflict escalation: that of intensification (which concerns the magnitude of the violence in terms of casualties) and that of expansion (which concerns the amplitude of the violence in spatial terms).

Finally, Chirine Mohseni's chapter examines the ethnic tensions between Kurds and Azeris in and around the city of Naqadeh (Western Azerbaijan) shortly after the Iranian Revolution. Favored by the Iranian state, the Azeris were socially and politically dominant vis-à-vis the Kurds, until the Iranian revolution challenged the ethnic hierarchy. The Sunni Kurds were marginalized and Shi'ism became a central element of the new political order. Violence between the groups was instrumentalized by the state to consolidate its influence. Chirine Mohséni points out, "the Azeris in the region, with the support of the state, held dominant social and political positions in comparison to the Kurds, (...) and the collapse of the old regime brought into question the hitherto legitimate ethnic hierarchy. Being Shi'ite became a key element in the relationship with the state and Sunni Kurds were marginalized."

1

"THE NARCISSISM OF THE MINOR DIFFERENCE" AND RELIGIOUS VIOLENCE

THE CASE OF THE ALEVIS AND SUNNIS OF CENTRAL ANATOLIA[1]

Benoît Fliche
Translated by John Angell

Of Turkey's two major religious groups, the Alevi and the Sunni, the Alevi represent a minority estimated to represent approximately twenty percent of the population. They are considered heterodox both by the Sunni and by the *Diyanet* (the religious affairs ministry), and are known for a certain casual approach to some key Islamic precepts.[2] They inherited a tradition of religious syncretism that dates from the Middle Ages in Anatolia and worships Ali, the Prophet's cousin and brother-in-law, along with his family members. Although the present study seeks to avoid stereotypes that portray the Alevis as more "tolerant" and "modern" than Sunnis, it is generally recognized that their attitudes concerning food, alcohol, and certain religious practices, like their non-respect of Ramadan, differ from stricter Sunni practices.

Furthermore, unlike Turkish Christian minorities, their denomination is not institutionally recognized by the Turkish government, which, like the Sunni, considers them heterodox.

My efforts to differentiate between Alevi and Sunni is not intended to suggest the existence of an Alevi "community" by contrast with a Sunni "community." My position is that the two groups are not socially constituted, but instead simply reflect separate denominational categories. There does exist an endogamic barrier between the two groups, however, but this does not necessarily qualify them as "communities." Rather than social groups, they constitute two categories, to use a distinction first drawn by Brubaker (2001). Furthermore, there are significant "ethnic" and/or religious variations among Alevis: a *Türkmen* Alevi would not appreciate being taken for an Alevi *Türk* or worse, for a *Sıraç*.[3]

Daily interaction between Sunnis and Alevis is marked by a certain hostility, however, that is expressed primarily through "friction" that helps to maintain the dividing line between them and reinforces fairly strict denominational endogamy. Although mixed marriages remain rare, they have become increasingly common. The Alevis are stigmatized by the Sunnis, who do not even consider them to be Muslims and hold them to be "even farther away than the *gavur* [the 'infidels' but 'People of the Book']." They are considered impure—their meat is not even considered *halal*—and are alleged to engage in orgies during which "they recognize neither their daughter nor their mother." Hostility sometimes gives way to violent events, for example at Sivas and in Istanbul's Gazi neighborhood during 1990s.[4] During the left-right conflicts of the 1970s, they were also the target of pogroms, a topic addressed later in this essay. In fact, they were the only victims of collective violence during this period, although there were other isolated attacks and a few fatalities during gunfights between partisans; the only collective massacres of the period specifically targeted Alevis (Sinclair-Webb, 2003), most memorably at Kahramanmaraş.

The differences between Sunnis and Alevis are not substantive, however, and the history of their relationship is arguably a fitting illustration of the "narcissism of the minor difference" that Freud described (Freud, 1921, 1962). During the 1990s, this Freudian construct gained popularity among social scientists outside the field of psychoanalysis, particularly anthropologists trying to explain social situations in which etic differences were associated with violence that in some instances reached genocidal proportions. From an emic perspective, these differences would be perceived as insurmountable and even intolerable.

Three examples of how scholars have employed this Freudian notion include an article by Blok (1998), in which he applies the narcissism of phenomena as Bourdieu described it in *The Distinction*, the work of Ignatieff (1998) in the Balkans, and Bromberger's work (2001), in which he posits a Mediterranean system of "complementary differences," constructed through a mirror effect, that is in a kinship if not precisely a filial relationship with Freud's original formulation.

In 2007, the Norwegian philosopher Kolstø revisited these and other applications of Freud's formulation to the social sciences, asking whether narcissism and the minor difference could provide the basis for general explanation of ethnic conflicts. He concluded that conflicts cannot be explained by examining objective differences, but that researchers should instead focus on perceptions and public representations of difference. In other words, we should turn towards the political and the meanings that politics imprint on difference. This perspective is linked to a broader debate about the how conflicts are articulated at various scales (small and large). As Sahlins has demonstrated, political violence tends to center on local conflicts, particularly when influenced by a process of structural-cum-symbolic amplification (Sahlins, 2005). Further, as studies by Xanthaxou (1999), Bax (2000) and Kalyvas (2006) have shown, macroscopic conflicts provide windows of opportunity for violence to express itself at microscopic levels.

In this article, I will adopt a different, if complementary, approach to these "political" interpretations. I will not specifically consider the issue of violence, which is sometimes difficult to access empirically. Rather, this chapter aims at understanding why there exists such intolerance vis à vis Alevis.

In order to explain conflictual relationships between Alevis and Sunnis, I will first demonstrate the tenuousness of the differences between the two categories before describing the violence against the Alevis over the past thirty years. After showing why classical sociological theories fail to fully account for this hostility toward Alevis, I will leave empirical demonstrations aside to try to propose more theoretical trails capable of better grasping these frictions that have sometimes transformed into violent acts. Grounding my analysis in the "narcissism of the minor difference" and in the concept of "identification" as interpreted by Lacan (1961–1962), I contend that unless research in this area takes the unconscious into account, its results are doomed to remain somewhat uninterpretable.

My aim is however not to be at odds with a system of explanation, via another that would be considered as more efficient because it invokes the unconscious. The aim of this chapter is perhaps even more ambitious in that is seeks to bring some elements of a field (psychoanalysis) into another, that of anthropology and sociology, despite these two disciplines' rare recourse to the tools built by Freud or Lacan.

This transfer is in any case not ensured, since establishing the unconscious as a central hypothesis in the explanation of social phenomena is by no means self-evident. Indeed, I am acutely aware that in attempting this "transfer", I run the risk of alienating the social scientist who may feel uncomfortable with this weakly delineated track.

My analysis focuses on Sorgun, a region of the sub-prefecture of Central Anatolia with which I acquired familiarity over a ten-year period (Fliche, 2007). I contend that my observations of the situation in the region with regard to the Alevis and Sunnis are generalizable in several respects, offering the dual advantage of a specific field of study that provides both rich ethno-graphic data as well as a high degree of exemplariness.

Are There Objective Differences between Alevis and Sunnis?

Sorgun has a reputation as a strict city characterized by a certain moral auster-ity. During Ramadan, not a single café, where the city's smokers gather for a few puffs, can be found open. Lighting a cigarette in the street during the holy month is to risk public opprobrium. The city is an orthodox space, as are many of the surrounding villages, despite the fact that about one-third of the popu-lation of the region's villages (29 out of 93) are Alevi. Eight are mixed: for half of them, as far as I know, diversity as a phenomenon started after 1980, with the demographic boom and some villages becoming market towns. The other remain "recent" phenomena and date back to the founding of the Republic (1923). Even if both communities have collaborated for collective works, there is however a strict separation in everyday life. There are generally two villages in one: an invisible frontier separates Alevi from Sunni neighbor-hoods. There is nothing extraordinary in this division. The phenomenon exists in entirely Alevi villages, as Jérôme Cler showed recently (2013): the political, religious and ideological division cuts the village of Abdal Musa into several quarters almost entirely impermeable to one another.

The differences between Alevis and Sunnis initially appear to be significant, but ethnographic observation reveals that the two groups share an array of practices associated with "classical" Islam. For example, Alevi villagers sum-mon imams for important occasions such as burials and circumcisions, and some also attend mosque on Fridays and during other holy periods such as Ramadan. Sunnis and Alevis also share a common sacred geography despite divergences between major religious landmarks; the Sunni refer to Konya and Mevlana or Hacı Bayram in Ankara when asked to name a great *türbe* near Sorgun, whereas the Alevis tend to mention Hacı Bektaş Veli in Cappadocia, although they also mention Hacı Bayram. Still, in terms of daily practices, both groups rely on the same mausoleums and saintly shrines for solutions to everyday problems, evidence that the practice of hope has no boundaries in terms of denominational differences, provided that they are effective.

In the past, the Alevis were known for other practices with origins in their nomadic past, including feast days related to the raising and herding of sheep and religious practices like annual *cem* ceremonies. *Cem* were held during the winter and were officiated by *dede* (priests), assisted by *aşık* (bards), and each family invited the entire village together in order to resolve conflicts and disagreements from the previous year. These occasions were marked by three practices that the Sunni found "shocking," including attendance by both genders, mixed dancing, and the consumption of alcohol. Since the 1970s, however, they have essentially disappeared, and only a few formal differences between Alevis and Sunni remain. One exception is a sort of "casualness" and even irreverence about Muslim dogma that is observable among present-day Alevis, who drink beer on the morning of the *kurban bayramı (Aid el Kebir)* and laugh at the call to evening prayer by the *muezzin*.

It is far from clear that this irreverence is actually of Alevi origin, however. Mahmut Makal's interpretation, for example, describes in some detail the "heterodoxy" that prevails in Sunni villages on the Anatolian plateau, particularly concerning questions of ritual purity (Makal, 2010). Relatively unorthodox behaviors are also readily observable among the Sunni. Sunni neighbors are quite happy, for example, to seek refuge in the warmth of their Alevi neighbors' homes to drink a few beers or glasses of *rakı* instead of staying in their cars in the middle of the fields during−20°C nights, where they run the risk of hypothermia and being attacked by packs of feral dogs.

The religious differences between Alevis and Sunnis are relatively minor, but this cannot necessarily be said of their political differences. In Turkey, there is a common idea that the Alevis, unlike the Sunnis, are "big Kemalists" or Republicans, but the real differences in their relationships with the government and the Republic merit closer examination. In their relationships with the Republic, Shankland (2003) noted profound differences between Sunni and Alevi villagers in the Tokat region, a region that borders Sorgun, describing the Sunni as being in a state of ideological homology with the government and as not having to make particular efforts to conform to their position within the Turkish Republic. On the other hand, he noted ideological divergences between Alevis and the Sunni government, and he found that their commitment to the Republic was significantly shaped by their values and beliefs, like the disappearance of the *dedelik* (a "caste" of priests who cannot marry among themselves). Shankland deemed this system to be incompatible with the egalitarianism promoted by the Turkish Republic. As an anthropologist, he felt that differences in the two denominations' different relationships with the government explained why Sunni villages exhibited greater flexibility and stronger demographic growth. In the Sorgun region, there does not seem to have been a similar phenomenon of "Alevi" migration later, but the question of the two groups' relationship with the administration does provide an important explanation for the region's ostracism for the past eighty years. In fact, the entire Yozgat district, which includes Sorgun, was until very recently excluded from every government economic development program. This exclusion is traceable to a revolt in 1919–1920 that was led by a few members of a powerful local Sunni family, the Çapanoğlu, who founded the city of Yozgat in the early nineteenth century (Küçük, 2002). The uprising was principally supported by Alevis, who feared suffering the same fate as the Armenians four years earlier (and in which they had participated, according to several reliable witnesses).[5]

The revolt was rapidly quelled, but it had significant consequences for the region. Many inhabitants contend that Yozgat was punished for the rebellion, and Atatürk reportedly forbade state financial support of the region. It is difficult to verify this assertion, but it is true that there was no industrial investment by the state at the time, and that throughout the twentieth century, the Yozgat district remained one of the least developed areas in Central Anatolia.[6] It is worth asking whether there were differences in how the Alevis and Sunnis managed the scarcity of resources during most of the twentieth century, and whether one group experienced greater discrimination by government institutions.

An initial observation is that the scenario is somewhat different from the conditions observed by Shankland in Tokat. As in Tokat, with few exceptions, Alevi villages did not develop during the twentieth century, and, if they remain lightly inhabited, it is due to their unfavorable geographical location. Alevi villages are primarily located on poor soil compared to Sunni villages because of the Alevi's previously nomadic existence; they became sedentarized in this region only around the time of World War I, settling in former pasture-lands that had poor accessibility and lacked basic infrastructure like roads. It is nevertheless difficult to be certain whether this imbalance can be explained by denominational differences beyond a certain non-causal correlation, and caution is preferable in drawing the conclusion that the Sunni benefited more from investment in Sorgun or other regions. The rare state-funded improvements appear to have been devoted to "priorities" that included larger villages that functioned as hubs; the few well-situated Alevi villages have benefited as much as Sunni villages from such state development projects, and the determining factor seems to continue to be geographical and not denominational. One of the arguments against the likelihood that the state intentionally treated Alevis differently than Sunnis turns on the question of literacy. According to the 1965 census, there was no significant difference in literacy rates between the two groups, both of which showed relatively low rates of 35 per cent of the adult population.

The inequalities appear as a result to stem from the structure of the resources made available by the authorities, who, if they did not re-balance inequalities, did nothing to accentuate the differences, at least until the 1980s. Beginning in the 1980s, in fact, there was a discernible and systematic black-mail effort to "build a mosque against public works". The Alevis must build mosques, which, as good followers of Ali, they spurn in the hope of public works in their villages like roads, electricity, and telephone lines.[7] The majority of mosques in Alevi villages were constructed during this period, reflecting the government's attempt to "orthodoxize" the Alevis ever since the 1980s by sending imams to staff their villages' newly-built mosques.

The last question of difference concerns migratory patterns. Here again, no major difference between the Alevis and Sunnis is observable in terms of emigration, another contrast with Shankland's observations in Tokat. In an effort to escape their arid lands, the Alevis were among the first of the region's inhabitants to attempt to emigrate to Europe. They shared a similar apprehension with the Sunnis about moving to the land of the *gavur* (infidel), but the Sunnis, whose circumstances were better to begin with, joined the move towards international migration later than the Alevis. Certain Alevis who did emigrate rapidly became wealthy and returned to Sorgun after a few years, and an Alevi neighborhood grew up in the 1960s on the city's north side.

As regards the question of Kemalism among the region's Alevis, there is a common idea that the Alevis are "naturally" attracted to Kemalism or are the "natural" allies of Mustafa Kemal Atatürk. The "naturalness" of this ostensible support (Massicard, 2005) merits closer examination, however. In this region of Anatolia, it is in fact difficult to establish a link between the Alevis and Kemalism, as illustrated by the fact that between 1965 and 1995, nearly half of them voted with considerable consistency on the right, often for parties identified with religious conservatism. Only a minority of the villages voted unanimously for the left and supported the "historical" Kemalist party, the CHP. In short, although not all Alevi villages voted majoritarily for the left, all of the villages that voted left (approximately fifteen) were Alevi.

It is not at all certain that the Alevi tend to be Kemalists, and there is a logical problem if they do, because it would lend legitimacy to the government's record of excluding them from investment and improvements in the region ever since the 1920s (Tapia 1996). Attributing Kemalism to the Alevis therefore requires ignoring a few important historical facts, among them Alevi support for the 1919 revolt against Atatürk (Küçük, 2002).[8]

The differences between Alevis and Sunnis obviously need to be placed into perspective. The "political" violence (as will be discussed in the conclusion, the quotation marks are warranted), particularly during the 1970s, must be addressed, however (Bozarslan, 1999). The differences appear to have been related to a broader left-right division, and furthermore, the violence of the 1970s is generally characterized as political. I will demonstrate below that this political interpretation is perhaps not a full explanation, and that the violence may arise instead from another difference that underlies conflicts that continue to persist into the present day.

Friction and Conflict in Sorgun in the 1970s

Sorgun is a small city that bears the same name as the region and whose economy is primarily centered around agriculture and coal. It has grown considerably due to internal migrations in the 1960s following the discovery of brown coal deposits, but the development of mining did not transform the city into an industrial center, and many migrants continue to work in the mines even while inhabiting an urban center. Until the 1970s, the Alevis did not feel that they were in danger outside their villages. In fact, some of them sold their land and moved to the city, but that changed during the 1970s, when Sorgun was not spared the eruptions of violence between political extremists that afflicted the country at the time.

This phenomenon manifested itself in several incidents that degenerated into two attempted pogroms against Alevis living in the northern part of the city. The first event occurred after one passer-by, a teacher, lit a cigarette in public during Ramadan. A riot that lasted several hours ensued and forced the unfortunate teacher to seek refuge in an Alevi's shop. The second incident was triggered by a rumor that a bomb had been found near a mosque. Small conflicts became an "everyday" occurrence, with sometimes tragic consequences. For example, a "communist" teacher who had just been transferred to Sorgun was killed, and an elementary school student died from a bullet wound received during a conflict among high school youths. A young man accused of being a communist was also tortured, and radical rightist partisans used glass to carve three moons, the symbol of the MHP (*Milliyetçi Hareket Partisi*, the extreme right Nationalist Action Party), into his chest. The span of these two events is not easy to trace. They were narrated by two informers, more than twenty years after they had happened. To the best of my knowledge, they occured in a short period of time during the 1970s.

The reaction of neighborhood Alevis was to organize a system of self-defense that included watches and arms training, as well as purchases of arms and munitions, clearly with the help of the army or the police. But the situation became more dangerous beginning in 1979, particularly for young people, prompting many Alevis to return to their villages, where they were forced to begin all over again, building houses and resuming farming. These years completely altered the Alevis' perception of the city of Sorgun, where they had once felt secure but that had become a perilous place where they no longer felt they belonged. Furthermore, life in Sorgun having become so unbearable that after the military coup d'état of 12 September 1980, welcomed "with relief" by the Alevis despite the violence associated with it, many of them departed for Ankara or for Europe.

In the Sorgun region, violence appears to have been limited to the urban environment. While the city had become dangerous for Alevis, they were safe in their villages, whose spatial layout does not in any event make entry by unknown parties easy, and invading them would require real, organized commandos. Entering into an "enemy" village would mean exposure to direct violence (some of my informants admitted being armed with Kalashnikov rifles... "that we hid in the 1980s and never found again"). Furthermore, Turkish rightist groups, unlike the followers of Guévara and Mao, who believed in a rural guerilla war, did not have a "ruralist" strategy. Not that rightist militants did not employ propaganda, but their strategies did not include the rural world, and even if they were on the alert, the villages remained outside the conflict.

Although I am not entirely persuaded that this provides a full explanation of the political context of the period, it is also important to note the high level of reciprocal knowledge that the villages maintained among themselves. Friendly relations between Alevis and Sunnis were and are common and sometimes sustained across several generations between two families, despite radically divergent political leanings. I witnessed a Sunni family that had become very conservative paying a courtesy visit to a very progressive Alevi family because their grand-parents were close friends.

Furthermore, relations between villages were not necessarily hostile and were regulated by specific accords that enable Sunni neighbors of one of the Alevi villages where I lived to freely restock their supplies of *çorak* (a clay-bearing soil used in the manufacture of roofs) in exchange for the privilege of gathering *madımak* (Polygonum cognatum) in the Spring without concern for their safety. In fact, my interviewees indicated that conflicts between villages were relatively rare prior to 1970. Of the three Alevi villages with which I am most familiar, I was able to document only two altercations in villages with populations of different denominations. Even these incidents arose not from religious issues but from typical rural disputes about livestock straying onto a neighbor's grazing land. Real violence in the villages themselves was, and continues to be, limited to the dangerous uncultivated zones of the open countryside, where it is unthinkable to roam without a rifle, a revolver, or a machete, both as a defense against wild dogs and wolves and because "you can run into your enemy at the next bend in the road." In effect, village violence is generally restricted to "family small murder" and follows a very different logic than conflicts based on ethnicity or identity. A further notable fact is that in matters of alcohol, Sunnis turn to the Alevis for their supplies, either to drink in their villages or at home, or simply to resupply. The Alevis, unlike the Sunnis as far as I could observe, illegally produced alcohol like wine and rakı and kept vineyards for that purpose (viticulture is no simple matter at more than 1,000 meters in altitude, where winter temperatures descend to –20°C in winter). In short, the region's violence occurred primarily in the urban spaces of Sorgun, where there was a weaker degree of inter-group familiarity.

Sorgun was by no means unique in that respect. The urban world witnessed the same type of violence against Alevis, in a political confrontation context. Undeniably more present in cities than in the rural world, anonymity is a dimension that ought to be considered.

Interpreting the Logic of Differentiation

Yozgat was among the most dynamic cities in Central Anatolia (Bozarslan, 1999). Situated about thirty kilometers away, Sorgun was influenced by three Turkish political groups. My informants have been clear in confirming that although every faction was present in the city, rightist groups were in the majority. The dividing line between left and right that ostensibly defined the line between Alevis and Sunnis could appear obvious at first glance, but in reality, this was far from the case. First, as discussed earlier, because the "Alevi equals leftist" formula is patently false. Indeed, not all Alevis voted for the left, even if the majority of voters on the left were Alevis. Represented differently, "Leftists belong to the set of Alevis"—but not its inverse—is the correct formula. Leftist militants nevertheless argue that the inverse was the case, which is their means of asserting that the dividing line was within the political rather than the religious domain: "there are also leftist Sunnis." We are thus faced with a political interpretation of the conflict. For the other side, the extreme right takes "the left belongs to Alevis" to be accurate, but they go a step further in their definition by also asserting the validity of the "Alevis belong to the left" formula. Thus, all Alevis are communists (*kızıllar*, or reds) or *Kızılbaş* ("red heads").[9] This is in no way an error of logic but an equivalence between being Alevi and being communist, yielding the logical sequence that indicates that communists are bad, Alevis are communists, and therefore all Alevis are bad. This gives the impression of a political interpretation of the conflict, but in fact, this inversion corroborates the conclusion that differentiation grows not out of political affiliation, but out of denominational difference.

The incidents that triggered the riots are inevitably tied to religion; a cigarette lit during Ramadan and a "bomb found" near a mosque. The outrage does not derive from rightist ideology but from Islam, in all likelihood because it provides more material for generating outrage and thus for politicizing Islam than is offered by "rightist." In other words, the ideology of the right is less able of supplying "identificational objects" to the individuals whom the militants intend to politicize, whereas Islam offers a profusion of such objects.[10] It is not clear precisely what communists were blamed for, in fact. Their crime was being atheist and being Alevi. Gourisse's argument (2014) tends to support this assertion when he notes that the MHP's mobilization was founded essentially on religious elements. In order to determine whether someone was in the enemy camp, his knowledge of the Qu'ran was tested, particularly in Kahramanmaras. Moreover, we have seen that the differences in such matters between these two groups were definitely slight.

It is conceivable that this represents a violent side-effect of a narcissism of the minor difference involving religious knowledge, but before drawing this conclusion, the hypothesis regarding the transformation of ethnic hierarchies (Vaner, 1984) needs to be examined. At the bottom of the social scale until recently, the Alevis had subsequently prospered somewhat, which made them the object of Sunni jealousy and vindictiveness. The established hierarchy of identities was called into question by the shift in Alevi status, which in theory also provoked their intolerance for the Sunni. This hypothesis needs to be considered here because it has been found to pertain in other contexts, as demonstrated in studies by the Africanist anthropologist Nicole Sindzingre. Nevertheless, in the case of Sorgun, this hierarchy of identities tells us something different. Why refuse this transformation of the hierarchy since the categories are not social groups? Being Alevi does not provide access to particular resources via membership in a group, and furthermore, it is not readily demonstrable that the Alevis were substantially wealthier than the Sunnis, and their social ascension is therefore undoubtedly somewhat of a fantasy. Of course, the order of perception can surely be invoked, however, such as "the Sunni perceived that..." in order to explain that they arrived at the point of initiating violence. But that does not answer the question of why it was intolerable for the Sunnis that the Alevis experience some elevation in their status. And explaining the rise of tolerance is ultimately the fundamental question. Because the differences between the two groups obviously are determined in the social sphere, but also, and simultaneously, on another stage—the unconscious.

My hypothesis is therefore that there is a confrontation between left and right, and between Alevi and Sunni that could take some local social logics. The political and violence related issues articulate around a religious differentiation, around a very light differentiation on minor issues at stake (at least for an external observer), around something close-to-nothing that makes it all, a violent effect caused by the so called narcissism of the minor difference.

On a Different Stage

As discussed earlier, the differences between Alevis and Sunnis are minimal from an etic point of view and very important from an emic perspective. I think that from an etic viewpoint, this difference was less pronounced at the beginning of the twentieth century than it is today, but that the orthodoxization of the state since the founding of the Republic, accelerated after the 1980 coup d'état, has considerably widened the rift between the two faiths. Again, studies in ethnology and rural sociology as well as eye-witness reports relativize the idea that heterodoxy was restricted to Alevis. Claims of a greater degree of freedom and emancipation among Alevi women do not withstand the readily observed everyday domination by men, and Alevis have nothing over the Sunnis in this regard. Is this just one more example of the "narcissism of the minor difference" between Alevis and Sunnis? We are ultimately faced with the reality of very slight objective differences regarding the important roles of women in daily social life in these groups.

Rather than a return to Freud, the following is best conceived of as a slight detour through his original thoughts about the term "narcissism," which has been somewhat compromised and refers to a specific field that is beyond the scope of the present essay. Freud demonstrated that the narcissism of minor differences centers on questions of identification, which is not to be confused with the question of identity. On the contrary, in *Group Psychology And The Analysis Of The Ego* (1921), Freud emphasized that the irritation one senses when confronted by others' differences arises from narcissism. Less than a conflict of interest, it is instead perhaps (Freud is cautious here, so let us also be) an expression of egotism:

> In the undisguised antipathies and aversions which people feel towards strangers with whom they have to do we may recognise the expression of self-love—of narcissism. This self-love works for the self-assertion of the individual, and behaves as though the occurrence of any divergence from his own particular lines of development involved a criticism of them and a demand for their alteration. Difference suggests, then, an alteration of the subject. (1922, 55–56).

But these differences can be effaced:

> But the whole of this intolerance vanishes temporarily or permanently, as the result of the formation of a group and in a group. So long as a group formation persists or so far as it extends, individuals behave as though they were uniform, tolerate other people's peculiarities, put themselves on an equal level with them, and have no feeling of aversion towards them. (1922, 56).

In this way, Freud places a hurdle in his reasoning: identification. If the group holds together, if one is able to get beyond the flaws of others, it is because of this process of identification:

> What we have learned from these three sources may be summarised as follows. First, identification is the original form of emotional tie with an object; secondly, in a regressive way it becomes a substitute for a libidinal object tie, as it were by means of the introjection of the object into the ego; and thirdly, it may arise with every new perception of a common quality shared with some other

person who is not an object of the sexual instinct. The more important this common quality is, the more successful may this partial identification become, and it may thus represent the beginning of a new tie. (1922, 65).

The third source is of particular relevance to the present article.

Identification and the Identificational Object

Freud underscored the fact that the process of identification is not homogeneous. The construction of the idea of the ego is the result of multiple identifications in primary infancy that are not necessarily homogeneous among themselves. This ego-ideal, the result of multiple primary identifications, does not explain phenomena of collective euphoria and even violence that are observable, for example, during a soccer match. Something else transpires: during these events, there is a substitution of the ego-ideal by an identificational object. The identificational object replaces, generally momentarily, the ego-ideal. Why momentarily? It could be argued that a structure does not function for a long duration in this mode of identification. Even if we are not fans of Fenerbahçe (one of Istanbul's largest soccer clubs), it is difficult to organize our lives as a function of this identification. The ego-ideal often presents flagrant contradictions with the identificational object and ends up gaining the upper hand.

We can envision, however, the relatively typical case in which the ego-ideal finds itself in perfect resonance with the chosen identificational object, which ultimately influences it, becoming the organizing element of the psychic structure. The identificational object, in taking its place within the ego-ideal, allows immediate narcissistic gratification. In an assuredly cavalier way, I am surmising that psychism works in such a way as to be economic, and that the specular relationship between an ego and its ideal is more draining than the relationship between an ego and an identificational object is simple, which lessens the amount of psychic work involved.

Ultimately, certain social contexts contribute to the substitution of the identificational object for the ego-ideal, which explains social matrices such as school and the army and of identificational material. As seen earlier, religion in Anatolia during the 1960s and 1970s presents a greater amount of identificational material than ideologies or political parties. This explains why the extreme right used religious themes to mobilize the population instead of extreme right ideology.

Identificational Object, Narcissism, and Violence

How can we understand the fact that soccer fans commit violent acts based on narcissistic wounds that can seem minor, like losing a match, when in other areas of their everyday lives they endure often much deeper narcissistic injuries, like domination in the world of work? The same can be asked regarding the caricatures of the Prophet or, more recently, the defilement of the Qu'ran in Greece. Why react violently to the lighting of a cigarette in the street during Ramadan or some other minor event when one's daily life is filled with major narcissistic injuries that ought to be be far more traumatizing?

Once again, "identity" does not enable explanation of this kind of problem—I can be Muslim and reports of the Qu'ran's defilement can fail to move me, but only until I find myself in a particular context with which I identify. The arguable hypothesis would be that the "narcissistic loop" is more rapid when the identificational object imposes itself because it takes a form that is "simpler" than the ego-ideal, i.e., a heterogeneous coalescence of primary identifications. In these moments of replacement of the ego-ideal by the identificational object, the same narcissistic mechanisms function to support the ego and change the image sent to the ego. With an identificational object, the image is clear. Any threat to this image directly threatens the ego—a defiled Qu'ran, a lit cigarette—and the image of the identificational object is objectively dimmed ... the ego registers the narcissistic wound instantaneously. Its response is more direct and often appears, seen from outside, totally disproportionate. Because the information is treated directly, the wound becomes apparent, and the stronger the identification with the object, the more deeply the wound is felt. This does not necessarily apply to the violence of an attack, but to the narrowness of the specular relationship established between the ego and the object. The ego reflects itself directly in the identificational object, the ego-ideal being less easily discernible. The reaction that is observed, when the ideal is threatened, is often less direct. This is why we sometimes have the paradox in which an individual who is called an idiot reacts less violently than if his object is accused of being an idiot. Which in turn explains the widespread technique of demeaning an idenficational object instead of the subject himself.

This is perhaps an essential point that pertains to the relations between the Alevis and the Sunni. The Alevis, because of their fundamental allegiance to The Call, constitute an insult through their very "deviant" conduct to the identificational object, thus wounding the Sunni. The Sunni reaction that seeks to expel these "heretics" from Islam arises from a narcissistic injury. The Alevis are intolerable because they soil the identificational object by refusing to accept it as it is. They recognize the Qu'ran but not as the unaltered word of God. For them, it is not a holy book, although at the same time they acknowledge its sacred character, if altered by political manipulation and the flawed interpretations of Mankind. Conceived in this way as a "historical" work, the Qu'ran is thus no longer holy, and it can therefore be the object of other writings, which the Alevis are not reluctant to compose in the form of supposedly more "true" and more "authentic" "alternative" Qu'rans. But this enlightenment in terms of the identificational object is insufficient, and another element that is required for an explanation of the relations between Alevis and Sunni is the case in which something is the object of identification and an identificational object is needed.

For the present, this argument has remained at the level of identifications "with". There is a difference—and an articulation—between "identification with" and "identification as". To undergo identification by the other, one is adopted via an identifying object, and we are thus in the mode of identification as, identified with one of our possible belongings (man, woman, Alevi, Sunni). In other words, we are identificationally adopted by means of an identifying object that allows us to be classified by the Other.

This identifying object can become an identificational object for the ego. Identification "as" can induce identification "with." When we speak to an individual identified as Alevi in Turkey as "an Alevi", which transmits an image back to him, literally, of an Alevi. In this way, someone offers me an identificational object "Alevi". I have the possibility, to a greater or lesser extent, of confirming or disconfirming the place of this object. Do I accept it as an identificational object or do I refuse it? Do I therefore identify myself with it, or do I not? It is not simply a matter of confirming a categorization, but of supporting a specular relationship between an object imposed upon my ego and me (which in turn arises from the expression "project an image"). Obviously, this identifying object is also formed based on the entirety of the information that I give about my belongings. If I carry Ali's sword around my neck, I will be identified as Alevi: the identifying object corresponds to the identificational object.

Moments of strong divergence between the identifying object and the ego-ideal are more interesting to examine. Devaluation of the identifying object typically provokes an emotional reaction. Being identified as an Alevi is to be treated as an Alevi, which evokes the literature on stigmatization and stereotyping. It is nevertheless important to note that the most often encountered response in such a situation is that the individual who experiences reification via identification responds in the same mode, i.e., that of identification.

The contexts of identification can be further explored, particularly as regards the case of anonymity. It is rare that a familiar individual is addressed in the same way as an unknown person, which explains why such modes of interaction usually occur in urban settings and not in rural or other spaces where individuals tend to know each other. Identification has a particular relationship with the unconscious, but it can also participate in conscious phenomena. One can consciously refuse an object of identification (or categorization), and one can similarly induce an erroneous identification of oneself. In Turkey, this takes on a typical form, the celebrated *takiye*, in which one appears how one is not and is what one does not appear to be, a perfect example of consciously manipulated phenomena of identification. In short, these are instances of manipulation of the identificational object in order to join a group, but also of manipulation of identifying objects that enable one not to be identified. This is evident in the case of the Alevis and Sunnis of Sorgun, for example when an MHP moustache is shaped like "wolf fangs" or the "moon" to signify the extreme right as opposed to the "Stalin-style" moustache, which signifies the extreme left, but also in the case of the false MHP moustache that is worn by leftist Alevis for administrative procedures. An interesting example of *takiye* is the following: several years ago, an Alevi candidate for migration to Europe was badly welcomed while arriving in a café in an Alevi village he did not know. Indeed, he was wearing a superb MHP moustache and had—rapidly, since tension has risen to the next level—to explain that he was not MHP at all but was in the middle of administrative procedures before his departure.

Signifying the Forbidden Signifier: A Question of Incest

The Alevi are supposedly anathema because they cast a shadow on the identificational object by refusing to accept it as it is. It seems to me, however, that the relationship between Alevis and Sunnis does not result from this one minor difference because, as opposed to the Christians, the Alevis accept the identificational object precisely when they should refuse it. It is with this that the Sunnis take issue.

For Lacan, Freud's "minor differences" are related to the function of the "unary" trait:

> This is what prompts me to say that what we have to articulate here is that in inverting, if I can say so, the polarity of this function of unity, in abandoning the unifying unity, the Einheit, for the distinctive unity, the Einzigkeit, I am leading

you to the point of posing the problem of becoming, of articulating step-by-step the solidarity of the status of the subject as it is linked to this unary trait, with the fact that this subject is constituted in his structure and his sexual impulse, between all of the afferences of the body, of its privileged function.

Concerning the first fact, the subject's ties to this unary trait, I am going to add the final point today, considering the path sufficiently articulated, by reminding you that this fact, which is so important to our experience and put forward by Freud, what he calls the narcissism of minor differences, is the same thing that I call the function of the unary trait, because it is no less than the fact that based on this minor difference—and to say minor difference, that does not mean anything other than this absolute difference that I was speaking to you about—this difference that is detached from any possible comparison, is based on this minor difference, inasmuch as it is the same thing as the big I, the Ego-ideal, that every narcissistic intention; the subject constitutes itself or not as the bearer of this unary trait, which allows us today to take our first step into what will constitute the object of our next lesson, in other words, the return to the functions of privation, frustration, and castration. (Lacan, 1961–1962, 156).

In the case of the Alevis and Sunnis, there are obvious problems in terms of the logical structure of differentiation. The other sects that are based on the Book have distinct relationships with Sunnism, by refusing this unary trait—which makes everyone as "1" different from the others, rather than a zero—it was signified that there is alterity in the others. Up to that point, no really serious problem exists: the difference of position with respect to the unary trait implies the absolute difference established by the unary trait.

Heterodoxy causes scandal by not refusing the unary trait, even as its position ought to exclude it. There is no difference of position with respect to the unary trait and, as a consequence, it does not fulfill its function of imposing absolute difference. The situation is comparable to true homonymy, where two individuals share identical first and last names and refuse to adopt another distinctive trait on the pretext that each is the only individual who should carry that particular name. There is confusion between the two individuals and despite it, nothing differentiates them from each other even as they continuously proclaim their difference. The difference cannot be established by the unary trait, and that is precisely the problem, which is why everything turns on a "nothing that does everything." The unary trait is not instituted clearly because it cannot be. The Alevis do in fact recognize the Qu'ran and Mohamed as Allah's Prophet. How, then, can one group be clearly and legitimately differentiated from the other? A difference nevertheless exists, and it is situated in the relationship with the Other: God and/or His discourse (the Qu'ran).

The Alevis designate themselves as Muslims and accept the Book, but at the same time they refuse the discourse by questioning the cause—"the Qu'ran is not the real Qu'ran." Is it really the Alevi's alcohol consumption and mixed-gender prayer that horrify the Sunnis, or is it the fact that they cannot accept the Alevi's refusal of a literalist view of the Qu'ran? What do the Alevis say when they are drinking? That the Qu'ran's word as spoken by the Sunnis is false. The Alevis believe that taking the Qu'ran literally is an error, which is tantamount to saying that the letter itself, and thus the Qu'ran, is false. They begin with the idea that refuting the authority of the letter is not refuting God, but it is refusing the symbolic order of the Sunnis without saying one is from an entirely different faith and without really affirming that they relate to a different God. Taking the dissident position is tantamount to finding fault with the other without truly differentiating oneself from him, thus placing oneself in a position of being irreverent, or even of being someone who treats these matters lightly and with humor, whereas one's interlocutors find nothing amusing about it because it unsettles their doctrinal space (see Lacan's Seminar V). It is not by chance that there is a rich corpus of Alevi jokes. And what do they say, these jokes, if it is not to thumb their nose at the the Sunnis' formal relationship with the Other?

Here is an example of an Alevi joke, collected in the field in 2001:

This is not a fable. It happened in Çorum. Some people really wanted to have a boy. The father had daughters but no son. One day he was watering his garden and he made a wish and addressed Allah: 'Give me a son, and after his military service you can have him back, I'll give him to you.' Sometime afterwards, his wife became pregnant and they finally had a son. He grew up and left to do his military service. When he came back, everybody welcomed him and embraced him. His father, at the moment he embraced him, remembered his vow and started thinking that his son was going to die. He didn't tell anybody anything, but his face darkened. His wife noticed this and asked him what was wrong. He told her about his vow. His wife said to him "and what if you went to see the religion man (*hoca*)? Maybe he has a solution, a sacrifice, for example." They decided to go see a *hoca*. They paid him in advance, saying that the price was unimportant, and they explained the story. The *hoca* picked up the bill, then took out an old book in Arabic. He looked through it a little. He looked and said "this is worrisome, I would like to make a talisman (*muska*), but, you know, this is serious. I advise you to go see the müftü.[11] He'll just save you some time." The farmer left to go see the müftü. Who was fairly good friends with the Alevi village. The farmer arrived with a hundred pounds and explained the situation. Maybe the müftü couldn't say that he couldn't do anything: "we do not interfere with the affairs of God. But I offer you a piece of advice. You know this Alevi village. They are the only ones who can find the solution. You tell your problem to the first person you see." The farmer left and went to the village. He saw a farmer coming with his big moustache and a shovel over his shoulder:

"Hey! Compatriot (*hemşehri*), one minute. The müftü sent me, do you know him?"

"Sure, he's a friend of mine."

And the farmer told him his story. The Alevi listened and twisted his moustache and finally, he said "you shouldn't have said things like that..." then he started thinking... "and, were there any witnesses? No? So there's your solution—deny your word and let Him just leave!"

It is crucial for the Sunnis that Alevis not be recognized as Muslims. Admitting that they have a different unary trait but are nevertheless tied to Islam would undermine the foundation of the Sunnis' own unary trait as Muslims, since only one Muslim faith is possible. The Alevis are thus necessarily non-Muslims for the Sunnis. But they are not exactly anything else, either—they are not Christians, Jews, or pagans. They are not people of the Book, nor are they among those who could be of the Book. Therefore, in some sense, they are Muslims. Once this point is unconsciously attained, how can these people whose difference is unspeakable be pigeon-holed? The answer is that they have to be placed in the null position, the position of "nothing at all," a vacuum, a lacuna in the field of signifiers. And there is no more fitting linguistic hole in the Turkish language than the one that simultaneously designates and does not designate "incest"—no word joins this English word to other signifiers: incest is quite simply not signified in the Turkish language.

The Sunni accuse the Alevis of practicing *mum söndü* ("the candle went out"), meaning orgies, "in which the father no longer recognizes his daughter, and the son does not recognize his mother." This accusation of incest is typical of the kind of stigmatization that could be casually discounted as "fair" revenge for the many Alevi jokes about the Sunni if it did not tie the Alevis to a crime that possesses no signifier in Turkish. This hole in the language cannot simply be ignored, and it demands our attention, especially because it represents an allegation against a significant category of the population. In this way, the Sunnis place the Alevis in a signifying void, defining them as insignificant, as meaningless. The reverse, however, does not hold—the Alevis recognize the Sunnis as Muslims, if not necessarily as good Muslims— they are imposters, bigots (*yobaz*), hostile to every idea of "modernity,"[12] who are obsessed by the letter of the Qu'ran but who neglect its spirit. The Sunnis are, however, verbalized and signified, while the Alevis are consigned to a gap in the language that is substituted for by the metaphorical expression *mum söndü*. My hypothesis is that by placing themselves in a critical position with respect to the master code, the Alevis manage to escape from it and to become unnameable, or more precisely, because they cannot be covered by a signifier, they become un-signifiable. And to signify their un-signification, they are linked to a crime for which no signifier exists—incest. They become incest through metonymic contagion, which explains the horror that they elicit in Turkish society to this day.

Out of this unspeakable difference, this "nothing at all," we remain short of the "minor difference," because the unary trait has such great difficulty emerging. It surfaces more readily during a long period of violent political confrontation. It is therefore impossible to ignore the context, the environment. In the case of Sorgun, several characteristics appear: an important anonymity, a strong politicization and an easy access to arms. This is why I consider it important to say that these explanations are complementary rather than they exclude one another. The political violence context is the result of a politicization of difference of a politicization that creates difference: the identificatory objects, and "outraged community"—in reference to the special issue of *SAMAJ* (Blom and Jaoul, 2008)—are so many ways of acting politically. With armed confrontation between left and right, it was possible to pronounce an unspeakable difference in other ways, and to do so violently. In fact, tolerance consists of appropriating for oneself what comes from the Other, and tolerance towards the Alevis is impossible, because even if they are different, they are not Other.

2

CULTURAL DIVERSITY
AND ETHNIC HIERARCHY

THE USE OF CATEGORIES
IN THE KURDISH CONFLICT IN TURKEY

Clémence Scalbert-Yücel
Translated by Adrian Morfee

An essential aspect of a conflict, especially if it is seen as an identity conflict by one of the parties, is the definition of groups. The categories used to legitimize, explain, or deny cultural differences shape political practices and public perceptions. A transformation in discourse about the other would thus imply a modification in the conflict. The hypothesis put forward in this article is that the recognition of "cultural diversity" in Turkey, and especially of the existence of the Kurds, leads at one level to a transformation in the way the conflict is defined[1] and in political practice, but at another level serves to entrench the old categories underpinning the ethnic hierarchy. The recognition of cultural diversity has an even greater effect in transforming the conflict since it is accompanied by the emergence of what is called "civil society" whose members, by producing discourse, become actors within the conflict.

This chapter concentrates on the image and discourse of the Kurdish populations and "problem" as generated by TV series produced in the 2000s for private Turkish TV channels. A dual discourse progressively emerged as of the late 1990s before being consolidated over the course of the following decade, with the new rhetoric of "cultural diversity" henceforth existing alongside older forms of rhetoric relating to the Kurdish question, perceived as a development or civilization issue. The coexistence of these two discourses clearly brings to light the relative value of identities and the process by which a hierarchy is established between them. These television programs drew upon a common and limited discursive pool[2] relating on the one hand to "diversity", and to the "Kurdish question" on the other. This pool is redeployed extensively from one TV series to the next, from one cultural product to another, as well as feeding these cultural products into the pronouncements of associations and public authorities, and vice versa. Furthermore, the fact that multiple actors approach the problem by drawing on the same discursive pool "reinforces the belief in the problem" (Lahire, 1999, 113). The TV series therefore need to be considered within this larger discursive space. The role played by the state within this discursive space also merits study. Whilst there are diverse (especially privatized) actors, the influence of the state would nevertheless appear to be central. This article will therefore follow on from the work of Yaël Navaro-Yashin showing how, with the introduction of the liberal economic policies of Özal as of the 1980s, the doxa of "civil society" often served to bolster the state.

Thus "cultural diversity", though not officially recognized in any text, is no longer taboo in Turkey, and is on display every day in the public sphere and in the media. Television, cinema, music, and literature act as a reminder that Turkey is not in fact made up uniquely of Turks. "Diversity", once seen as capable of dividing the country and thus as a threat, is now shown on a daily basis. Does this discourse on diversity play a role in bringing the conflict to an end by generating recognition, as would seem to be implicit within such discourse, or does it actually sustain the conflict? For at the same time this discourse about the Kurdish "question" and its "solutions" is largely unchanged, with the themes, stereotypes, and values being fundamentally similar to those that state discourse has conveyed ever since the creation of the Republic. The meta-image of the Kurds, though initially produced and conveyed by state discourse,[3] is now widely disseminated in the public sphere by the media, associations, celebrities, etc. The sharp increase in the number of discourse producers is, however, a new phenomenon (dating from the end of armed conflict and open "polarisation" in the early 2000s), and something that substantially modifies the "Kurdish problem" and its "solutions".

The first part of this article will present the conditions in which it is possible for a new discursive form and new discursive spaces to emerge, and new discourse producers too, i.e. TV series. The second part, based on an analysis of three series (*Sıla*, *Tek Türkiye*, and *Tatlı Bela Fadime*), will examine the nature of this discourse, distinguishing between discourse on "diversity" on the one hand, and that relating to the "Kurdish question" on the other.[4] Finally, the third part of this article, about the reality-effect of discourse, shows how the TV series and their producers—among other new actors—are involved in formulating the Kurdish problem and solutions in a particular way, with state ideology remaining central to their approach.

The Transformation of The Discursive Field

The Conditions of Possibility of Transformation

The emergence of identity as a discursive register, as well as of discourse about "cultural diversity" and a "cultural mosaic", is linked to several internal and external factors.

The sharp increase in the number of TV series is first of all linked to the liberal policies and privatization of the audiovisual sector under Turgut Özal in the 1990s. The emergence of a large private audiovisual sector has sometimes been analyzed as part of the "development of civil society against the state", but as shall be seen here it is also a central element in the "production and reproduction of thralldom for the Turkish state" (Navarro-Yashin, 2002, 130). The liberalized market was on the lookout for new products and "identities are, to an important extent, produced in the context of a marketplace" (Navarro-Yashin, 2002, 111). A factor internal to the production sector also helps explain the interest in "diversity". In a competitive sector[5] producers looking for originality opted for new places to film. Interest in filming in the regions really started with *Asmalı Konak* ("Vine Mansion", 2002), an extremely popular series shot in Cappadocia and which became a sort of archetype for a successful TV series. Diversity (and related themes such as travelling, adventures along the way, and self-discovery and discovering others) also provides ideal material for a screenplay.

Elise Massicard has underlined how the post-1980 period, corresponding to the end of the military regime and the introduction of liberalism, put an end to the dominant political register and marked the "synchronization of Turkey with international politics, characterised since the 1980s by the flourishing of particularistic movements and the politics of recognition and difference, under the impulse of the 'end of the great [universal] narratives' such as modernity and progress" (Massicard, 2005, 94). International contributions, especially those of the United Nations (with the Habitat 2 conference held in Istanbul in 1996 for example) and of the European Union also played a role in this process of synchronisation. Following on from the Helsinki summit in 1999, Turkey became a candidate for joining the European Union which "announced her preference for the discourse of unity in diversity" (Kaya, 2003). Ayhan Kaya points out that the semantic slippage in European discourse from "minority" to "cultural diversity", whilst in part rooted in the Union itself, had additional specific causes in Turkey. During his visit to Turkey in July 2000 the EU Commissioner for Enlargement, Günter Verheugen, put forward a draft Accession Partnership Document in which the term "minority" was used. This sparked strong criticism, and in the final version of the document the term "minorities" was replaced with that of "diversity" (Kaya, 2003).

The existence of Kurdish mobilisation, its rapid growth in the 1990s, and the cultural activities this encouraged, played a major role in the development of discourse on cultural diversity in the country, within both various state bodies and protest movements. In 1990, when the war between the PKK and the Turkish army was escalating and there was increasing support for the PKK among the Kurdish population, Turgut Özal recognised the "Kurdish reality" during trip to the South East. These changes combined to open up a breach in the definition of Turkishness and ended up transforming certain aspects of public policy and cultural practices.

Discussion about constitutional citizenship (*anayasal vatandaşlık*) thus started in 1992 (Doğan,1992) before really taking off in the spring of 1994 with the anniversary of the Constitutional Court. The possibility of redefining citizenship (in a way susceptible to include different populations) was once again the subject of debate, and the expression "cultural mosaic" emerged. Whilst Demirel spoke of "constitutional citizenship", the Prime Minister Tansu Çiller, in his 1995 New Year speech, replaced Atatürk's famous "Ne Mutlu Türküm diyene" ("How happy is he who can say he is a Turk") with "Ne mutlu Türkiye'nin vatandaşıyım diyene" ("How happy is he who can say he is a citizen of Turkey") (Ciller, 1995 and Fikret Bila, 1995). Bozkurt Güven, the author of a book about Turkish identity and chief adviser to the president, when asked by a journalist: "does the expression 'Ne mutlu Türküm diyene' include different ethnic groups" answered as follows: "of course it includes them. Atatürk saw and took into account different groups—the Circassians, the Kurds. [...] He was fully aware of this diversity. He tried to create a 'supra-identity' embracing this diversity. He said, let's create a supra-identity from these various ethnic groups and call it Turk. It's not to everybody's liking, but in Turkey there is a mosaic structure. In Anatolia there is a cultural mosaic" (Hasan, 1995). Discussions were thus engaged once again about definitions of Turkish identity and citizenship, as evidenced by debates about the report drawn up by the Working Group on Minority and Cultural Right published in 2004 (Oran, 2007).

Cultural policies were thus progressively liberalized, and the floodgates opened in 1991 with the authorization to publish and to broadcast audiovisual recordings in Kurdish. Kurdish music and literature progressively emerged on the legal market. Twenty years later, the public channels TRT 6 and TRT Arapça were broadcasting entirely in Kurdish and Arabic respectively, and all the private TV channels were airing series presenting diversity.

The "mosaic" rapidly conquered the market for cultural production, as did "diversity". The "ethnic" sections in bookshops and record shops emerged (Muhidine, 2000), and cinema and the television took these things up. The TV series, introducing socio-political and ethnic themes, were often described as "more than just a TV series" (Biçer, 2009). *Yabancı Damat* ("The Foreign Groom"), for instance, telling a story set in the shared territories and histories of Greece and Turkey, was described by the press as a "bridge of friendship". More recently *Elveda Rumeli* ("Farewell Rumelia"), about the Balkans in the late nineteenth and early twentieth centuries, has been described in the following terms: "this simple TV series has become an 'instrument for remembrance' of a deeply buried stage of our history" (Biçer, 2009). TV series became a means for the Turkish population to discover the past and present, both as a response to their curiosity and helping in turn to generate further interest.

The Themes of the TV Series—Between Tradition and Terror

TV series about the South East appeared in 1998. They are based around the theme of terror or that of custom. The two themes became progressively interlinked as of 2007.

Deli Yürek ("Crazy Heart", 1998) was the first series to address the "Kurdish question". It opens on a "terrorist" attack that the hero, a commando in the

South East who is on leave in Istanbul, tries to foil. It was the first in a string of series based on the themes of the deep state, and the links between "terrorism", the Mafia (and drug mafias in particular), and foreign forces seeking to divide the country. Most of these series on the theme of terror—which functioned as hymns to the greatness of Turkish-ness and were often extremely insulting towards religious minorities—were written, directed, or produced by Osman Sınav, whose sympathies for the ultra-nationalist right show through. In 1997–8 he directed *Sıcak saatler* ("Hot Hours") about the war in Bosnia, and the well-known *Kurtlar Vadisi* ("Valley of the Wolves", 2002–2005). His *Pars Narkoterör* ("Panther Narco-Terror", 2007–2008 for Show TV) and *Sakarya-Fırat* (2010 for TRT), partly shot in the East, provide a direct treatment of the war between the army and the PKK, and the links between the PKK, drug traffickers, and the international Mafia.

A new sort of TV series about the East appeared as of the 1999–2000 season, about six months after the arrest of the PKK leader, Abdullah Öcalan. These series totally ignore the conflictual dimension and the war raging in the region between 1984 and 1999, openly reverting to former rhetoric about the backwardness of the region. They are devoted to "tradition" and "custom" (*töre*) and were sometimes described by the press as "aşiret dizileri" or "ağa dizileri" (tribal or agha series). The first in this genre was *Aşkın Dağlarda Gezer* ("Your Love Wanders in the Mountains", 1999 for TGRT) inspired by and starring the singer and actor Özcan Deniz. It is based on a vendetta and the impossible love story between two people from warring families. The series, shot in Harran (in the Urfa region), unfolds in a "timeless past".[6] Although Harran is undeniably a mixed region (as is Mardin in later series), the story is anchored in Kurdish society, as indicated by the first names, costumes, and accents. Stereotypes about the Kurdish regions (tribalism, religion, tradition, and smuggling) are very present. The theme of custom, which is central to later series, also appears here. After *Aşkın dağlarda gezer*, however, these stories are situated in the present, as is the case for *Berivan* (2002), *Gurbet Kadın* ("The Woman Far from Home", 2003), *Ezo Gelin* ("The Bride Ezo", 2006), *Aşka Sürgün* ("Exile in Love", 2005), and *Sıla* (2005), among others. These series confirmed the use of elements such as costumes (the *keffiyeh*, headscarves for women, etc.) and accents which went on to become stereotypical. The use of the Kurdish language, with some lines being subtitled, and some songs, also progressively emerged.

From *Tek Türkiye* (2007) onwards, the themes of war and "terrorism" (or drug trafficking to finance it) are overlaid on the still dominant theme of custom, such as in *Bir Bulut Olsam* ("If I Were a Cloud", 2009), *Aşk bir Hayal* ("Love is a Dream", 2009), and *Aşk ve Ceza* ("Love and Punishment", 2010).

A Wide Range of Producers

The theme of tradition was introduced in 1999, primarily by actors of Kurdish origin and first among whom was Özcan Deniz. *Aşkın Dağlarda Gezer* was inspired by a story about his family. Of Kurdish origin,[7] it would seem that at this precise stage of his career he chose to play the Kurdish card.[8] In 2005 Mahsum Kırmızıgül, a singer from Diyarbakir, acted in *Aşka Sürgün*, the TV series produced by Tomris Giritlioğlu. He subsequently went on to adopt this theme in the films he directed (*Beyaz Melek*, "The White Angel", 2007; *Güneşi Gördüm*, "I Saw the Sun", 2009). Whilst Özcan Deniz's role as a legitimate representative of the Kurds in the broad sphere of cultural production in Turkey was both brief and half-hearted, Mahsum Kırmızıgül still assumes and reinforces such a role presenting the discourse of peace and fraternity, whilst drawing on a shared discursive pool (the differentiation between East and West, tradition, backwardness, education, etc.).

The fact that Kırmızıgül should act in a production by Tomris Giritlioğlu is certainly not entirely neutral. Giritlioğlu, after a career with TRT, created her own production company, Sis Yapım, specialising in socio-political productions and remembrance, especially in series such as *Hatırla Sevgili* (Remember, My Love) and *Bu Kalp Seni Unutur mu*? ("Can this Heart Forget You?") about the troubled political history of the country, the film *Güz Sancısı* about the anti-Greek pogrom, the series *Karayılan* about relations between the Armenians and Turks during the war of liberation, and *Kasaba* ("The Market Town") about Alevi Kurdish farm workers. A committed participant in left-wing politics during her time at secondary school and university she enlisted advisers such as Etyen Mahçupyan and Murat Belge to help her carry out her projects (Kalyoncu, 2000). She stated that she wanted to tell young generations about the past and gave priority to "projects which bring out our social mistakes" (Kocal, 2006 and Caliskan, 2007). She did not choose the easy option politically, and her projects were sometimes suspended, at times due to their lack of commercial success.[9] Others were very popular.

Most Production, a company set up in 1985 by Mustafa Oğuz and his wife Gül Oğuz, produced and directed *Sıla*. The distinguishing features of the company were its ideal of development and involvement in social projects. Gül Oğuz was a founding member of the Social Volunteers Foundation

51

(Toplum Gönüllüleri Vakfı) whose mission is to promote "social peace", "solidarity", and "change" to young people whilst "respecting differences". The foundation's fundamental principles include local participation and education. Although Gül Oğuz did not "claim to put an end to custom" nor resolve the problems in the East with her series *Sıla*, she did wish to present and "draw people's attention" to these issues.[10] She wanted to use a highly commercial product to work for a cause (the condition of women): "I can no longer just pretend these things don't exist", she observed.[11]

Other liberal companies have also produced fine examples of this sort of production, such as Erler Film (especially with *Gürbet Kadın* and *Aşk bir Hayal*). This company is headed by Türker İnanoğlu, who was born in 1936 and is part of the Yeşilçam generation of the Turkish cinema industry. His company, founded in 1960, expanded quite quickly and played a full part in the Yeşilçam film industry, in which many Christians were active. He was personally and professionally affected by the exodus of the Greeks from Istanbul to Greece in successive waves over the course of the 1950s and 1960s (Scognamillo, 197–199). These personal and professional experiences, under the impulse of the nationwide trend for cultural diversity and remembrance, would appear to have resulted in specific projects such as *Yabancı Damat*. His *Tatlı Bela Fadime* also featured Turks with Greek origins.

Tek Türkiye, lastly, is an internal production by Samanyolu, a religious channel with links to Fethullah Gülen. The producer, Salih Asan, supports the thesis of fraternity and also points out that *Tek Türkiye* puts forward a vision of responsibility towards the problems currently facing Turkey. In his opinion, the real measure of the series' success is that it shows a young man leaving the mountains.[12]

These series, produced and broadcast on a number of national channels, reached all the various publics and involved a very wide range of producers. The recent movement of private channels towards the public channel TRT (with *Sakarya—Fırat*—2010) shows how the private and public sectors share one and the same discourse. Whilst it is important not to over-interpret and overestimate the political dimension of these actors (there are other, perhaps less "committed" producers also taking part in the creation of this discursive pool and drawing on it), it is nevertheless the case that each of these actors (from the extreme right to the liberal center and taking in the *fettulahcı*) has something to say about the country's history and current state—and indeed says it. The emergence of what could be described as "fashions" and the reproduction of virtually identical images means that one may justifiably speak of circulation around and based on a shared discursive pool.

Discourse Implicitly Structured by Ethnic Hierarchies

Despite the differences between producers, discourse about cultural diversity in general and the Kurdish question in particular is comparatively homogenous. Two levels of discourse exist alongside each other, the one relating to "diversity" as found spreading through the public sphere, and the other relating to ethnic hierarchies. Such hierarchies are nothing new, but were problematic given that the very idea of cultural diversity was denied. Once this idea was recognized it was possible to openly display ethnic hierarchies.

The unity lying behind diversity

Tribal and agha series take place (either entirely or in part) in the peripheral regions of the country where the population is both different and the same. Spatial distancing is the first step in the process of differentiation. These distant regions are discovered by the hero, an outsider who finds himself projected into "another world",[13] that of Eastern or Oriental Turkey. The hero comes either from the Turkish upper or educated middle classes, or else from the East in which case he has studied in the West or abroad. The viewer embarks on a sort of "ethnographic" voyage of discovery of the strange and often violent ancestral practices of the men and women of the East. This didactic technique brings out the differences and thus generates identification. The viewer identifies with Sıla, the lead character in the series of the same name (for we are in the same situation as her, knowing nothing of the customs of the East and discovering them as she does). It is she who observes the other: "Don't look at what is happening here from the perspective of Istanbul" Boran says to her, her husband's tribal leader (*Sıla*, Episode 8). Yet everything in the way it is written leads us to see this "other world" from the perspective of Istanbul and that of the "average Turk".

It is not wholly innocent that the favored spots for shooting these series are Mardin, and Midyat in the same province. Very shortly after the progressive lifting of the state of emergency in the early 2000s, "the region turned into an object of spectacle and a place of political pilgrimage for Kurds and Syriac Christians who wanted to return to their evacuated villages, as well as for human rights activists, journalists, academics, local and international NGO agents, supranational actors and state officials who variously wanted to report the experience of violence under the emergency law and implement projects to improve conditions" (Biner, 2007, 33). Mardin became especially attractive after its application in 2001 to be named as a UNESCO World Heritage Site. Since then it has been widely presented by the media as a "remote and mystic city of the 'Turkish Orient' with a unique architectural heritage, and as a kind of Babylon with a peaceful co-existence of its multi-religious and multilingual communities" (Biner, 2007, 34). Mardin has been built up into a symbol of multiculturalism (Öktem, 2005) and so provides the ideal backdrop to these series.

Discourse about the peaceful coexistence of the peoples is central. When Boran explains to Sıla that "for centuries Turks, Kurds, the Syrians, Yazidis, Arabs, Sunnis, Alevis have all lived together as brothers" here (*Sıla*, Episode 5), any tensions and conflicts which have raged in the region are clearly glossed over, as they are in most discourse currently produced about Mardin (Biner, 2007). Gül Oğuz explained the choice of Mardin to shoot *Sıla* as follows: "it's very unfamiliar here, it's very beautiful. It's like Jerusalem, with three religions and five cultures. I initially chose it because of its visual qualities [...] And then conversations came and fed into the scenario. For example an Assyrian came and said: "we are each of us a different fruit, one of us an apple, another a pear, yet another a peach—but at the end of the day we're all of us fruits and we all live in the same garden".[14]

In *Sıla*, as in *Tek Türkiye*, the various peoples of Turkey are described as "brothers". Zeynep, the schoolmistress in *Tek Türkiye* who comes from the Kurdish village but was educated elsewhere, explains to her pupils why she chose to get them to put on a play about Çanakkale:

> My grandfather, along with his brothers the Lazs, the Circassians, the Yörüks, and the Zazas, gave his life for this country. Çanakkale is the best illustration of this brotherhood. And our grandfathers are buried side by side in Çanakkale even. Let us too be rid of these perverse games and, side by side, be a united Turkey. Let us bring to the surface the brotherhood lying beneath the earth, children! (*Tek Türkiye*, Episode 19).

Discourse about diversity within unity is even present in very nationalistic TV series such as *Kurtlar Vadisi* and *Pars Narkoterör*, whose two heroes are a policeman with a Cherkess mother and a policewoman from a Kurdish background. Differences in origin or language are no longer a threat to the nation with which it is possible to identify.[15] Even the PKK combatants can be reintegrated within the nation. As a soldier says to his brother the policeman: "this young lad arrives ... in the mountains where he had 40 people under his command ... Who knows how many soldiers' lives he took? And so we had to bring him in. But he too is a son of the Fatherland ... he has understood where he went wrong ... it's up to us to forgive him and protect him" (*Pars Narkoterör*, Episode 1).

And so the story that emerges is of "diversity" in a united Turkey, even in the most nationalistic TV series. The only difference is the way non-Muslim minorities are perceived. In Osman Sınav's productions they are excluded from the nation and presented as traitors. In *Tek Türkiye* there is no mention of them. But they are present in more liberal productions about the East (Erler Film, Most Production) via the figure of the Mardin Christian, and so whilst the main character is always Muslim there is a Christian in the supporting role (a friend or "blood brother" of the hero).

Lastly, the way the stories are put together and the characters built up via the extremely widespread theme of adoption—and the associated one of education—also feed into this discourse. In many of these series the viewer learns that the hero who is visiting and observing the East is not really a stranger. The hero, educated, often wealthy, from Istanbul or Ankara, and working as a doctor, businesswoman, or schoolmistress, was born in the East but adopted by a family in the West where they grew up and were educated. The primitive East is seen through the (critical) eyes of this person who is both same-and-different: Sıla the businesswoman, Tarik the doctor in *Tek Türkiye*, and even the policewoman in *Pars Narkoterör* who comes from Van and returns to her region with her fiancé. The schoolmistress in *Tek Türkiye* was not adopted but studied "elsewhere" and returns to the village to carry out her mission as a schoolmistress. In *Tatlı Bela Fadime*, the viewer learns that the grandfather of the Istanbul boy who saves Fadime was a Black Sea Greek from Fadime's village.

The discourse of brotherhood and the narrative technique of adoption emphasize how, despite their diversity, they all belong to the same "family".[16] The different individual is civilized by education, thus becoming a Turk. The different individual, now named as such—all the ethnic groups are publicly referred to—is allowed to retain certain of his or her characteristics, now rendered harmless by the rhetoric and policies of "cultural diversity". Openly displaying this "cultural diversity" is a way of consolidating the process that generates an ethnic hierarchy, for not all identities have the same value. The way the Kurdish population is treated in comparison to other Muslim populations is explicit.

The Consolidation of the Ethnic Hierarchy

In addition to the spatial differentiation—constitutive of difference—and the theme of brotherhood—constitutive of unity—is temporal differentiation, which generates sameness. The primary discourse of TV series about the East, based on the theme of custom, is grounded in the use of an "evolutionary Time" defined by Johannes Fabian as follows: it "promotes a scheme in terms of which not only past cultures, but all living societies were irrevocably placed on a temporal slope, a stream of Time—some upstream, some downstream. Civilisation, evolution, development, acculturation, modernization (and their cousins industrialization, urbanization) are all terms whose conceptual content derives, in ways that can be specified, from evolutionary Time" (Fabian, 1983, 17). The Kurdish regions are anchored in a (virtually) immobile past. The lexical field relating to time, the decors such as the fine old buildings of Mardin and its surrounding region, and the props and costumes all aestheticize the place whilst anchoring it in the past.[17] Not all the series are as aestheticizing as *Sıla* is, and *Tek Türkiye*, for example, made for a popular audience, is simply shot and draws heavily and very effectively on symbols.

The way this Orient is inscribed within the past is also characterised by the continuing existence of custom or *töre*. Custom is used to characterize a violent and virtually savage East, in a more negative but just as Orientalizing way. *Sıla* even goes so far as to say: "the only thing I know is that it is hell here" (*Sıla*, Episode 9). Custom is presented as unjust and cruel, as wholly unworthy of acting as a legal point of reference. This is clearly brought out by the title song of *Sıla*, by one of the most popular singers in Turkey, Sezen Aksu. The continued existence of custom explains why the tribal system also persists, a reminder of ancestral times. The tribal leader owns the land and everything that lives on it (*Sıla*, Episode 1), and the fate of all the individuals he "owns" depends on him. But he is, finally, merely the person who implements the all-powerful custom.[18] The *töre*, via the intermediary of the agha, lay down the rules governing the family and kinship relations and, more generally, relations between men and women. It is because they are still operative that the tribulations of the individual (and especially the woman) persist. These TV series show the primitive customs of the men of the East (vendettas, honor crimes, suicide, forced marriages, polygamy, levirate marriages, *berdel*,[19] etc.), all seen as linked to the *töre* and primarily victimizing women. As seen below, education is the way to remedy their continuing existence and the solution to all the ills afflicting the region.

The only way of presenting the ethnic hierarchy is by comparison. Like *Sıla*, *Tatlı Bela Fadime* is situated in another world, that of the Black Sea, with its own specific characteristics. Fadime, presented from the opening credits as "Karadenizli", is defined more by the region she comes from than by her ethnic

CULTURAL DIVERSITY AND ETHNIC HIERARCHY

status.[20] Most of the distinctive and stereotypical elements of the Lazs—
Karadenizli (Meeker, 1971, 323–324, 329) are deployed from the credits
onwards (with traditional costumes and dances, violins, and plates of ancho-
vies). The accents are specific and everybody carries a weapon, notably the
women. It is on this specific point that the stereotype (about the honor of the
Lazs and their love of weapons) is turned back on itself, for Fadime's father has
run off with a Russian woman but he is weak and afraid of his wife who is
pursuing him with a rifle. This inversion creates a comic effect, and is one of
the points differentiating the systematically serious way the East is treated
from that of other regions and ethnic groups.

Tatlı Bela Fadime, like *Sıla*, addresses the issues of forced marriage and
"honor crimes". However, unlike *Sıla*, *Tatlı Bela Fadime* treats these themes in
an openly humorous manner. Sıla is forced into marriage by *berdel*, and signs
the civil marriage certificate holding a weapon behind her back. When she
flees, the men of the tribe set off after her so as to enforce custom (*töre yerine
bulacak*). Fadime, having saved a young man from Istanbul (but from a Greek
family in the region) from drowning, takes him into her house. He tries to kiss
her while she is sleeping. Thinking her honor has been stained, both she and
her family decide they have to marry. The young man is married by force in
front of the Imam, holding a weapon behind his back. He runs away during
the celebrations and Fadime, armed with a revolver, sets off in pursuit so as to
"cleanse her honor" (*namusu temizlemek*). So whilst the stories might be virtually identical, role inversions and the comic effect this produces establish an
important difference between them. The terminology used also differs, for in
Sıla it is a matter of *töre*, in *Tatlı bela Fadime* a matter of *namus*.

Namus, or "sexual honor", in turn an integral part of "social order" or *şeref*,
is a "grand and weighty" term throughout Turkey (Meeker, 1976, 245). Hülya
Tanrıöver has observed that *namus*, which is "very dear to Turkish culture"
and acts as "a point of resistance to hegemonic values", goes uncontested by the
TV series (Tanrıöver, 2004, 232). Fadime's conduct to "cleanse" her *namus* is
never brought into question by her family and the village community. The
only criticism comes from the mother of the Istanbul family who offers money
to the Karadenizli family to spare her son from marrying a "*köylü*" (village
girl). This criticism is wholly undermined by the fact that it comes from an
unpleasant and superficial character.

The image of the *töre* is entirely different, as seen above. Gül Oğuz makes a
clear distinction between them and *namus*: "it is of course a form of slavery
[...] Custom is not experienced as the honor of the woman but rather as a

chain enslaving both women and men".[21] Everything in the series stigmatises the *töre*, associated with "criminal practices" (going as far as murder). Accordingly, the series merely reinforce the more general vision propagated by national institutions and a whole host of associations, circumscribing honor crimes (representative of the archaic tradition) to the East and the Kurdish populations as studied by Dicle Koğacıoğlu. They thus partake in what Koğacıoğlu has called the "ethnicization of the tradition effect" (Koğacıoğlu, 2004).

This difference in treatment would seem to suggest that Kurds are still perceived as problematic. The East is always portrayed in a serious manner and is no laughing matter. The "ethnographic" journey and didactic tone insist upon the problem of the East, described once again as a "civilization" problem. The lack of education explains why the problem persists and is the source of all the area's ills. The problems of women and tribal violence are linked to the lack of education *Sıla* tells viewers. These problems, as well as the problem of manipulative "terrorism", are bound up with the lack of education *Tek Türkiye* tells viewers. As Bernard Lahire has pointed out, focusing on a unique cause partakes in "the constitution of social problems" and prevents us from "conceiving of the existence of multiple and congruent 'factors'" (Lahire, 1999, 113). There is thus a single solution to the problems of the East—education. The TV series presents businesswomen, doctors, and policeman of Kurdish origin—though nevertheless civilised—whose mission is to civilize the East in turn. Civilizing via education is a way of producing the self-same.

Does "Civil Society" Reproduce the State's Project of Civilising the Kurds?

Writing for Social Change

The TV series and their producers wish to get across a social and political message, and openly preach social change and the evolution of the East towards "modernity". They produce a specific discourse which clearly partakes in the practice of social change.

As seen above, the way the scenarios are constructed makes it possible to bring out that individuals thought of as Other are in fact the same, or can become so via education. Contemporary differences between this "West" and "East" are clearly explained by their position within "evolutionary Time". The need for change is clearly announced from the first episode of *Sıla:* Boran, the (good) tribal leader—the modern agha whose image is also built up in *Asmalı*

Konak—is opposed to certain customs he judges to be unfair, criminal, and dangerous. At his wedding he requests that the traditional gunshots are not fired into the air, arguing that certain customs need to be changed and forbidden. His cousin, Cihan, a figure of the bad agha, refuses and fires his gun in the air. These gunshots mark the beginning of a struggle between the good modernizing agha and bad conservative agha. The catchphrase *töre değiştirmek* ("change custom") becomes the slogan of the series. In *Tek Türkiye* it is especially the Imam who points out that certain *töre* are bad and need to be changed (Episode 2); and Tarik the doctor, like the Zeynep schoolmistress, who both clearly have a "mission" (Episode 9) to tend to the sick and to educate people. Their determination is unwavering. These heroic, fictive missionaries doubtless serve as examples in real life. The image of the "missionary" is an old one, as shown by certain examples from the early days of the Republic.[22] The opening credits of *Tek Türkiye* could not provide a more explicit illustration of its main message, portraying various Kurdish characters (identifiable as such by their clothing and first names) against the greyish walls of a miserable village, before the character of Tarik the doctor appears and the decor of these sad walls fades into a sunny blue sky announcing better days ahead.

And so various techniques are used to get across the production's message. Changes to good and bad characters are used:[23] the bad characters—those who want to follow custom because it is custom or because it serves their own personal interests—gradually die off or change to become "good". The good characters seek to "modify" the status quo, stand up against primitive *töre* and push everybody, especially girls, to go to school. Bad characters are for the preservation of the *töre* and against education, etc. A recurrent technique the producers draw upon in their mission is the insertion of micro-events and mini-tales of a didactic, moralizing, and normative nature, echoing current affairs and the social and political agenda. This may be seen from the first episode of *Sıla* with the gunshots scene. The director Gül Oğuz observed about this: "even if it can seem comic, I will continue" [to include such lines].[24] The use of a wedding scene became a classic for these series, and in each of them the attitude of the characters towards the revolvers signaled if they were good or bad. It is not insignificant that Muharrem Buhara, a scriptwriter specializing in children's series and who worked on entertainment-information programs such as *Bizim Sınıf* (Durgunoğlu, Özuygun Kuşcul 2008), should have worked on the writing of *Sıla*—even though such techniques were not strictly applied.[25]

Furthermore, far less "committed" producers also took up these themes because they were popular and a proven success. This means that there is a circulation and very pronounced intertextuality between the series which repeat each other, refer to each other, reproduce each other (but which also reproduce themes and images present in other cultural products, such as popular novels, or other political and social spheres), and which make up the shared and limited discursive pool both feeding into the work of each producer and to which they in turn add. This shared discursive pool is therefore not limited to the world of TV series.

Civilisation Projects

Discourse on the sources of the problems in the East and on civilisation is not a new phenomenon, but what is new is the emergence of new actors (foundations, associations, commercial companies, and cultural producers) who support and add to a single, given discourse which has the state and its principles at its center. The significance and benefits to be derived from the private sector becoming thus involved in questions hitherto the preserve of the state is something emphasized by both the state and the new actors. The first episode of *Bir Bulut Olsam*, about the opening of a school by "philanthropists", is particularly revealing here: during the opening ceremony a character remarks: "we will see what citizens are able to do in cooperation with the state!". This exclamation is a clear instance of the intertextuality between the TV series on the one hand, and the exchanges between fiction and reality on the other. It is impossible not to see a reference to the script of *Sıla* and the practical involvement of its producers.

The commitment of producers has transpired in the real world too. Following on from *Sil Baştan* (Start from the Beginning, Kanal D, 2004), an early series about the East and custom, Gül Oğuz lent her name to an Institute for women that was being built in Diyarbakır (in the municipality of Bağlar). In 2007 she invested in the building of a primary school in Soğutlu in the region of Mardin. At the opening ceremony Gül Oğuz declared: "these children will bring light to this land, they will bring new life to it, they will bring work and bread. They will set up thousands of schools and factories. Our dream will become a reality".[26] The school project, its building, and its opening, are included within the script of the series, and the opening ceremony was broadcast live on ATV with the music and title song of the series, fiction and reality thus meshing together. This mode of pronouncement—commonly used in Turkish series today (Vovou & Koukoutsaki-Monnier, 2007)—makes the message of the series all the more practical and reinforces the practical role played by discourse producers.

Although the construction of the school was not entirely carried out within the framework of the Ministry of Education's "Eğitime 100% Destek" campaign (100 per cent support for education—which enables volunteers, associations, private companies, etc, to finance the building of schools and benefit from tax exemptions), the Mardin Vali commented on the similarities during the opening ceremony, declaring that, thanks to philanthropists (hayırsever), education in Mardin was making significant steps forward.[27] This campaign, launched in 2003, is only one of many to promote schooling—and especially the schooling of girls—set up in Turkey as part of the UNICEF "Education for All" project in 2003. It was around this period that campaigns were set up, either inspired or launched by the state, or by foundations and associations supporting, relaying, and contributing to the dominant discourse about education. Whilst there is not space here to present these campaigns in detail, it is worth mentioning certain aspects of some of them so as to bring out the existence of this shared discursive pool relating to problems in the East on the one hand, and the role played by the state in this discursive pool on the other.

The aim of the "Haydı Kızlar Okula" campaign (Come on girls, off to school!), the main project of the "Campaign to Support Girls' Schooling" (Kız Çocukları Okullulaşmasına Destek Kampanyası) launched in 2003 by UNICEF in collaboration with the Turkish Ministry of Education, is to bring about equality in the schooling of boys and girls. It started in the ten Kurdish provinces of the East where the rate of schooling was very low amongst girls. It was launched by the Ministry as part of the UNICEF programme, but nevertheless draws upon contributions from "civil society organizations" and private actors. On its website, a page entitled "what I can do" suggests to the media that they "prepare TV series about the education of girls".[28] Ideas are thus put forward to "civil society organizations", celebrities, and ordinary citizens.

Many campaigns for girls' schooling were set up by "Çağdaş Yaşam Destek Derneği" (Association to Support Modern Life), an Ataturkist association that was set up in 1989. This "civil society association" working "above political parties" nevertheless works in very close "collaboration with state institutions" on occasions.[29] It also calls upon the aid of the private sector. Two campaigns both provide an example of this collaboration between state institutions, civil society organisation, and the private sector, and clearly illustrate the existence of this common discursive pool: "Çağdaş Türkiye'nin Çağdaş Kızları-Kardelenler" (Modern Girls of Modern Turkey—Snowdrops) and "Baba Beni Okula gönder" (Send me to school, Dad!). The first, in collaboration with the telecommunications company Türkcell, finances several thousand grants for young girls in the East to study in the West. It has received widespread support from celebrities from the world of "culture". Ayşe Kulin visited families of girls receiving grants in the East and described the miserable environment they lived in and their closed horizons. This misery was opposed to the light of knowledge offered by schools (Kulin, 2004). Kardelenler has also received the support of Sezen Aksu, a very famous singer and liberal, and a vocal supporter of a solution to the Kurdish problem and the recognition of cultural diversity.[30] She made an album whose profits went to financing the campaign. The video of the song "Kardelenler" presents numerous similarities with the discourse of the TV series: a Kurdish village, a girl, and the singer. The girl is first filmed in black and white, and the singer in color. They then hold hands, upon which the girl appears in color too. They go through the village collecting the girls who are busy working and take them to school. They put on their school uniforms and enter the school over which the Turkish flag is flying. The video presenting the Baba Beni Okula gönder! Campaign (in collaboration with *Milliyet*) opens on a schoolmaster taking the register in his class. The boys answer from the classroom that they are present, whereas the girls answer present from the fields, the chicken run, their bridal room, etc. An indignant voice-off states: "that's not where they should be, they should be at school".[31]

Conclusion

The example studied here of TV series shows that whilst discourse on cultural diversity makes it possible to name and describe different ethnic groups, it still has its limitations. It is based on ancient stereotypes and whilst it does preach diversity, this is only as part of unity. This discursive shift goes hand-in-hand with changes in state policies, with the definition of Turkish-ness being debated and a wider range of cultural practices authorized, leading on to new demands and new forms of demands issuing from particularistic movements.

On the other hand, this discourse about diversity does not emerge on its own and reinforces the ethnic hierarchy by bringing it out into the open and calling on a wide range of actors. The narrative structures and use of "evolutionary Time" is a way of presenting Kurds as fledgling Turks. Education plays a central role in this evolution toward civilisation. Thus the new form of "cultural diversity" consolidates a long-standing situation of domination. Whilst providing everyone with a new opportunity to voice their views on the subject, the discursive pool that producers draw on and add to is limited in scope and the discursive habits established over the course of the past century are not brought into question, whatever the point of view. The "secret violence" of cultural diversity "consists in camouflaging its own violence", one might be tempted to say, paraphrasing Michel De Certeau (1993, 55). By camouflaging it in this way it can also be propagated to new actors, and sometimes even those seen as being on the side of "protest".[32] Furthermore, this balance is not uniquely symbolic since such rhetoric legitimates the involvement of each individual. Nevertheless, as observed in this article, there is a wholly relative "transformation" of discourse and its concomitant immediate effects on the redefinition of terms and actors in the conflict. The long-term effects are no doubt more complex.

Further work is no doubt required. The comparison needs to be taken further by working on other ethnic groups, and especially the Roma. But as this article has attempted to show, what is especially needed is to analyse these forms of discourse and images—and conduct fuller analysis of discursive habits—taking into account the far larger cultural, social, and political spheres within which they circulate, are perceived, and are reproduced. TV series are but one of many possible areas of observation. A long-term project of this sort—based on the existing literature—would make it possible to deconstruct this "discursive and imagistic screen" (Lemaire, 2003, 144) through which the reality of power relations are filtered.

3

ETHNIC AND REGIONAL FERMENT IN IRAN

THE GILAN EXAMPLE

Christian Bromberger
Translated by Françoise Gillespie

When contemplating ethnic conflicts in Iran, the observer is immediately struck by the situations of Baluchistan, Kurdistan, and to a lesser extent Azerbaijan. In other provinces the tension, and its expression, is certainly not absent, but is less heavily politicized. Why are there such differences in intensity of demands? Two paths are generally explored to explain these disparities.

The first path takes into account both the specificity and the liveliness of cultural identities: the greater the gap between the ways of being and the attitudes of a given group, and those that are expressed at the core of the nation, the more pronounced such differences will be, the more intense the friction (and conducive to conflict), and the more vehement the claims. The strength of activism could therefore rest upon objective and subjective factors. It could rest upon the conjunction of a substantial identity—scrutinized by the alien observer—and of a performative identity, expressed by actors. Congruence between substantial and performative identities has been dis-

65

cussed in the past. Identities that are proclaimed are selective, they result from choices and omissions, they move according to context. They are different to what a substantive and contrastive analysis of facts may reveal, while subjective[1] and performative markers of identity refer to a society's genuine characteristics (language, religion, customs and historical events), if only by enhancing them.

If one is to question the "objective" and "subjective" contents of identities, it is necessary to take into account the geo-demographical contexts in which these identities appear, are expressed, and are claimed. Identities interlock, be it from the local to the regional, ethnical, or national. There exists great friction between classes, be they of similar scope (between micro-regions for example), or between inferior and superior classes (between a micro-region and a region for example). Such friction can arise between competitors on the same level same level—as a test of their own superiority—or between an encompassing authority and its subordinates, when regionalists denounce "small countries" for their lack of loyalty, or when the latter accuse regionalists of stifling them.

The second path suggests an opposite move: rather than starting from groups and their cultural differences—between themselves and the state norm—the idea is to start from the state, its very nature and its acceptance of differences (or lack thereof). The Jacobin model, for example, promotes a hegemonic culture that is not adapted to ethnic or regional specificities. On the contrary, the imperial model (the Ottoman or the Austro-Hungarian Empires, for example) allows for diversity as long as it does not question the order of the general structure. Federalism or confederalism (the Helvetian system, for example) are other systems that accept cultural and institutional differences. Whatever the model, the authority of the central power plays a critical role in determining the modes through which differences are expressed. In less democratic situations, the cultural expression replaces the political, since it is the only alternative to open revolt.

This contribution will follow these two paths, by briefly presenting the situation of minorities in the Iranian state and their historical background, then by questioning the case of Gilân, a province of northern Iran, not known for its violent outbursts, but with a certain editorial fever and cultural abundance that express a will to further autonomy. Does a strong feeling of identity, along with the reminders of humiliating encounters, contribute to this cultural activism? What sort of reaction do these soft regionalist claims trigger, both beforehand—by an authoritative state not so inclined to accept initiatives that could escape its control—and after—by local subdivisions (small ethnic groups, micro-regions) wishing to promote their singularity and feeling under-represented by a regional project that appears hegemonic to them?

Ethnicity Taboo in Iran Today

Early each year the Supreme Guide of the Revolution proclaims a theme, or slogan, for meditation throughout the year. At the start of the year 1386 (2007–2008, the Iranian year starts at vernal equinox), Ali Khamenei proclaimed *Ettehad-e melli Ensejân-e eslami* (National unity, Islamic cohesion). By adopting such a slogan, Ali Khamenei clearly signaled that national unity and Islamic cohesion are at the forefront of leadership concerns. The Supreme Guide's annual slogan, however, is far from being the only indicator among the government and their supporters of a national sensitivity regarding these issues. To merely say the word *qomiyat* (ethnicity) or to speak of Kurds and Balochis alone is sufficient to arouse suspicion of secessionist Zionist plotting backed by "hostile forces" abetted by "world arrogance". Researchers interested in ethnic groups and known protesters are quickly arrested or refused entry visas.[2] In short, there is mistrust in high places of the "deceptive uses of ethnicity, a concept that lends itself to conspiracy" in the words of the *hojjat-ol eslam* Yunesi (as quoted by William Samii, 2000, 126):

> It is true that during the two years preceding the Supreme Guide's watchword, troubles were numerous in the peripheral provinces: riots in Mahabad in July 2005 following the death of a young Kurdish activist shot by security forces; armed actions carried out by the PJAK (Free Life Party of Kurdistan, formed in the spring of 2004); A major demonstration in Tabriz, in May 2006, involving some 200,000 people, following publication of an article and cartoon lampooning Turks in the newspaper *Iran*; Unrest in Khuzestan in response to a persistent rumor according to which the government is preparing an ethnic restructuring of the province to benefit the Persian population at the expense of Arabs; armed attacks by a Balochi group, Jundallah (People's Resistance Movement of Iran), including an attempt on two of President Ahmadinejad's bodyguards during a presidential visit to the region... At this new year 1386, national unity and Islamic cohesion seem like so much damaged goods. How did the situation become so tense?

Islamic and Imperial Unification

Iran is an ancient multiethnic empire that became a centralized nation state only under the Pahlavi dynasty (1925–1979). Reza Shah and his son

Mohammed Reza pursued a deliberate policy of linguistic unification by imposing the Persian language in education and the media. Cultural or ethnic expressions of regional diversity were tolerated but only so far as to accommodate folk festivals and the like, but never anything that might be construed as undermining national unity. A 1925 article in the newspaper *Ayandeh* (Future) illustrates and foreshadows this project. The columnist wrote: "Achievement of national identity means that the Persian language must be established throughout the country, and that regional differences in clothing, customs and the likes must disappear" (quoted by Atabaki, 2005, 31). Provincial boundaries similarly provide evidence of the drive for unification with respect to pre-Islamic dynasties. Reza Shah used terminology (*ostân*—province—*shahrestân*—equivalent of a French county) reminiscent of the Sassanids for naming territorial divisions (Chehabi, 1997, 235) and ensured that provincial territories were not contiguous with the ethnic groups inhabiting the area, so that, for instance, the area inhabited by the Kurds extends far beyond the limits of the provinces of Kurdistan, while Sistan and Baluchistan form a single province (see Hourcade, 2004, 518), the Bakhtiari people are divided between Khuzestan and Chahar-Mahal, etc.

The Islamic Republic has certainly been more tolerant of linguistic pluralism, enshrining this in Article Fifteen of the constitution. The constitution recognised the equality of all languages then spoken in Iran, under Persian of course, the sole official language. Whatever their pluralistic initiatives in the linguistic sphere, however, was more than counterbalanced by intolerance in the religious sphere; unification and standardisation of religious practices figured heavily in the modernization program, and the imposition of an Islamic lifestyle stringently imposed.

Moreover, the long war against Iraq (1980–1988) strengthened nationalist sentiment, which, together with population displacements, contributed to the unification of customs. These events have been so effective that it appears the peoples of an empire are now the minorities of a nation state: abused minorities, but nonetheless loyal to the nation in the face of several challenges to their loyalty. A telling case is at the outset of the Iran-Iraq War, the Iraqi regime believed that some of these minorities would rally to the cause of their "Arab brothers" in Khuzestan, but national loyalty prevailed over a hypothetical ethnic solidarity.

Does this mean that identity politics have vanished under a unified state? The situation is actually much more complex and in the 1990s took a strange turn for various reasons. First, with respect to issues of regional power, following the breakup of the Soviet Union and the reorganization of Iraq, Iranian minorities who previously occupied peripheral positions found themselves supported by independent states (Azerbaijan, Turkmenistan) or autonomous regions (Kurdistan) inhabited by newly enfranchised ethnic relations. To the southeast the Balochis are supported by a Baluchistan Province, which enjoys relative autonomy within the Pakistani federal system. Examples of cross-border ethnic and national self-affirmation generate renewed interest in ethnic identity, especially as there is no lack of structural cause for complaint. These minorities (Kurds, Turkmen and Balochis, excepting Azeri Turks) are completely or predominantly Sunni in an authoritarian Shi'ite state. Such "pan-Shi'ism" (William Samii, 2000, 133) is particularly visible and present since the Islamic revolution. Article Twelve of the Constitution, states that the official religion of Iran is Twelver Shia Islam and affirms that other schools of Islam will be respected and that regulations will be adapted in localities where there is a non-Twelver majority. But the reality is quite different. Sunni mosques were destroyed or closed in several cities and there are none in Tehran so that Sunni faithful must attend payer services in the Pakistani embassy or on a vacant lot in the event of great collective ceremonies. Not a single Sunni is a member of the government and it is difficult for Sunnis to access positions of official responsibility, even within their own provinces. In short these people feel a sense of rejection and have developed relationships between themselves and with Central Asian republics, such that one may speak of an "Oriental Sunni Arc" (Dudoignon, 2006), counterpoint to the "Shia arc" formed by Iran and southern Iraq, Bahrain and southern Lebanon. The sense of marginality suffered by these minorities is heightened by their relative poverty: Kurdistan, parts of East and West Azerbaijan provinces and Baluchistan belong to the disadvantaged northwest and southeast (Hourcade et al, 1998, 160–161). These minorities suffer therefore a quadruple marginalization: spatial, cultural, religious and economic.

Gilan: A Polyethnic, Stratified Society

Wedged between the heights of the Alborz Mountains and Caspian Sea, Gilan province occupies a marginal position within the Iranian national space.[3] Benefitting from a subtropical, humid climate, it is a landscape inlaid with rice paddies, citrus gardens, mulberry plantations and fields of tea—a lush green landscape lying in startling contrast to the ocher tones of the Iranian plateau. The mountains are mainly occupied by pastoral peoples, the

Gilaki to the east and the Talyshi to the northwest, the latter forming a clearly individualized group within the province, an "ethnic region" in the words of Marcel Bazin (1980). Taken as a whole, the provincial population forms a stratified multi-ethnic society, (Bromberger, in press) each group having a differential advantage with regard to the most prized resources. At the top of the scale are the Gilaki, followed closely by the Talyshi of the coastal plain. These two groups dominate regional rice and tea production, and, historically, sericulture. The Gilaki also have the upper hand on key sectors of commerce and administration, even if they face competition for administrative posts from Persian bureaucrats originating on the plateau. The mountain people of the wet slope of the Alborz Mountains, (the Gilaki and most Talyshi) special-ize in cattle and sheep husbandry and occupy a peripheral position within the region and a lower status than their Gilaki neighbors. The Sunni faith of the Talyshi population inhabiting central Gilan Province no doubt contributes to their marginalization as an ethnic group (Bazin and Bromberger, 1982, 14–15 and Map 4). At the bottom of the social scale are seasonal migrants and immi-grants from other provinces. Seasonal migrants, mostly Khalkhali, a Turkic group from the arid mountains of neighboring Azerbaijan Province, find work in Gilan during the winter months doing menial labor (clearing fields for example), as masons or as peddlers. These migrants are also specialists in mari-time fishing, a relatively "skilled" labor in which Gilakis who live by the sea have no interest, treating the activity with indifference and even repulsion. In the province, Kurds are another stigmatized minority. A number of Kurds were settled on the coastal plain under Reza Shah—notably, the settlement was in fact a result of forced migration intended to present a barrier against the threat of a Russian invasion—and have a monopoly on buffalo husbandry, a specialty for which their Gilaki neighbors have the highest disdain. These buffalo herders are further stigmatized for their religious belief. They are con-sidered *Ahl-e Haqq* and qualified, as elsewhere in Iran, as *Ali Abdullah* (those who claim that Ali is God, the height of impiety).

A process of economic integration has no doubt been underway for the past thirty years: the Gilakis participate in greater numbers in marine fisheries, the Khalkhalis and Gâlechis have permanently settled the villages of the plain and taken up farming. At the same time, the Khalkhalis, and more generally, the Azeris have become active in the urban economy, notably in the construc-tion and trade sectors. In short, the traditional hierarchy has weakened even though it remains objectively perceptible, whereas a subjective hierarchy may be inferred from ethnic stereotypes and "skills" attributed to one or another population... In announcing the proposal to create an autonomous province of Tâlech, the reaction of a significant Gilakis is outrage: "What! These people who provided us with maids now want a province!"

The Thrust of Regional Sentiment and Cultural Activism

Whatever the friction, Gilan does not stand out among Iranian provinces for its ethnic claims or conflicts as do Baluchistan or Kurdistan. Rather, Gilan is often portrayed rather lightheartedly, famed for its cuisine and for the alleged frivolity of its women (Bromberger, 1986). From within the province however, there is a growing regional sentiment that varies in intensity and shape according to location. This movement is rooted in an anti-establishmentarian history rich in protest activity that has proven a fertile ground for political mobilization. Between 1915 and 1921, Gilan was the threshold of a peasant rebellion framed by the urban elites that led in 1920 to the short-lived Soviet Socialist Republic of Persia, with its capital at Rasht. This was not a 'regionalist movement', yet served to instill in the local culture a memory of political mobilization. How then does this regionalist sentiment translate into the language of contemporary regionalism?

Actors for a Regionalist Approach

It is useful to identify the main instigators, or entrepreneurs of regional protest movements, as well as their target audience. Largely, the instigators belong to an intellectual elite comprised of teachers, students, aspiring academics and professors, the latter of who are often forced out of their posts as a result of their dissidence. The audience for public events is more varied however, ranging from casual observers seeking personal freedoms to lofty regionalists using public events to deliver a message of protest; deep-seated regionalist convictions, the desire to voice largely unheard regional grievances, and even just simple entertainment value figure among reasons for attendance. Regional events then serve as a substitute forum in a context of restrained political discourse.

The Agenda: From Place Names to Journals

The revolution provided the opportunity to restore old place-names that in Pahlavi times had assumed heavily imperial connotations (Bandar-e Pahlavi was restored to Anzali, Bandar-e Farahnaz, Kiyashahr, etc.). The search for demotic place names, particularly in Talesh, assumed an ethnic subtext; one stark example was the renaming Hashtpar, capital of Talesh County, to Talesh, in keeping with the local language.

Perhaps the most striking feature of the cultural activism that has gripped the province is the proliferation of cultural associations and publishing activities. Gilan boasts a strong tradition in these areas (particularly in the field of publishing, see Nozâd), a tradition closely associated with the region's active political history. There were no less than eighty-four newspapers and magazines in 2007, with ninety more awaiting authorization; it also hosts forty publishing houses, publishing one book per day, on average.

Although small in area, Gilan Province is among Iran's three most prolific provinces in term of publishing output.[4] Among these publications, all created or recreated beginning in the 1990s (with marked acceleration during the presidency of Mr. Khatami, 1997–2005), are a dozen that are either ethnographic in scope, or advocate a regionalist editorial program. The bi-monthly *Gilevâ* (the local name for a west wind) is the oldest (founded in 1992) and most widely distributed of these magazines, with a 1000 subscriptions and a total distribution of about 4,000 copies per issue.[5]

Edited in Persian, the journal publishes a number of Gilaki texts. Among other journal titles, one might cite *Gilân-e Mâ* ("Our Gilan") and *Farhang-e Gilân* ("Culture of Gilan"), a publication of the Regional Office of the Ministry of Islamic Guidance, and duplication of local editorial initiatives, a topic I discuss in greater detail at a later stage. Even more surprising is the number of reviews supported by Talesh, a community of fewer than 500,000 inhabitants. Talesh supports six reviews/journals, including *Tâlech* ("Monthly"), *Bahâr-e Tâlech* ("Tâlechi Spring") *Tâlechyâr, Tahqiqât-e Tâlech* ("Quarterly Review of Taleshi Research"), *Nasim-e Tâlech* ("The Taleshi Breeze"), *Zamime*, an annual supplement devoted to Talesh published by *Farhang-e Gilân*, and the official journal mentioned above.

These publications are varied in scope; ethnographic and historical studies, economic analyses, hagiographies (particularly those of local or regional significance), local poems and proverbs, demands for the preservation of local languages, and protestations against the county's current status as a provincial backwater all feature, to various degrees, in the publications. Gilân, popular under the Pahlavis for its beach resorts and supposed moral freedom, is today disparaged for the same reasons. The journalistic scene allows for a counternarrative celebrating the heritage of the region, with gastronomy, literature, legendary histories and local grievances finding expression within it. One particular showing of cultural pride is to be found in the writings of A. Abdoli (e.g. 1386/2007), a Tâlechi rhapsodist, who argues that Zoroaster was from the region. Among other significant and recent publications of regionalist inclination, we should note dictionaries of Gilâki, Tâlechi and even Tâti, a minority language spoken in the province. For a long time the only Gilâki-Persian dictionary was that published in 1953 by Mr. Sotudeh. Since the 1990s, a host of new dictionaries have been produced, including Gilâki-Persian, Tâlechi-Persian and even comparative dictionaries of Tâlechi, Tâti and Azeri.

Sources of Conflict: Regionalism, Ethnicism and Localism

The publishing landscape is not only distinguished by its scale, but also its reflection of varied, and often diametrically opposed, political opinions. This is readily deducible from a quick comparison between two major publications, *Gilevâ* and *Tâlech*; the latter consistently calling for an autonomous province of Talesh, while the former are strongly in favor of a unitary-state model.

In addition to the publications themselves, there is a dense network of associations supporting them. These operate on both a local and regional level, typically in Gilan and Tehran respectively, adding yet another layer of complexity to the agendas expressed in the journals. The geographical scope of these organizations varies considerably; one association, *Siyâhkalihâ*, represents the small town of *Siyâhkal* and its surrounding countryside; another association, Rudsar, beyond representing the city, represents the eastern limits of the province; in Talesh, an association located in Fuman seeks to represent western Taleshis exclusively. Nor do all these groups concern themselves with cultural or administrative issues. One particularly welcome development is that of associations promoting environmentalist causes.

The major discontinuity, however, occurs between the two groupings of Gilâni expatriates based in Tehran where the regional debates are framed. Prior to 2006, both groups were chaired by the same person, a Tâlechi university professor of environmental sciences. The dispute arose over the adoption of a regional project. The Gilâni members of the association were hostile to the creation of a province of Tâlech as demanded by the militant Tâlechi. The situation rapidly escalated with the Gilâni charging the Tâlechi with separatist intentions, of being Zionists backed by foreigners. The Gilâni in turn accused the Tâlechi of wanting to dismember Iran by joining Tâlechi militants in

Azerbaijan who in 1993 formed a short-lived autonomous republic that was quickly suppressed by the Azeri authorities in Baku. Tâlechi activists challenged these criticisms, advocating the creation of a federal state where the province would benefit from greater economic, social and cultural freedoms. Feeling at "the periphery of the periphery", disadvantaged in a province which is itself relegated to inferior status, they simultaneously challenge the hierarchy which subjects them to the Gilaki within the Provincial system and the state's centralizing policies. The discomfort is all the more vivid when one considers that the Tâlechi conceive of themselves as sandwiched between Gilaki Shi'ites to the south and, to the north, Azeri Turks who claim that the largely Turkified Astara County, although Tâlechi in name, be attached to Ardabil province (Bromberger, 2007).

Publications and associations, the third register upon which is written the record of regional sensitivities, are constituted by cultural events that abound and are themselves sources of conflict. Festivals (*jashnvâre*) of regional culture are a popular genre much in demand. Onstage, a succession of poets, singers, girls in regional costume and amateur actors interpret the phases of agricultural labor (the transplanting and weeding of rice beds, for example) or pastoral activities (churning of butter, spinning of wool) or skits taken from local folklore. Above all, these festivals celebrate local personalities, living or recently deceased whose memories are praised or to whom prizes are awarded (another popular exercise in Iran). On such occasions, nationalists and federalists do not sit in the same row. If, on the other hand, the festival is held in Tehran where the audience is composed of more than provincial expatriates, regionalists from other provinces will attend as a sort of fraternal expression of regionalist sentiment. Since the establishment of an open-air museum in Saravan, Gilan province, at this author's initiative (Bromberger, 2007b), the museum can also host such events. The revitalization of lost rituals is also part of the regionalist repertoire. Among these are the celebration of the *No-ruzbel*, or Gâlechi New Year, celebrated on the 15th Mordad (6 August) and not on the vernal equinox as the Persian New Year, and *Tirmâsinza* (13 Tir, the fourth month of the year, and so, on 19 November for the Gâlechi community). The first event draws several hundred people in a village located at 1400 meters elevation, where a bonfire is lighted (photo 1) to celebrate the New Year. The second is a divinatory practice, said to foretell the fate of participants in the ritual. These ceremonies had not been performed for over thirty years and were revived in 2006–2007. New rituals were launched, such as the celebration of the lilies (*gol-e susân*) on the heights of Ammarlu, which has been observed since 2005, and for which the public gathers for tightrope walking, popular music and picnics. A thousand people attended in 2008.

One should also note that these events are organized during the daytime at high elevations and far from surveillance. Generally, a local celebrity, living or deceased, is honored and participants do not hesitate to speak frankly, criticizing the regime directly or indirectly. We should finally mention events that are celebrated regionally but which are not regional in nature, as for example, the commemoration of the martyrdom of Mirza Kuchek, leader of the movement that led to the creation of the ephemeral Soviet Socialist Republic of Persia. Some celebrate the revolutionary hero in his home, the restoration of which was supported by community contributions. Others celebrate his martyrdom near his mausoleum, where the character's aura and religious piety are evoked by word and image.

The State's Response

Numerous points of tension existed between regionalists; the conflict, and indeed at times intersection, of interests between federalists, nationalists, provincialists and ethno-provincialists gave rise to the conflict. Nonetheless it was not restricted to this, and we must also consider external conflict with the state. Much of the government's official language is characterized by themes of national unity, emphasizing repeatedly the notion of "loyalty to the motherland". A May 2006 article in the official *Iran News* carried the headline, "Loyalty of Iran's Ethnic Groups Not in Doubt". In the article the columnist noted, "The majority of Balochis, Kurds, Arabs, Azeris and other ethnic groups are patriotic and nationalistic Iranians with absolutely no separatist tendency". This loyalty is displayed during the week of "sacred defense" when, during the military review, representatives of different ethnic groups dressed in regional costume parade in formation. Any deviation from these standards of loyalty, especially in ethnically sensitive areas (Baluchistan, Khuzestan, Kurdistan), is, as we said earlier, severely sanctioned and punished. In less sensitive areas, such as Gilan, the response of the state assumes a more subtle form, at least in appearance.

Once an association has been identified as having dissident tendencies, state officials or regime supporters invariably respond by creating their own structures to counter their influence.

In addition to the director's admonishments concerning the duty of loyalty, one must add those of clerics who, when celebrating the martyrdom of Mirza, compared the martyred hero with clerics who defended their country during the Holy War with Iraq (1980–1988). Posters read slogans, "May the 11th Azar (2 December), day of the fighting cleric, of the martyr General Mirza Kuchik Jangali and of martyred clerics from the province of Gilan be praised!" One must never concede to one's opponents the exclusive use of a popular symbol! We find this same situation in Tehran, where members of the House of Gilân (Jacobins sympathetic to the regime) and those of the House Tâlech (Federalists and Democrats) stared at each other as unblinking porcelain dogs. But power does not delay in its attempt to neutralize opponents through the use of entryism; by operating a change of venue in 2007, the authorities regained control of the House of Tâlech, now directed by a Tâlechi occupying an official position.

The tactic is the same with respect to publications: *Farhang-e Gilân* is, as mentioned earlier, the official journal of the Ministry of Islamic Guidance and a hindrance to the various independent reviews. But it is in regional events that the use of public power is the most spectacular, and where, by disruption or pre-emption, provincial authorities are able to recover the initiative. Here are two examples: during the 2008 *No-ruz Bel*, the provincial Heritage Service themselves organized the ceremony. As people gathered on Malakut Hill to listen to regional musical groups, a dissident group pre-empted the programming asking the crowd to chant *"Khalij hamishe fârs"* (Persian Gulf Forever), a slogan and theme unrelated to the event. Later, once the bonfire was lighted, local firefighters were summoned to extinguish it. The year before, the heritage services produced a poster for the event that was not released until the day before the festival ceremony while the festival organizer was occupied with a visit to the local gendarmerie. In June 2008, approximately 1,000 regionalists and casual observers gathered for the annual Festival of the Lilly, held on the heights overlooking Gilân where three-quarters of the remaining wild lilies are carefully protected. The Environment and Heritage services supervised the event imposing arbitrary rules: one may play musical instruments and sing, but one may not dance. Another example of arbitrariness, this one reported in Tehran, occurred where an ethnic cultural center (*Farhangsarâ-e aqvam*) provided space for regionalist events, its director insisting on the links between regional cultures and national culture. Regionalists are not fooled by such stratagems and can only support them. But how then, should they react, when, during a show or outdoor event, a speaker takes the microphone to denounce international Zionist conspiracies or to thank the *amâken* (secret police) for their contribution to the event's successful organization?

Conclusion

Conflicts and resentment are not lacking either among regional movements or between regional movements and the state. The situation is probably not as aggravated in Gilan and Tâlech as it is in other peripheral regions. No Gilâki or Tâlechi representative attended the Congress of Nationalities which met in London in February 2005, while members of Kurdish, Balochi, Turkmen, Azeri, and Arabic Khuzestan did. One of the principal demands of the Congress was greater federalism, an option that the Iranian government attributes to "the cabal of global arrogance". Conflicts driven by minorities seeking recognition of their cultural and political rights are not so very different from conflicts that could be used to destabilize the central and centralizing power of the government of the Islamic Republic, and certainly could not be overlooked as a stratagem employed by a hostile power bent on the government's overthrow. However, proponents of a federalist approach and of a relaxation of central authority are not at all conspirators manipulated from abroad. Conflicts of varying intensity between the center and the periphery pose the problem and define the nature of the Iranian state. Whatever happens, issues of ethnicity, regionalism, localism and diversity of religious affiliation will continue here as elsewhere despite the fact that when identities breakdown they tend to be reasserted with ever greater ostentation and vehemence.

4

THE MANAGEMENT OF IDENTITIES IN AND BY TURKEY'S POLITICAL PARTIES

Elise Massicard[1]
Translated by John Angell

This paper grew out of my surprise that, while like France, Turkey envisions itself as a universalist and unified republic, Turkey confronts far more significant problems of identity. In fact, Turkey's identity-related problems, which have centered on specific ethnic and denominational issues since the 1980s (Ayata, 1997; Bozarslan, 2000), have recently increased in intensity. Identity politics has since become a means of claiming and proclaiming particularist rights, which are often expressed in terms of correcting wrongs or of demanding recognition. This development has been associated with various tensions and very high levels of conflict, particularly, but not exclusively, regarding the Kurdish question (Kılıç, 1992). More broadly, growth among a range of movements has been accompanied by an increasing tendency to interpret social problems through the lens of a wide range of identitary interpretations. For example, the Islamist movement is read through issues of identity. Political actors have been forced to take action concerning the growing importance of identity issues compelled to find ways of managing them, although such questions are often settled and regulated outside "legitimate" policies.

The present essay is intended to analyze how the principal actors in the political arena, the political parties, manage these identitary tensions both within their constituencies and externally. I will address the subject by cross-referencing different levels of observation and analysis, based on the hypothesis that the multiple constraints and modes of management vary at national, local, and individual levels and that only an analysis that accounts for the coexistence and articulation of these different levels can provide an understanding of how identity is managed, which can appear paradoxical on initial examination. The analysis of the interplay among different levels of analysis, that is, the focus of this article, derives from several different scholarly sources. On the macro level, my interpretations are grounded in previous studies of Alevist mobilization at the end of the 1980s that gave voice to the Alevis' demands for recognition (Massicard, 2005b).[2] At the local level, the study grows out of my previous research regarding political parties in Adana between 2006 and 2009, particularly of the CHP (People's Republican Party).[3]

The choice of this metropolis of approximately two million inhabitants in southern Turkey is related, among other factors, to its "multicultural" character—a relatively politically correct term frequently used by my interlocutors to designate the population's diversity. The principal groups that compose the local population include the Turkophones, often described as "Türkmen", Arabophone Alevi groups[4] (also called Nusayri), who settled in the area at the end of the 19th century (Keser, 2008), and Kurds. The Kurds were traditionally seasonal laborers in the rich plains of Çukurova, particularly during the cotton harvest, and began to settle in Adana in the 1970s, followed by a larger influx when many took refuge in the city after the war in the southeast. The Adana area has experienced a period of socio-economic difficulty that began two decades ago and is tied to problems in agriculture and agro-industry, primarily cotton, and to the development of its neighbor and competitor Mersin as the primary commercial center of the region. This pattern was accompanied by the transfer of a number of government subsidies from Adana to Mersin, and several factories subsequently were closed (Emiroğlu, 2007). As a consequence, unemployment is very high and is exacerbated by significant internal migration, leading to Adana's status as one of Turkey's most economically unequal cities.

The region's tensions and social problems are often framed in terms of identity. Adana and its neighbor, Mersin, are the only large cities in Turkey outside of the Kurdish areas where the vote for pro-Kurdish parties is significant (approximately 9 per cent, compared to 5 per cent in Istanbul.)[5] Tension between so-called ethnic groups is frequent.[6] Adana has a reputation for violence, which forms part of its image, and the Adana civil courts are known throughout the country for the memorable episodes of violence. Tension between groups often leads to outbreaks of violence.[7]

We are faced with two questions: how can we account for the fact that this localized tension and sporadic violence between groups do not become generalized? And why, despite the political actors in Adana interpreting these incidents in terms of identity, does "visible politics"—that which is expressed through the mainstream media—(Sartori, 1976) make such infrequent mention of them? The goal of this article is to analyze the way in which in this context the parties that position themselves as "universalist" manage the identity dimension.[8] Demands based on issues of identity, which are illegal, are quasi-taboo for the political parties, which are reluctant to become public relays for these sorts of demands, particularly on the national level. The parties consider the identity dimension as a central parameter in their relations with voters, however, and they incorporate it for this purpose, particularly in terms of personnel management of candidates and party officials. In order to face this double constraint, they use specific modes of communication that are characterized by connotation and ambiguity. There is in fact a kind of unavowed representation of identity within the parties, a paradoxical form of transfer of identitary tension into the field of politics; this process takes place without being reflected in the public space, without overt expression of demands, in short, without politicization in the sense referenced by Lagroye (2003).

Identity as an Illegitimate, But Effective, Basis for Mobilization

Avoiding the Subject of Identity: The Illegitimate Status
and Powerful Constraints of Identity

It is appropriate in discussing the macro level to begin with an examination of the broader context, particularly official conceptions of society and of the government that influence the legitimacy of the various discourses and the different forms of political mobilization and action. The political parties' margin of maneuver concerning questions of identity is strictly limited by laws that stipulate that the "the right to found a political party cannot be exercised with the purpose of (...) making distinctions based on language, race, religion, denomination, or region."[9] Party rules and regulations are not allowed to contain any clause that refers to religious or denominational differences among prospective members. Nor can the parties' names include the titles of religions or denominations or expressions that are related to them.[10] Furthermore, articles 14 and 69 of the 1982 Constitution stipulate "political parties cannot affirm that within the territory of the Republic of Turkey there are minorities based on national, religious, cultural, denominational, racial, or linguistic differences.[11] Nor may they remain indifferent to such affirmations by other parties." The articulation of any community based on identity by means of a political party is thus illegal and illegitimate, and parties are forbidden from expressing identity-related claims or demands. This had led to the forced closure by the Constitutional Court of numerous Kurdish nationalist parties for threats to the integrity and indivisibility of the state.

A marked increase in particularist (i.e. identity-based) demands since the 1980s has paradoxically occurred simultaneously with the increasing institutional reaffirmation of the doctrine of national unity, which provided the principal justification for the 1980 coup d'état, probably in reaction to armed opposition in the southeastern part of the country that culminated in the early 1990s. The growth in particularist demands has in fact placed them at the center of public debates and state interventions (Neveu, 1999b). This change is clearest concerning Kurdish nationalism and political Islam. Indeed, these two movements not only proclaim individual identities, but they also directly challenge the construct of official national identity, which is founded on the exclusion of both Kurdish-ness and of political Islam (Yörük, 1997). For government institutions and certain political figures, because both movements demand the institutional integration of diversity, they call the very foundation of the nation into question. This means of framing the question by authorities has resulted in highly specific sanctions against the two groups.

The classic method of delegitimizing social movements in this political context is to "identitarize" them.[12] One example was the hunger strikes of 2000–2001 that were publicly described as "Alevi", which had the dual effect of delegitimizing an opposition movement and of criminalizing the Alevis (Massicard, 2002b).[13] This identitarization of a movement is the equivalent of accusing it of favoring particular interests over the general interest and thereby presenting a threat to national unity. This argument negates any aspirations of movements or organizations to representing particular groups that are considered a public threat.

As a consequence, political figures have had to make appeals to the "obligatory consensus" (Copeaux, 2000), in an attempt to express themselves within the rhetorical boundaries of national unity and interest and hence gain legitimacy. This maneuvering is all the more crucial for particularist movements, which are most in danger of becoming stigmatized as separatists. Particularist demands are thus not publicly expressed in the language of diversity, as would be the case in an openly multicultural setting, but with reference to the supreme values of the nation, most notably of unity. Although it is considered illegitimate to publicly demand that difference be acknowledged, it is legitimate to join the fight against non-discrimination and equality. As I have shown in previous research, drawing perspective on a framework inherited from Goffman (1974), the principal framing employed by Alevist movements—and particularist movements in general—is that of national unity (Massicard, 2002a). Accordingly, the Alevis argue that because they were a founding element of the Republic of Turkey, they constitute to some extent a guarantee against dangerous Islamists who could potentially provoke religious schism (Massicard, 2006). This process imposes specific constraints on the forms of legitimization that political figures are able to evoke, the possibilities for alliances between political groups, and how they manage the issue of identity. However, it should be noted that the relative legitimacy of these groups' activities is currently in the process of changing, especially in view of the growing influence of European norms on how political legitimacy is defined in Turkey. The EU framework is generally quite sensitive to identity issues, with EU norms providing Turkish groups with new mechanisms and resources for transcending national constraints.

As shown above, these constraints allow us to better understand the complex relations between the different groups and movements, especially between particularist and "generalist" groups. In fact, "generalist" political entities like parties and labor unions tend to attempt to maintain a certain distance between themselves and identity-based movements and organizations, rarely allowing themselves to become standard-bearers for particularist claims that might compromise and delegitimize them.[14] This holds true even when an identity-based organization claims to be fighting for the same cause as a generalist group. This is one reason that the parties do not publicly or nationally support or represent particularist demands, with the notable exception of Kurdist parties, which are constantly threatened with closure, and of the MHP, whose platform is official Turkish identity and which is therefore exempt from being considered "particularist". The leaders of different parties, even those that sympathize with the Alevis, withhold comment on the Alevi question in order to avoid being suspected of being an Alevi party or of supporting a particular group (Schüler, 2000, 199). For generalist entities, it suffices to maintain and reaffirm their separation from the rhetoric of identity in order to avoid being suspected of favoritism, regionalism, or of concealing a minority-based core membership. Generalists tend to criticize, for example, the chauvinism or retrograde nature of identity struggles, as illustrated by the following episode. Kemal Kılıçdaroğlu, originally from Tunceli and a Kurdish-speaking Alevi, was elected head of the CHP in 2010, marking the first time that a large party was led by an Alevi. His election had triggered a debate regarding his Alevi identity that centered on whether the CHP had "come to terms" with his Alevi electoral base. It is interesting to note that Kılıçdaroğlu has always remained discrete regarding his identity and never refers to it openly, in an apparent effort to allow it to be forgotten. This tendency yields in effect a partitioning between the modalities of mobilization and organization, even when the claims of the "universalist" party and the "particularist" organization are broadly similar. As a consequence, numerous leftist Alevis complain of being "excluded" and accused of religious propaganda by generalist organizations (for an eye-witness report, see Şener, İlknur, 1995, 95).

A further reason why the parties avoid making their ties to identity-based organizations or even identities in general apparent is the fear of alienating a segment of their supporters. In fact, questions of identity, especially the Kurdish question, often lead to tension and even hostility that makes them especially difficult for parties to control. One episode was decisive in this regard. Prior to the 1991 legislative elections, the social-democratic SHP[15] party entered into an alliance with the nationalist Kurdish party, HEP in the southeastern provinces.[16] Debarring the HEP from competing in the elections at this key moment, when it was a matter of tipping the balance in favor of a political or a military resolution to the conflict, might well have resulted in a Kurdish boycott, the legitimisation of Kurdish claims on the international stage, and an increased militarization of the movement. Certain HEP MPs elected on the SHP list took the oath to the national assembly in Kurdish. They were excluded from the SHP in the ensuing scandal. Fighting against the PKK intensified, and the HEP was itself banned in 1993.[17] In the west and center of the country, the SHP was accused of having allowed the PKK to enter Parliament, but the nationalist Kurds did not consider that it represented their interests. The SHP thus proved itself incapable of maintaining the role of mediator in a situation of increasing tension, and it lost votes on both sides, having failed both to take responsibility for its relationship with Kurdish nationalism, and to avoid the negative consequences of that relationship among the wider electorate. This episode influenced the attitude of leaders of social-democratic groups towards minorities in general (Schüler, 2000, 198), and the resulting partitioning had a direct impact on the ability of political figures to form alliances and generate support.

The Role of Identity Questions in Generalist Mobilization

The idea of a wall between generalist parties and issues of identity needs to be critically examined, however. In effect, generalist mobilizations were and are unable to completely ignore the identity factor. In fact, an intensive period of several weeks of observations of the CHP in Adana led me to the conclusion that party officials and members interpreted intra-partisan developments from an almost exclusively identity-related perspective. As one concrete illustration of this paradox, when I asked a CHP official in Adana to offer his assessment of the list of candidates for office in the 2009 municipal elections, he mentioned the identity of every candidate.

Clearly, how constraints are managed differs as a function of scale, and at the local level, the contexts of political action are different, and generalist parties can maintain often implicit relationships with figures associated with identity movements. As long as these alliances are not echoed nationally by the media, they do not create problems of legitimacy. In other words, parties that make efforts not to appear "particularist" on the national level can very well play the identity card at the local level (depending on the modalities described below). But the logic behind these local maneuvers depends heavily on how group relations are configured locally and are difficult to adapt to the national level (Massicard, 2012). In addition, parties sometimes attempt to mobilize the local population by drawing on their "identity bases", which are often clearly fragmented within a single party's membership (Wedel, 1999). In a context in which individuals know each other, such affiliations are known and accepted. In mobilizing their membership depending on specific identities, the parties are attempting to consolidate themselves and to reinforce the support of their different constituencies. Schüler (1998) has demonstrated the decisive role of ethnic and religious groups and compatriotism (*hemşehrilik*) in the construction and growth of the base of the SHP. This supports the hypothesis that "generalist" parties can find it advantageous to approach certain identity-based groups, particularly to the extent that these groups can provide access to networks with relatively high degrees of internal organization.

I have argued in a previous work (Massicard, 2013) that mobilization and engagement with the base of a universalist party like the CHP in Adana takes place primarily not through party organization itself, but via inter-acquaintance and common interests among groups (see also White, 1999, 171–172). These individual groups constitute a fundamental organizing unit for party operations, particularly the formation of coalitions and the work of mobilization. These groups also possess a social existence outside the party, relying on multiplex ties that are often extra-partisan and sometimes extra-political. Because not all groups are formed and organized in the same ways, diverse kinds of bonds are observable among them. Some bonds are political, meaning that collective militancy in the past can provide the catalyst for a group. Other bonds are extra-political, including ties of kinship and neighborhood, ethnicity, "country" (*hemşehrilik*), and alumni networks. The importance of such groups to a partisan organization that utilizes networks of acquaintance is that they enable the enlistment of numerous individuals who are in relationships of reciprocal obligation. In another context, Obershall demonstrated that one fundamental factor in mobilization is a group's prior organization, which can take two forms: communitarian or associative. Communities:

> also produce horizontal bonds and feelings of solidarity in the interior of a collectivity that can be activated for the pursuit of collective goals and the formation of conflict groups. [...] Instead of preventing mobilization, the group's preexisting organization contributes to motivation to participate, to the extent to which it provides both pre-established communications networks, already partially-mobilized resources, the presence of individuals who possess leadership abilities and a tradition of participation among the members of the collectivity. (Obershall, 1973, 119, 124).

The interest of mobilization using inter-acquaintance groups is obvious in terms of their prior existence and proximity to a large number of individuals (Massicard 2013; see re. the *hemşehri* Massicard, 2005a). Both inter-acquaintance and social control provide obligation channels that foster mobilization.

Because of the rarity of institutionalized channels for mediation with society, the parties often try to recruit or promote individuals who can mobilize the vote of an inter-acquaintance group or an assumed community: "the notables with the potential to mobilize blocs of votes become important to parties and vie with each other to negotiate with the parties the preferential allocation of public resources in exchange for votes, which enables them to sustain themselves or to obtain leadership positions at the local level" (Massicard, 2004, 102–103). As a consequence, individuals seeking to make a career in the parties often promote themselves as representing a numerically important group or as having the ability to mobilize numerous "captive" votes. Such groups can include tribes,[18] but they are also very often identity-based groups. In fact, in Adana—perhaps because of the prevalence of the identity-based interpretation of political phenomena—identity groups are often in themselves considered to be political entities that can be mobilized as a single voting bloc. This explains why some party members and officials were surprised by the fact that the choice to include a member of a leading Kurdish family to lead the CHP organization of Adana's main district had very little impact on the party in attracting Kurdish voters.

Numerous officials have offered explanations in terms of "primordial" ties that can in theory provide an almost natural ground for political solidarity. Consequently, within the CHP federation, the "Southern Group", primarily composed of Arabophone Alevis settled in the southern part of Adana, is often described as the "Arab group" by outsiders (similarly, people refer to the "Kurdish Bektachis" or the "Kurdish group"). This phenomenon extends to the case of one group that often describes itself as "Türkmen" based on having formerly belonged to a cooperative, despite the fact that the group's identity is not based on "Turkishness." This is probably because ethnicity functions as the basic idiom of politics while also helping distinguish the group from other groups. This identity-based interpretation, however, should not be taken at face value, because it is more a simplification than a reality. The "Southern Group" is in fact primarily composed of Arabophones, although this does not signify that this "identity" connection forms the basis for the group (which, as a matter of fact, makes no claim to a particular identity). On the contrary, it is constituted as a group through a political mobilization effort based on dormant militant networks from the 1970s that were reactivated and later extended, an effort that helped attract voters towards the CHP who had been more oriented towards parties of the liberal right until the 1990s.[19] These groups are not preexisting social groups that could be inserted as-is into the party, as would be suggested by an interpretation strictly in terms of absorption of preexisting social or identitary divisions by the parties. Instead, they are constituted by deliberate efforts to form a group. And, while ethnicity does unquestionably provide a sort of mobilizeable bond for forming a group, and above all a framework through which a variety of groups can be organized, it does not provide an immediately or automatically transposable organizing principle in terms of politics. If the belief that ethnicity does transfer readily into politics persists, it is because certain party officials and candidates themselves retain the image of a "captive" clientèle in order to make themselves appear more important. But beyond this "identity" interpretation of division and difference lie more complex realities. As we have seen, the identity dimension is considered important by party officials, leading to the question of how, in this context, officials manage the identity factor both internally and externally.

How Political Parties Manage the Identity Factor

Several approaches to managing identity among parties can be identified. The analysis presented in this section will examine how the parameter of identity is integrated into the management of human resources before turning to an examination of specific modes of communication.

Identity as a Parameter for Managing Human Resources

The identity factor, whose discursive articulation is highly constrained, is first managed at the level of "human resources", which is to say the personal or *ad hominem* level. This takes on particular significance in Turkey, where there is a distinct tendency for various social and political domains to become personalized. In the present case, although the identity demands of particular groups are not considered legitimate, the presumed identity of individual political figures plays an important role, at least in terms of how they are publicly perceived.

The fact that in Turkey the personality of party and elected officials is so important requires some explanation. On one hand, I have observed that in the parliamentary arena, although the parties' positions on particularist issues are always discreet, an individual official's discourse can be far more explicit, and legislators can be seen openly fighting in the name of their constituencies, or for the recognition of a particular difference. For example, only the very limited number of elected officials whose Alevi identity or ties to the Alevi cause are widely known and form part of their political and electoral trajectory are able to proceed in this way. It is also worth recalling that patronage and nepotism are highly prevalent and that the parties function principally as organizations for the redistribution of positions and advantages of every kind among members and constituents (Schüler, 1998), practices that usually operate through intermediaries in the form of party or elected officials. A former SHP minister, an Alevi Kurd, explicitly told me that he favored his own "*mil-*

let" (nation, group) in the exercise of his political functions.[20] The extent of such practices is difficult to measure, but it is perceived as a significant and even politically decisive factor. In December 1992, one year after the DYP–SHP coalition came to power, Seyfi Oktay, the Alevi Minister of Justice of the SHP, was accused during a parliamentary session of having recruited 12,500 Alevis.[21] The roles were reversed when the DYP controlled the same ministry, and in May 1996, when Ş. Ulusoy, an SHP legislator from a family of Alevi religious dignitaries, criticized the "anti-Alevi purges" that had taken place there.[22] This discernible favoritism and its direct impact on the average Alevi's prospects explains general Alevist organizations' voting pattern: a broad list of possible options is first announced, but full public commitment is typically delayed until full candidate registers are announced and an enumeration of Alevi candidates can take place, the results of which are almost invariably proportional to the number of pledges. It is easy to understand how, as a result, particularist organizations perceive the listing of candidates as a major factor, even more than the positions of political parties, which rarely explicitly defend questions of difference.[23]

In parallel to this process, party officials consider denominational, ethnic, and regional identities as important data in choosing candidates and party officials. In Adana, one commonly accepted vision is that the vote is based mainly on the identity factor: the Arabs are broadly believed to vote for the leftist parties, the Kurds supposedly vote either for the Kurdist parties or for the AKP, whereas the Türkmen vote is divided between the MHP, the AKP, and the CHP. It is also widely assumed that the vote of a group will be larger if it is represented among the candidates, because the groups want to see themselves represented. According to my observations, local CHP officials in Adana attempt to obtain the votes of each group while avoiding the appearance of being the party of a single group, ultimately a somewhat dangerous balancing act. Following the results of internal elections that preceded the 1999 legislative elections in certain religiously mixed areas, the leadership of the CHP worked to create a balance between Alevis and Sunni.[24] In cities like Adana, the parties administer calculated doses of information about candidates' identities, and during the process to determine the CHP candidate for mayor of Adana in the March 2009 municipal elections, party officials attempted to anticipate their possible losses of "Türkmen" votes if an "Arab" was appointed as candidate. They then tried to balance the candidates at different levels, ultimately counter-balancing the "Arab" candidate for mayor who was supposed to "hold" the Arab electoral base (considered a sure win in any event) with a "Kurdish" mayoral candidate from the biggest and most important district in the province. The goal of this balancing act was to reinforce the electoral support of the significant number of Kurdish voters in this strategic district. Similarly, identity assumes a major role in the development of the campaign strategies, and especially on the focus on given groups.[25] The same type of process is at work in choosing members of the central committees of the parties, where an effort is made to represent different groups. During internal party elections, one classic tactic for delegitimizing a team is to claim that they represent a particular group to the detriment of the general interest. In one example, during highly animated internal elections in the CHP at the end of 1997, a former district mayor of Seyhan of Arab origin was accused of "using ethnicity as a basis for doing politics" and of wanting to "establish an Arab Republic", an accusation that he vigorously contested.[26]

This balance does also depend, however, on the targeted electoral bases, and their representation (or lack thereof) among party officials. In Adana, for example, Arabs are poorly represented in the AKP, both among officials and candidates. This is because the predominantly Alevi Arabs seldom vote with the AKP, and hence the AKP does not view them as a viable voting bloc. For that reason, they focus on the Kurdish and Türkmen votes. Ultimately, the political stakes of identity should not be interpreted as an absolute value but seen in relative terms with regard to the other parties and candidates. During the 2009 municipal elections, CHP officials judged a candidate put forward by another party to be a direct competitor for votes because he was an Arab. This kind of identity-based human resources management has consequences, and the presence of elected office-holders from a particular group contributes to the reproduction of that group's electoral support. It is clear from the above discussion the extent to which the identity factor is integral to the functioning of parties, among other factors, both as a means of representing the largest possible number of constituencies but also of focusing a party's efforts primarily on certain social groups.

During the pre-election period, there is rampant speculation about candidates' identities in private conversations, and some candidates and officials calculatedly maintain ambiguity about their identities, appearing in different settings and implying certain details without ever confirming them. Information about identity can be a valuable resource that is as a result sometimes kept secret, particularly in the case of semi-private acquaintance networks within organizations, which are omnipresent in contexts characterized by factionalism (Schüler, 1998). Within the context of this dual constraint, it is possible to identify several specific modes of communication that relate to how the identity factor is managed.

Specific Modes of Communication

As has been described, generalist movements often implicitly attempt to address "identitary" audiences. In order to manage the fragmentation of identities, organizations employ specific communication modes. Without claiming to have studied these phenomena in a systematic way, I argue that three discursive strategies appear to be prominent: the management of ambiguity, of the implied, and of the publicity of situations involving inter-action. The political semiology of these strategies merits further and more systematic exploration.

Inclusivity

The first category of semiological strategy consists of targeting specific audi-ences or evoking identity issues while at the same time avoiding particularist modes of communication. There is a striking absence of references to Aleviness and the defense of Alevi rights; indeed, recognition of such differences hardly ever appears in electoral platforms or party literature. When such subjects are mentioned, it is through an appeal to general principles like "secularity", "equal treatment", or "non-discrimination", and not through references to a particular group. For example, a 1987 DSP[27] tract stipulates "no denomina-tional community (*mezhep*) will enjoy preferential treatment by the authori-ties. The children of different religions and denominations can receive religious instruction in the public schools according to their religious vision" (DSP, 1987, 86). This formulation enables them to avoid explicitly referring to the Alevis, who are nevertheless encompassed by the deliberately vague and broad category of *mezhep* (which can be understood as including every inter-pretation of Islam), thus allowing Alevis to comprehend that it is implicitly addressed to them.[28] Such inclusivity practices allow specific audiences to be addressed without excluding other groups, and only when countering accusa-tions of being anti-Alevi do party officials explicitly employ terms like "Alevi".[29] Although it is not advisable to project a public image of being pro-Alevi, it is acceptable to side-step accusations of anti-Alevism, which would constitute discrimination, and as such a threat to national unity.

Ambiguity as a Resource

Another somewhat similar procedure consists in appealing indirectly to certain identity groups through the use of symbols, signs, and connotations. All that is required is to refer to figures whose connotation is ambiguous or comprehensible to certain audiences while being less or differently interpretable by other groups. For example, in the legislative elections of 2002, a DEHAP (Kurdish nationalist party) poster represented a famous statue of the sixteenth-century rebel poet, Pir Sultan, a figure simultaneously of the extreme, even revolutionary, left, while also possessing an Alevi connotation.

The poster emphasizes the poet's revolutionary dimension by showing a flame at the tip of the poet's guitar—the party's symbol—thus simultaneously evoking a Kalachnikov rifle.[30] On the other hand, Alevi connotations are reinforced by the extract from a Pir Sultan poem, appropriated as a leftist and Alevi slogan and signifying "Come, let's band together." This can be read as either leftist or Alevist, depending on the audience's sensitivities. Clearly, even though the identity connotation is part of the presentation, it is not always obvious. Maintaining ambiguity enables broad audiences to be addressed while excluding as few as possible. Similarly revealing is the choice of music for the 2004 campaign of the CHP mayoral candidate in the Şişli neighborhood of Istanbul that has a significant Alevi population.[31] The primary melody comes from an Alevi religious song whose words have been changed but is nonetheless immediately recognizable to Alevis. The melody is also known in other circles but not as Alevi because it was incorporated, minus its Alevi connotations, into the national folk music repertoire during the 1930s and has enjoyed considerable air-time on the radio. The same message can thus be read differently, with the identity factor only one possible interpretation; Alevis feel specifically addressed by the music, but non-Alevis, unaware of the Alevi connection, do not feel excluded by it.

The Management of Publicity and the Partitioning of Information

Another party communication strategy for deriving an advantage from identitary fragmentation is appealing to different identities simultaneously. This is achieved by controlling publicity, which can be described as occuring along two primary axes: the oral-written continuum, and spatial partitioning.

Although written references to identity are exceedingly rare, oral references are very frequent, a noticeable gap between written and orally communicated party platforms and campaign literature. During the campaign season, party officials express more explicit promises orally than they allow themselves to write. For example, during Alevi festivals, representatives of nearly all of the parties offer veritable showers of electoral promises regarding Alevis. D. Baykal, the CHP leader between 1995 and 2010 with a minor interruption, was criticized by a number of Alevis for "not even pronouncing the word 'Alevi.'" It was seen as acceptable that the party not directly convey Alevi demands, but less acceptable that he not even pronounce the term in this kind of context.

Oral electoral promises are generally restricted to these relatively closed settings. Similarly, in Gazi, an Istanbul suburb with the reputation of being simultaneously Kurdish, Alevi, and leftist, I noted the DEHAP posters described above; I never noted them in any other neighborhoods. Although I was not able to assess the precise geographical distribution of these campaign materials, I believe there is a phenomenon of territorialization that leads to a partitioning of the advertising discourse of the parties that, although not rigid, is amplified by the media, who relay the messages beyond their target audiences, occasionally provoking indignation and public debate.

Conclusion

Despite the question of its legitimacy and its virtual invisibility as a public issue, the identity factor represents a prominent feature in the Turkish political scene, particularly among parties that claim to be universalist. Diversity and identity are thus integral to the field of politics, but the nature of their integration is paradoxical: it is not the object of publicity or public expression of the positions and demands of the different groups involved, and thus does not constitute what Lagroye calls politicization (2003). It can therefore be hypothesized that this paradoxical integration contributes to the non-politicization of tensions related to identity. In fact, it may even contribute to their attenuation to the extent that the modalities used to manage identity leads to an unspoken representation (or at least a presence) of the presumed groups within each party, a form of integration that caters to different electoral factions within the political parties.

As we have seen, the management of identity issues needs to be understood within the context of multiple constraints that simultaneously, though in different ways, affect organizations and individuals. The significant attention that the parties devote to publicity management, the importance of acquaintance groups and the syndrome of personalization suggest that only a focus on actual interactions and specific contexts can provide an understanding of the way political parties manage the identity factor.

It also seems important to distinguish between levels of action and to iden-tify the specific constraints associated with each level. In other words, the identity dimension is managed quite differently at local and national levels. In pursuing this line of inquiry in future research, it may be appropriate to focus more specifically on the articulation between these different levels of action, both by organizations and individuals.

5

THE TRANSFORMATION OF A CONFLICT IN THE DIASPORA

SIKHS, MUSLIMS AND THE BRITISH STATE

Christine Moliner
Translated by Adrian Morfee

One of the most recurrent aspects in the transformation of identity conflicts in the contemporary world is their extension to the diaspora (as is the case with the Kurds, the Tamils, etc.). Does this simply involve "importing" conflicts from the home countries, or does it enter a distinct phase in being adapted to the local context? More specifically, the central question of this article is that of the role played by the host state's public policies in the transformation of conflicts into the diaspora: how do complex representations of the Other (that originate from the home societies) evolve in a migration context and how are identity frontiers reconceived? Several variables exert an influence over inter-community relations in this specific case: the British policy of integrating immigrant populations, which has changed considerably over the past fifty years; the different relations Sikhs and Muslims entertain with the host country; the temporal dimension of their experience as immigrants; and finally, the links between local, national, and transnational issues and conflicts.

This paper focuses on the relationships between Sikh and Muslim communities in Great Britain over a period of several years (from the end of the 1990s to 2010). Particular attention is paid to the local context, and especially the role played by British integration policies, and the sharp turn they took in July 2005. Multiculturalism, perceived as responsible for the ills plaguing British society in general, and more specifically for the July 2005 attacks, gave way to a new credo of community cohesion.[1] As shall be seen, whilst this policy develops a discourse based on living together and interfaith dialogue, it actually exacerbates conflicts between communities, and especially those relating to the distribution of local resources. What needs to be accounted for here is the way in which new tensions have appeared over recent years, leading in particular to strategies of differentiation and the emergence of rhetoric of aggression, and this despite a positive dynamic in the transformation of inter-community relations and the emergence of a shared (geographical/cultural) diasporic identity. One of the decisive elements in this shift has been the policy adopted towards British Muslims since 2001. The state, by its favorable treatment of Muslims (such at least is the charge brought by other minorities), has produced a situation that Sikhs perceive as unfair.

Before proceeding further, it is worth making a few observations about methodological aspects and fieldwork conditions. In an earlier article (Moliner, 2007), I presented the results of a fieldwork survey carried out between 1998 and 2000 relating to British Sikh identity, though not specifically to Sikh—Muslim relations. In this article and as part of a discussion of how to study representations and constructions of alterity, I pointed out how in my interviews with British Sikhs I had encountered a tangible phenomenon of self-censorship relating to any direct expression of hostility towards other communities, a very similar phenomenon to that observed ten years earlier by the sociologist Gerd Baumann in Southall (Baumann, 1996). I thus refrained from asking direct questions about relations between Sikhs and Muslims, opting instead to privilege participative observation and informal interviews. And it was in fact these which provided the most interesting information, supplemented by community literature produced by the gurdwaras (Sikh places of worship) and various Sikh organizations in Britain.

The fieldwork carried out in 2009 and 2010 was conducted very differently, and I explained to my interlocutors that the research project related specifically to relations between British Sikhs and Muslims. The people I met were therefore primarily (Sikh and non-Sikh) actors involved in dialogue between the two communities, who had taken part in a weekend of dialogue in Northern Ireland in July 2008.[2] Over the previous ten years several local conflicts (in particular in Slough, to the west of London, and in Birmingham and Bradford) had resulted in the deterioration of relations between the two communities, and had even become a subject of concern for several organizations and local actors specializing in conflict management who were thus receiving public financial support as part of the new policy of community cohesion.

In this chapter, I will first discuss the historical construction of Sikh-Muslim antagonism, and the role played by colonization and the subsequent partition of their region of origin, that has translated into contested memories and contentious relations between the two communities and the two Nation-states of India and Pakistan. How does this seemingly "inherited" and imported conflict evolve in a migration context? As will be discussed, British Sikhs and Muslims share a common migration history to the host country. They have rediscovered their common regional identity and shared heritage in the diaspora, which have been revived through popular music and the emergence of a British Asian youth culture. Despite these profound commonalities, local factors are responsible for the recent deterioration of inter-community relations, mainly the competitive politics of assertion and quest for recognition pursued by each community, vis-a-vis the British state, and British politics regarding ethnic minorities, reconfigured by the war on terror the country is engaged in.

Identity Reconfigurations

The Social Construction of an "Historical" Antagonism Between Sikhs and Muslims

In a previous article (Moliner, 2007) I described Panjabi Sikhs and Muslims as *frères ennemis*. Independently of the frequent misuse of this French expression its heuristic value is clear: amicability and enmity should not be conceived in a dualistic fashion as two opposing and unrelated poles to be studied separately, but are in fact intimately bound up with each other and built in tandem.

These two communities originally come from the northwest of South Asia. They share a very strong regional identity (*Panjabiyyat*) but were separated during partition with the Sikhs (and Hindus) fleeing towards India and Muslims towards Pakistan. The extremely violent events during partition left deep scars at both the individual and collective level. The violence also played a fundamental role in the formation of the two Nation-states, and in the elaboration of aggressive national representations and categorizations of the Other as the enemy.

The political, material, and symbolic border between India and Pakistan has served since independence to mark this partition both physically and in people's minds. This border, which was relatively porous in the 1950s, has become one of the most militarized in the world and an entire administrative apparatus operates making it virtually impossible for Indians and Pakistanis to cross the border. Therefore, separated since partition, Panjabis have followed a similar migratory path to the West, especially to the former colonial metropolis. We will here discuss some aspects of this post-colonial diasporic encounter.

The Sikhs form an ethno-religious group which has progressively acquired its autonomy from the Hindu matrix, with colonization and a social and religious reform movement (the Singh Sabha) bringing about a redefinition of Sikh identity. This redefinition is based partly on establishing hermetic boundaries between the three religious communities, Sikhs, Muslims, and Hindus.[3] Sikh collective representations of the Muslim as a radical and threatening figure of alterity draw on a corpus of liturgical and historical texts. The confrontation with the Mughal power from the seventeenth century onwards figures predominantly in Sikh historiography and is interpreted as a struggle against tyranny and religious fanaticism. The creation of the Khalsa (a religious and military order) in 1699, one of the major events in Sikh history, is even presented as a direct response to repression by the Mughal power. In the following century this anti-Muslim rhetoric was euphemized under the influence of the Singh Sabha, whose priority (to establish Sikh religious identity as totally separated from Hindsuism) lead to the designation of a new enemy, namely the Hindu (Moliner, 2007).

Antagonism, however, resurfaced with the communal riots of the 1920s and 1940s, during which Sikhs and Hindus clashed with Muslims. The memory of past conflicts, carefully kept alive by each community, played a crucial role in triggering the mass violence perpetrated during partition in 1947 which forced 12 million Panjabis into exodus and cost the half a million lives.[4] The particularity of these events, seen by some as akin to genocide, is that both victims and oppressors were drawn in equal proportion from all three communities. Yet the collective memory of this tragedy, which has been perpetuated within each community, projects the evil and horror onto the other camp, and has in fact been reinforced. Furthermore, the nationalist discourse of the two new states and the official accounts of violence during partition have legitimized and reinforced these antagonistic memories.

This phenomenon amounts to a partition of memories, and has been facilitated by the fact that territorial division has been accompanied by a genuine ethnic and religious cleansing, to the point where nowadays there are hardly any Hindus or Sikhs in Pakistani Panjab and very few Muslims in Indian Panjab.

The chapter will now turn to the commonalities shared by Sikhs and Muslims, fashioned by a similar post-colonial migration history.

A shared migratory identity?

Sikh and Muslim Panjabis share the same migration history. Mainly from rural backgrounds, they moved to Great Britain in the years of economic reconstruction after the Second World War and provided a large and cheap pool of labor. Most of them came from the same dominant caste (the Jats) and originated from a limited number of pockets of emigration, with the Sikhs coming from Doaba (in the center of eastern Panjab), and the Muslims from Mirpur (in Azad Kashmir) and the districts of Faisalabad and Jhelum (Western Panjab).

They also followed very similar migratory paths. The first migrants were part of a process of chain migration and depended on their clan (*biradari*) to help them settle (Ballard, 1983). They were highly concentrated in the same regions, primarily Greater London and the Midlands, and in the same inner city districts, and started off in the same unskilled jobs and with the same social standing. But from the 1970s onwards, a process of socio-economic differentiation got under way and Sikhs had their families come and join them earlier than Muslim migrants. With the arrival of educated and skilled migrants, East African Sikhs moved up from unskilled industrial work to more diversified sectors such as retail and the liberal professions. This is why the Sikhs and Indians were generally less affected than the Pakistanis (and Bangladeshis) by the severe industrial crisis of the 1970s, and why they now enjoy a superior social and economic profile (Singh and Tatla, 2006).

According to the census in 2001, there are 336,000 Sikhs in the country (out of a total of 1 million Indians) and 747,000 Pakistanis (2001 census, Office for National Statistics).

A British Asian identity has taken hold amongst the second and third generations, transcending religious, ethnic, and national frontiers. The category of Asian in Great Britain, like other minority identity constructions, is both something that is imposed on people and which they lay claim to. Thus 'British Asian' identity as experienced by young people emerged in part as a reaction to the racism of the dominant society. Above and beyond this reactive dimension, young people may be seen to identify with this category in a more positive way. This identification is based on the objective shared points given above, on rejecting the divides and conflicts of their parents' generation, perceived as meaningless in Great Britain, and on their perception of a strong degree of cultural overlap (food, clothing, and social norms). Various more narrow senses of belonging can co-exist within this pan-ethnic category, but they nevertheless transcend religious and/or national frontiers, such as regional senses of identity of which *Panjabiyyat* as one of the most flourishing examples. This term, of comparatively recent usage, is generally translated by Panjabi identity, and refers to the cultural heritage, social practices, and shared values that are common to all Panjabis, be they Hindu, Sikh, or Muslim, Indian or Pakistani, and which extends to the diaspora (Roy, 2015). It is generally marked by nostalgia for the unified Panjab of pre-partition days, idealized as a space and time of communal harmony.

In its most widely and frequently used sense *Panjabiyyat* has primarily a cultural content, with the question of language acting as the vital element of this regional identity.

The literary circles of the Panjabi diaspora—composed primarily of writers, intellectuals, academics, and teachers, the oldest among whom remember a unified Panjab (many of them originating in Lahore and nurturing an indefatigable sense of nostalgia for it)—place the promotion of their language and literature at the center of their activities. Young people identifying themselves as British Asian or British Panjabi are also active in this area. The question of language is in fact highly complex, as it operates both as a powerful link and as a factor of division, thereby working to undermine the potential of *Panjabiyyat* to act as a pan-ethnic identity category bringing people within the diaspora together.[5] Hence British Sikhs have been single-handedly conducting a campaign over the past twenty years demanding that the BBC accord a more prominent place to Panjabi in its radio programs (in various sub-continental languages), arguing that it is the mother tongue of a large majority of South Asians in Great Britain.

The reinvention of *bhangra*, a traditional Panjabi form of music, by the diaspora has popularized *Panjabiyyat* among young people. These songs and dances originated in the rural Panjab to celebrate the spring harvest, and were exported to Great Britain by the first generation of migrants. The first groups appeared in the 1970s (Baumann, 1990). Over the course of the next two decades *bhangra* became a mass cultural phenomenon and an emblem of their identity for young Panjabis thanks to the development of the audiovisual industry and the influence of the British black musical and cultural scenes. Music produced by the diaspora was even re-exported back to India and became very much in vogue in Bollywood films in particular.[6]

Panjabiyyat has since then enjoyed renewed vigor in the sub-continent, helped both by the success of *bhangra* and the films celebrating it (such as *Veer Zara* for example) and the development of initiatives seeking to bring about a rapprochement between the two Panjab.[7] Civil society on both sides of the border has been very active in this field, especially since the reopening of the border in 2004. Since then there has been a spectacular increase in the level of exchange of all forms between Indian and Pakistani citizens (in what is referred to as citizens' diplomacy) crossing at the Wagah checkpoint half-way between Amritsar and Lahore, with pacifist gatherings, theatre tours, concerts by artists committed to the reconciliation of the two countries, cricket tournaments drawing crowds to Lahore, Chandigarh, and Delhi, and pilgrimages (of Sikhs from the Indian Panjab and the diaspora to their sacred places in Pakistan).

Lastly, South Asian intellectual and artistic circles in Great Britain have drawn on the heritage of partition and its ramifications for the diaspora. For a long time partition was hidden from public view in South Asia, with official histories insisting on the independence and birth of the two young nations. But in India, following the lead of the Subaltern Studies, a bottom-up history of partition was put together in contradiction with official histories and focusing on the question of the extreme violence that took place during partition and its role in the formation of rival nationalisms. After the publication in India of works in which the victims of partition were given the opportunity to voice their side of the story, an increasing number of survivor testimonials were gathered in Great Britain too.[8] One widely applauded UK-based journal published an interview of Panjabi elders who survived the partition violence and owe their life to a member of a different religious community (Maini, Malik, & Malik, 2008).

The Man Mela Theatre Company has been exploring this theme for the past fifteen years via its adaptations of short stories by Sadat Hasan Manto, the great partition writer, and by putting on plays by contemporary writers such as Mazhar Tirmazi. In 2007 the company presented to the British public *Voices of Partition*, a performance commemorating sixty years of the partition of British India, that included workshops, presentations, oral history and a play, presented at the Edinburgh Festival in August 2007. This performance was also accompanied by a workshop organized in Panjabi with Sikh, Hindu and Muslim women from Smethwick (Midlands), seeking to compare and contrast memories of partition and local community relations.[9]

Reinventing the Conflict Within the Diaspora

The Points of Conflict

Despite the many commonalities between British Sikhs and Muslims, particularly the renewed interest in their common cultural heritage and shared past, several areas of contestation and conflict have surfaced in the past twenty years, that have the potential to seriously damage the relationship between the two minority communities.

Recurrent themes fuel the mounting tensions between British Sikhs and Muslims: the question of Muslim proselytizing and radicalism, the status of women in Islam, and the prohibition of mixed couples and of exogamous sexual relations. The most prominent of these is the question of Muslim proselytizing, especially at universities. Proselytizing by Christian fundamentalists is also condemned, with the Sikhs seeing themselves as easy targets in the face of what they deem to be aggressive proselytizing by these two religious communities. The question of conversions is an essential component in representations of the self and of the Other. The Sikhs thus see Islam and Christianity as proselytizing religions and, despite thousands of Western converts to Sikhism, they see themselves as a non-proselytizing religion.[10] This results in a feeling of being threatened and vulnerable when confronted by these two communities, seen as aggressive and numerically dominant.

Inter-religious tension in the host country is thus seen as a repeat of past conflicts, those of the twentieth century overlapping with those of the eighteenth century. Forced conversions to Islam under the Mughal Empire still impinge heavily on the collective imagination, and on the place Muslims have in it. Nevertheless, it is important to point out that these conflicting memories are not merely the legacy of the past that refuses to be forgotten, that they are not purely imported from the Subcontinent, but are in fact reinvented. In this specific case they are just as much a product of British society and of its Islamophobic tendencies, with the persecutions undergone in the eighteenth century being lumped together with the 11 September 2001 and the July 2005 attacks in London.

In particular, the Sikh writing exhibiting this point tends to share two features: that they are both written and published in Great Britain. They seek to warn young British Sikhs against what supposedly erroneous representations of Sikh history and ideology promulgated by some British Muslims, in particular in schools and on university campuses (Sidhu, 1998; Sidhu and Singh, 2001)

A new term, *takfirism*, conveys this sense of unease: it refers to the insulting use of the term *kafir* by certain British Muslims to designate non-Muslims. This was identified as a core issue by the Sikh participants in a weekend of dialogue organized between British Sikh and Muslim activists in Northern Ireland in 2008. The alternative report written by four of the Sikh participants (who disagreed with the official report) refers to 'the impact of "kaffirism (sic)"-based attitudes in the Muslim community on social cohesion, stating that: Sikhs feel they are perceived as "kaffirs" by significant sections of the Muslim community. This term is in widespread usage regards non-Muslims. Sikhs believe the word "kaffir" is a hate word, and should be treated as racially and religiously hostile in UK law.[11]

The status of women is another sticking point. Sikhs are eager to present Sikhism as an egalitarian religion, encouraging the participation of women in religious and social spheres and forbidding any form of discrimination, and in particular the practice of *purdah* (veiling of women and segregation between the sexes). Certain practices are, to their eyes, representative of the status of women in Islam: polygamy, the veil, and divorce by triple *talaq*.[12] A leaflet published by a Sikh women's organization, the Sikh Woman's Awareness Network discusses this topic and provides a comparative study of certain beliefs and doctrinal points relating to women in the two religions (salvation, education, hereditary rights, gender equality, the entitlement to pray, dress codes, menstruation, and marriage), through long quotations from the Koran and from the Adi Granth (the sacred writings of the Sikhs) (Sikh Woman's Awareness Network, 1998). The normative and textual approach adopted accentuates points of divergence between the two religious traditions and, conveniently, glosses over the question of actual social and cultural practices, which are shared by all Panjabis independently of their religious affiliation and which equally tend to confine women to a subordinate position.

The third topic, and no doubt the most contentious one, is that of exogamous sexual relations, which gives rise to a complex admixture of emotions, phantasms, and collective representations in both communities, drawing on memories of partition. Endogenous marriages are still the norm amongst British Asians and exogamy is socially frowned upon, especially by the family and community of the woman. In South Asia, women are considered repositories of their community's honor (*izzat*), and so potentially as an instrument for its dishonor. It is therefore the duty of the men of their families to ensure that the community's social norms are respected and to enforce behavior in compliance with these norms. This patriarchal control of women, of their bodies, and of their sexuality is generally analyzed in reference to the traditional norms and values of the society of origin. However, it is in fact far more a product of their experience as migrants and of the resulting complex relationship between ethnicity, gender, and social class, and is specific to the social constructions of masculinity amongst marginalized groups (Westwood, 1995).

The prohibition of relations with those outside one's own community is thus not specific to the Sikhs, but in their case it is exacerbated where Muslims are concerned. A constant concern relating to the alleged seduction and/or kidnapping of young Sikh women by Muslims is expressed both in interviews and on various websites and online forums.[13] Although no case has as yet resulted in legal proceedings, this is a particularly sensitive and potentially contentious question as it is bound up with both aspects of the argument being put forward here, the fear of forced conversions and the status of women.[14] These social constructions inevitably bring with them the specter of partition, mass rapes, and the forced conversion of women. They feed into the tensions, especially in West London and the Midlands, and are often the starting-point of localized micro-conflicts which are then built up by the two communities into an inter-community conflict threatening social peace.

Official categories and strategies of differentiation

The official categories and classifications also play an important role in the ongoing process of disjunction between British Sikhs and Muslims. Such is the case, for instance, with the Asian category which emerged and became established in the 1980s in contradistinction with the category of "Blacks", a holdall term covering all the formerly colonized minorities. For British Asians however, it was more a matter of differentiating themselves from other migrants (in particular from the West Indies) than of giving body to any shared identity (Modood, 1988). And so following on from the mobilization of British Muslims against Rushdie, non-Muslims called for new categories to enable them to differentiate themselves from Muslims. An additional step was taken in the 2001 census with the introduction of a question on religious belonging, existing alongside ethnic and national categories (White, Mixed, Indian, Pakistani, Bangladeshi, Black, and Chinese). It was thus possible to establish the numbers of the various religious communities (and for example to see that the number of Sikhs had been overestimated against that of Hindus). But it also led to the production of demographic and socio-economic statistics by faith groups, crystallizing phenomena of internal differentiation.

For the desire of Sikhs to differentiate themselves from the Muslims is also based on the fact that British Muslims are seen as lagging behind in socio-economic terms, something which appears to be confirmed by statistical studies showing they have a far higher unemployment rate, perform worse in education, and are more heavily dependent on social services. This theme cropped up during the interviews I conducted:

> You know why Sikhs need a separate category? Because their needs are different...Muslims have the highest rate of dependence towards social benefits; on the contrary, Sikhs have the highest rate of house ownership. So there are socio-economic differences.[15]

> The way the figure of the good and bad immigrant is constructed also takes part in this process of differentiation: During the summer 01 riots, it was the Muslims against everybody else. But the British media blamed the 'Asians'. But no Sikh nor Hindu took part in it, so they thought 'why are we being tarnished, we don't want to be considered as Muslim'.[16]

A Sikh journalist takes a similar stance:

> There is the feeling that Sikhs are hard-working, successful people, while Muslims are just here to claim social benefits. So there are economic grievances and a sense that we Sikhs gave our blood for this country, that there is a special relation between us and the British that the government should acknowledge.[17]

This desire to differentiate themselves is all the stronger amongst Sikhs as their external symbols of belonging, the beard and turban, paradoxically make them look like radical Muslims, and this misperception means that they have been attacked on several occasions since 11 September 2001, both in Great Britain and in the United states.

Policy Transformation as an Explanatory Factor

British sociologists have established a line of descent between colonial representations of and policies towards colonized populations and the integration policies adopted by postcolonial Great Britain.

A policy of assimilation in the 1950s and 1960s gave way over the following decades to antiracism and multiculturalism, based on recognizing and valuing cultural differences, in conjunction with a policy of equal opportunities. Urban riots in summer 2001 in the North of England, followed by the July 2005 terrorist attacks in London, led to a radical questioning of this political and ideological framework, and multiculturalism was officially abandoned in favor of a policy known as community cohesion.

Multiculturalism, and especially its anti-racist aspects, certainly helped improve the integration of immigrant populations and the way they were taken into account by British society. Yet by targeting communities it also played a role in institutionalizing the minority identities defined along the more and more exclusive lines of religious belonging for South Asians. According to its detractors, one of the perverse effects of multiculturalism was to have played a hand in legitimizing the most conservative and orthodox definitions of communal identity. Thus British Asian community leaders are primarily religious leaders, and it was faith-based associations which received the lion's share of public funds and which managed to mobilize immigrants—far more successfully than pan-ethnic or secular organizations did—around, therefore, religious issues (turbans for the Sikhs, halal meat in canteens for Muslims, and so on). In the pursuit of public funding and political recognition, immigrant communities were thus encouraged to emphasize their supposed internal homogeneity (the Muslim community versus the Sikh community, the Hindu community, etc.), their cultural particularities and, as part of this process, minority identities as defined along religious lines became reified and institutionalized (See Garbaye and Schnapper, 2014).

Public discourse about and policies for immigrant populations therefore evolved radically, emphasizing racial belonging in the 1960s and 1970s, then ethnic belonging, before focusing on religious belonging from the 1990s onwards (Singh, 2005).

Regarding demands made by minority populations, British Sikhs were the pioneers here, and from the late 1950s onwards they exerted considerable influence over the drawing up of policy at both the local and national level (Singh, 2005). Their mobilization to be entitled to wear turbans (at work, at school, on motorbikes) was crowned by a decision of the House of Lords in 1982 according them the status of an ethnic group. This enabled them to benefit from British anti-discrimination legislation (defined in Great Britain on ethnic lines, not religious ones), unlike Muslims who as a religious group are debarred from invoking it. Inspired by the success of the Sikhs, Muslims have been in the forefront of inter-community competition for the recognition of particular benefits since the early 1990s. Their mobilization against *The Satanic Verses* and against the two Gulf Wars indicates that despite being politically underrepresented, Muslims have acquired a capacity for collective mobilization around specific themes.

Has the recent introduction of the new policy known as community cohesion changed the situation? The riots of summer 2001 in the North of England (in Bradford, Burnley, and Oldham) and the attacks in London in July 2005 sounded the death knell of multiculturalism, seen as responsible for all the ills of the country, and in particular the non-integration of certain parts of the young immigrant population. The Cantle Report, one of the four reports commissioned by the government after the 2001 riots and published under the title of "Community Cohesion", prefigured the new policy which was gradually put in place (Kalra, 2002). This seeks to foster social cohesion, inter-community harmony and dialogue, and interaction between the various components (both immigrant and non-immigrant) of the British population to enable common values to emerge along with a notion of common destiny. In a way the new British model may be said to be similar to the French model of integration, though with one major difference, that of the role played by religious issues, as seen below.

The Department for Communities and Local Government is in charge of drawing up and implementing social cohesion policy. This includes various aspects, those studied here are inter-religious dialogue and preventing violent extremism.

Inter-religious Dialogue

The religious dimension plays a very important part in British public policy, which recognizes "faith communities as an important component of the local community and value the experience, skills, and diversity they bring to wider society" (Communities and Local Government, 2008). Religious institutions and communities are therefore considered by local governments as the privileged partners for drawing up local policy, urban renovation programs, and tackling unemployment and delinquency. Inter-religious dialogue is a firmly established practice in Great Britain. It was initially an ecumenical initiative, between the various Christian churches and then, with the influx of migrants, expanded to include other religions. As part of a recent policy shake-up, the Inter Faith Network bringing together a whole host of associations throughout the British Isles, has become a leading partner for the CLG, as it "contribute[s] to community cohesion through deepening inter-faith understanding and cooperation". As may be seen, interfaith dialogue is accorded a new political and social role, defined as follows: "build up trust, mutual understanding, and respect; help defuse inter-community tensions; reinforce community cohesion; foster cooperation on local issues and work jointly on social and educational projects".

This was the framework for the dialogue weekend involving a group of Muslim and Sikh activists organized in July 2008 in Northern Ireland by Faith Matters, a not for profit organization working to reduce interfaith tensions and encourage dialogue between different faith groups in the UK. The same body, financed by the CLG, has set up an ad hoc committee of leading Sikh and Muslim figures which meets every three months.[18]

Preventing violent extremism

The aim here is to identify and provide financial support to leaders and community organizations "capable of taking the initiative to fight violent extremist influences" and thus "support Muslim youths", "support Muslim women" reinforce the "capabilities of Muslim religious leaders", and organize "local forums against extremism and Islamophobia" (Communities and Local Government, 2008).

A Young Muslims Advisory Group was set up in October 2008, and composed of twenty-three "young Muslims" chosen to advise ministers and policy deciders on issues affecting their daily life. This was set up in the search for suggestions on how to "apprehend websites which incite radicalisation" and "increase the involvement of young Muslims in civic life" (Communities and Local Government, 2008).

Considerable sums of money are thus devoted to supporting this "moderate Islam" seen as a rampart against "extremism", and tasked by the government of "putting its own house in order", so to speak. The Preventing Violent Extremism Fund handed out £6 million to seventy local authorities identified as being a priority on being set up in October 2006, and an additional £45 million between 2008 and 2011.

The Consequences of the Policy Shift on Inter-Community Relations

Claire Alexander, in an article analyzing the 2001 riots and the policy responses to them, and in particular perceptions criminalizing young British Muslims, is highly critical of the new policy of community cohesion (Alexander, 2004). According to her, cultural differences, previously valued by multiculturalism, have been seen as a danger since the riots, especially when these differences are associated with Muslims. The supposed cultural specificities of Muslims are constructed as incompatible with modernity and the British national framework: Alexander speaks of the "pathologization of Muslim culture" (Alexander, 2004, 10). The two sides of public policy are indivisible: community cohesion (which can take various forms—interreligious dialogue, education and citizenship, the introduction of an oath of loyalty, and so on) goes hand in hand with the criminalization and containment of Muslims.

This policy thus contributes to the stigmatization of British Muslims, who are perceived as a major threat to the ideal of community cohesion. The notion of extreme violence automatically associated with them is of course part of this stigmatization, and takes on a virtually phantasmagoric dimension. Furthermore, it exacerbates competition between communities for the financial and symbolic resources dispensed by the local authorities, with non-Muslims feeling hard done by in comparison to the largesse showered on Muslims. This grievance was repeatedly articulated in the interviews carried out with British Sikhs:

> In fact the British government has started to pamper Muslims since the Rushdie mobilization. The government has become aware of the international dimension of the Muslim community, of the Ummah. So there was a deal between them & Muslim extremists: you can do whatever you want outside the country, but don't strike the UK. This deal was broken in 07/05. Now, a lot of money is spent to tackle extremism, and this money is not spent on other groups. For instance, here in Slough, a lot of money is spent on funding Muslim festivals, Eid parties and dinners, under the pretense of preventing extremism. And this is not fair![19]

The interview with a Sikh municipal councilor reflects the same sense of frustration:

> As a municipal councilor and a magistrate, I am regularly invited to several interfaith and community cohesion meetings & functions, but you know, I don't go there anymore, because it is useless. They are allocated a lot of money to curb this violent extremism, you see. This money is given to moderates, to "control" extremists, but they don't do what they should with it. For example, they spent huge amounts of money on religious festivals. Actually, the council says the money given by the government is for the Asian community as a whole but in fact it only goes to Muslims. And Muslims are very good at applying for money under the Asian tag, for their own purposes only...[20]

Grievances relate not only to the distribution of public funds, but also to that of symbolic resources and the recognition supposedly enjoyed by

Muslims at the expense of other communities. As the same municipal councilor explained: "I have a feeling that local authorities are only interested in the Muslim community problems."[21] A Sikh activist and member of an inter-faith dialogue forum states:

> It is a fact that the government is paying much less attention to Sikhs...Look at the way they have handled the fire in Bow *gurdwara*:[22] if it had been a *masjid*, it would've made the headlines in mainstream papers, and the police would be a lot more active. That is why there is a real sense of being neglected among Sikhs.[23]

This feeling of resentment is all the more pronounced as it is also based on the feeling that the authorities favor Muslims not because of their "merits" and their contributions to the host society, but solely on the basis of their "capacity to do harm". These pronouncements show very clearly the desire to differentiate oneself from the Muslims, the minority of the worst as referred to by Elias and Scotson (Elias and Scotson, 1997).

Conclusion

Relations between Sikhs and Muslims follow two paradigms: that of fraternity (*bhaichara*) and that of a historical antagonism, with the place accorded to each depending on the context. The meaning and value of these relations are far from being cast in stone, even though the paradigm of conflict is perceived as hereditary in the collective imagination of both communities. In the context of the diaspora, these relations are the outcome of several variables. The fact of being a migrant leads in itself to reconfigurations in the identities and boundaries between the communities, as well as to antagonistic constructions of the Other. The majority society acts fully on these processes.

This paper has principally focused on the role of public policy in the evolution of inter-community relations in Great Britain. As the example of British Sikhs and Muslims shows, the host state comes across as a key factor in these conflicts, deciding on the distribution of both symbolic resources (the "politics of recognition" as referred to by Taylor) and of material resources (funds allocated as part of the new policy against "violent extremism"), thus exacerbating competition between the communities.

Other elements, however, are beyond its control: the improving ties between Indian and Pakistani citizens in South Asia stand out in contrast to the logics of conflict observed in Great Britain, to a large extent preventing their being re-exported back to the countries of origin.

6

THE ORIGINS OF THE PROTEST MOVEMENT AGAINST ETHNIC HIERARCHY

THE AZERBAIJANI CAUSE IN IRAN

Gilles Riaux
Translated by Françoise Gillespie

Azerbaijan is the historical name of the great region of northwestern Iran, bordering on the republics of Turkey, Azerbaijan and Armenia. The Azeris of orientalist literature, the largely Turkic-speaking and Shi'ite people of Iranian Azerbaijan are known for their successful integration into Iranian society and enjoy a significant presence among the country's elites, unlike other ethnic groups, mostly Sunni, who find themselves marginalized in Iranian society. Azeri Turks have for long held an advantaged position in Iran's ethnic hierarchy, a fact that may explain why as a group they have a low historical propensity for opposing the central government (Ramezanzadeh, 1996). In Azerbaijan however, as in all of Iran, a protean project for recognition of traditional ethnic cultures is underway, primarily outside of the institutions of the Islamic Republic. This movement is expressed openly in books and magazines dedicated to ethnic culture. Prior to the Revolution, few books on ethnic subjects were published and those in print often circulated informally. Indeed, between 1979 and 1984, over 180 books were published in Iran (Gokdag and Heyat, 2004). The revolutionary period also marked an important, if only symbolic, victory for ethnic movements, with Article 15 of the Constitution of the Islamic Republic formally recognizing the equality of cultures and languages.[1] Even so, intense publishing activity and legal recognition of ethnic cultures remain marginal elements of the revolutionary period, which was marked essentially by a search for consensus (Khosrokhavar, 1993). Consensus for the overthrow of the Shah and for establishment of an Islamic Republic did not prevent a number of ethnic groups from formulating their own demands. These groups pointed out that the Revolution, far from being limited to a heroic struggle of the Iranian people against the Shah, was in fact the scene of multiple conflicts. The publishing frenzy of a small number of writers convinced of the need to write about Azeri-Turkish culture is symptomatic of the rise in the public space of a cause originating in previous decades and whose objective is the recognition of specific rights for ethnic groups other than Persian, especially with regard to cultural matters. Its emergence marks the beginning of a conflict between protesters campaigning to change relationships between ethnic groups and their opponents who do not consider such issues legitimate.

With respect to the Azerbaijani cause, if research is to focus on the transformation of the conflict, we must consider that the conflict itself is the product of protest opportunities introduced by regime change. It was the Revolution itself that created the conditions conducive to ethnic conflict, by raising the ethnic self-awareness of specific categories of the population who started to protest for recognition of their rights.[2] In this chapter, I have used the theoretical tools of the sociology of social movements, in order to consider the Azerbaijani cause as a challenge to the hierarchal system of ethnic identities. This has allowed me to avoid a binary approach and critical construction in terms of degree of social integration, a common approach in Iranian ethnic studies. Resource mobilization highlights the decisive role played by intellectual figures from the educated middle classes. Based on their cultural and social capital, these entrepreneurs have specific resources that give them the ability to carry out a redefinition and enhancement of 'turkishness' in its Azerbaijani specificity. This endeavor, while far from uniform, is constrained logically by resource limitations (Riaux, 2008). On the other hand, a critical approach taking into account resource mobilizations hardly accounts for the actors' terms of engagement and precludes acknowledgement of the essential role and dynamics of interaction with the environment (McAdam et al., 2001, 22). I argue instead that the origins of the Azerbaijani cause are the product of interactions between actors and their environment and develop a diachronic approach that considers the different periods of social action. My argument identifies a sequential theoretical framework for the study of early-stage ethnic movements. First, assertive identity strategies are produced by certain cognitive processes common to ethnic activists across successive movements; the interactions of these activists with national construction policies, whether domestically or abroad, feature decisively in their initiatives. The movements are then shaped by the different social positions and resources available to these actors, determining the movements' particular courses of action. Finally, the expression of ethnic demands in non-democratic contexts, begins to soften as periods of political transformation set in. Social movements tend to follow this outline, with each of the different formative stages playing a specific role in the foundation of ethnic movements.

This chapter studies the transformation of the conflict between activists (typically educated, middle class and Turkic) and state officials. A close examination of the dynamics and portrayal of interaction between these actors is therefore required, bearing in context any significant changes in the political landscape. With a view to this, I also try to explain the complex fluctuations in relative Iranian identity-values, exposing the fluidity of the ethnic hierarchy. These played a decisive role in the genesis of the Azerbaijani cause under the Pahlavis. Conflagration of the issues became possible only as a result of the political opening introduced by the Revolution, a period when the articulation of the ethnic cause was recognized through the relationships between participating individuals, groups and institutions. Thus, the conflict was not simply transformed by the change in ethnic hierarchy, but more specifically by the mobilizing opportunities afforded to certain social groups within the new system.

The Roots of Azerbaijani Claims During the Pahlavi Dynasty

Ethnic claims are seldom disconnected from a social environment, rather, in this case study they tend to feed on this environment marked by a devaluation of relative Turkish identities. Far from being generalized across the social spectrum, ethnic devaluation primarily affected the educated middle classes, opening the way for a challenge to the existing hierarchy from this specific social category, without recourse to open conflict with the state.

In Iran, ethnic identities are part of a hierarchical system that defines access to public and social resources. The Iranian hierarchical system must be regarded as an evolutionary system of regional dimensions, produced by inter-action between ethnic groups.[3] Under such conditions, the value of Turkish identity, considered in relation to other identities, may fluctuate. Several factors may explain these fluctuations: the demands of the actors in question, changes in prevailing ideologies or in state policies, events that alter the perception of identities (through the interpretive biais of the actors themselves) or demographic and economic trends that make some identities more or less relevant. This chapter will focus on the declining value of Turkish identity.

The Devaluation of Turkish Identity

Turks traditionally suffer from a bad image in the Iranian world. The naturalizing term *Tork-e khar* (Turkish donkey) is expressed in different forms in Iranian popular imagination: Turks are shown as clumsy, crude individuals who lack education and refinement. Yet, Turks have long occupied a privileged position among the Iranian elite. The major dynasties that ruled Iran since the great Turkish migrations of Central Asia were of Turkish origin. To this day, Turks play a dominant role in the army, an institution that was central to government interests throughout the nineteenth century and the main beneficiary of reforms. In the nineteenth century, Tabriz, the main city of Azerbaijan, was the most dynamic and prosperous city in Iran. It benefited from the proximity of the Ottoman Empire and Russia: goods, people, and ideas all transited through the city before spreading elsewhere in the country. Turks, or at least the Qajar aristocracy and bazaars, enjoyed privileged access to a range of resources that reinforced their pre-eminent social position and gave them a prominent place in the organization of ethnic hierarchy. However, adaptation and assimilation of Western ideas and techniques during this period (Richard, 1989) helped transform the relative values of identities, especially for Turks. Based on a comparison of writings by Western travelers from the beginning to the end of the nineteenth century, Xavier Planhol's work tells us, "In the space of a quarter century, the social status of Turks has changed. Latent disdain is now openly expressed." The reasons lay in the change of "model and master". Iran was guided by the West. The great Turkish dynasties and tribal confederations that had long dominated the country lost their luster, resulting in a loss of prestige and reinforcing cultural appropriation of the Western concept of nation (Planhol, 1984, 127). European orientalist knowledge has helped scholars propose a new Iranian identity, based on the Persian language and pre-Islamic history, both particularly suited to the paradigm of trans-national identities (Thiesse, 2005). In the name of this restrictive conception of Iranian identity, Turkishness was rejected as exogenous. According to Taqi Arani, "it is a disgrace for Azerbaijanis to be mistaken for Turks [...] To deprive Azerbaijanis of the honor of being Persians is flagrant injustice" (Arani, 1924). According to Goffman, "normative expectations, duly presented" developed, with respect to the "social identity" of Turks who must endeavor to hide their Turkishness (Goffman, 1963). Obvious signs of Turkishness in public spaces were discredited and the bearers stigmatized.

These normative expectations were relayed by official institutions that required the use of the Persian language and enforced a notion of Iranian identity as defined by the criteria of Iranian nationalism. Whether in education, the military or in cultural institutions, considerable efforts were made to give primacy to Persian identity and sublimate minority cultures. Such policies imposed a devaluation of the cultural capital inherent in minority languages, hampering intergenerational transmission and rendering standardization impossible. Schools were the starting point for enforcement of the exclusive use of the Persian language among new generations. Arani insisted on the need for a massive education effort in Azerbaijan: "If compulsory primary education is not yet feasible in all of Iran, it must be implemented in Azerbaijan at any cost; this is essential not only for education but also for political reasons" (Arani, 1924, 254). Mahmoud Afshar explained the political rationale for limiting the presence of non-Persian identity markers:

> what I mean by the national unity of Iran is a political, cultural and social unity of the people living within the present borders of Iran [...] Achieving national unity implies the institution of the Persian language across the whole country, the disappearance of regional differences in dress, customs, and other things, and the elimination of tribal leaders. (Afshar, 1925, 8)

The achievement of national unity claimed by Afshar came after widespread riots rocked the Iranian provinces, including Azerbaijan, with uprisings led by Sattar Khan during the Constitutional Revolution, and by Sheikh Khiyabani in 1920. These were crushed by the army, whose reinforcement coincided with the establishment of the Pahlavi state (Cronin, 1997). Once the revolts threatening national unity had been suppressed and before the state's coercive power could be fully established, the army was directed to weaken tribal power, to extend central government authority throughout the country, to destroy local authorities and disarm and pacify civilian populations. Once all of this had been accomplished, the army was to ensure homeland security (Cronin, 2003, 39). In December 1946, after nearly one year of existence, the Autonomous

Republic of Azerbaijan—formed with the support of the Soviet Union who had occupied northern Iran during World War II—was crushed by the army. Military victory was followed by a major crackdown and the exile of nearly 15,000 people who fled to the USSR. In the following decades, Azerbaijan was regarded as a potentially secessionist region and the scene of intense repression under control of security institutions. The memory of riots (perpetuated via oral and family traditions) and everday interactions with the institutions of repression, whether real or imagined, created a special relationship to the state, especially since these were subject to interpretation by the actors involved.

Demographic and economic growth also influenced the relative values of identities. The country's economic development, based on the exploitation of hydrocarbons, produced a concentration of economic activity in the capital, which then became the exclusive center of Iranian modernization in the 1960s and 1970s (Madanipour, 1998). The polarization of economic growth was detrimental to surrounding provinces that remained on the sidelines of the country's economic transformation. In the case of Iranian Azerbaijan, marginalization was visible in the decline of the province, and of Tabriz in particular, from positions of preeminence in early twentieth century Iran. Another consequence of the polarization of economic growth, displacement of rural populations to urban centers, was a significant factor in redefining Turkish stereotypes. As a rural, densely populated and little industrialized province, Azerbaijan was a primary source of emigrants. The influx of a poorly educated workforce, who often found it difficult to speak Persian, contributed to the introduction of stereotypes describing Turks as clumsy and crude. At the time of urbanization, they were seen as rough-hewn peasants fresh out of their rural surroundings. Speaking a heavily accented Persian, they ended up with menial jobs, poorly paid. They were however considered courageous hardworking men, who proved to be successful in the trading business. Popular imagination abounded in migration related stereotypes about Turks. Under the Islamic Republic, the decline of migration from Iranian Azerbaijan and increased migrations from other provinces (including Kurdistan), and especially Afghanistan, helped rebuild the system of ethnic hierarchy. But stereotypes die hard, and their pervasiveness continued long after the social processes that brought on their emergence.

The combined effects of these processes resulted in a decline of the relative value of Turkish identity in Iran and therefore, in restriction of access to resources, mainly symbolic. This development was felt essentially by a minority of the educated middle class, and led to the conditions for protest against ethnic hierarchization.

Awareness of the Azerbaijani Cause

The population did not universally and equally feel the fluctuations in the relative value of their identities determined; social class, origin and geographical location, age and gender determined discrimination.[4] The possibility of accessing resources associated with ethnicity was part of this complex web. Each spot of the social space was shaped according to the norms and specific logic of differentiated identity strategies. Because of the social specificity of scholarship engaged in redefining and upgrading Turkishness, I will focus my study on the educated middle classes. What they shared is access to modern education that in turn provided them with important cultural capital. Even if translation of a good education into economic success was easy in the 1950s and 1960s, providing access to enviable positions, it appeared considerably more difficult during the following decade (Kian-Thiébaut, 1998).

Ervand Abrahamian's work on the Second World War period, has shown how identity strategies, developed by the leadership of the *Tudeh*, the Communist Party of Iran and its breakaway branch in Azerbaijan, the *Ferqa-ye Demokrat-e Azerbayjan*, tied in with differentiated social positions. Abrahamian emphasized the homogeneity of the *Tudeh* leaders, who belonged to a young Tehran intelligentsia quite unprepared to address the issue of relations between the center and the periphery:

> As Western-educated intellectuals, they associated centralization with modernization. As Persian intellectuals, they favored the rapid expansion of the state educational system. As Orthodox Marxists, they viewed society through a class perspective, ignoring the ethnic dimension. Linguistic and regional issues were therefore ignored in all three of the major political statements made in the early years of the party. (Abrahamian, 1970, 301).

This generational, geographical and intellectual solidarity conflicted with the position of older communist militants who made up the *Ferqa-ye Demokrat-e Azerbayjan*. The latter came mainly from Azerbaijan and did not necessarily master the Persian language. They had experienced Marxism as a result of political commitments made over the course of the various revolutionary episodes that had marked the Caucasus and northern Iran in the early twentieth century.

The differentiated social positions that explained the conflict within the *Tudeh* and the autonomist shift of the *Ferqa-ye Demokrat-e Azerbayjan* diminished gradually with the extension of the modern educational system, the development of the educated middle classes and the limitation of exchanges between Iran and the Soviet Republics of the Caucasus.[5] These transformations occurred as the relative value of Turkish identity continued to depreciate while markers of Turkishness continued to disappear from the public space. According to Alain Dieckhoff, "if social mobility was promoted by the central government and offered real, economic and social benefits, the intelligentsia had only a residual interest in engaging in a strategy of dissociation even though a total loss of cultural identity may be enough for social promotion" (Dieckhoff, 2000, 58). In Iran, opportunities for implementation of the cultural capital acquired during formal education ensured high social mobility and prevented possible dissociative tendencies. The depreciation of the relative value of Turkish identity was perceived by the educated middle classes as a necessary step in the process of national standardization and considered part of the broader theme of modernization imposed at a fast pace by Mohammad Reza Shah to turn his country into a respected great power. The Turkic speaking educated middle classes were free to develop their own identity strategy, setting aside stigmatizing Turkish markers; they could refrain from expressing their Turkishness in order to affirm their full Iranian identity. The refusal to express Turkishness could be confined to the public sphere, but it sometimes extended to the private sphere and led to a total loss of cultural identity.

With regard to the educated middle classes, the stigma of identity presents a paradox that must be clarified to understand some commitments, exceptional for their rarity, but central to understanding the origins of the protests in Azerbaijan. Through access to the educational system, certain actors assimilated a modern culture largely defined by the Persianist criteria of Iranian nationalism. Their commitment to the prestigious Persian language endowed with its rich literary heritage, the heritage of classic Iranian civilization, the sense of occupying a special position in the Middle East, the assertion of national independence, indeed all elements at the core of Iranian nationalism, remained an unsurpassable horizon for all modern middle classes beyond political or ethnic divisions. As a result, the relationship to the world of the educated middle classes developed through the prism of identity imposed by Iranian nationalism. This raised the issue of coexistence, among Turkic-speaking educated middle classes, of an enhanced Iranian identity and a stigmatizing Turkish identity, regarded as backward and uneducated. Even though the identity strategy of setting aside Turkishness was widely adopted, there remained a minority of the educated middle class who were committed to the defense of Azerbaijani identity. Could such a commitment be affirmed against Iranian nationalism, but also through the prism of that same Iranian nationalism? Here, the explanation offered by the actors, according to which Azerbaijani national revival is a form of resistance against the excesses of Iranian nationalism, is over-simplistic.[6]

Unless, perhaps, we adopt a Foucaldian understanding of "resistance": resistance is not merely an adverse reaction to domination or its negation. It is "never in a position of exteriority in relation to power" (Foucault, 1978, 95). It refers always to the situation it opposes and acts as a counter-strategy, embedded in a multiplicity of power relations. If we understand resistance as being at the core, and not out of the power that causes it, we must consider Partha Chatterjee's approach to nationalism as a "derivative discourse". Chatterjee reflected upon the colonial context, characterized by the inability of post-colonial societies to develop identities independent of the dominant Western categories. Such inability makes nationalism a "different discourse, yet one that is dominated by another", from which it selects elements to build itself (Chatterjee, 1986, 116–122). The derivative approach can be used in the cause of Azerbaijan. Indeed, the new Azerbaijani identity was developed based on the criteria of Iranian nationalism, the dominant discourse in intellectual and political fields. It served as a model for operating a reinterpretation of the Turkish tradition of Iran and for establishing a new social order where Turkish identity, now Azerbaijani identity, would be endowed with virtues at least equal to those attributed to Iranian identity.

The choice of an identity strategy that is dissociative and highlights Turkishness should be viewed in the context of the relative depreciation of Turkish identity in Iran. There remained, however, a marginal choice, the logic of which requires explanation. These choices are to be found in recurring passages through the transnational space of aspiring entrepreneurs of the Azerbaijani cause who experienced specific interactions. Thus, several prospective entrepreneurs of the Azerbaijani cause had completed part of their graduate studies in Turkey. This led to cognitive dissonance with the educated middle classes in Iran, marked by the ideological prism of Iranian nationalism. The student experience in Turkey may well have led to Turkish stigmatization, thus making it possible to identify with the Azerbaijani cause. For others, socializing among militant groups close to the Azerbaijani cause, both in northwestern Iran during the Second World War and in Tabriz and Baku in the following decades, helped create awareness for the stigma of Turkishness.

These passages through the public space, while conditioning an intersubjective construction of the social world, were linked to commitments within it. They did not however, become a source of conflict prior to the Revolution. Indeed it is the Revolution that offered many in the educated middle classes—now aware of the ethnic issue—opportunities to challenge the ethnic hierarchy. In addition, the Revolution provided researchers with an abundance of publications, which helped them identify individuals, observe group structures and understand relationships among different players in the Azerbaijani cause.

Mobilizations During the Revolutionary Period

The Revolution offered the whole of Iranian society great opportunities to engage in politics. Members of the educated middle classes receptive to the Azerbaijani cause were not excluded, even if their ardor was marginal compared to the universalist passion that inflamed Iranian society at the time. The undeniable surge of publications dealing with Azerbaijani language and culture during the revolutionary period showed that the entrepreneurs of Azerbaijani identity were ready and seized the opportunity to act. The establishment of an Islamic republic, seen as a break with the Persian nationalist regime, created opportunities for change in the stratification of ethnic Iranian identities. As a result of their claims, two nationalist strategies have emerged in relation to the social positions occupied or perceived as being occupied by the identitary entrepreneurs. These strategies concern either the means of accessing state benefits via the mediation of elites close to the center of power, or by opposition to the state, via pursuit and accumulation of resources.

A Strategy to Reorganize the System of Ethnic Hierarchies

The first strategy emmerged among a group of Azerbaijani identity entrepreneurs rooted in the educated and priviledged middle-class families who rallied around the quarterly review, *Varliq*.[7] These men made up a solid, socially homogenous group. All were either educated at least to high school, and pursued academic, journalistic or executive careers. The group formed in Tehran, even though most were from Tabriz. In 1978, the group had founded the *Anjoman-e Azerbayjan* (Azerbaijan Society), a study group that met regularly in members' homes. The group's efforts focused on publishing the review *Varliq*, the first issue of which appeared in April 1979. The review dealt primarily with culture, language, literature and Turkish history, but also with cultural and societal problems affecting the Turks of Iran. An important characteristic of *Varliq* when viewed within the galaxy of ethnic Azerbaijani publication was its extreme longevity, a fact that can only be understood in light of the multiple private resources of its publisher and founding editor, Javad Heyat.

Born in 1925, Javad Heyat came from an aristocratic family. His father, Ali Heyat, was Chief Justice under the Pahlavis. After attending elementary and secondary school in Tabriz, he enrolled in medical school in Tehran before attending medical school in Istanbul and in Paris to specialize in cardiology. Back in Tehran, he began a brilliant medical career at Hedayat hospital where he performed the first open heart surgery in Iran. Javad Heyat wrote over 80 articles in Persian and a score in English and French for medical journals (Anon, 2004, 12). Following the Revolution, Heyat held various academic positions, became professor of surgery at the Free University and published three surgery manuals. At the same time, he also wrote several books on the history and language of Azerbaijan. In 1983, he participated in the first Conference on Turkic Studies at the University of Indiana in the United states, where he presented a paper on the Azeri language and literature before and after the Revolution (Heyat, 1983). He has received a number of honorary degrees from the University of Medicine in Istanbul, the Medical School of the Republic of Azerbaijan, the Turkish Language Academy in Ankara and the Academy of the Republic of Azerbaijan. In addition, he was Khamenei's personal physician, when the latter was President of the Republic.[8]

As this brief biography demonstrates, Heyat possesses unique cultural capital both as a leading figure in the Iranian medical community and as a recognized expert on Turkish affairs, in Ankara and elsewhere. His professional practice provides significant income to supplement the family fortune. His personal wealth has made it possible for him to finance a magazine that is not profitable and requires regular subsidies to carry on. It is thus quite natural that he should assume responsibility as Editor-in-Chief of *Varliq*. The journal's longevity is thus linked to the social capital of the Javad Heyat family and confirmed by his medical career. Heyat family connections have facilitated negotiation of the hazards of Iranian censorship, even under the most repressive regimes. The history of *Varliq* is thus inseparable from Javad Heyat who stands as its central figure.[9]

The transformative strategy for social ordering envisaged by the first group included a three-step process. It began with the publication of writings on Azerbaijani culture aimed at affirming the legitimacy of the Turkic identity in Iran and its recognition by political authorities. It included a comprehensive critical description of the components of Turkic identity, a task completed by the intellectual members of the *Varliq* circle. Many books were published, each based on the authors' respective specialties: Heyat wrote on the history and literature of Iranian Turks (1358a, 1358b, 1361),[10] Mohammad Ali Farzane published a grammar and two books of folktales (1358a, 1358b, 1361), Hosseyn Bigdeli wrote a review of Turkic literature (1358). In addition, collections of poems were published from authors like Sonmez (1358, 1359), Savalan (1357) or Bigdeli (1359) whose purpose was to unveil the soul of Azerbaijan. This intense activity was supported in a number of *Varliq* issues that included articles about Turkish culture and poems. The editorial line clearly expressed the notion of a Turkic revival following decades of oppression, thanks to the Revolution. In the second issue of the review, a poem by Notqi spoke of "the curse that tied up my tongue" and of "lost identity" to describe the effects of the Pahlavi regime (Notqi, 1979b, 3). It was this curse that the *Varliq* entrepreneurs sought to end.

The Islamic Republic appeared much less hostile toward ethnic groups than the old regime: Iranian nationalism was no longer the state ideology and many leading figures of the new regime were of Turkish origin. The apparent receptivity of the new regime to calls for the re-evaluation of ethnic hierarchies encouraged *Varliq* contributors' adherence to the legitimate register of commitment during the Revolution. This required affirmation of a common destiny with Iran, while defending the specificity of Azerbaijan, as stated in the editorial of the first issue of *Varliq*:

> Each and every people of the world has the historical and legal right to preserve its national culture, identity and language, no matter how long those peoples have had historical and cultural affiliations with other peoples throughout history. The people of Azerbaijan, together with the other peoples living in Iran, share a common destiny and have contributed to the creation of a common culture, and yet retain a national identity, character, and mother tongue (Notqi, 1979a, 3).

This common destiny then had to be integrated into the political upheavals of the time. The unanimity surrounding the overthrow of the monarchy naturally led *Varliq* members to take up the slogan, "Down with the Shah!" They found the old regime guilty of maintaining a policy of cultural repression against the Turks of Iran, and its fall was seen as just by Azerbaijani activists (Yashar, 1979). It was thus expected that the revolution would lead to restoration of Turkish pride and put an end to ethnic discrimination: Turkishness would no longer be stigmatized. To *Varliq's* readership, the Revolution appeared as an opportunity to recover resources, mainly symbolic, by reforming the system of ethnic hierarchization in Iran.

Adherence to the roll of legitimate commitment at the time of the Revolution helped make their claims acceptable to the new regime. The purpose was to influence the institutions of the new regime to recognize the enviable status of Turks. Some *Varliq* members tried to have a say in the constitutional debates that took place through the end of 1979. The first issue of the magazine, which read almost like a manifesto of the *Anjoman-e Azerbayjan* cause, called for recognition of the "national language and culture of Azerbaijan, the establishment of schools in the coming school year, a national media in the Turkish language, as well as the recognition of the right of the Azerbaijanis to use their mother tongue in the courts and other government offices" (Notqi, 1979a, 10). Hamid Notqi identified the most significant claims in the subsequent issue of the magazine: "the first four years of school must be taught in the mother tongue, then in both the Persian language and the mother tongue" and "radio, television and all media must serve the development of ethnic, regional and national cultures" (Notqi, 1979b, 12–13). These claims were part of the speech Notqi gave at the "Seminar on the needs of the Iranian nation for the Constitution" on 24 June 1979. The seminar was held at the University of Tehran after the Assembly of Experts was asked to draft the constitutional text. Also in the second issue, in an open letter to readers, colleagues, fellow citizens and the government, Notqi demanded recognition and enforcement of the promises made to the people of Iran for the acknowledgment of their rights and freedom, based on arguments from the Koran (Notqi, 1979b, 49–51). In addition to taking public stands, the most prominent members of *Varliq* approached some of their contacts more discreetly to make their claims known to the new political power. Such measures, although difficult to document, were effective, at least to Khamenei who expressed support for the magazine in a letter.[11] Through various forms of action, the people at *Varliq* worked for a reorganization of the system of ethnic hierarchization and a reassessment of Turkishness so that ethnic Turks would enjoy access to (almost) the same resources as ethnic Persians.

A Strategy for the Subversion of Ethnic Hierarchies

The second strategy was that of identitary entrepreneurs less well endowed than the first group, who, despite benefitting from a secular education, were less successful in transferring their cultural capital into the economic sphere. It is difficult to adequately account for this group's activities during the revolutionary period as their efforts are difficult to identify and the individuals associated with this group failed to organize into a structure. The actors in this group bore the brunt of competition between the various parties, groups and organizations seeking to establish themselves within a political space that had been profoundly shaken in revolutionary Iran. Nevertheless, overall ideas emerged through the publications of the time. *Ulker*, the first Turkish newspaper with articles in Persian appeared on the day following the departure of the Shah, 17 January 1979. It was the organ of *Tabriz Shairler ve Yazarlar Jamiyati* (Association of Poets and Writers of Tabriz) and called for recognition of cultural rights of ethnic minorities. The association had a youth section, *Genchi Shair ve Yazarlar Jamiyati*, which published *Genchlik* (Gokdağ and Heyat, 2004, 58). A literary magazine, *Dede korkut* was created; a speech by Balash Azeroğlu at the 7th Congress of Writers in Azerbaijan SSR, broadcast on Radio Baku, was published in one of the issues (Nissman, 1987, 72). One of the poems of the famous Soviet poet was published in Tabriz (1364). The Revolution also offered former players of the Autonomous Republic of Azerbaijan an opportunity to resurface. The most famous among them was Mohammad Biriya, former Minister of Culture of the Republic. He returned to Iran after his long exile in Azerbaijan SSR, he was quickly apprehended and died in detention. Nevertheless, one of his poetry books was published in Tabriz (1360). Mohammad Zehtabi did not meet the same fate as Biriya even though his publications were instrumental in articulating the Azerbaijani cause in Iran (1358, 1369, 1360). Alongside the former players of the Autonomous Republic were many left-wing activists. Some were too young, some had postponed their entry into the middle classes because of their activism, yet they were the driving force behind left-wing circles that developed in the 1970s. They were particularly active in the city of Tabriz, where commitment to the left was not inconsistent with support for the Azerbaijani cause. These men joined in the great revolutionary days that set Iranian cities ablaze and participated in the many organizations that gradually molded Iranian revolutionary society. Out of this uncoordinated effervescence, there emerged an atypical personality, Hosseyn Sadeq, recognized as such in the small circle of politicized intellectuals in Tabriz.[12] Hosseyn Sadeq played a pivotal role in the development of Azerbaijani nationalism by encouraging people from various backgrounds to get involved.

Hosseyn Sadeq was born in 1945 in Tabriz, then under Soviet occupation. After he studied in Turkey, which played a decisive role in his commitment, he returned to Iran. He was arrested by the Secret Police for secessionist activities in the 1960s and 1970s. His imprisonment brought prestige to his commitment but it prevented him from benefiting from the transfer of his cultural capital into the economic sphere. He was forced to remain a mere translator. Unlike Mohammad 'Ali Farzane, at the time of the Revolution, Hosseyn Sadeq was not sponsored by Javad Heyat to be reinstated in the modern middle classes. In 1979, he founded in Tabriz *Azerbayjan Yazijilar va Shairler Jamiyati* (Association of Writers and Poets of Azerbaijan), which brought together intellectuals close to left-wing circles. He launched three successive publications that experienced chronic problems and only lasted a short time: *Yoldash* (Comrade), *Enqelab yolunda* (The Road to Revolution) and *Yeni Yol* (The New Road). These publications shared a common pro-Soviet editorial policy and condemned vehemently the oppression allegedly suffered by the Turks under the monarchy. At the same time, he published several books steeped in the idea of a national revival to come (1356, 1357, 1360) as well as books of poetry under the name Duzgun (1358, 1359, 1360). In 1982, Hosseyn Sadeq was invited to Azerbaijan SSR for a conference organized to mark the 60th anniversary of the USSR by the Azerbaijani Society for Friendship and Cultural Relations with Foreign Countries (Nissman, 1987, 73).

The activist paths of identity entrepreneurs with little economic or social capital deeply affected their commitment to the cause of Azerbaijan. Limited resources led them to seek resources abroad. Such resources were readily available because many activists had lived or maintained contacts abroad and the USSR was eager to offer services through the Azerbaijan SSR, to extend their influence over a new regime whose future was still uncertain. The Azerbaijani Society for Friendship and Cultural Relations with Foreign Countries set up deliveries of books and newspaper subscription systems between Iran and the

IDENTITY, CONFLICT & POLITICS IN TURKEY, IRAN AND PAKISTAN

Azerbaijan SSR. The Soviet publication *Odlar Yurdu* (Country of Fires) was circulated in Tabriz. Many books published in the Azerbaijan SSR were transcribed or translated for publication in Iran. The low social and economic capital of these entrepreneurs, coupled with Soviet resources, implied a relationship of dependence with the Azerbaijan SSR. For several decades, the Soviet concept of nationality was imposed and a political syntax for the cause of Iranian Azerbaijan, now called Southern Azerbaijan (*Janub Azerbayjan*) was created. The Soviet concept of nation led to an autonomous approach to Azerbaijani identity defined by linguistic rather than territorial criteria. The political syntax for the cause of Iranian Azerbaijan was a proposed pseudo-Marxist reading of interethnic relations at the national level, in which Persians were assimilated to the ruling class while the dominated ethnic groups were called on to overthrow the government and make room for a new system. Such a reading gave a revolutionary role to Iranian ethnic groups and particularly to their forerunners (Nasseri, 1981).

The autonomous and revolutionary concept of Azerbaijani identity emerged clearly through the objectives given by Hosseyn Sadeq to Azerbayjan Yazicilar va Shairler Jamiyati. The objectives of a movement that defined identity in terms of linguistic coherence were to "defend the honor of [a] literary heritage nearly destroyed by the predations of the Pahlavi regime" and to prepare native language texts for the schools. These criteria were so clear that it would be necessary to "communicate the activities of our association to Persian-language newspapers in Tehran". It was also necessary "that the provincial and regional associations of the constitutional period be reactivated in a modern and progressive manner and have the state recognize Azerbaijani autonomy." The requirement of autonomy was similar to the territorial criterion of the Soviet concept of nationality. The administrative unit must allow establishment of institutions, including cultural, which distribute resources to entrepreneurs for the cause of Azerbaijan. Subsequently, it is necessary to "connect with other writers and progressive organizations in the world," placing the associations immediately within the Soviet fold. Finally, the idea of autonomy should "extend the concept of class among the people," thus giving the entrepreneurs of ethnic identity a revolutionary function dear to Leninism and to ethnic groups, that of a proletariat (Nissman, 1987, 50–51). The autonomous and revolutionary idea of "Azerbaijan-eity" is symptomatic of the strategy that would subvert the hierarchical system developed by under-capitalized identity entrepreneurs. Such a system would challenge the ethnic classifications of the existing order by imposing a new standard, one that links "non-Persian-ness"

126

with the revolutionary class. Such a strategy could not be deployed against the Islamic order imposed by Islamist militants or vigilante committees active on the streets of Iranian cities. This is particularly true in Tabriz, which experienced violent clashes between supporters of Ayatollah Shari'atmadari and Islamists between December 1979 and January 1980. As newspapers and various cultural events were gradually eliminated (Tagyeva, 1991), the identity entrepreneurs eventually disappeared from the public arena.

Even if the two strategies seem opposed, the Azerbaijani cause survived because of the cultivated relations of committed individuals and groups, but also because of republican institutional interest in the ethnic question. Against the backdrop of the war with Iraq and the repression of various forces which took part in the Revolution, Azerbaijani identity entrepreneurs confined themselves to the rather discreet business of cataloguing Turkish culture and heritage, an activity better suited to the individuals gathered around the *Varliq* review.

Conclusion

The strategies deployed by identity entrepreneurs of the Azerbaijani cause during the revolutionary period envisaged a challenge to the hierarchical system of ethnic identities prevalent at the time. If the perceived and real social status of such entrepreneurs explains the differentiated forms of action, their commitment to a particularist cause distinguishes them from their alter egos. The choice of an assertive identity strategy requires evaluation both of the resources necessary to pursue a cause as well as the process of engagement. This choice in favor of ethnic distinctiveness first appears as a result of the interaction of a prospective identity entrepreneur with his or her environment. In the case of the Azerbaijani cause, interaction with the environment should be considered as variable, and dependent upon identity values, especially ethnic, produced by multiple cognitive processes. By studying the relative value of Turkishness over time, it is possible to comprehend the roots of the Azerbaijani cause in a way that would not be possible if one were to consider solely the objective conditions of Turkishness within Iranian society. The question of relative social status is raised by the Islamic Revolution and transformed as a source of conflict and social mobilization. Finally, ethnicity, while referring to accessible resources and rules of compliance, is also part of the tangle of social stratifications proper to the state. It is when these relations undergo radical transformation that ethnic conflicts may appear in Iran.

7

VIOLENCE AND WAR IN THE MIDDLE EAST IN THE 1980s

Hamit Bozarslan
Translated by John Angell

During his lectures at the Institut d'Etudes Politiques in Paris, Professor Rémy Leveau enjoyed citing the fact that, like the years 1916–1917, 1919–1920, and 1948, 1979 represented a break in Middle Eastern history and signaled the beginning of a new ten-year historical cycle.[1] The seminal events of that year are worth recalling: the Camp David Accords, the occupation of Afghanistan (perceived as a "betrayal" by both the nationalist Arab left and the internationalist left), the Iranian revolution, and the occupation of the Ka'aba by militant Islamists, which signaled a shift from the "revolutionary idea" of the left towards an Islamism hitherto considered a "valet of imperial-ism". The result of this series of events was greater internal integration in the Middle East, and they gave birth to the idea of a "Muslim Asia."

Although each of these four events occurred within a specific historical context and they shared no causal relationships among them, they were read through the subjectivities of contemporary commentators as necessarily related, which assigned them new meanings and transformed them into the

129

signs of new "political realities" (Edelman, 1991, 196). The interpretations that resulted are so varied that researchers are faced with a gap between the specific contexts of the events and the grammar of alterities and enmities, the political convictions, and the militancy that underlies them. The increasing power of the Islamist movement is the most tangible result of this gap. As Sadat's assassination in 1981 and the Syrian Muslim Brotherhood uprising in Hama in 1982 showed, Islamism in effect became the dominant political syntax of protest in the Middle East throughout the entire decade. Only two zones—Kurdish and Palestinian, both characterized by a trans-border and supra-territorial dynamic—remained linked in any way "to the left".

Even more importantly, the historical cycle that began in 1979 was marked by three long wars that shook the region well beyond the confines of the conflicts themselves. The first of these conflicts, between Iran and Iraq, radically transformed both societies and, through a ricochet effect or amplification via proxies, played an important role in the political and military reconfiguration of the Kurdish and Lebanese situations. The second war took place on Afghan soil against the Soviet occupier and weakened the "Evil Empire", even contributing to the collapse of the Soviet Union. It also initiated a veritable military transfer from the Maghreb or the Machrek to Pakistan and Afghanistan. Third, the Lebanese civil war, which in reality began in 1975, worsened throughout the decade, leading to shifting allegiances among the different communities, but also to internal divisions within them. This allowed Lebanon to become the forward base for numerous military and paramilitary organizations. Compared to past events like the Kurdish and Israeli-Palestinian conflicts, these wars, which were responsible for more than a million casualties and made millions more homeless, were far more deadly, and they contributed to the spread of brutalization among Middle Eastern societies.

Each of these three conflicts drew to a close sometime between 1988 and 1989, but in each case, the end of the war occurred in its own specific context. The Gulf war reached its end because military victory in a classical war between two governments proved impossible. Afghan resistance ended with the Soviet withdrawal in 1989, leading to continued internal struggles between a number of factions. Finally, the Lebanese civil war was formally ended by the Taef Agreements, which were negotiated in Saudi Arabia and signaled the ascendancy of Syria, the Leviathan that had entered the conflict from outside as a "policeman" and arbiter in the Lebanese theater. The "Kurdish conflict" was exacerbated by the Iran-Iraq conflict and survived the end of this historical cycle, although it was profoundly altered by the massive use of chemical weapons in Iraqi Kurdistan, the exhaustion of Iranian Kurdish guerilla forces, and the intensification of the PKK's efforts in Turkey.

This period, although so decisive in shaping the Middle East and the current Muslim world, has not been adequately researched for at least two reasons. First, the widespread sense of relief that accompanied the end of this brutal cycle in the region appears to have prevented either public opinion or scholarly research from adopting a critical retrospective view of the immediate past. There is every indication that the collective unconscious preferred to leave to fiction and literature the task of recounting the vast individual, familial, and generational suffering experienced during this long decade. Second, the "acceleration of history" during the 1990s that was exemplified by the fall of the Eastern European regimes, the second Gulf War, the collapse of the Soviet Empire, and the Balkan Wars caused observers to turn their attention elsewhere.

At the risk of straying from the topic of this article, it is important to remind readers that this transfer of interest dashed hopes in the Middle East as well as in Afghanistan. In the mid-1990s, the region's increasingly interconnected conflicts were stalling, and the need for outside arbiters became increasingly urgent. As Ghassan Salamé pointed out at the time, "never has the theory according to which empires are as often born from an appeal from the periphery as through the expansion of the center been so amply illustrated..." (Salamé, 1994, 19). It must be acknowledged, however, that the United states, the only power able at the time to respond to this "call to empire," missed the opportunity to construct "an empire" in response to the demands emanating from these "peripheries". The choice of freezing the conflicts as they ended and postponing their meaningful resolution and the political "double walling" of Iran and Iraq by the Clinton administration ensured that the future "revenge of the world's complexity" (Hassner, 2002) would catch the world unawares.

This article deliberately seeks to avoid engaging in military history or the vast domain of international relations, choosing instead, twenty years after the facts, to understand the impact of the sequence of events and wars of the 1980s on the evolution of the phenomenon of violence in the Middle East. My objective is not to provide an overview of Muslim societies during this period. And, although I formulate a number of research hypotheses, numerous highly important questions will remain unanswered for the simple reason that their analysis will entail significant interdisciplinary and comparative research. Finally, references made in this article to groups of combatants with sociological profiles, ideological aspirations, and very different patterns of socialization (Islamist opposition, Kurdish militants, Lebanese militias...) are not intended to suggest that I reify them as interchangeable "agents of violence". My purpose is rather to examine to what extent, during a period of radical deregulation observed in more than one area, non-governmental actors were able to broaden their field of action, often at the cost of their autonomy and their capacity in controlling the process in which they were engaged.

The Weakening of the Status Quo

One characteristic of this historical cycle is located in a new kind of articulation that it allows between different types of conflict such as the Cold War (which configured the Middle Eastern landscape although it did not originate in the region), the impressively long Iran-Iraq conflict, the Afghanistan War that unleashed unprecedented activity in Pakistan and throughout the Middle East, the Lebanese civil war, which drew external agents into its highly local vortex, and finally, the "peripheral" Palestinian and Kurdish conflicts. Each of these conflicts was endowed with its own historicity, and each was also redefined by the conflictual landscape of all of the others and contributed in its own way to the weakening of the logic of the global and inter-governmental status quo that, for better or worse, had prevailed in the region since the Suez War.

The occupation of Afghanistan unquestionably represented the greatest challenge ever to be offered to the tacit Americano-Soviet agreement that immunized the lines separating the two blocs by forbidding direct military intervention. Well into the 1970s, the global Cold War system constituted the regulatory framework for different conflicts in the Middle East and elsewhere in the Muslim world and over-ruled each conflict's particular historicity. But Moscow's flagrant violation of this rule at the end of December 1979 showed that the Cold War could no longer supply a reliable protective framework for the region's governments, which contributed considerably to their anxieties. Even as the articulation among local conflicts and the Cold War was more pronounced than ever, the cleavage lines were no longer drawn according to the logic of strict global bipolarity, including the evolution of the Afghan conflict. There were additional reasons for the weakening of the grip of the Cold War, however. Beginning with the revolution, Iran had eluded America's influence and provided a model of universal emancipation and of a Shiite communitarian *da'wa*, ultimately emerging as a regional actor in its own right. For its part, Iraq, Iran's adversary, and Syria, its ally, maintained ties of military dependence with the USSR, albeit without becoming vassal-states. Their bilateral ties with different European governments and even, in the case of Iraq, with the United states, allowed them important room to maneuver.[2]

The status quo between governments was similarly weakened. In fact, the Iran-Iraq war temporarily ended the sacredness of borders that had ensured governments' "collective security" for several decades. Without taking on the attributes of a direct confrontation, the tensions between Baghdad, Damascus, and Ankara underscored a decline in the Westphalian logic that had configured the region following World War I. Finally, the Lebanese civil war, in which Israel, Syria, and to a lesser extent Iran and Iraq were militarily involved, shattered the tacit accord between regional and international powers that had allowed Lebanon to function as a buffer zone and a reservoir of resources that was available to all parties.

The conflict-creating order that arose as a result probably did not threaten the existence of the region's governments, with the singular exception of Lebanon, but it made them more "precarious". The region's governments were obliged, completely against their will, to relinquish their monopoly on the instruments of violence in order to survive, thanks to the enforcement of their place as *primus inter pares* of violence, and as a consequence, they ceased to operate as the lone actors on the regional stage. One can thus raise, *a posteriori*, the question of "who profits and who suffers from the state's monopoly on violence," (Bourdieu, 1992, 92–93) and of who benefits when the state is no longer able to reproduce this monopoly.

It is during this decade, in fact, that non-state actors, among them Iraqi and Lebanese Shiites (along with additional denominations of the latter), Iranian, Iraqi, and Turkish Kurds, a variety of political organizations such as the Mujahids of the People in Iran, the *commandants* in Afghanistan, and groups that could even then be described as Arab jihadists, acquired access to the instruments of violence. These groups managed to participate in in-progress wars without completely giving up their own objectives, whether political, national, or communitarian. In the follow-up to the three wars, a true military transfer among non-state-sponsored groups was organized, enlarging their field of activity, even when it meant that they became mercenaries for one government or another. Reports during the heat of events in the 1990s and 2000s often referred to "Afghan Arabs", whose ranks actually included Bosnians, Kurds, Turks, and others and undoubtedly numbered several tens of thousands.

But equally important to an analysis of the entirety of this historical cycle is an assessment of the region's overall military mobilities, without excluding the Syrian Army, which maintained a significant presence on Lebanese soil throughout the decade, Kurdish military camps in Iraq, Iran, and Lebanon, or Iraqi and Iranian groups in third countries that included, sometimes with rapid turnover, tens of thousands of fighters. As Bertrand Badie and Marie-Claude Smouts have asserted, the logic of dissemination of the 1980s conferred "international importance to civil violence {...} that was fed by the weakening of governments, transfers of allegiance, and the rise of particularisms, but also by the growing international capabilities of infra-state groups" (Badie and Smouts, 1992, 105).

The decade was marked by a steady transfer of the domain of violence and coercion from the state to non-state entities. Every group that was formed slowly slid from being composed of enlisted members of regular state military towards being manned by irregular troops, an evolution that was inevitably accompanied by increasing articulation between the two. The regular military seemed unable to conduct a war without resorting to irregular, non-state groups for several reasons. As part of this bargain, a given state's military is forced to relinquish control of a particular territory or population to non-state bodies, allowing these groups to themselves monopolize the instruments of violence and its accompanying police functions within their fiefdoms, and hence to control forced recruitment and armed mobilization. In this way, on an infinitely larger scale than in earlier times, a juridical nightmare seems to have come to pass that is directly contrary to the notion that the activity of war is a legitimate armed conflict between states. Much to the epistemological irritation of Carl Schmitt (Monod, 2006), the "violence of war" obliges the state that initiates it to increasingly include the "partisan", and even the "motorized partisan", in its war-like undertakings, blurring its own participation in the game of international legitimacy. Making use of these irregular groups becomes an undeniable asset for states, which as a consequence possess highly effective additional instruments for pressuring their adversaries. The drawback, of course, is that these same instruments prove that the state—previously defined as a "bordered power container" (Giddens, 1987, 120)—is no longer in full control, thus unmasking the enormous but empty contradiction between the principle and praxis of the state. The state continues to "fear *founding* violence, in other words, violence that is capable of justifying, legitimizing, or transforming legal relationships, and thus of presenting itself as having the right to make laws" (Derrida, 1994, 86). In the singular context of the 1980s, however, the ability of the state to ensure its perpetuation via its praxis depends paradoxically on the very actors who threaten the state's own claims to exclusive sovereignty.

VIOLENCE AND WAR IN THE MIDDLE EAST IN THE 1980s

Articulation of States of War and States of Violence

Whether it occurs in the border zones between Iran and Iraq, on Afghan territory, or in Beirut, whether it is inter-governmental, anti-colonial, or civil, war
is, above all, precisely what it refuses to be in juridical terms: an institutionalized, organized act of violence. For this reason, it always exerts a considerable
impact well beyond military history. Even if the state of scholarly research does
not currently allow more than the formulation of a handful of hypotheses, one
can nevertheless observe that under the impact of war, the state is transformed
into a field of multiple actors of coercion—including death squads, militias,
individual interest groups, and fragmented intelligence services—who share,
sometimes at the cost of bloody internal conflicts, the benefits of conflict. The
brutalization of the 1980s, however, transcended state power, and by transforming itself into a massive theater for the enlistment of "irregulars," these
wars and conflicts allowed the emergence of what Frédéric Gros calls states of
violence, in other words, of a social order in which the boundaries between
state and non-state, interior and exterior, and public and private are no longer
distinct.[3] The "discontinuity" that governs the passage from a state of war to a
state of peace gives way to an axiological continuity also marked by violence
(Gros, 2005). Under the generic name of "war", coercion and violence are
sometimes placed at the service of a power that is weakened by the very revolution out of which it was born (Iran), and sometimes at the service of the conflictual constitution of a field of ethnic or denominational protest (the Kurdish
and Shiite zones); at other times, coercion and violence are at the service of a
militia that necessitates the control of a community or a locality (Afghanistan,
Lebanon), and ultimately, in every one of these conflicts, of privatized businesses. Whatever the setting, and whatever ultimate references are cited to
legitimate it—whether political, religious, national, or communitarian—coercion and violence by state, anti-state, para-state, or forces at the margins of the
state also reproduce themselves on the "internal front", in the core of every
group involved. Omar Carlier's remarks concerning the "party" in Algeria seem
highly relevant to any protagonist who bears arms: "to be conqueror" one has
to "win twice: within ones party and for one's party" (Carlier, 1995, 71), and,
similarly, in one's "camp" and for one's "camp".

The Regime of Subjectivity and the Ethos of the 1980s

New forms of violence, from rural guerilla action to militias, and from political assassination to urban insurrection, belong to a regime of subjectivity that

is overwhelmingly melancholic, even tragic. The contrast between the (quasi-) joyous subjectivity of the Palestinian militancy of the 1960s and 1970s, even if it was not victorious, and the successful war of Islamism during the 1980s on the Afghan front, is particularly striking. Is it because of the disappearance of a universal frame of projection like the "left" of the 1970s, which ascribed the militancy of Muslim societies to something besides this "particular thing" that is Islam? Or is it because of the Iraqi-Iranian conflagration that consigned Islamic societies to lethal conflicts against themselves and not against some "Zionist" or "imperialist" enemy? What can be said about the enormous cost of the Afghan jihad's victory in terms of human lives? These questions merit scholarly attention based on the memoirs that militants and combatants have begun to publish.

One thing is certain: there is a link between the regime of subjectivity of the 1980s and the militant ethos that developed in the aftermath of these wars. The mourning ceremonies, the cult and albums of martyrs, and the echoes of distant combat that galvanize the Zarqaoui generation are all elements of a subjectivity that "radicalizes the world through sacrifice" (Baudrillard, 2002, 16). As for the ethos itself, it transforms a committed individual into someone who bears of guilt for this world and into the hope for deliverance through suffering to which he submits himself.

As illustrated by the examples of Abdullah Azzam, Ossama al-Maqdisi, Ayman al-Zawahiri and Osama bin Laden, as well as Abou Moussab al-Zarqaoui, the notion of *hijra* has played a central role in the definition of sacrifice among the Afghan Arabs, constituting a moment of distance through the pain that is the prelude to the return to earth that will provide deliverance from the ultimate battle of purification. But the exile of Abdullah Öcalan and thousands of his fighters from Turkey, and of Messoud Rajavi and his followers, can also be interpreted as a form of *hijra* that inescapably leads to an armed return to the "land of infinity" (i.e. Kurdistan). The final, quasi-Biblical battle that would then take place is supposed to allow both the reconquering of a colonized nation or of a confiscated revolution, and the construction of a new man who no longer bears the guilt of the world on his shoulders. These expatriate militant tendencies gave birth to new figures, respectively the *mujahid* and the *gerilla*, who are simultaneously remote because they act from a distant land and omnipresent because they are immortalized through narrative. They are distinguishable from the Palestinian *fidai*s and the Kurdish *pechmargas* of Iraq and Iran because they are modeled on the image of the perfect leader and as a result constitute prototypes of the society to come.

The notion of martyrdom is likewise redefined by the moment of re-foundation in the *hijra* or by the armed struggle conducted on the ground. This is how the PKK martyrs engaged in the fight against the Israeli army between 1982 and 1983, or how the Afghan Arabs, beginning with the legendary Azzam the Palestinian, fuel resistance through self-sacrifice in a distant land. Through their deaths, they complete the eschatological fusion of a cause, a time-witness of combat (years of foundation and re-foundation in exile), of a place in which the cosmic drama is staged (Afghanistan-Pakistan, Lebanon), of a leader, of an inner circle of founding fighters and martyrs, and finally, of a narrative. Or perhaps, through consensual sacrifice on the ground, like in Iran or Lebanon, they fulfill the meaning of revolution by conjuring the failure of the *mujahideen*,[4] elevating a community, in this case of Shiites, to the rank of inheritors worthy of the first martyr, Hussein, who bears the suffering in a nation and, though his martyrdom, of its re-founding. One can see how, whether religious or not, the construct of martyrdom that has been so polysemic throughout the twentieth century gains new meanings through axiology and thus achieves true semantic and symbolic simplification. As Georges Simmel predicted, "the conflict of a war or group {...} often carries a degree of clarity and resolve inside the group that they did not ordinarily possess" (Simmel, 1990, 210).

The new sacrednesses engender new symbols of heroism that take the place of the models of the *fedai* and the militant that had dominated the imaginaries of protestors in the Middle East during the 1960s and 1970s. If the guerilla method (*gerilla* in its local adaptation) became the trademark of the PKK, the last and certainly most radical avatar of the rising left of the previous decades, in Afghanistan, it is the figure of the *mujahid* who became the standard-bearer. This figure describes two categories of combatants—Afghans fighting under the orders of their *commandants* (Massoud Ahmad Chah (1953–2001), Ismail Khan, Zabiollah as well as Haqqani) and the young "Arabs" who came from far away, sometimes abandoning wives and young children. Many of them left behind the wealth and comfort of their social positions or placed their fortunes at the service of the *jihad*, which they further contributed to through their ascetic lives, like Bin Laden, or by their deaths, like Azzam. In Lebanon, finally, it is the militia member who became the most visible figure in the conflict, a figure who dominated the urban space through taxation, protection, and war, using force to claim his territory and imposing himself as much as a philosopher as he does as a romantic warrior figure, or else as an entrepreneur of privatized violence.

Ideology and Axiology

The analysis of the role of ideology in the wars and violence of the 1980s yields an image of singular complexity. Clearly, the exercise of violence as a long-term commitment requires a system of representation and a belief that makes it sacred and establishes a horizon that defines victory, or at least an eschatological vision. The "ideologies of the 80s" had a powerful ability to attract recruits and provided a totalizing framework that gave meaning to obligatory consensual sacrifice. These ideologies were able to explain the world by referring to a long history, to the "corruption" of the present, and to the projection of a purified future cleansed of the system of *taghuti* or injustice and oppression. If revolutionary Iranian (and to some extent Lebanese) Islamism, the Jihadist ideology that defined the Afghan resistance, and Kurdish nationalism remain extremely effective in mobilizing people to this day, it is because they are able, each in their own way, to articulate an eschatological reading of history, a requirement of commitment defined as the construction of an identity as a new man, and the demand for self-sacrifice. In a sense, their success depends on their ability to persuade individuals to voluntarily accept the obligation whose achievement is necessary for collective emancipation. Beginning in Lebanon, where the first suicide attacks occurred in 1983 (one of them by a Christian communist), and later in Kurdistan of Turkey, where the first self-immolation took place in the Diyarbakır prison in 1982, the cause inhabits the individual to the point of driving him to self-sacrificial violence.

It would be impossible to minimize this ideological "density". However, when we attend to the axiological level in the concrete field of the praxis of violence, we observe that the adhesion to a *da'wa* does not differentiate contesting movements from each other. Articulated in wars and viewed through the reality principle, violence becomes a means of sustaining a vast logistical system that involves daily management of rearward bases that sometimes contain thousands of people, the protection of the leader, and the safety of fighters in transit. Violence can only reproduce itself over the long term if it can transform itself into a system. Regardless of the predisposition of the militants to self-sacrificial acts as a sign of their fidelity to a cause, no individual actor can elude the imperative of the movement's durability, all the more confining because everyone takes part in a process that no single one controls. They are obliged to accept unpredictability as a shared horizon, and the existence of the system requires them to model themselves on the same matrix and according to the same axiological codes, to banalize and legitimize, sometimes against their own inclinations, identical behavior, even when they contradict the premises of their founding ideology. This requirement means that every member must position himself in a vertiginous chain of configurations from which the possibility of decisive victory is lacking, to change allies according to the emergency of the moment or to tactical opportunity, and to respond to situations as they arise while anticipating situations that could potentially arise in the immediate future. Worse still, this trial by fire unfolds over a long period during which no single fixed organizational framework constitutes a stable element, when internal fragmentation is an inevitable side-effect of conflict, and where the possibility of access via violence to the legal or illegal resources of war serves as a way for new groups to attract recruits that arise from their own socializations and are ready in turn to join the action and further perturb the entire conflictual landscape. The multiplication of state actors on the stage of violence also creates the terrain for the proliferation of non-state actors, expanding the possibilities for new alliances and allegiances. All of this means that the rules of the game sometimes become irrelevant at the very moment they are taken for granted.

Conclusion: The Leviathan and the "Partisan"

The articulation between war and violence inevitably poses the problem of the state's authority. The more the Weberian state, defined as an "organ", enters into a symbiotic relationship with external forces and experiences internal fragmentation, the more it becomes militarized and hence transformed, despite the coercive resources at its disposal, into a "weak state {incapable} of creating legitimacy by guaranteeing safety and other services" (Holsti, 1996, 117). Not only do resources other than those available through profit and coercion become rare and no longer adequate for the exercise of effective control over a given territory, but in certain cases, the reproduction of the Leviathan itself simply becomes impossible.

It goes without saying that situations are not analogous among different countries: after the long Iran-Iraq war, for example, both states were able to reproduce themselves, but with a loss of the legitimacy—nationalist in Iraq, revolutionary in Iran—that had provided meaning to the war. The question of the Leviathan was of a different character in Afghanistan, where, against all expectations, Najibullah's "communist" administration that succeeded Babrak Karmal's regime was able to hold Kabul for many years, although its survival was a default solution to the Afghan crisis established by the military protagonists. The impossible conquest of state power by victorious warlords engaged in a civil war prevented the investment of the capital by any particular one among them. The state took years to reconstruct itself, beginning in 1994 and working from the system's periphery. The Taliban, who were not veterans of the war and were even formed after the Soviet withdrawal, overwhelmed the Afghan government using Pakistan as their base. Their ability to control a large portion of the country confirmed, at least partially, the Gellnerian hypothesis that saw in religion the potential arbiter of certain conflictual systems (Gellner, 1981).

The singular historicity of Afghanistan, where even if they were victorious, the *mujahideen* failed to gain ascendancy, provided the religious authorities with an infinitely more important role that that of simple arbiter—they imposed themselves as order and authority at the cost of sacrificing all pretenses to politics and to the divisions that it implies. In Lebanon, the impossibility of producing an internal Leviathan became apparent as soon as Israeli forces departed in 1985. Syria, enthroned in 1989 as Lebanon's protector through very free interpretation of the Taef Accords, imposed itself as the new Leviathan who came from outside for the simple reason that no alternative system of conflict arbitration had been reached. While gaining acceptance of the non-disarmament of Hezbollah, its ally, Syria organized the disarmament of the militias, sometimes by force. It is, however, not at all evident that the militia members can be counted among the losers of the war. Most of them joined the army, thus demonstrating that violence can be profitable, and the supposed "neutralization" of Samir Geagaa and Michel Aoun led to a "freeze" of the grammar of enmity of the civil war that simply was reactivated again after 2005.

Finally, if non-state actors (the Kurdish parties in Iran and Iraq, the Iraqi Shiite organizations, the Mujahideen of the Iranian people) were the great "losers" of the end of this historical cycle, they nevertheless conserved the resources necessary for their conflicts, in terms of legitimacy and allegiances, which would enable them to exist over the long term. Even the most weakened among them have shown themselves very capable of capitalizing on their "historicity," in other words, of using "knowledge about the past as a means of breaking with it—or, at any rate, only sustaining what can be justified in a principled manner" (Giddens, 1991).

As we suggested elsewhere (Bozarslan, 2014, 2015), this knowledge will prove to be of undeniable use to them in understanding the 1990s, but also in the first decades of the new century.

8

SELF-RADICALISATION OF A YOUNG INDIAN JIHADIST IN GREAT BRITAIN

THE QUEST FOR ETHICS
AND LONG-DISTANCE SUFFERING

Aminah Mohammad-Arif
Translated by Adrian Morfee

There are countless ways of studying conflicts based on ethnic, linguistic, and religious differentiation, and their transformation over time (Brubaker and Laitin, 1998; Hobsbawm, 1993; Kalyvas, 2006; Poletta and Jasper, 2001). The entry point chosen here is the "suicide mission" of a young Indian jihadist, Kafeel Ahmad, who, together with an accomplice, planted bombs in London in 2007 and then tried to ram Glasgow airport with a car. The decision to study a single trajectory is not arbitrary; I had, as fate would have it, met and interviewed the (future) jihadist, this before his resort to violence.

Beyond the individual trajectory, the case of this jihadist is interesting for several reasons. First, it highlights the variability of scale at work here, which is symptomatic of a transformation in conflicts of differentiation. Contemporary jihadism primarily pits individual actors (the jihadists themselves) against collective actors (the state and, in some cases, society), and the action, which is pre-eminently individual (Bozarslan, 2004; Elster, 2005; Gambetta 2005), is carried out in the name of an entire community (even though the community in question does not necessarily identify with the action) and of a cause perceived as collective (washing away the humiliation of the Umma). This case also shows that the dynamics of a conflict may be apprehended from a micro-logical angle (the actions of one or two individuals), even though the action has potentially macro-logical repercussions: the feeling of terror—however diffuse it may be—as experienced by the population as a whole, whilst the community as a whole (Muslims) find themselves in the media spotlight, and fear a backlash from the host society (in a diasporic context).

Second, the fact that a young engineer with no known propensity for violence and acting independently of any external framework, which is to say without any exogenous indoctrination, actually carried out these acts is fairly intriguing and raises a certain number of questions. How does one go from a "banal" identity differentiation (an expatriate becoming aware of his or her Muslim-ness in a non-Muslim land) to the stage where the feeling of difference appears to be so insurmountable that it spills over into violence? And is it solely an "exacerbated" awareness of difference that triggers the self-radicalisation and the shift to violence?

Third, it raises methodological questions about the issue of jihadism using suicide missions as a modus operandi. Several authors have rightfully pinpointed the shortcomings of framing it in terms of motivations. For instance, Talal Asad notes that "Trying to pin down motives is difficult [...]: when and how did the intention of undertaking a suicide mission come to be formed? Which desire predominated—killing oneself or killing others? [...] How does one set about answering such questions if the perpetrator is no longer alive?" (Asad, 2007, 40). As a matter of fact, motivations "may not be clear even to the actor" (Asad, 2007, 64). Besides, hardly any of the typical motivations put forward provide satisfactory answers to the case studied here, whether they be economic deprivation (of the individual or of the surrounding) (Kalyvas and Sanchez-Cuenca, 2005),[1] revenge (Kalyvas and Sanchez-Cuenca, 2005) or resentment (Elster, 2005),[2] religious sacrifice and the quest for martyrdom (Strenski, 2003), resistance to political oppression (Kalyvas and Sanchez-Cuenca, 2005; Jayyusi, 2004), the lack of political imagination, as stemming from the belief that politics and religion are mutually exclusive (Etienne, 2005), suicide bombing as a war strategy (Pape, 2005), and so on.[3] But when exceptional primary sources are available (such as interviews uncovering the personal world of religious and political meaning of the future jihadist), can one then provide more convincing answers? This article will show that such sources do help to shed a light on the process, but only to some extent.

The sources I am using here include two long interviews that I conducted in July and August 2006, that is to say one year before the attacks, as part of a research project on born-again young Muslims in Bangalore.[4] Let me be precise here that although Kafeel was already religiously and politically radicalized when I met him, his trajectory nonetheless suggests that the idea of resorting to violent action had not yet taken hold in his mind at that time. The interviews present therefore the interest of not falling into the trap of (self-)justifying discourse. More important, despite certain grey areas, Kafeel's answers to my questions fit in sufficiently well with the elements from the other sources. These sources include several email messages we exchanged, an email message he sent his brother and which was available online, and an interview with his family in 2008. Of great use were also the articles in newspapers covering the affair and particularly Bilal's trial: as Talal Asad notes, "it is only at the trial of someone who has failed to complete the operation that the motive of the suicide bombers can be adduced" (Asad, 2007, 45). True enough, but Kafeel's trajectory was somewhat different from Bilal's and hence requires a distinctive analysis as the elements collected during Bilal's trial, and the sources concerning Kafeel's case, suggest that the motives of both perpetrators may not have been fully identical. In this article, I shall focus mainly on Kafeel's trajectory because of the original ethnographic material at hand.

By drawing extensively on this material, I will show the role of two driving forces, long-distance suffering and the quest for ethics, both taken to extremes on account of moral outrage (at the Iraqi war), behind Kafeel's decision to resort to violence.[5] But such factors cannot solely be held as premises for action, for whilst a significant number of Muslims throughout the world, and young Muslims in particular, experience strong political emotions (like indignation), it only results in a minute number of them resorting to violence. Other explanatory factors (wholly external to motivations *strictu sensu*) need to be taken into account, such as the role played by chance.

After a description of the attacks, I will first seek to map Kafeel's personal trajectory and then examine his religious and political trajectory. I will end with a section on chance as an ultimate explanation in the recourse to violence.

The Attacks

Let us now take a look at the facts themselves. On 29 June 2007, Kafeel Ahmed, a young Indian aeronautics engineer, and Bilal Abdullah, a young

Iraqi doctor, planted two booby-trapped Mercedes loaded with gas cylinders, petrol, and nails in the centre of London at around two o'clock in the morning. One of them was parked in front of the main entrance of Tiger Tiger, a busy nightclub, and the other in front of a bus stop in nearby Cockspur Street. But a faulty connection with the mobile phones that were to act as detonators meant that the homemade bombs assembled by Kafeel did not explode. They were subsequently safely disposed of. The next morning, Kafeel wrote an email message to his brother Sabeel Ahmed, seemingly a "will" left in the drafts of his Gmail account. A few hours later whilst on the way to Scotland with Bilal, where both of them were based, he sent an SMS to his brother telling him how to access this message on Gmail. A little later, with Bilal alongside him, he tried to ram the main entrance to Glasgow airport with a burning jeep. But the car crashed into one of the pillars, and despite several attempts Kafeel did not manage to enter the airport with the vehicle. Bilal then threw petrol bombs out of the Jeep at passers-by, whilst Kafeel opened the window and doused the outside of the vehicle with petrol, before throwing a petrol bomb too. He got out of the car and was immediately engulfed in flames. He tried to stop the airport security services from approaching him but was finally overpowered, the flames which had burned all his body were put out, and he was handcuffed whilst being filmed by an amateur video maker. Suffering from 90% burns he died one month later in hospital, apparently without it having been possible to question him. Bilal, for his part, jumped out of the vehicle and was immediately arrested. Other individuals in their entourage were also arrested shortly after, including Sabeel, who was accused of having attempted to cover the tracks leading to his brother, a cousin in Australia who had a SIM card in his possession given to him by the Ahmed brothers, as well as several friends of the two jihadists. Nearly all of them were doctors, and the media dubbed the affair the "doctors' plot". In reality, as well as the fact that Kafeel was not a doctor, only Bilal was sentenced, in December 2008, whilst Sabeel served a sentence of a few months before being deported to India.

There are several murky areas in Kafeel's trajectory, but investigations concluded that there was every reason to believe that the cell behind the attack was composed of only two people: Kafeel and Bilal.

The trial offered Bilal[6] the opportunity to explain the reasons behind his actions. In particular he said how angered he had been as a student at the degradation of Iraqi hospitals in the 1990s following on from economic sanctions, and then at the sufferings endured by the civilian population during the occupation of his country. Holding the Americans and the British responsible for the situation in Iraq, he said he wanted to give Britain a "taste of fear" and "a sense of what life was like in a war zone", but denied having wanted to kill, though he failed to convince the British courts of this.[7]

The Geographical Trajectory—Imposed and Chosen Moves

Kafeel's geographic trajectory is composed of both "imposed" or even "obligatory" moves, and others that were "chosen". These started very early on in his life, at the age of one when his parents, both doctors from Karnataka, emigrated to Iran, then came back briefly to India after three years before emigrating once again, this time to Saudi Arabia.[8] Like most Indian children of migrant parents in the Gulf countries, Kafeel attended local Indian schools. Contrary to initial suppositions put forward in the media who were quick to establish a correlation between time spent in the Middle East and his radicalisation, the few years he lived in Saudi Arabia and in Tehran would not seem to have had any impact whatsoever on Kafeel, who was still a child at the time. He did not refer to these years at any stage during the interviews, not even when asked if he had lived abroad.[9] Rather than seeing this as an attempt to dissimulate, which would not fit in with the rest of what he said, it would seem rather that this period played hardly any role in his religious and political trajectory.

It is hard to assess the years spent in India. Kafeel returned there aged thirteen to continue with his secondary schooling. He was followed by his brother, and then his parents who settled in Banashankari, an affluent district to the south of Bangalore where his family still lives. His parents opened a clinic which they ran until their retirement. They enjoyed a certain level of visibility and social capital within the "community". In 1997, Kafeel enrolled in an engineering school (UBDT Engineering College) in Davangere, a small town in Karnataka about 300km from Bangalore. On graduating, he left India to continue his studies in the United Kingdom. After having spent four years in Ireland and England, Kafeel, the oldest of three siblings (his brother was a doctor and his younger sister was a medical student), was obliged to go back in June 2005 to look after his father who was suffering from Alzheimer's. In December, he found a job with Infotech Enterprises, a company specialising in outsourcing for the aeronautic industry, and which counted Boeing and Airbus among its biggest clients. He earned about 50,000 rupees a month apparently, a tidy sum, but not a huge one in the urban context. He worked there until August 2006 before resigning for personal reasons for, according to his brother, he wanted to continue with his doctorate. Did his status as a member of a minority group in his country of origin have any impact on his radicalisation? It would appear highly doubtful, at least in the light of what he said during the interviews, when he stated he had never personally suffered any discrimination, either in India or elsewhere. His answer to the question was: "Personally, never, though I have heard other people who have been discriminated against. I believe I was lucky". Furthermore, India hardly figured on his map of injustice (cf. *infra*). Finally, whilst the known instances of his political mobilisation did take place in India, they related to transnational events (the Danish cartoons and Chechnya) and not local ones.

It is rather the diasporic experience as an adult that he mentioned at great length during the interviews,[10] combined with a very specific temporal context (the period after 9/11 and its repercussions on the identity construction of many Muslims around the world, together with the decline in organised forms of violence in favor of isolated acts) which would appear to have played an overwhelmingly determining effect. 2001 marked a new stage in the young man's life. A brilliant 22-year-old, he left India, this time on his own initiative, to read towards a Masters' degree in aeronautics at Queens University in Belfast. He stayed there until 2004, and then enrolled at Anglia Ruskin University in Cambridge where he started working on a doctorate in Computational Fluid Dynamics. This is when he met Bilal, with whom he developed a very close friendship. As will be seen further on, it was this diasporic experience, resulting from a move undertaken by choice, which led him to reconfigure the relationship he had towards religious issues, which in turn had repercussions on the way he perceived the world, and on his sense of ethics. It opened up new political horizons to him, on the basis of which he drew up his map of injustice, focusing extensively on international issues. It enabled him to interact with individuals, and that potentially nurtured a pre-existing propensity towards radicalisation (a personal idiosyncrasy) (Fillieule, 2001). His (chance) meeting with Bilal and their subsequent frequenting of the Hizb ut Tahrir are indicative of the singular nature of his socialization, arising from the fact that he was an expatriate, something which tends to exacerbate political and religious identities. Such an exacerbation can sow the seeds of conflict that, under the influence of (sometimes chance) trigger events, can ultimately lead to violence. But nevertheless, this is not a "classical" case of long-distance nationalism[11] (since India was not on Kafeel's map of injustice, nor was it targeted by the action), but is rather a strongly emotional form of identification with the "Umma" or "Qaum" (the "community" and by extension "nation") of Islam and their sufferings, with in this instance both the identification and the sufferings being experienced remotely.

THE QUEST FOR ETHICS AND LONG-DISTANCE SUFFERING

*The Political and Religious Trajectory—Individualism and the Search
for an Ethics*

An Individualised Relationship With Religious Issues

Kafeel's action explicitly referred to the concept of *jihad*, which is rooted in religion. This section will start by examining his eminently radical, intellectual, and especially individualistic relationship with Islam, specifying from the outset—though it hardly seems necessary—that religion alone does nothing to explain his radicalisation or recourse to violence. Kafeel's marked interest in religion is rooted in his family environment:

> Initially, it was my parents who would talk to me about Islam, teach me. It was more of obeying them, and you know listening to them, and then it came to a point when I started reading, and again that was probably because my Dad would say "Why don't you read this book?", I would go read it and he would ask me about it, that kind of reading. And then I developed a genuine interest. And that's why I started reading and still continuing. My Dad would say read about the Ja'fari fiqh, read about the Shaf'i fiqh. I read that, bits and pieces, I have my own interest.

> We have discussions now and again. We are very open at home. I would put forth an argument and we would have a discussion on it. Mom and Dad would have an opinion on it, we would sit around and discuss and reach a conclusion, that's the way it is.

> It is not necessary that I read the same books as my Mom and Dad. Their literature is in Urdu, my literature is in English, so it's a good way of interacting, the ideas that we have read.

For Kafeel, then, who was from a family of Hanafi Sunnis, it was not some simple form of "Islam by filiation" or passive obedience of his parents, but rather an intrinsic personal interest as suggested both by what he said ("genuine interest", "my own interest") and by what he read. His autonomous approach to religion may also be seen in the following: "I don't want to join the Jama'at-i Islami just because my Dad joined the Jama'at-Islami. I have got a certain number of differences with him over some issues [...]"

Kafeel, unlike his father, was not in fact an active member of the movement. Although on his father's advice he read the texts by the founder of the JI, Abdul Ala Maududi (and in particular his commentary on the Quran), he did not see himself as belonging to this movement, feeling closer ideologically to the Ahl-i Hadith, the Indian version of the Salafists.[12] He explained that what attracted him to the Ahl-i Hadith was that they did not discriminate between schools of law: "The A-i-H is the most accommodating because if someone prays according to the Hanafi opinion, I don't see them looking down at him."

Nevertheless, he rejected the idea of being affiliated to any movement, declaring at several stages during the interview: "I am a Muslim, full stop". But he was close ideologically to Salafism, something that dated back to his time in Great Britain: "I don't have much of an experience with the Ahl-i-Hadith, in fact, I came to know about them only after coming back to India. I had heard about them very vaguely before I went to the UK. In the UK, I heard of the Salafis."

In addition to his discovery of Salafism, his diasporic experience was a decisive moment in his religious and identity trajectory. It was while he was in Ireland that he left his beard to grow so as to assert his Muslim identity, he said, even though his interest in religion did not date from this period. Nevertheless, the "trigger" moment in his physically "marking" himself by his beard dated from his time in the diaspora (even though the way he described it was fairly surprising and almost trivial):

> In fact, the reason why I started sporting a beard was because I wanted to be recognized as a Muslim, when I was in Belfast. I wanted to be known as a Muslim, not because I did not want to blend into the society or any such things, they were not uncomfortable dealing with the Muslims because why should they be?

> *Was it like an awakening in Belfast?*

> Not really, I probably was doing what I always wanted to, have a beard. When I was in Belfast, I grew a bit lazy, shaving around. (Laughter). I started realizing that maybe it's about time. I always thought that it was something I have to do. But I was always putting it off.

Independently of its sources and areas of influence, his interest in Islam, expressed here with a powerful identity dimension and generated by the diasporic experience, was expressed primarily by his desire to be identified as Muslim by the Other. For Kafeel, this was accompanied by a ritualism which impregnated his daily life: canonical prayers, fasting, frequent pilgrimages to Mecca (both with his parents and then on his own), complying with the ban on interest and similar practices.[13] When asked about the importance prayer had for him, he answered:

> Salah is a relaxing factor. Takes me out of this daily run-around business, it gives me time to reflect on my life. Also, it is an obligation, so I would do it very, very strictly and I feel all the Muslims should do the same. It's an obligation towards

God. Obligated by the Prophet (s) and Allah (swt). It's a constant reminder of the hereafter and the truth that everybody is going to die. The aim is for the hereafter.[14]

Kafeel's ritualism was accompanied by a literalist interpretation of Islam, in accordance with Salafist ideology. His answers to several questions, such as polygamy for example, shows this: "Allowed. That's final". Equally, the question was put to him for example why it was important not to eat pork. Whereas other young people similarly committed to Islam draw on medical reasons to try to rationalise why it is forbidden by the Quran, Kafeel opted for a strictly literal interpretation: "Because it is forbidden, that's it". This almost amounts to a deliberate refusal to rationalise, a commitment to non-rationalisation arising from a deliberately literalist approach and not some passive imitation of inherited rituals (*taqlid*).

But independently of its literalism and ritualism, Kafeel's Islam partakes especially of a logic of subjectivising and individualising religious issues, as shows for example his response to the following question:

Which of the following statement comes closest to your view?

– Everything in life is determined by God
– God allows man to have some free choice in life?
– God gives man total free choice

(Reply) Could I place my own? Human being is given freedom of choice, freedom to follow religion or not to follow it. The choice I have taken up is to follow the commandments given by Allah (s.w.t) to Prophet (s.a.w). Although there is freedom choice (third), I will take the choice to go for the 1ˢᵗ option.

This individualisation includes and transpires in his resistance to any framework: it would seem that Kafeel never at any stage joined a collective body (except the Islamic Students Society of Northern Ireland, but this is a student association and not a tightly structured organisation). It is true that he frequented the Hizb-ut Tahrir but without becoming a full-fledged member. Even his religious practice could make room for a highly individualistic dimension, for instance on several occasions he went on the "little" pilgrimage (*umra*) on his own, going directly from Great Britain. Whilst in Bangalore, he attended various organisations without joining any of them. His religious trajectory gives the impression of a perpetual individual quest. At times, he attended the Sunday meetings[15] of the Ahl-i Hadith, and at others those of the JI-affiliated BIFT (Bangalore Islamic Foundation Trust), as well as frequenting a Quranic Study Circle. The only condition for him was to be able to interact, but he did not believe in passively received religion: "I attend lectures, seminars, programmes of every organization, if I know there is a lecture here. On one condition, that there is a Q and A session. As long as they have a Q and A session, I don't mind who is organising." In Great Britain, he also went to all Islamic events that seemed worthy of interest, such as Q&A sessions and talks (Tariq Ramadan, etc.).

Behind this apparent ideological dispersal (picking things from various *fiqh*, etc.) lies a vision of Islam which is deeply rooted in the Texts, the sole source of ultimate legitimacy and the incarnation of ultimate religious authority (as a typical "born-again Muslim" Kafeel accorded but little weight to the opinion of traditional authorities). According to his mother, when the family were discussing religion: "Kafeel would always ask, what do the Quran and the Hadith say? He would always check in the Quran and the Hadith."

It is worth adding that Kafeel's perception of Islam included an eminently totalising dimension: whilst remaining pragmatic, he said he was in favour of a sharia state: "We should have complete sharia law. [...] I would prefer to live in a place where there is the sharia, unfortunately there is not any place at the moment."

When asked if in his opinion there was an ideal country he answered: "An ideal place would have been where Sharia is in totality, which is kind of utopian idea at the moment, perhaps. When it becomes a reality, it would be my favourite place to live in. But as such, anything goes."

But this totalising vision did not lead to any social ghettoization, far from it in fact. Whilst religion shaped much of his daily life, he said that he still ate in fast food restaurants (provided it was halal), listened to music (except rock, Hindi film soundtracks, and *qawwali*, not because it is a form of Sufi music, but because it employs too sophisticated a form of Urdu), read short stories and novels (but not The Da Vinci Code because it's too long), watched films (but not Hindi films as they are too long and too boring), and enjoyed cricket and football (which he played with his friends). The fact that there was no schism is all the more interesting as many other young people interviewed who had "returned to Islam" had for their part abandoned these practices which they saw as contrary to Islam. Did Kafeel experience this situation as generating an unbearable tension between his religious ideals and his daily life made up of highly profane practices? This is not an easy question to answer especially as Kafeel seemed very "at ease with himself" during the interview, calm, self-confident, and often using the words "fun", "enjoy", and so on. Rather than this being a matter of compromise (something which he rejected, or at least said he did), it would appear that he did not see any incompatibility between certain mundane practices and his own "textualistic" interpretation of Islam. In a way it was his ultra-literalism that meant he was able to go on leading a material life, as there is nothing in the Quran forbidding these practices. But above and beyond the fact that this situation reveals the relative flexibility of interpretation afforded by Islam, what is especially interesting to note is that Kafeel's social and ethical radicalism remained largely theoretical, not transpiring in any lifestyle strictly modelled on his ideals. Furthermore, his self-radicalisation, which went far beyond family teaching and developed independently of any organisational framework, left him free of any form of constraint, and offered him considerable room for manoeuvre, meaning he was able to "negotiate" his own individual personal reform.

The Relation to the Other and to Politics

Kafeel's relation to the Other is also symptomatic of the fact that there was no relational ghettoization. When asked if he had non-Muslim friends, the answer was: "Yes, school friends, college friends, degree friends, work friends, UK friends" this was followed up by a question about Shias: "Yes, [I had a] Shia friend, he was not very religious, he did not like to discuss about religion. In fact, there was a Qadiani in Cambridge University as well. We would just keep out of that topic, you know what I mean. We would just talk about cricket or football."[16]

When I told him that in Pakistan Shias were not always considered to be Muslim, he appeared surprised: "Oh really, but they follow the Jafri fiqh, that's just a difference of opinion".

His vision of Great Britain is equally interesting, and he said that he appreciated its cosmopolitanism, to such an extent that he regretted having had to go back to India:

R: It was really good. I really enjoyed over there, I miss my time over there. I was probably more social over there than I am here, somehow I was able to fit into the society more than I am able in India for strange reasons. I used to get along very well with various nationalities, locals and somehow it's not very often that you see people going from the Subcontinent and feeling very comfortable. Maybe I had very good company. I hardly ever had the craving to come back. If it were not for a genuine reason, probably I would have stayed over there. If it was not for my parents, I would probably go back, but this is not going to happen.

Who were you interacting with?

(Reply) Nothing specific. I would go around with anyone. When I was in Belfast, most of my work colleagues and friends were Irish and not many Muslim friends as such, in fact there are only 2000 Muslims in Belfast. Among the Muslims, we knew practically everyone of us, because we all went to the same University and there was only one *masjid*. There was really a very wide scope of interaction. In Cambridge, it was a little more international, a very dynamic place. Because of such a wide range of nationalities, even my colleagues were from all over the world, from Australia, South England, Israel, Holland, a very dynamic, healthy, international environment.

At the individual and social level it would seem that belonging to different ethnic and religious groupings did not generate any marked feeling of conflict.

But despite the value he attached to cosmopolitanism and his interaction with people from different ethnic and religious origins, when it comes to the collective and especially the political level his propensity to interpret any situation, especially those perceived as a negative experience, via Islam took on another dimension, and sowed the seeds for potential conflict. And so independently of his ritualism, Kafeel harboured an eminently political vision of Islam. He no doubt inherited this from his father who was, as observed earlier, a very active member of the Jama'at-i Islami, an organisation that embodies an ideology conjoining religion and politics more than any other does. But once again, Kafeel did not follow his father's example "literally", and his relation to politics reveals how he linked family influence and the desire to distance himself, resulting in his acquiring a form of ideological autonomy:

> I have got a certain number of differences with him [father] over some issues, like voting for example. It's an opinion that the JI has included in their ideology. From what I read, it is a later add-on, it was not in the original ideology. They should not get involved in politics, they can have a political say, not necessarily get in, how can you support criminals and goons?

In fact "political vision" is understood here as referring not just to politics *per se* (elections, etc) but as a system of "ethics", as suggested by the following:

> In the UK, there are lots of debates about whether we should get involved in politics or not. Actually, some of the Salafi groups are in favour of voting. I took a decision after reading both sides. There is an article written by the Hizb-ut Tahrir on the fallacy of voting. It's a very logical argument. Some Muslim organizations (Muslim Association of Britain and Muslim Council of Britain) would promote voting. The Tablighi Jama'at said that they did not want to get involved; they did not even want to discuss. After reading all these opinions, the HuT had an opinion based on a very logical and intellectual frame of mind, with a bit of input of *halal* and *haram* in it. It was the most intellectually strong argument that I have read. After I read the *halal* and *haram* aspects of it, I came to the conclusion that voting was not the kind of thing to do. There are other ways, for instance lobbying, for instance parallel organizations, they can have your own shadow govern-

ment, just like in the UK, you don't necessarily get involved in the voting, you just keep tabs on it, you write, you promote in the media, you develop a public opinion, this is politics, this is permissible, whether the other is not really. I am not actually comfortable with either, like creating opinion, I am not a very vocal person as such. Try to have accountability. If the Minister for education wants to raise the fees for higher education, then you bring up arguments why it is feasible for the students, have a debate, have a political forum. This is politics but this is not getting involved in the dirt of politics, making false promises. If you want to be a good Muslim, you can't be a politician.

[...]

Once you involve yourself in politics, there is a lot of money involved, there is lot of honour involved, I have seen some of the guys who did get themselves involved, who started changing their opinion on the basis, to compromise. That's dangerous. Let's say we have a block of community and its votes, it's enough to get the person in power, and if the person does actually win, what guarantees do we have that the person is actually going to stick to his promises because he has never done it in the earlier occasions. Jack Straw said that he is going to this, to do that, he went to Blackburn (70% of the population is Muslim) and the Muslim population voted for him, but what happened in the end, he was in favour of the war in Iraq.

These comments (such as "I took a decision after reading both sides") are also symptomatic of his individual quest, and thus of an autonomous approach, which seemed to be virtually a constant concern of Kafeel. He did not merely "absorb" the teaching of a given organisation (the HuT for example), but was also interested in the doctrines of other movements (such as the JI or the TJ).

In any case, whilst political involvement *strictu sensu* (the electoral game) only inspired him with negative feelings, that does not mean to say that he was uninterested in eminently political issues, far from it in fact. He closely followed situations in various parts of the world where Muslims are subject to various forms of violence (physical, moral, or economic) and where present or past intervention by Western powers plays a role. When asked what *jihad* meant to him, he answered:

[It] means struggle, to keep up the daily prayers, to read the Quran on a daily basis, it could be a struggle to help your parents, to be kind to them, to help the needy. Life is a struggle.

Is fighting poverty a form of jihad for you?

(Reply) Depends on how you look at it, fighting against poverty just by giving money is probably *zakat*, fighting to change the reasons why the situation was created, is *jihad*. I know that there is a pathetic situation in Africa. If you go back and look at the reasons why the situation was created, it goes down to the capitalist system and the whole colonial system which went there, plundered, looted, and left the people and the state where they are now and military regimes, which have nothing to do with the people, were oppressive and were supported by the Western governments. So that's the reason why the situation is what it is in Ethiopia, Somalia, Sudan, a capitalist economy and the colonialist thinking within the Western powers. Fighting them is definitely *jihad*.

What about Iraq and Afghanistan?

(Reply) In Iraq, Afghanistan, it's an occupational force which is sitting in these two places and the people over there are freedom fighters, so I would categorize them as a *jihad*.

And in Kashmir?

(Reply) It's not clear what the people want there, the freedom from India, or they want to be independent or they want to join Pakistan because you always get conflicting ideas. Besides, there is no occupying forces as such over there, there is a government over there run by Kashmiris, so it's difficult to say whether it is a *jihad* or not. I am not sure about it, but I have no doubts about Iraq and Afghanistan but they are not the same, I would not classify both of them as same. In Kashmir, it is more a confused internal conflict, because Kashmiris are ruling Kashmiris, not like some Keralites or Tamilians going and ruling over there.

This answer about *jihad* is interesting on several different levels. First of all, it is symptomatic of the importance he attached to individual reform, at least in theory, and to ethical issues. Secondly, it shows that his reactions, and hence emotions, were focused on international issues, whereas he analysed "local" issues (South Asia) with greater critical distance and in a less emotional way. He thus seemed to view the destruction of the Ayodhya mosque in 1992 and the 2002 Gujarat pogroms, the two great "moral shocks" for Muslim Indians, in a fairly neutral and detached way (Cf. Jasper, 1997). Kafeel viewed them as political manoeuvring in one case, and a (highly risky) inter-linking of politics and religion in the other: "Ayodhya was a political game to come to power. Gujarat is something else, it's a mix of politics and religion. Post-Ayodhya, what happened, politics propelled religion."

Beyond the subjectivity of political "emotions" and perceptions of injustice, this difference in reaction according to the type of conflict (highly local versus global) is probably, at least in part, symptomatic of Kafeel's radicalisation in diaspora. But the way he interpreted the conflict in Kashmir, which is traditionally considered by global jihadists as one of the worst places of Muslim oppression, also suggests that for Kafeel injustice was defined first and foremost in terms of the sovereignty of a people or community. He interpreted the issue of Kashmir as a purely internal affair not involving any foreign occupation, and it did not therefore generate any emotional response from him. On the other hand, other conflicts where the sovereignty of people is (more clearly) brought into question, with the involvement moreover of powers "traditionally" known for and decried for their imperialism and not merely by jihadist circles—the United states, Russia, Great Britain—generated far more emotional responses. The fact that Kashmir did not appear on Kafeel's map of injustice, in addition to enabling him to transcend a vision of politics which could otherwise come across as parochial, also reveals the largely autonomous nature of his radicalisation in the way he could ignore the official "lists" of jihadist organisations.

This autonomy is largely rooted in the use of the internet, which has become one of the main routes for the self-radicalisation of would-be young jihadists. His extensive use of the internet is confirmed by the investigation of the Indian police, which concluded that he frequently consulted Internet sites detailing the suffering of Muslim populations in promoting jihad. It is worth noting that Kafeel, having been forced to return to India, had a more restricted social life than in Great Britain, with most of his time being spent in family and professional circles. It was therefore highly likely that he would devote part of his free time surfing jihadist forums, transformed into the platforms to compensate his feeling of loneliness and reinforcing his feeling of belonging to a wider community.

In any case, independently of the discourse and modes of his radicalisation, Kafeel's positions resulted in his (self)-mobilisation—far before he ultimately resorted to action—which would seem to have arisen from an autonomous decision on his part. One of the known instances of his mobilisation for example is his involvement in two demonstrations in Bangalore against the Danish cartoons, one that he attended "spontaneously" after receiving an SMS, and the other organised by local community leaders. Another sort of mobilisation is even more closely bound up with questions of autonomy and, if the information is correct, attests to a higher level of activist involvement, it being reputed that he organised on his own initiative a meeting denouncing the situation in Chechnya.[17]

Nevertheless, neither his universe of meaning nor the combination of endogenous factors (personal idiosyncrasy, his experience within the diaspora, his self-ideologization via the Internet, etc.) and of exogenous factors (local context, timeframes) fully explain why this ultra-idealist, without any apparent propensity to violence (even condemning the 11 September attacks during the interviews and at no stage putting forth an apology for violence) and from an apparently stable family,[18] tipped over into ultra-violence, nor why he felt he was fulfilling a religious duty (for a political cause)—why, in other terms, jihad ended up making such perfect sense to him that he decided to resort to action. To reuse the title of an article by Nicolas Mariot, "Does one have to be motivated to kill"? (Mariot, 2003). Kafeel was certainly motivated in absolute terms, but his motivations (those at least which are known) did not necessarily result in the obligation to kill or to be killed. Especially as many other young Muslims, just like Kafeel, and having lived abroad or not, harbor similar feelings of moral outrage at what they see as flagrant injustice against their community. Some of them sublimate the individual feeling of outrage in time-consuming and psychophagic ritualism, by "conventional" collective mobilisation (taking part in demonstrations), etc. But that does not mean to say that they resort to violence. His own brother, for instance, did not resort to violence despite having followed a very similar trajectory (the same family milieu, same strong paternal influence on his religious education, same expatriation, same return to Islam, same perception of injustice at the fate of Muslims, etc.).[19] Thus other dimensions need to be taken into account, such as the important role played by chance.

Chance—The Ultimate Key in the Recourse to Violence?

Whilst in no way clear-cut, the role played by chance in Kafeel's trajectory transpired in various ways. Firstly, it was chance that Kafeel met Bilal, whom he admired for his knowledge of Arabic and of the Quran.[20] Bilal was born in Aylesbury, England but returned to Iraq at the age of five. It appears that he spent the rest of his childhood and adolescence there. He came from a family that traditionally numbered many doctors, and started studying medicine at the University of Baghdad from which he graduated in 2004. He returned to England to complete his training, and it was during this period that he met Kafeel in Cambridge. In May 2006, he returned to Iraq where he spent three months, during which time he was in contact with insurgents according to the prosecutor. He then returned to Great Britain, highly radicalised apparently, and started working as a young doctor in a public hospital, the Paisley Royal Alexandra in Scotland. A second chance occurrence, it would seem, is the fact that Bilal's return coincided with that of Kafeel, who had just left his job in India so as to carry on with his doctorate, arriving in Great Britain in

September 2006 when the two met up again. The following month Kafeel went back to Bangalore but returned to Great Britain in May 2007. A few weeks later Kafeel, then aged twenty-seven, and Bilal, twenty-eight, carried out their failed attacks.

During the trial, Bilal asserted that it was Kafeel who was the instigator of the attacks. But according to the conclusions of the enquiry and witnesses from his entourage (such as Shiraz Maher, a former Hizb ut Tahrir sympathiser), it was in fact Bilal who was the principal instigator. It was not clearly established if the Emir referred to in the email message Kafeel sent his brother was Bilal himself, or if someone based in Iraq had inspired him.[21] In any case, and notwithstanding Kafeel's strong degree of self-radicalisation and self-mobilisation, his friendship with Bilal no doubt triggered a group dynamic. As Elster notes it, "peer pressure is an important factor in generating and especially in sustaining the motivation of suicide attackers" (Elster, 2005, 239).

The trial also sheds some light on the reasons behind the choice of the date and place of the attacks, once again showing the non-negligible part played by chance. Bilal first explained the choice of date:

> One of the plans was to choose a day when (Gordon) Brown was taking over from Tony Blair. That was postponed because I was working up to that time and we were not able to finish all the shopping. I was working so we cancelled that idea and left it to the next week until we had finished shopping, some minor stuff, some petrol and some walkie-talkies.

And then the choice of place:

> It was a day out to the city to find some suitable places to leave the devices, like 10 Downing Street, Parliament and Buckingham Palace, places we had in mind, places we had heard about. Mostly we were wandering around on tour buses. We were looking at how protected these places were and if it was possible to leave a car outside. In conclusion, we decided it was very difficult to leave a car outside prominent Government buildings. We decided to leave the car in central London.[22]

Apart from the fact that these observations are so trivial as to be almost laughable, they reveal how certain highly material constraints can significantly water down the original symbolic aims.

As for the choice of Glasgow airport, it would seem to have been largely due to its relative proximity to where Kafeel and Bilal lived, as well as its visibility. It is doubtless one of the most important infrastructures in the region, and the period coincided with the summer holidays, implying that there would be a strong concentration of people in the airports. But it has to be acknowledged that it was mainly a last-ditch choice made after the failure of the London attack.

Thus chance probably played a non-negligible part in Kafeel's ultimate act. The way the action was planned (and especially the way the vehicle was loaded) suggests the intention to resort to self-sacrificial violence, an intention which for Bilal gave way under emotional stress (fear). During the trial and thus the public declaration of his motives, Bilal neither assumed nor laid claim to any such intent, opting simply to deny it for his defence, and stating that he thought Kafeel wanted to drop him off at the airport. And so, though it is impossible to draw any hard and fast conclusions, the way events occurred would not appear to suggest Bilal Abdullah attempted to set fire to himself, and instead would tend to confirm what the judge said during the trial: "I am satisfied you both intended to die in the process and Kafeel duly did so. But I suspect your own courage deserted you at the last minute."[23] But if we are to trust the description of the facts given during the trial, even Kafeel's resorting to self-sacrificial violence would not appear to result from any long and "carefully thought through" intention to die, such as that of a suicide bomber pressing the button on a belt of explosives. While his action may be reminiscent of the Russian anarchists who "often chose to end their own lives with their last bullets rather than fall into the hands of the authorities" (Kalyvas, 2005, 227), it might also have been brought about by an ego that had been bruised by the failure of the attacks, especially as it was Kafeel who had made the bombs. So it is seemingly the case that self-sacrificial violence sought as much—if not more—to wash away the (personal) humiliation at the failure of the London attack than it did to wash away the (collective) humiliation undergone by Muslims around the world. It is also worth noting that the potential quest for glory by self-sacrifice, which is often described as an important factor in the literature on jihadism (Abou Zahab 2006), does not appear to have been a major consideration here. In any case, quite apart from the meaning of the act, the self-sacrificial violence was far from being inevitable, at least for the observer, even though it doubtless became such for Kafeel at a given moment, for reasons arising from a tight-knit combination of emotions, ideals and ultra-personal considerations.

Conclusion

It is true that Kafeel is a global jihadist belonging to his times, corresponding to the wave of violence fuelled by the Iraq war, with his repeated moves (engendering a fragmentation of cultural landmarks to the point where Indian-ness comes across as an accessory), his self-radicalisation (with a marked resistance to any formal framework in his case), the role played by the internet (both for self-radicalisation and learning how to make bombs), the choice of a Western country as a target, the way of operating, the amateurism of the act, the choice of infrastructure for the target (an airport) and the signature he used in his farewell email to his brother (Abu Abdulrahman, reminiscent of the "classic" testaments of jihadists operating within the framework of an organisation). He is also typical of his times in his choice to wage a deterritorialised war, and his abstract feeling of powerlessness in the face of an acute sense of injustice, engendering long-distance suffering, and leading to what ended up becoming an intolerable level of outrage.

So whilst the war in Iraq, which is morally unacceptable to a large majority of Muslims around the world, provoked virtual and symbolic anger, it would also seem to have had deeper repercussions on the psyche of a small minority, such as Kafeel, for whom their refusal to accept it reaches extreme heights. Like others before him, he sought to move from being an outraged yet passive observer to becoming an actor for whom denunciation was not an acceptable alternative for action, and who put an end to his own sufferings by violence, or at least believed that he could do so. It is also worth observing that it is paradoxically as if long-distance, and hence imagined, suffering had a stronger effect than suffering which, if not experienced, was at least closer to home. Kafeel, who in all probability never went to Iraq, went through with his action, whereas Bilal, who had directly witnessed the sufferings of Iraqis, and hence could have been motivated by revenge, held back at the last moment.

In any case, Kafeel's radicalisation also has certain specificities, and the world of meaning which emerges in the interviews shows that his radicalisation is rooted in a complex combination of religious and political issues, including their subjacent corollaries—ethics and identity. This might appear tautological given that this combination is theoretically at the very heart of jihadism. Nevertheless, and as certain studies have shown, not every individual involved in some form of jihadism, whether it includes self-sacrificial violence or not, necessarily places Islam at the heart of their identity (Devji, 2009). Some would appear to be virtually non-politicised, never having taken part in any form of mobilisation, and/or feeling largely unconcerned by collective utopias (be they theories of an Islamic state or otherwise), as was the case for example of those behind the 2006 attacks in London (Devji, 2009). But in Kafeel's case religion is not some simple instrument for justifying and legitimising his acts, and his ultra-ritualism shows that his religion shapes much of his daily life even though it does not result in any mental and/or social ghet-toization. For him, an Islamic state made sense (he read Maududi and Sayyid Qutb with interest), however abstractly, as shown by the interviews as well as by his frequenting the Hizb ut Tahrir, even though when he resorted to vio-lence it would appear that this utopia stopped making sense at a certain moment. This latent radicalisation, in combination with factors relating to gender and age (young men are more susceptible to use violence as a resource) and strong emotions (anger and indignation at the feeling that the sovereignty and thus dignity of the collective entity he identified most strongly and emo-tionally with, that of the Umma, had been trampled on), thus ended up cul-minating in jihadism. Even though the process of radicalisation itself extended over a relatively long period of time, the stage of resorting to violence would for its part seem to have unfolded over an extremely short period of time, under the impulse of a chance meeting.

Finally, the importance of timeframes and contexts is worth underlining as it exerts a strong influence on the way differentiation conflicts evolve: Kafeel's action was carried out during a period in which organised forms of violence had declined and more individualised forms predominated. Jihadist attacks as a means of operating, and as a language and ultimate form of political action, had become commonplace (both in terms of their frequency and their visibil-ity), and this independently of whether or not they involve self-sacrificial violence. But jihadism itself has evolved over recent years, with a form of ter-rorism which was once more or less channelled and even organised either by bodies such as the Algerian AIG or Pakistani Lashkar-e-Taiba or else by net-works such as Al-Qaeda, having been supplanted or supplemented by a form of jihadism conducted by individuals operating independently of any frame-work and who thus mobilise alone. This self-radicalisation, primarily taking place within diasporic populations—who are particularly inclined to ques-tioning their identities—and drawing on the Internet as a technical and ideo-logical trajectory, is thus rooted in a complex combination of exogenous shifts (the decline of organisations which might act as a framework, such as Al-Qaida) and endogenous forces (long-distance suffering and the quest for an ethic). And it is in fact this combination (and in particular the absence of any framework) that enabled Kafeel to preserve his autonomy of thought and action in his daily life. In any case, however specific the example of Kafeel might be, it is nevertheless representative of a form of violence where long-distance suffering, arising from moral outrage, has an overly determining effect, to the extent where whilst not being the sole explanatory factor it is nevertheless a variable in its own right.

9

CONFLICTING EMOTIONS

THE 2006 ANTI-"DANISH CARTOONS" RIOT IN LAHORE (PAKISTAN)

Amélie Blom

"We avenged the Prophet!" These were the words shouted by the Kouachi brothers as they came out of the office of the French satirical journal Charlie-Hebdo on 8 January 2015, having murdered most of the editorial team. The attack was in retaliation for the re-printing of the controversial cartoons initially published in the Danish daily newspaper *Morgenavisen Jyllands-Posten* ten years before. The "Danish cartoons controversy" operated in a mirror process from its very inception and events interestingly followed a script similar to that of the "Rushdie affair" in the late 1980s (Blom, 1999). The controversy similarly turned into a transnational discursive war opposing abstract conceptual pairs: freedom of expression vs. religious feelings; humor vs. insult; tolerance vs. fundamentalism; enlightenment vs. obscurantism. Incensed by what it perceived as the growing self-censorship of European artists and writers when publicly talking about Islam in a post-9/11 context, the editorial team of *Morgenavisen Jyllands-Posten* decided to conduct an *in vivo* experiment by inviting cartoonists to draw the Prophet of Islam "as they saw him". Among the twelve "cartoons" that were published on 30 September 2005, three, clearly depicting the Prophet Muhammad, provoked an international wave of protest worldwide resulting in total in about 140 deaths, six of them in Pakistan.[1]

The anti-Danish cartoons riots that happened in Lahore on 14 February 2006 offers an interesting micro-political site for analyzing how the culture of violent dissent has evolved in contemporary Pakistan and how emotions operate in this process. On that day, the military-controlled government led by General Musharraf (1999–2008) lifted its ban on all outdoor meetings for this long-distance outrage to be publicly expressed. The protest in Lahore, organized not by the usual "Islamist suspects" but by a small Barelwi group, the Tahaffuz-e-Namoos-e-Risalat Mahaz ("Front for the Protection of the Honour of Muhammad's Prophecy", or TNRM), turned into a riot, a rare phenomenon in the city.[2] Lahore is the second-largest city in Pakistan—with a population of about 7 million people—and the political, cultural, and economic center of the Punjab province (60 per cent of the population). Contrary to Karachi, it is not ethnically divided: 85 per cent of its population is Punjabi-speaking and 94 per cent is Muslim. It is also a Pakistan Muslim League (PML) stronghold: a party then divided between the ruling pro-Musharraf faction (PML-Q) and that led by the exiled former Prime Minister, Nawaz Sharif (PML-N). The city has often been the nucleus of anti-government movements: the anti-Ahmadi[3] riots in 1953, the 1968/69 movement against General Ayub Khan that led to his being ousted from power, and the 1977 *nizam-i-mustafa* ("system of the Prophet") movement that resulted in Zulfikar Ali Bhutto's downfall.

As tautological as it might seem, no organization can mobilize potential protestors if these are not initially affected and moved, or "emotionally disturbed" (as one the participant to the Lahore's demonstration put it). Based on interviews with some of the protestors who took to the streets against the "Danish cartoons" in Lahore, this article defends the need to take the role of emotions seriously in our understanding of how group's differences are shaped in social protests and how this can eventually lead to violence. The role of emotions in protests can be studied from "the micro-level processes by which bystanders become participants, to the emotional repertoires that activists draw upon when pitching their case in different settings, to the organizational mechanisms through which particular emotions are managed, to the macro-structural shifts responsible for making certain emotions legitimate motivations for protest" (Goodwin, Jasper and Polletta, 2004, 414). This research map proves very useful for our understanding of the cartoons riot in Lahore, and this at two levels: First, because emotions (anger and love in particular) are "a way of being-in-the-world, a relationship between oneself and one's situation" (Solomon, 1984, 250); they shaped the way such a disturbing event as "cartooning the Prophet" was qualified as an attack in need of retaliation. Secondly, as public performances, emotions can also have "significant structural and action consequences" (Flam and King, 2005, 4). Indeed, the riot in Lahore erupted not in a vacuum but in the context of a (not so carefully) staged drama of righteous anger.

Some Words on Methodology

In addition to my personal observation of the Lahore demonstration, as well as press articles and TV programmes, my primary material includes interviews with eight protestors (all male, no women participated in the protest) in May 2007, conducted in Urdu and in English. Identifying protesters a year later proved slightly problematic, with the exception of the protest's chief organizer and leader of the TNRM, *maulana* Muhammad Sarfaraz Naeemi (later killed in a suicide-attack). In his late 50s, he is a prominent *alim* in the Barelwi tradition and heads the Dar-ul Uloom Jamia Naeemia, a madrasa located in Garhi Shahu, a working-class district nearby Lahore Railway Station.

   All interviewees lived in Lahore's popular districts and belonged to the same social milieu, one that can be called—for lack of a better word—the middle-class, a "residual category" of neither poor nor affluent (Daechsel, 2004, 30). All of them were sons of low-rank civil servants, apart from Waqas, a 22-year-old "street boy" from the Old City (*androon sheher*) who took part in the riot, and Ahmad, a 39-year-old former boxer, born in the Old City as well. Nadeem, aged 23, went to the protest alone but left "when the atmosphere became violent".[4] He came to Lahore to study law at the Punjab University and asserted his dislike of the "religious parties" despite sharing their views. This was not the case for Farhan, described by his friend as a "typical inflexible Jamaati guy, very committed to the Islamic cause". Aged 31, he also migrated from a village to study at the Punjab University. He is a former member of the Jamaat-i-Islami's student wing, the Islami Jamia-i-Tuleba (IJT), and an experienced protestor. His friend Ramzan, a 27-year-old maths teacher, who had studied at a Deobandi madrasa also attended the protest. And finally Hasnan, born in Lahore, a 17-year-old student at the Mohammedan Anglo Oriental (MAO) College, participated as well. His favorite pastime is *naat khawani* (reciting religious hymns in praise of the Prophet). He is a regular devotee at a Barelwi mosque in the popular Chauburji district. The interview was conducted in its premises and in the presence of its *khatib*, Qari Tausif, a 35-year-old activist of the Jamiat-ul Ulama-i-Pakistan (JUP, a Barelwi political party formed in 1948).

'Emotional Commotion'

Only two demonstrators I interviewed had actually seen the cartoons, the others relied on the way in which the local media, English- and Urdu-speaking alike, framed the issue: the "'blasphemous' cartoons against Prophet Muhammad, PBUH". "It was something that disturbed me emotionally" says Farhan, while Waqas recalls that he "got angry as soon as [he] heard on TV that they had been rude to our Holy Prophet". This was the emotional trigger of an outrage that could not be seen but was strongly felt. Affects at their pre-reflexive level are certainly the hardest to analyze but cannot be ignored, as proven by Hasnan's testimony. After stating that, "I learnt on TV that some people made caricatures of the Prophet", he immediately put his right hand on his heart and adds "May God forgive me but they say they were *caricatures* [stressing the word] ... this provoked a big commotion in Islam and among its people. It's obvious that in our hearts, a great shock arose". The emotion that this young protestor tries to describe means, in Urdu, a shock related to fear (*halchal*, "commotion", also means "panic" and *haul*, a sentiment of terror). This shock is, later on in the interview, compared to "a lightning bolt that struck the heart of those who love the Prophet".

The publication of the cartoon provoked, what James Jasper terms a "moral shock", creating "such a sense of outrage in a person that he or she becomes inclined towards political action, with or without the network of personal contacts" (Jasper, 1997, 106). "Look, out of respect, we keep no pictures of the Prophet in our houses or even our minds, how can we possibly allow others to do it?" explains Ahmad angrily.[5] This informed what has been convincingly defined as "the essential political emotion": anger (Holmes, 2004, 123). But anger is born out of what was certainly the most "managed emotion" (Hochschild, 1983) during the mobilization: love for the Prophet (*ishq-e-rasul*). Farhan explains this love as a reflex emotion: "Love for the Prophet is such that we cannot bear anything ridiculing it. There is nothing to be explained, it's not a scientific thing or a contract. It's a relation of love". All protestors mentioned it, irrespective of their doctrinal affiliation, or lack thereof. For Hasnan, it is "the most important quality of a Muslim". That

"Europe" addressed its apology to "Muslims", and not to the "Prophet" was therefore baffling: "The problem is not us but the personality they made cartoons of", says Farhan.

Yet, anger is also "a judgmental emotion": when angry, "you are the judge, and the other person the defendant" (Solomon, 1984, 250). The protest organizers' framing of the issue played a crucial role in this respect. When asked how he discussed the issue during his *khutba* at the mosque, *imam* Tausif replied: "I informed people that this act was blasphemous and that the punishment for the blasphemer is death". This was a potent frame in a country where the Blasphemy Laws condemn as a crime punishable by the death penalty if related to the Prophet, any "deliberate and malicious acts intended to outrage religious feelings". Blasphemy is, indeed, a quintessential form of outrage that implies drawing a line between what is tolerable and what is not according to one's religious beliefs (Favret-Saada, 1992, 253). Appeal to the inherent relationship between the Prophet's "honor" and one's own drew this decisive line, as demonstrated by the very name of the "Front for the Protection of the *Honor* of Muhammad's Prophecy". This, more than anything, moved people to view protest as not only be useful, but also truly fulfilling, bringing a sense of gratification, "not of achieving a utopia but of striving for one" (Jasper, 1997, 135). Interviewees used the more common word "*izzat*", a term which covers "a whole complex of emotionally charged values including honor, respect, reputation, shame, prestige and status" (Dusenbery, 1990, 242) and is applied to relationships within and between families. Indeed, Ahmad compared the publication of the cartoons to insulting a family member in the most dishonoring way imaginable: "never mind, please, but it is as if someone took pictures of your mother without clothes".

Protestors, nonetheless, also displayed moral balance, evaluating the legitimacy of their attitude by questioning that of their distant opponent. They discussed with great passion freedom of speech. Farhan claims that, "tolerance in European countries means that human beings are all equals, even exceptional people such as Prophets. But in Islam, sacred personalities are not our equals. Our concepts are not the same". Hasnan, the young *naat* singer, conveyed the point through a poetic metaphor: "man should talk in such a way that flowers come out of his mouth, but its thorns should not wound the other".[6]

Organizational Dynamics and the Compulsory Expression of Anger

"I defeat those who denigrate the Prophet." This is how Ahmed Riza Khan, the founder of the Barelwi movement and then twenty years old, replied when asked by a host to introduce himself (quoted in Metcalf, 1982, 300). This is the mantle that the organizer of the Lahore protest, *maulana* Sarfaraz Naeemi, wrapped himself into. Naeemi, is not only a professional "mobilizer" on causes revolving around the "Prophet's honor" and blasphemy,[7] but also the heir in a line of Barelwi *ulama* who transmitted to him a given repertoire of "outraged protests". Naeemi's father founded the Jamia Naeemia in 1953, and the very same year started to campaign in the anti-Ahmadi movement. The very name of the Front also attests the transmission of an emotional repertoire of protest: it is borrowed from the *Tehreek-i-Tahaffuz-i-Namoos-i-Risalat* formed by another Barelwi *imam* in February 1989 to lead the protest against *The Satanic Verses*.

Why are issues related to the Prophet's honor so prominent in Naeemi's activist trajectory? The answer lies in the "morally valued and compulsory collective [...] expression of feelings" (Mauss, 1969, 277), along with the "socially legitimate emotions that the situation itself prescribes" (Latté, 2006, 11). In Pakistan, Barelwis in particular are supposed, and expected, to feel strongly about the Prophet: assessing his prominent position and exalting his greatness is at the core of their identity. As put by *imam* Tausif again, "the reason we came out on the road [in protest] was the emotions that any Muslim *should* have had". Defending Muhammad's prophecy is therefore also a "feeling rule", a "guideline for the assessment of fits and misfits between feeling and situation" (Hochschild, 1979, 566). It is one of the rare issues on which Barelwi *ulama* take the lead of collective protests, such as the 1953 and 1974 anti-Ahmadi movement and the 1988/89 anti-Rushdie campaign.[8]

The Enemy's Provocation

"How to provoke a worldwide crisis with twelve little drawings?" asks Jeanne Favret-Saada (2007) half-provocatively. But these were far from insignificant. It would be misleading to oppose a Muslim emotional crowd to rational, harmlessly funny, Danish cartoonists. Protestors' emotions were very much a reflection of those that motivated the cartoons: fear, anger, exasperation, and a desire to assert a moral superiority and stigmatization (we can laugh at everything while Muslims are easily manipulated by intolerant and violent preachers). This was palpable in most of the drawings (the Prophet as a terrifying sexist villain, suicide-bombers driven by sexual frustration, etc.). *Maulana* Naeemi explains: "they showed the Muslim with a scary face, like a terrorist about to devour someone". This was a very sensitive representation in the post-9/11 context. The cartoonists wanted to warn people against the deviant usage of Islam for violent aims, but from the receptors' point of view (many of them sharing the same concern), they implied that "Muslims" in general— their Messenger was pictured—were to blame. For Ahmed, the "most insulting" image was the Prophet stopping suicide-bombers at heaven's gate: "The Prophet is standing, a loose woman at his arm, and says 'go, do suicide bombing and you will be rewarded with a *hoori*!'"[9] Contrary to the common reading of the anti-cartoons protest as proving Muslims' inability to laugh about their religion, popular humor is not mistaken about the allegorical dimension of the *hooris* (that the drawing denies).[10] What was unbearable was the perceived intention to harm.

Indeed, the outrage was felt as a result of perceived provocation. All the interviewees were absolutely convinced that the cartoons were "a conspiracy against Islam" by "them" (Europe, the West, America). The attributed intention to harm is how "the righteous anger that puts fire in the belly and iron in the soul" could be placed in a convincing "frame of injustice" (Gamson, 1992, 32), with a proper script and a villain to blame. Farhan explains: "*they* say that these cartoons happened just by chance but I don't believe them. It was pre-planned". For *maulana* Naeemi, "Bush was behind all this, he targets Muslims because he is an extremist Christian", a significant anti-parastasis[11] echoed by Hasnan: "The people who committed this [the cartoons], I call them rebels, extremists actually". That the allocation of blame was framed as a "conspiracy theory" is neither irrelevant nor irrational. This particular "regime of justification" helps protestors, when they speak from the "world of inspiration" (emotions) to the "civic world" (street protest, for instance) and the "world of opinion" (the media), to lower the impressions of "spontaneity" and irrationality attached to their emotional reactions (Boltanski and Thévenot, 1991, 19). It acts, as well, as a "pragmatic constraint" that "freezes the anxiety" generated by the "bad intentions" attributed to the other (Thévenot, 1995, 150); it rationalizes an intolerable situation (Why would anyone want to hurt me? Why are "they" so insensitive to our love for our Prophet?). It ensures that the grievances engage a group, hence calling for public recognition (otherwise it would be nothing more than a personal suffering). Finally, it works as a strategy of "self-aggrandizement" (Boltanski, Darre and Schiltz, 1984, 23), enhancing the status of the victim (How frightening I might be, hence powerful, if such great powers try to hurt me!).

Yet, protestors were eventually put into "attack mode" (Jasper, 1997, 106) by another widespread and decisive way of reading the situation: Muslims were not only "attacked" but "tested". "The cartoonists wanted to test whether or not Muslims would rise in the name of their Prophet," says *imam* Tausif. Their resilience was also at stake. For Farhan, it is Muslims' capacity to resist the spread of European values which was checked: "European countries thought that they can tease Muslims as much as they want and Muslims will get used to their notion of tolerance". This explains why joining the 14 February demonstration was described as a matter of fighting back.

The Crowd: From *Communitas* to Destruction

The Lahore protest was preceded by a wave of demonstrations in the country. Yet, the two main organizers of the 14 February protest in Lahore—the Qaumi Tajir Ittehad (QTI), the largest association of local traders, and Maulana Naeemi—expected it to be peaceful. They were proved wrong. The issue at stake was such that, in addition to the JUP, many other political and religious parties joined such as the Jamaat-ud-Dawa (JuD) and both factions of the PML.[12] Indeed, the distant conflict thus turned local.

The protestors—about 5,000 to 10,000—formed a greatly heterogeneous crowd: Barelwi madrasa students, traders, shopkeepers, party activists, students from government colleges, youngsters from popular districts (the "wheelie boys" thus called for their motorbike stunts or "the kind of guys who stand in front of girls' colleges" as a friend farcically describes them), lawyers, journalists, low-rank civil servants, etc. Some had also come from the city's surrounding villages. The crowd was nevertheless homogeneous in terms of class: residents from posh areas were almost entirely absent.

The protest was far from apolitical: slogans invariably blamed the Pakistani government for its inability to "protect Muslims" and for its alliance "with the US". This was inscribed in the route of the protest itself. It started from Data Sahab Darbar[13] in the Old City to reach the Punjab Assembly after going through Mall Road (or The Mall). This road is the nerve of the city, linking the Northern Old City to the Southern upper middle-class and elite residential areas, a major shopping centre, a concentration of colleges and universities and the place where most of the government's buildings are located. The spatial set-up of the demonstration itself was, indeed, part of the many dispositions for the emotional dramaturgy of anger to take place, and a major reason for it getting out of hand as well. *Imam* Tausif remembers that when he joined it, "emotions were very high, each party was holding its flag, people were holding banners demanding that the cartoonists apologize to the entire Muslim world and do *toba* [vow not to do it again]". The Lahori demonstrators mainly formed an expressive crowd. They wanted everyone to know that they occupied the moral high ground and could "fight back". As put by Nadeem, it was a matter of "talking to the world [and] send to the cartoonists the message that for the Muslims it is a very important issue so they'll stop printing these cartoons", of "express[ing] our emotions in our actions" (Farhan). All along the procession route, a symbolic duel was fought between loved and hated characters. Slogans were raised in praise of the Prophet and "villains" were booed: not so much the cartoonists but "Denmark", "the Jews" and the "Bush-Mush (Musharraf)-Blair" trilogy, hence transforming the issue into a conflict between singular, and more familiar, personalities. The "outraged community" was called upon to act as a sanctioning judge in this fight between good and evil and to personify a reclaimed dignity. It was the embodied *umma*; an identity that, far from being an "artifact", was "felt, expressed, reinvented, claimed" (Cefaï, 2007, 258) and put in presence of itself. As remembered by Hasnan "we were holding each other's hands [...] we were lost in our love for the Prophet". As stressed by Victor Turner, it is precisely in conditions on the peripheries of everyday life, such as a street protest, that the "wind of existential *communita*" can better be felt and the *communitas* itself experienced as an "eternal now" (Turner, 1974, 243, 238).

Yet, this fight between a public good and a public wrong ended in uncontrollable anger and the consequent destruction and looting of The Mall. The pattern of violence was similar to many other riots (Janowitz, 1979): first, attacks against emblems of public order and once the security forces show signs of weakness, rioters split into small groups, smashing offices and shops, burning motorbikes and cars, and looting western fast-food shops and their offices. When they tried to rob an ATM machine, two rioters were killed by a private guard. One group set fire to the old Diyal Singh Mansion where a Shehzan bakery was located, while others attacked the Pakistan International Airlines' office, travel agencies, outlets of the Norwegian mobile company Telenor, etc. The evolution of the targets clearly show a progressive lifting of inhibitions: rioters took a police official hostage—when he tried to calm the rioters—and beat him up, and finally broke off the police cordon at the provincial Assembly and set one of its rooms on fire. The Rangers (a paramilitary unit) stayed in the city for twenty days. At the end, 135 protestors were arrested, a hundred buildings were vandalized, and 400 cars and motorcycles damaged (Khan, 2006).

Many of the protestors I interviewed were shocked by the riot. Farhan, the former IJT activist and an old hand at demonstrations, put the blame, interestingly, on a bad management of emotions:

IDENTITY, CONFLICT & POLITICS IN TURKEY, IRAN AND PAKISTAN

Usually, groups who organize demonstrations know how to control the crowd when it becomes too emotional. But in this protest, people from neighborhoods, the common public, came to express their emotion, they had no leadership, no coordination, they were not part of any system.

Indeed, when the Barelwi leadership tried to address the crowd, it proved useless. *Imam* Tausif remembers: "our *ulama* said on the loudspeaker: 'Stop the [rioters], brothers! They're not our people, they're creating chaos!' But no one listened". But Nadeem gives another picture: "some people were totally uncontrollable but others were instigating them". There were, certainly, disconcerting facts: violence erupted as soon as the protest started while men carrying guns and law-enforcement officials in civvies were spotted guiding the crowd. Yet, the crowd was not simply "imitative": certain acts of violence made sense, such as attacking a Shezan bakery allegedly owned by an Ahmadi, others not. When a man tried to push the crowd to attack a Christian church, shouting "kill the *kuffar* (infidels), burn them!" People looked at him indifferently thinking he was a "crazy drug addict". To understand the inner logic of violence, we need to go "inside" the crowd (Weisbrod, 2002, 555).

A Rioter's Testimony: The Street Boy and the Policemen

Waqas is 22 years old and lives in Rang Mahal, in the heart of the Old City. His participation in the protest was primarily a matter of a peer group's "programme" in the colloquial language of Lahore's street boys: "My friends called and said 'hep, what's up man [*kia programme hai yaar*]?' There's a strike tomorrow on this cartoons thing, let's go". Though quite shy, he laughs constantly when recalling his "heroic deed" on that day. He casually explains: "Two policemen passed in front of us, we trashed them badly, took our bikes and run away". When I asked him if they had done something to him, he replied even more casually: "No, I just felt like it [*dil kar raha tha*]". His childhood friend adds in the same laughing tone "He's our Shahrukh Khan, angry even before meeting his enemy!"[14] But Waqas corrects him: "yep, it was an old anger. Police fined me a lot of times. They always ask for more and if you don't have the money, they give you a *chalan* [fine]".[15] After a short silence, he adds: "So what? Beating up policemen is no big deal, they beat people all the time no?" His friend, pursuing the movie metaphor, adds: "him and his brother, they always get a 36 at the lottery![16] They're the famous *badmash* [goons] of Rang Mahal". As a matter of fact, when we met, Waqas's elder brother was in jail (he had opened fire in a street fight) using a police car to visit his family.

170

After beating the policemen, Waqas and his friends joined the protest and chanted slogans in praise of the Prophet. When they reached the lower portion of The Mall, they saw "the police beating up a lot of people, people threw stones at them and the police fired back tear gas". They then saw other people destroying buildings: "we got emotional and did it as well, but we just joined. We broke windows, KFC, Telenor signboards, traffic signals but no cars". He then describes different groups of rioters:

> When we left, we heard that they killed a guard, but it's not us, those were just bandits [*dakoo*]. There were also Jihadis there. Those who started the violence were students, from MAO College and Diyal Singh College. Someone had told them what to do, what to break. I also saw two boys opening straight fire but those were just 'show-offs' [*shokhe larke*]. And those robbing bakeries and food outlets were villagers, daily laborers (added in a despising tone).

Waqas's testimony clearly demonstrates the limit of the "frustration model" to explain violence; an explanation of the February 2006 riot incidentally favored by many among Lahore's liberal elite. Waqas is not part of a *lumpen-proletariat* marauding mob: his father is a property dealer and the family recently moved to a well-furnished house in a middle-class locality. Sure, some deprived youngsters used this opportunity to rob any valuable goods they could get their hands on. Generally though, group belonging and not social class, that mattered here. Waqas is what is locally known as a *lafanga* (ruffian), *aawara* (literally vagabond) or, in Punjabi, a *wela jea banda*, which has the double meaning of an "idle" or "free guy" (from any commitment). These diverse labels describe a well-defined category of young men who easily get into fights and who don't study or work out of choice. When mentioning the Pakistani employees who lost their jobs because of the riot's destruction, Waqas dismissively replies: "that's up to God". For the "*wela jea banda*", those compelled to work are "losers". His way of life is to have fun with his (exclusively male) peer group, "play cricket and watch TV", spend a lot of time out in the streets and do motorbike stunts.

This does not mean, at all, that Waqas's anger was not meaningful. Raised in the Barelwi tradition, he feels strongly about the Danish cartoons' "insult". Yet, he does not dwell on intricate conspiracy theories, contrary to students, but says: "They had been rude to our Holy Prophet, for us he is a God just after God and I got angry. I swear I would kill the guy who's done these cartoons if ever he comes in front of me!" Taking a fighter's posture, he adds, "We can insult their God as well and see how they'll get angry!" In his social universe, where a *gustakh's* (a rude person) comment leads to an immediate fight, you don't react by breaking diplomatic relations or calling for public apologies: you silence your opponent, even if miles away, by showing your strength. "If Muslims all over the world were united, no one would dare saying anything to them," he concluded. And it is the people's responsibility to do. He explains: "The government didn't take any action on this. Only the people did something". When I ask him "what did the people do?" He replies, "Many things, they broke shops, cars and official buildings, they destroyed foreign companies so that they get out of our country, they burnt effigies of the British Prime Minister". Waqas is proud to have been, somehow, the voice of the people on this day. His moral valuation was also clearly visible in his narrative of legitimate targets during the riots: no Pakistani shops, cars and bikes. He clearly dissociated himself from the "robbers" and the "show off boys" (violent out of greed and vanity). His own violence had a righteous flavor: vengeance, against the offending "West", and the local police.

The emotional and moral frames prescribed by any given social interactions are never fully constraining: they are precarious and sometimes they break when experiencing dissonance (Goffman, 1974). This happened during the Lahore riot at the time of the first encounter with the police, on the Lower Mall: it displaced the locus of the demonstrators from a show of love to the Prophet and hatred against "the West" into a "police and thief" game. The police, totally unprepared, were indeed forced to push back rioters, here and there, thus increasing the playful dimension of violence. More importantly, it sent mixed signals: in some parts of the procession it displayed empathy, chanting slogans with the crowd, in others it used repression; an ambiguity mirroring that of Waqas's day-to-day interactions with the police.

The second important situational dissonance that Waqas underlines is the inner conflicts within the crowd: first, the presence of Jihadist militants. Truly, the TNRM was immediately engaged in "emotional warfare" (Goodwin, Jasper and Polletta, 2004, 417) with rival doctrinal groups, whose very presence was also felt as a provocation. *Imam* Tausif recalls: "A group of people from the JuD tried to join us but our [Barelwi] *ulama* asked them to put down their flags, they refused and we had an argument with them". The competition between diverse Islamic groups for the monopoly on the "inner essence" of Muslims in Pakistan is increasingly fought on a wider public arena, such as TV channels and, importantly, the streets of Pakistan's main city, where various religious sects struggle for public visibility and "re-negotiate their relationship (among themselves and with the state)" (Freitag, 1989, xii). In the context of Pakistan's religious sectarianism, this is particularly important, especially in

Punjab where Barelwism has, historically, its core of supporters. As a result of General Zia's (1977–88) pro-Deobandi and Ahl-i-Hadith inclinations, Barelwi *ulama* were progressively put on the defensive. Polemics became more intense and increasingly opposed them to the state,[17] as well to new Jihadist groups. The presence of Jihadist groups was not the only one to foster unconventional emotions. As Waqas recalls, "college boys started the violence", a point made by other interviewees as well. When a group of college students tried to remove a picture of President Musharraf and Chaudhry Elahi (the PML-Q Punjab chief minister) on the Lower Mall, they were baton-charged by the police and they attacked, in return, a police station. The wider context of students' politics in Lahore sheds light on this incident. Though banned, student unions survived as the youth arms of Pakistan's political parties.[18] Their rivalries since the late 1980s had been extremely violent in government colleges and universities, particularly so in MAO, Diyal Singh and Islamiyya colleges where the "college boys" of the 14 February protest were coming from. The violence that erupted may then have been a result of an internal "PML campus war".

The Local *Imaginaires* of Violence

Waqas' testimony therefore shows that the Lahore riot formed a part of larger incidences of everyday violence, occurring in a wide range of social and political contexts (family, colleges, streets, etc.). It provides another crucial piece to the puzzle of the triggering of violence. When at the very beginning of the interview, he said, "I would kill the guy who's drawn these cartoons" he immediately added "I'll kill him at once like Ghazi Ilamdin Shahid did."[19] This allusion is quite fascinating because it refers to a dispute over printed words and the application of the blasphemy law in pre-partition time. Waqas explains:

> Sometime ago, Ghazi Ilamdin Shahid killed a guy who had published a book against Islam but the British government had him hanged. He was a resident from my neighborhood, Rang Mahal, there is a Ghazi Ilamdin Chowk (square) a minute away from my home, many places are named after him, clinics, schools, etc. each kid knows about him.

Although participants often described the rioters as "teenagers who watch too much Indian movies and want to be hero" (as put by Ramzan), the quest for heroism proves much more complex. It needs to be contextualized within the rioters' local *imaginaires* of violence—an *imaginaire* kept alive and meaningful by other riots that had happened in the city since the late 1920s. The pattern of riots (but not of demonstrations in general) in Lahore from the late 1920s till today demonstrates a progressive domination of a vocabulary revolving not on socio-political conflicts anymore but on competing religious narratives.[20] One of the first riots in pre-Partition Lahore was that alluded to by Waqas. The next one, in 1935, also took place in the Old City but this time over the "Shahidganj Mosque".[21] The second major wave of riots happened during the dreadful 1947 "communal war of succession" of India-Pakistan's partition (Talbot, 2006, 44) which was, also, particularly intense in the areas from which the 2006 protestors were coming from and in The Mall as Hindus and Sikhs owned most of the shops and buildings (such as the Diyal Singh Mansion which was burnt down during the riot).

In post-Partition Lahore, riots continued to centre on a public assertion of "Muslim-ness". This was the case of the 1952–53 anti-Ahmadi campaign, which soon turned, like the anti-Danish cartoons riots, into anti-upper class violence and compelled the Army to step in.[22] In 1977, riots erupted again in the Old City during the *nizam-i-mustafa* movement. In November 1979, when false rumors spread that the United states and Israel had seized the Grand Mosque in Mecca, a mob set Lahore's American Cultural Centre on fire. In 1992, as a counter-reaction to the Babri Masjid destruction in India, crowds attacked Hindu and Jain temples in the Old City. Riots then erupted out of the wave of sectarian killings in 1997 and in 1998. Then came, of course, the anti-cartoon riots.

The State's Politics of Self-Expression and the Violence of Emotions

Although riots in Lahore were often used as tools of partisan objectives,[23] we still have to explain why they so often look like "moral crusades" (Gusfield, 1986). We have to look here at the "emotional-institutional context within which social movements do their emotion work" (Flam, 2005, 19). This is hard to ignore in South Asia, where the post-colonial state inherited a politics of social control precisely based on the assumption of the "emotional subject" as shown by the case of Ilam Din. Then it gradually consolidated, through state sponsorship, with what has been forcefully conceptualized as the "politics of self-expression", which focused the public debate on a conception of individuals as "inward-looking and self-contained subjects whose sole purpose was the self-expression of their inner essences" (Daechsel, 2006, 1–2). This peculiar political culture, formed in 1930s-50s was particularly pervasive among the Lahori middle class milieu; a major actor during the anti-Danish cartoons protest. The notion of "middle-class" is certainly problematic yet describes well a group whose social mobility depends on education, emigration and, more than anything else, on "mastering the art of wheeling-dealing [...] learning to give and take bribes, mobilizing friends and relatives' influence [...] to access to governmental authority" (Qadeer, 1983, 171). The early Muslim League ideologues and the Urdu conservative press—two critical transmitters of the "Danish cartoons outrage"—thus popularized a political culture revolving around symbolic matters and meant to "stimulate an affective emotional state of empowerment" (Daechsel, 2006, 57). They also shaped the vision of Pakistan as a meta-historical collective whose Muslim inhabitants' right to exist is constantly threatened in a universe of perpetual warfare and conspiracies.

The Lahore riot clearly proved how symbolic wars opposing individuals' essence and "meta-historical collectivities" continue to be an appealing idiom of protest even after Zia's time.[24] General Zia's Islamization programme meant, basically, that "debates about democracy, economy, education, culture, women's issues, human rights' issues as well as the functioning of bureaucracy, judiciary and army drew heavily on the divine sources of morality, authenticity and accountability" (Waseem, 2007, 153). Zia did not just rely on the colonial legacy of the "emotional subjects" entrusted in the Blasphemy Laws but also altered them to effectively excommunicate Ahmadis, introducing more stringent rules in 1984.[25] The historical affinity between these laws and anti-Ahmadism elucidates why rioters selected their targets in "a repertory of traditional punishment" (Zemon Davis, 1973, 81), setting a bakery on fire after rumours spread that it was owned by an Ahmadi is one example. Zia then imposed the controversial article 295-C[26] in 1986, which dramatically shifted the institutionalized "rules of emotions" by authorizing the state to kill its inauthentic subject in wider and even more ambiguous situations. In Punjab, the PML has proven in the last two decades to be the best gatekeeper of self-expressionism. This party, dominant in Lahori politics and an important actor in the anti-Danish cartoons protest, supported, for instance, a bill to make death a mandatory punishment for blasphemy in 1992, and agitated for the restoration of the "religious column" in the National Identity Cards and Passports.[27]

The Mall operates as a crucial socio-physical marker of this abstract fight pitting the "authentic Muslim" against "Westernized Other", in addition to the more traditional rivalries with the "Hindu Other" and internal opponents. It is, indeed, one of the rare streets where the Westernized elite's lifestyles somehow fuse with the more traditional ones characteristic of the Old City. With its Pizza Hut, Mac Do and foreign banks, yet conservative traders and shopkeepers, it is the place where the "cultural war" so much feared by Farhan is fought:

> These cartoons are part of a cultural war against Muslims. Do you really think that these multinational companies are here just to make profit? No, their slogans are not valueless: "Enjoy the dirt" says the ad of Surf Excel or 'if you feel like it, ask for more', that's the Pepsi one. But you don't just do what you feel like doing or enjoy getting dirty in a Muslim society!

Conclusion

At the micro-level, emotions such as anger and love, linked to specific moral judgment (honor) and cognitive appraisal (Muslims are being tested by a worldwide conspiracy), eventually motivated protestors to react. At the meso-level, during the protest itself, the emotions displayed proved hard to manage and a riot broke out. They were indeed highly conflicting: a desire for eternal *communitas* yet destructive anger, of morally valued feelings and yet outlawed emotions. Based on the testimony of a rioter, I argued that this was informed by the inner conflicts and emotional warfare at work within the crowd. This testimony also reveals the significance of historically shaped local *imaginaires* of outrage. This led me to address the wider emotional-institutional landscape that makes certain emotions and symbolic causes legitimate motivations for violence. The February 2006 anti-Danish cartoons protest in Lahore reveals the complex interlinkages, which are at play in several other riots between righteous anger, emotional warfare within the crowd, day-to-day patterns of violence and the pattern of the state's symbolic violence.[28]

10

QUETTA CITY AND THE BALUCH GUERRILLA

ISSUES AT STAKE IN POLITICALLY MOTIVATED
URBAN VIOLENCE

Luc Bellon

The city of Quetta has been subjected to an unprecedented wave of urban attacks since 2006, ranging from the destruction of public goods (with gas installations being blown up, railway tracks destroyed, breaking down electric lines or lamp-posts, etc.) to targeted assassinations.

Quetta is the capital city of the Baluchistan Province of Pakistan. One of its main characteristics is its location at the interscetion of the Baluch and Pashtun tribal lands (parts of the city being built on Pashtun land, others on Baluch land), who are the main two main tribal groups of the province. It forms a colonial and post-colonial "enclave", an "island" encapsulating the state administration, the army, immigrant populations and tribal societies (Gazdar, Kaker and Kan, 2010).

Most of these attacks have been attributed to Baluch Nationalists.[1] Although Quetta has often been the scene of sporadic violence—bomb and missile explosions have regularly resonated in the streets since the 1970s—this has rarely caused substantial physical or human damage.

The systematic and intensive use of violence by Baluch Nationalists within the city is, therefore, a new phenomenon. The scale of urban violence mirrors that of the province-wide Baluch uprising (the nationalist armed struggle that was sparked off in early 2000 is the most intensive Baluch guerrilla warfare the Pakistani state has faced). The question I look to explore is whether this surge of violence in Quetta is an anomaly, or a mere continuation of the nationalist struggle itself? One way of answering is to look at the specific traits of this urban warfare. The form taken by the violence in Quetta is entrenched in the social and political makeup of the city itself. This paper will describe the main historical and political features of the urban configuration in which this violence has taken root, as well as the social and territorial divisions.

The main focus here is to understand the extent to which this new violence enhances, or modifies, existing relationships within the city. It is not to reveal "why" or "how" this violence suddenly erupted in the urban configuration, nor to evaluate the degree to which this violence is violent to those who are targeted by it.[2] Instead, the aim is to shed light on the social relationships to which this violence contributes—disregarding the initial intentions behind the violent acts themselves. In other words, this paper looks at how this violence is perceived by the inhabitants of the city. More specifically, it focuses on those who, whilst not the authors of the violence, see it as meaningful and legitimate. How do they perceive its incidence on the larger social configuration of the city? The main hypothesis is that apart from the obvious and explicit political motivation behind these attacks, the perpetuation of violence acts as an opportunity to challenge relationships and the way they are interpreted within the city.

The present analysis is based on field research conducted in Quetta in 2007 and 2009, as well as on the consultation of secondary sources. In 2009, I specifically focused my observations on Kili village, situated in the middle of a reputed Baluch militant area.[3] Kili was developed as a village four generations ago by people who belonged to a single Baluch tribe, originating from a region 200 kilometers south. Kili is now occupied by a more heterogeneous population, comprising of other Baluch tribes, Pashtuns and Punjabis. Yet, the members of the original tribe still make up the majority of the population and control most aspects of political life. In the village, I met mostly sympathizers of the armed struggle. I focused on the changes that occurred in the city due to the increasing violence, and how this violence is seen or understood by the village inhabitants.

By attending to the reaction of Quetta inhabitants who see justification in this violence, but who are not its authors, it is possible to highlight their role in producing the implication that this violence can have at micro-level. It is by combining their point of view with the wider historical and political context of the city that it is possible to identify some of the effects of the Baluch politically motivated violence in Quetta.

After describing the urban context of Quetta, I will give an overview of the nature and scale of the violence itself, focusing specifically on attacks attributed to Baluch nationalist armed groups. This violence being unprecedented, I will describe the transformation of the Baluch armed struggle from being solely rural to integrating the provincial capital city into the conflict. I will then show that Baluch inhabitants, who are not directly involved in the violence, translate these urban attacks as a frontal opposition to the state. Taking a closer look at the Baluch-Pashtun relationship and its evolution, I will describe some of the stakes deriving from the ongoing violence in Quetta.

The Context and Scale of the Baluch's Urban Guerrilla

The British administration initially moved into the area of Quetta to establish the last military outpost on the road to Afghanistan, and subsequently transformed it into the 'headquarters' of the 'agencies' which they administered in Baluchistan (Bruce, 1900; Thornton, 1888; Scholz, 2002). In the absence of any significant commercial route, they established a communication and transport network—including a railway line from the coast of Sindh which reached Quetta in 1887 and the border of Iran in 1917 and 1922 (Scholtz, 2002, 106–110)—thus turning the small town into an administrative, commercial, cultural and transport hub for the region (Thornton, 1888, 81–82), following the classical development process of "colonial towns".[4] On land which originally belonged to a Pashtun tribe (Bruce, 1900, 71), they established a garrison (*cantonment*), administrative quarters (*civil lines*) and a residential and commercial centre populated by civil servants, administrators, railway workers and traders—most of whom were settlers belonging to the Sikh, Hindu, Christian, and Punjabi communities. The areas immediately surrounding this core are principally Pashtun to the north-east, and Baluch to the south-west. The demography has been further influenced by large-scale migration from Afghanistan. A first wave of Shiite Hazaras settled in 1906, and again during the rule of General Musa Khan Hazara (who was Governor of West Pakistan from 1967 to 1969).[5] Following the outbreak of war in

Afghanistan, the early 1980s saw another wave of migration, mainly composed of Pashtuns.

The Baluch zones were not initially part of the city itself and were seldom, if at all, populated. But the commercial development led Baluch populations—including the inhabitants of Kili—to settle on the land adjacent to the city and belonging to the Baluch Shahwani tribe.[6] The development of agricultural markets and the expanding administration also offered job opportunities to illiterate tribesmen (Scholtz, 2002, 117). Situated along today's Sariab Road, these zones became officially part of "urban Quetta" in 2002.

Quetta's mixture of populations does not reflect the demographic composition of the Province at large, where indigenous groups of Pashtun and Baluch are in a majority. The figures in the following table are drawn from the 1998 census, and show the proportion of different ethnic groups, as categorized in the census itself (Gazdar et al, 2010, 14).

Table 1: Ethnic Groups in Quetta (in per cent)

	Urban Quetta		Rural Quetta (District)	
	1901	1998	1901	1998
Settlers	71.8	31.0	41.5	31.0
European	13.4	0.0	7.3	0.0
Pashtun	11.0	23.7	18.0	24.6
Baluch	2.3	24.6	30.0	23.7
Other Indigenous	1.5	20.7	3.0	20.7

Source: 1998 census data compiled in Gazdar et al., 2010, 14.

These figures reveal a large-scale shift in the demography of the district over the course of almost one century: the Europeans of the colonial period disappear entirely, settlers diminish in proportion in the urban area, though not in the rural area, the proportion of Pashtuns in the whole district increases, and the Baluch move en masse into the city, with their proportion of the total urban population rising from 2.3 per cent to 23.7 per cent. Interestingly, the disparities between the various groups are also tremendously reduced. Urban Quetta was progressively 'indigenised' as the Baluch and Pashtun population increased in size and political power.

The end result is the presence of a cosmopolitan city in the middle of relatively hegemonic tribal land, and a place of potential political compromise.

Despite numerous population movements over the last century, the urban territorial divide between the different groups remain relatively clear cut. The majority of migrants live in the city centre, near the administrative area. The Pashtuns have established themselves on their lands adjacent to the centre. The Baluch are mainly concentrated on what used to be Shahwani land, to the south and slightly towards the edge of the city centre. Two major enclaves of Hazara migrants have emerged. The (Pashtun) Agfhan refugees have been more prone to disperse, though there are still a few pockets of concentration.

This geographical segregation translates into the reinforcement of group identities, thus giving considerable importance to territory, both in terms of settlement possibilities, as well as economic competition. With an economy mainly based on trade and traffic, to be a majority in an area also means controlling the trading route and the commerce which it hosts. But despite recurrent territorial disputes, especially between Baluch and Pashtuns, the city has never experienced open conflicts relating to land claims. The only cases of land expansion have occurred via legal transactions with tribal land being sold to the administration, individuals, members of other tribal groups, or settlers.

This ongoing community divide within the city reflects Quetta's evolution from a post-colonial outpost and buffer-zone between two Empires to an urban and economic hub (Gazdar et al., 2010, 33). The vibrant economy of the urban centre provided the local elites with an opportunity for legal and illegal trade with the rest of the province (especially in natural resources and agriculture products) and with the neighboring Afghanistan and Iran. Pashtun and Baluch tribal groups developed routes to transport goods to and from the city, while the leaders of nationalist parties often came from their ranks, thus enhancing their political influence in Quetta. Migrant populations from Afghanistan (mostly Pashtuns, Hazaras, and Uzbeks) also benefited from this trend; and while Pashtuns continued to work mostly as traders, Hazaras diversified enormously, opening small businesses and, more significantly, entering the administration. Finally, Quetta was an obvious source of power for religious groups during the Qandahar-based Taliban regime, and since then they have used the city as a rear base.

It is within this complex social environment that the wave of Baluch nationalist violence erupted from 2003 onwards. As mentioned, this eruption is unprecedented both in scale and type. The founding members of the Baluch Student Organization (BSO)[7] and an active political worker in Quetta during the 1973–1977 Baluch insurrection (see next chapter for details) remembers that,

Map 1: The City of Quetta

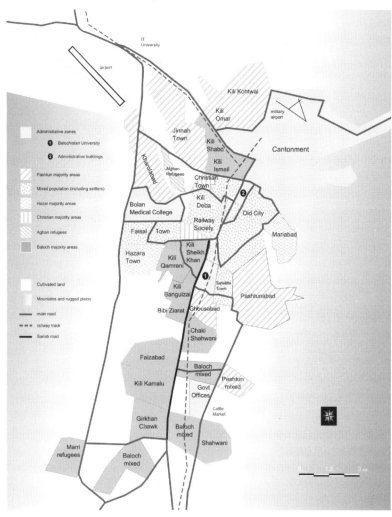

Source: compiled and drawn by the author, 2010.

Bomb blasts occurred at the time of Zulfiqar Ali Bhutto, but it was political. It was not like this target killing. They had a cause of political grievance. There was not a single fighting that ever happened in Quetta. Only bomb blasts, but which never created any casualty. Only one casualty happened, which was the bomb carrier himself—perhaps he did not know how to handle it—who died in front of the governor house. His name was Majid. He wanted to throw the bomb on the Governor House, but it exploded in his hands. In Quetta, this was the only casualty. (…) Even in the 1960s there were many skirmishes, but the city was never disturbed.[8]

The following main trends shown in figure 1 were identified by compiling the available data.[9]

While the total number of attacks remains high (one to two attacks a week on average for the past 6 years), they have changed in nature. The number of bombs and rockets, which formed the majority of occurrences until 2006, declines considerably, whilst target killings rise constantly. These target killings take the form of firearm assassinations or grenades thrown from a vehicle into a gathering place or shop.

The attacks attributed to Baluch nationalists have become truly deadly since 2006. As indicated by Figures 2 and 3, their attacks target the security forces mostly, but also include government officials and medical or educational staff and buildings. Public infrastructure (drains, railway tracks, gas pipes, and pylons) are generally damaged by bombs. The attacks are overall increasingly precise. Whereas previously the press and individuals I interviewed were unaware of who was responsible for the explosions, the attacks now seem to carry clear political messages. The murder of the provincial min-

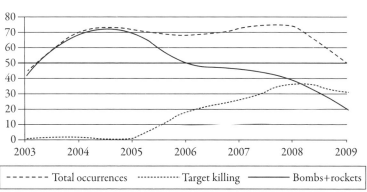

Figure 1: Number of attacks attributed to Baluch nationalists

Figure 2: Number of people killed by attacks

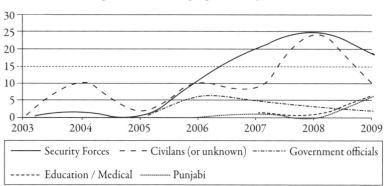

ister for Education on 26 October 2009, for which the Baluchistan Liberation United Front (BLUF) claimed responsibility,[10] is a typical example.

Since 2007 Punjabi settlers have become a definite target, though the number of attacks remains relatively low. The killing of those widely held to be "innocent Punjabi barbers"—rather than confirmed politicians, dignitaries, or high-ranking government servants, i.e. anyone against whom a legitimate political grudge could be held—is generally seen as the victimization of a group of city dwellers, who are socially discredited because of their economic activity (barbers) and because they belong to the country's dominant ethnic group.[11] To the eyes of many Baluch, these killings bear a different meaning. But when analysing the root causes underlying this point of view, it is first

Figure 3: Number of people targeted by attacks

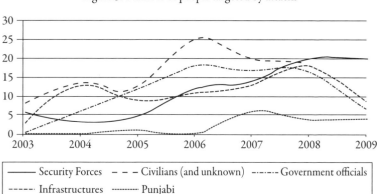

useful to go over the evolution of the conflict and how it was progressively imported into Quetta.

The Gradual Urbanisation of Guerilla Warfare

Since 1947 the Pakistan army has faced five successive rebellions in Baluchistan. Although not always abiding by the same dynamics, they are now seen by Baluch nationalists and sympathizers as "wars of national liberation". The first insurrection occurred in 1948, following the official incorporation of the Kalat state into Pakistan. Low intensity mobilization, principally based on tribal affiliation with the Kalat leader's (*Khan*) family, led to several guerrilla actions against army posts, and the subsequent retreat of a group of men to the surrounding mountains.

In 1958, a second guerrilla calling for the independence of Kalat state mobilized 750 to 1000 men in the same region (Ziring, 1999, 163–214 & 325–335; Afzal, 2001, 144–6; Feldman, 1972, 204–5; Mazari, 1999, 84).[12] While some consider this rebellion as the real starting point for the Baluch identity movement and its nationalist posture (Breseeg 2004, 300–4), the mobilization was still based on circumscribed tribal links and only concerned a limited territory. The armed confrontations were restricted to remote and mountainous areas.

The third conflict was triggered by the *Parari*[13] guerrilla movement between 1962 and 1969. Not only did this conflict last longer, it also spread over a much larger area than the 1958 uprising, running from Jahlawan (southern half of the Province) to the Marri-Burgti areas (in the North-East). It was also characterised by a pronounced Marxist ideology (Harrison, 1981). The guerrilla continued to focus on rural areas, using urban centres (mainly Quetta and Karachi) for logistical support.

The fourth insurrection, from 1973 to 1977, was conducted principally by Marri and Bugti tribesmen, but nevertheless affected most parts of north-east Baluchistan, taking in a larger area than the 1960s conflict. The Baluch People's Liberation Front (BPLF) and several spontaneous independent groups came and fought alongside the *Parari* movement, the instigator of the uprising.[14] Urban areas, especially Karachi, were used more intensively than previously, but activities there were still limited to networking. The guerrilla continued to struggle against army battalions in the mountains of Baluchistan.

Since 2000, Baluch nationalists have sparked off a new rebellion, whose scale (in terms of mobilization and territorial coverage) is larger than any of the preceding ones.[15] The armed struggle is conducted by four major groups: the BLA (Baluch Liberation Army), the BLF (Baluchistan Liberation Front), the BRA (Baluch Republican Army), and the BPLF (Baluch People's Liberation Front). The arrest of 250 to 300 militants in 2000 led to the murder of a judge in Quetta. In 2003 and for the first time in their history the Baluch nationalist parties came together in a coalition, named *Baluch Ittehad* (Axmann, 2008, 284)[16] which agreed on a common platform supporting the armed struggle. In 2004, a new guerrilla front was opened on the coast of Gwadar, in Makran Province, where the political opposition to the Central Government's economic development plans for the region was transformed into armed rebellion (Axmann, 2008, 261–92). In 2005, tensions flared again in the north, especially in the Bugti area, leading Nawab Akbar Khan Bugti, a 79-year-old tribal leader, to join the mountain guerrilla.

In August 2006, Nawab Akbar Khan Bugti was killed during a military operation. On 20 November 2007, the guerrilla leader Balaach Marri was also killed near the Afghan border. The two deaths coincided with a major shift in the guerrilla movement, which stepped up its urban operations, ranging from sensitization campaigns to targeted killings.[17]

One of the main victims of the targeted killings, the Police, was unable to control or prevent the recurrent aggressions.[18] Consequently, the government ordered the deployment of a federal paramilitary contingent, the Frontier Corps (FC), in the city (Abbas Hassan, 2007). This led to the occupation of urban spaces by forces endowed with heavy military gear (such as automatic weapons, grenades, machine guns, mini tanks, sandbag shelters, bulletproof jackets and helmets) at the city gates, on major road and railway crossings, around administrative quarters and Cantonment, in front of the residences of important elected representatives and political leaders, inside university premises (Baluchistan and IT Universities), and patrolling incessantly up and down Sariab Road ("Sariab Road", to the south of the city and passing through Baluch majority areas, has come to designate the Baluch areas and nationalist strongholds in Quetta).

The FC's official mandate is to prevent any armed action. They have therefore setup permanent check-posts, and regularly prevent people from entering the city. They also occasionally shut down institutions such as the Baluchistan University (August 2009), and play a role in government censorship by closing down offices of critical voices such as the daily Urdu newspaper *Asaap*.[19]

This ostensible military presence in the city and the accompanying government actions contribute to the feeling of insecurity and tension among citizens, including those demanding more security in the streets. This situation is aggravated by grievances concerning the many "disappeared" co-tribesmen including, they claim, non-activists. It is estimated that since 2000 somewhere between 900 (official sources) and 8000 people (Baluch activist sources) have disappeared in Baluchistan as a whole. The combination of a stronger FC presence—despite its efficiency in curbing the number of target killings since mid-2009—and the increased number of disappearances has led to a notable feeling of frustration amongst many of the people I encountered. The *nazim* (mayor) of Kili, who has been in office for the past eight years, offers the following analysis with regard to the implications of this situation for Baluch areas in Quetta:

> The guerrilla against the government has started in the mountain (...). In the city, with the help of the media, all these exactions which happen in the rural areas have been shown. When thousands of Bugti tribesmen were displaced because of the military operations in their area, the media talked about their living conditions in the Jalalabad camps, which were miserable. They also reported on all the disappearances which happen everywhere. So the people wanted to protest against these things. There have been many demonstrations, including women and children showing the pictures of their brothers, fathers or husband whom had never come home. So, in order to suppress this movement in the urban area, they have deployed the army. Now, the big difference is that most of the people support the Baluch fighters! Because they are convinced that it is the government which does all this. They have put the army everywhere, so the people think the government is here to suppress them. So much of the tension comes from the presence of these armed forces.[20]

The army presence, while offering a definite shield against armed outbursts, has also contributed to tensions in the city, and incites some individuals who had not been particularly politically oriented before, to start sympathizing with militant activists.

State Reaction and Reaction to the "Punjabi" State

The radicalization of some of the citizens can be illustrated through the case of Ghulam, a small-scale public construction contractor and a non-political volunteer social worker in his free time. A feud in his tribe, in which he was indirectly involved, meant he needed to seek protection. As he saw it he had two options: he could either approach an established government-affiliated party, or else one close to Baluch revel groups. Because of the military presence and actions outside and within the city, he chose the latter option and became an active member of the BRP (Baluchistan Republican Party)[21] because "all other Parties, like the one in power right now and the rest, they cannot do anything. They cannot protect me". He thence became a potent advocate of the Baluch cause. The BRP being openly in favour of the armed struggle, he was "disappeared" for almost seven months. During this time, his wife and children went on hunger strike for several months in the heart of Quetta to request his liberation. He had been recently freed when I spoke to him, appeared frightened to speak and angry against the Federal government.

Not only did Ghulam take a radical stance, but his wife and children moved into the public sphere too. Until then, women had seldom been publicly involved in political struggles, especially amongst the Baluch. Yet Ghulam's family is not an isolated case. Over the previous four years, news reports had regularly shown processions or gatherings of women, and declarations by the Baluch Women Panel (BWP) frequently broadcast. Demonstrations of women and children chanting anti-state slogans and carrying banners and photographs of missing people have been recurrent in the city since 2006. Several heads of families narrated how their children refused to sing the national anthem at school. In June 2009, for the first time, the women's branch of the BRA (Baluchistan Republican Army) claimed responsibility for bombing two shops in the centre of Quetta. This involvement of women within the public sphere is a significant shift of dynamics in Quetta's social and political context.

At the time of my fieldwork, Quetta was the scene of growing resentment against the state, especially amongst Baluch populations, in turn feeding popular support for violent acts committed within the urban setup, such as the bombing of infrastructure, political target killings, and in some instances the targeting of civilian members of the Punjabi populations.

In 2007, Baluch sympathizers of the armed struggle expressed reservations about the emerging trend of victimizing Punjabi barbers. They found these hard to justify, and often suggested that the attacks were carried out by Pakistani Intelligence in order to discredit the Baluch armed struggle. Two years later the views of the same individuals were less assured. While most of the media and (non-Baluch) public opinion continued to condemn these killings, the same sympathizers were now convinced that the Punjabi civilians who were killed were in fact informers for the intelligence agencies. One of them claimed that "the BLA never killed anyone innocent. It has its own information cell to identify those who occupy our territory, or those who give information to government agencies. These are the matters of the guerrilla; we have no way of knowing better than them".[22]

The state is not only personified by the military presence in the streets, but also by the Punjabi population who is increasingly seen as its faithful representative. In this light, the recent targeting of individuals belonging to the Punjabi population is seen by many Baluch citizens living in Quetta as a political act against the domination of the Federal state.

The targeting of Punjabis has led to their large-scale migration from Baluch majority areas (such as Kili), selling their property to move to the city centre or other Pashtun areas in the province. I did not find anyone in Kili averse to these departures. The accounts I collected do not see the absence of settlers as having any significant incidence on their social space. The *nazim* expressed the following position about this population and the threat they are faced with:

> We are compelled to take the votes from the settlers because, as a city *nazim*, there is a need to get the votes. So if the settlers represent 48 votes, we are compelled to be in contact with them. (...) Before, there were many settlers here, but they have moved because of the violence. Most murders do not take place here, but in the city centre where most of the Punjabis live. Yet here, they are still afraid and they leave. If they leave, they do not tell the *nazim*. They do what they want. I am not responsible for everyone, and if they want to go, I cannot keep them from doing so. If I tell them to stay and they get killed, then they will consider me responsible for the murder. The government would like the *nazim* to do everything, including police work; but we cannot do that. (...) To me, it is up to them to decide whether they stay or leave.[23]

The *nazim* further justifies the distance he takes regarding the plight of Punjabi families living in his zone of influence by his fear of attracting disapproval from the Baluch nationalists. In these circumstances, the Punjabi population is dangerous to support and easier to neglect. All my discussions with Baluch villagers in Kili corroborate this lack of interest for the predicament of these displaced families. Even when showing sympathy for their fate, the villagers never mentioned neighborly relations, acting as a good host, extending protection, or any other social behaviour which they would otherwise be prone to boast as values specific to the Baluch culture. This situation is in ways similar to the radical shift, observed by Elisabeth Claverie (Claverie, 2004, 15–30), by which "neighbours" become "enemies" in the context of conflict, with the opposition principle thus prevailing over integration in a social network. On his end, the *nazim* has both taken up office as mayor, and is supported by voters who also oppose the state. By choosing not to protect the Punjabi settlers; the *nazim* is also taking an ostensible stance against the state, which has not gone unnoticed. In fact he today keeps a low profile, avoiding his own domicile for fear of being abducted by the "agencies".

Since Punjabis personify the state in the eyes of Baluch nationalist sympathizers, they have to show their sympathy and solidarity for the nationalist struggle if they are to stay in such quarters as Killi. The PIB political party (*Punjabi Ittehad Baluchistan*) was set up in late 2006 with the main objective of obtaining protection for the Punjabi population of Quetta, by asserting their political neutrality regarding the skirmishes between the Baluch and the government. Despite their official slogans supporting Baluch and Pashtun civilians, they did not convince the Baluch nationalists. On 27 May 2007 an explosive was thrown at the house of Dr. Aziz Qureshi, the PIB President. In November 2007 the killing of Balaach Marri triggered riots during which the PIB offices were burned down. The people I interviewed generally consider the PIB as an opportunistic party seeking to protect its followers without supporting the Baluch cause.

It must be recalled that most of the Punjabi families migrated to Quetta in the late nineteenth century when the British established the city as an administrative centre for Baluchistan. Despite having been settled there for numerous years, they still bare the stigma of their outside origins, and are seen as being imported by the state to govern tribal populations. The Punjabis are increasingly targeted by armed attacks in as much as they are stigmatized as "colonizers"; and while many Punjabi families have no affiliation with government institutions, they still need to prove they have no involvement in any government schemes. Some go so far as to argue that protecting them is tantamount to opposing the guerrilla movement and the equivalent of coming to terms with the government. What seemed negotiable in the 1970s—securing the rights and protection of civil populations established in the Province for several generations—is no longer discussed today. The unprecedented trend of large-scale Punjabi self-exile from certain quarters of the city, and from Quetta itself, can be partly understood by the fact that they have constantly been marginalized from the tribal social space.

As settlers, Punjabis are not considered part of the city, and their departure leaves many Baluch indifferent. Yet to what extent do the other groups of inhabitants really belong to this place? The demography of Quetta has been shaped by circumstances and numerous waves of migration. It was established according to the administrative needs of a colonial power at the crossroads between two major tribal groups, and in accordance with the economic needs of a growing urban hub. As a result, nobody really claims ownership of the city. The question as to which group had power over this urban centre prior to the British is still a matter of discussion amongst Baluch and Pashtuns, but the recent Baluch uprising has tended to leave it to one side and not taken any firm stand on it, treating the control and ownership of Quetta as a secondary concern.

Multiple Ownership of a Negotiation Playground

The city of Quetta is at the confluence of the Pashtun and Baluch tribal zones. Both people keep an old dispute alive regarding its ownership. The fact that it was originally built on land belonging to the Pashtun Kassi tribe is an accepted fact by both parties. But the Baluch claim that the town was given to the Khan of Kalat, at the head of a Baluch Confederacy (Samin, 1987),[24] by the Afghan king Ahmad Shah Abdali (1722–1772). When the British first asserted control over the region to set up garrisons and ensure access to Afghanistan (1839–1840) they took part of the Khan's territory on lease, including Quetta, the Bolan Pass, Kachhi, Jahl Magsi and Noshki (Baluch, 1990, 252–3; Hugues, 1877).[25] From then on, Quetta became what has already been described as a buffer zone and colonial enclave, slowly evolving into an urban and economic hub. As the nationalist ideologies developed amongst both Baluch and Pashtuns, the ownership of Quetta became a growing territorial stake and reached its peak in the 1970s when both were arguing as to where the boundaries of "Greater Pashtunistan" and "Greater Baluchistan" should meet. The pragmatic stake of possessing the already developed provincial capital had to be reconciled with an ideological principle grounded in history. Both groups claimed the territory on different historical basis: one arguing that the land originally belonged to the Kassi tribe, the other that the administrative rights had legally been transferred to the Kalat Confederacy.

Apart from the historical debate, Quetta is subject to economic competition where the Pashtuns are in the lead. Their economic predominance is linked to several factors, the most prominent of which are: the greater economic development of Pashtun areas during the colonial years (Hussain, 1986); the fact that Pashtuns and Punjabis took over the trades vacated by departing Hindus and Sikhs in 1947 (Holland, 1985, 226–7); the large-scale arrival of Afghan refugees since 1979, who hooked up with Pashtun networks once they left the camps; the access to lucrative smuggling routes from Afghanistan; the fact that their tribal land was situated in areas suitable for the development of agriculture activities (Titus, 1996, 292–93); and a wider international commercial network (Spain, 1962, 22). As a result, the Pashtuns now dominate trade in Quetta, and in Baluchistan in general. Through trade, they have conquered entire areas of the urban space, thus reversing the Baluch expansionist tendency analysed by Fredrik Barth in 1963 (Barth, 1981, 83–102).[26]

The relationship between Pashtuns and Baluch was a recurrent theme in my conversations about Quetta and its recent changes. Interestingly, the question of ownership is always left in abeyance, or eluded with sentences such as: "we will see this when the time comes". During one of these discussions, a *mawlwi* (religious scholar) of Kili observed:

> Quetta is a good example of the friendship that prevails between Baluch and Pashtuns; because the respective areas are clearly separated and defined. The Pashtuns are not against us, but they are not for our struggle either. But because the areas are separate, we remain in good terms. The issue on which we fight is the government subsidies. (...) There can be some tensions, for example on the question of quotas,[27] and these types of things. But we think that the Pashtuns should be a free nation. Pashtuns are the same as Afghans. The question as to who owns Quetta is not a problem. Of course, some people say things ... but they will decide. There will be a type of *jirga*. When we will be free, we will decide together.[28]

I repeatedly heard, from Baluch and Pashtuns alike, that the territorial ownership of Quetta is not a central issue today. During an interview, one member of the Baluch Student Organization (BSO) thought that the Pashtuns were "very active" in the 1980s and 1990s, but now "the situation has changed". According to him, the Pashtuns did not think that the Baluch movement would go this far, and they now have to deal with this new situation,[29] thus suggesting that the ongoing conflict, of which target killing is a part, offers a possibility to renegotiate, at least partially, the social relationship with the Pashtun tribes. The new political leverage over the Pashtuns can be measured in economic terms. Since 2006 Baluch organizations have very frequently called "shutter down" (imposing shops to close) and "wheel jam" (banning all public and commercial transport from the streets) strikes in Quetta, sometimes lasting for several days. Given that most shops are Pashtun-owned, these repeated events paralyzing most commercial networks have put considerable pressure on the Pashtun economy and, consequently, on Pashtun political representatives.

The relationship between the two groups remains ambivalent. Here, side by side, are two quotations, one from a Baluch nationalist sympathizer (Sangat) and one from a Pashtun who is heavily involved in tribal and mainstream politics (Khan):

> Sangat: Pashtuns are very happy. Today it is the Baluch who are oppressed, while they, they wait for their turn. There is no collaboration between us. (...) To

answer your question as to who controls Quetta, what happened in the 1980s [when two transporters, respectively Baluch and Pashtun, clashed and provoked a conflict leaving a dozen people dead][30] is an example: no *jirga* took place, nothing, but we managed to solve the problem. Since then, no such tension ever arose. There have been skirmishes on the University campus, as usual, and some threats. But Pashtuns cannot afford to fight against us, because of the trade; which means that the Pashtuns are lucky to have such good clients as us. (...) You will not see any Baluch in the Pahstun areas, whereas the Pashtuns are everywhere. (...) It is the same thing for us: we cannot afford to fight against them.[31]

Khan: Quetta is governed by the Pashtuns. If it goes on like this, the Baluch will continue selling their land, and there will be more and more Pashtuns in the city. (...) People come to see me from everywhere (...) especially regarding this misunderstanding between Baluch and Pashtuns. These are the major tribes. Without the Baluch, the Pashtuns are weak; and without the Pashtuns, the Baluch are weak. If they say: "we have the Gwadar Port", we can say that we have the boundary with Afghanistan and Iran. The fact is that both parties are in a strong position. So, we need to do something before the situation becomes bad between our two nations. Separation is... what can I say? Baluch and Pashtuns are already separate. What they do, they do on their own. But the situation in Baluchistan is now so difficult, and this province is so backward, that we have to consider ourselves like brothers.[32]

Both of them remember the confrontation between the two transporters, the subsequent spontaneous popular uprising and the numerous deaths, as the last major Baluch-Pashtun conflict in the city. Describing the event, Paul Titus's principle analysis is that "the main effect of violence on the transport industry and the Quetta politics has been a polarization along tribal lines" (Titus, 1996, 289). Indeed, those I interviewed stressed that this particular conflict and similar ones are better solved by negotiations between the two groups via the mediation of a tribal authority, than by the government judicial system. Along this line of thought, Khan asserts: "those who go to the police regret it, and come back to see the tribal chiefs. The more the security situation deteriorates, the more our workload [as tribal chiefs] increases".[33] The same tribal logic applied with Ghulam who, instead of seeking support from government representatives or supported organizations, went to the BRP (Baluch Republican Party) which he deems best suited to protect him from his tribe's vendetta.

But rather than considering this polarization as an effect of violence, I would argue that violence itself and its resolution are based on an existing polarization occurring along tribal lines and extensively underlying social relationships within the urban context. In the case of the transporters' rift of the 1980s, influential members of both groups intervened and a compromise was reached which prevented the recurrence of such outbursts. Today, although the Baluch-Pashtun ethnic divide is all-pervasive in political mobilization, government jobs, and resource allocation, instances of open conflict between the two main ethnic groups remain relatively rare (Gazdar et al. 2010, 30).

In other words, the way violence has developed in Quetta over the years, with the recent numerous bomb attacks and target killings, is more a symptom of the nature of the city's social fabric, than a cause of radical transformation or shifts. The effect on the other hand, beyond the original (political or economical) motivation of the act itself (control over a traffic route, acquiring political strength, weakening the government's writ, etc.), is a possible renegotiation of the balance between the existing polarizations. Being at the crossroad of the two major tribal groups, and being home to both government representatives and settler populations, Quetta is naturally the main arena for these negotiations. While everyone owns part of it, nobody owns the city as a whole, thus creating a microcosm reflecting the different types of social and political relations that prevail in the province and the country at large.

Conclusion

Whilst the Baluch nationalist politically motivated violence in Quetta has not created group polarization in the city, it did have an effect on existing forms of polarization, creating opportunities for renegotiating group stances. It has stimulated a reaction against Punjabis in as much as they personify the Federal Government's presence in Baluchistan, something considered by many politically oriented Baluch as state colonization. Justifying attacks against Punjabis feeds into the existing tendency to exclude this group from the Baluch social fabric and networks. Similarly, the violence is translated into a show of strength of the Baluch in general, offering an opportunity to renegotiate the ambivalent relationship between them and the Pashtuns. The violence destabilizes and discredits government institutions, thus enhancing the existing propensity to turn to other decisional and regulatory mechanisms based on tribal structures and economic stakes. Baluch and Pashtuns are drawn towards negotiating their power relations, their interdependence, and their respective relations with the state.

Although control over the city of Quetta is often seen as the most conspicuous source of rivalry between Pashtuns and Baluch, this has, in fact, become a secondary matter. The guerrilla attacks target infrastructure, institutions, and powerful figures or individuals symbolizing state occupation. Yet they have not led to an increased territorial control by the Baluch. In no instance has the violence committed by Baluch guerrilla fighters been viewed as territorial conquest of the city. The goal is not to control or to conquer Quetta as a whole, and the question of who owns the city, which would spark off direct confrontation between the two groups, has been put on hold.

This being said, the localized competition to take over urban spaces remains intense (especially through the acquisition of real estate, an area in which Pashtun and Hazara populations continue to have the upper hand). Territorial boundaries within the city, which were already relatively clearly defined, have been further strengthened during these years of violence. Certain areas have become out of bounds to "outsiders", such as the Baluch zones of 'Sariab Road' for the Punjabi population. This homogenization of urban zones can also be observed in Pashtun-Afghan areas (Kharotabad and Pashtunabad), as well as Hazara (Mariabad and Hazara Town). While the central areas are still mixed, territorial partitioning on its immediate outskirts continues to crystallize. The "villages" (*kili*) are each controlled by a dominant group. This does not reflect an attempt by specific groups to establish a homogenous presence in the city, but corresponds to the assertion of their identity within circumscribed territories. Similarly the goal of violence in Quetta is not territorial conquest. The violent acts committed by Baluch nationalists add themselves to a complex series of social and political tensions. The capital of the Province is an arena where the government can be destabilized, rather than a territory to be occupied, re-conquered, or liberated. With its scattered and heterogeneous population, Quetta remains a city of circumstances, a city of negotiations between groups, living up to its original purpose imagined by the colonial administration. The political arena it has become is today fostering the crystallization of goup identities emerging against destabilized national institutions.

11

GRADUATING TO VIOLENCE

THE ESCALATION OF STUDENT STRIFE
AT KARACHI UNIVERSITY, 1979–1989[1]

Laurent Gayer

« [...] *Jab shabab par akar*
Khet lahlhata hai [...] »

When the young arrive
The wind starts blowing over the fields.

Habib Jalib (1928–1993), "*Jamhuriat*" (Democracy).[2]

Social sciences and political science in particular have generally been more concerned with the "root causes" or "raw conditions" (Horowitz, 1989) of political violence than with the way it unfolds. Dominant approaches have hitherto focused on why men rebel, kill, and get killed, rather than how. But this search for "background explanations" (Collins, 2008, 20), based on the study of motivations and opportunities (Boix, 2008), exposes itself to several pitfalls. The first consists in assigning motivations to these actors—and particularly those involved in acts of self-sacrificial violence—without even bothering to consider what they have to say about their own actions (Horgan, 2009, 15),[3] resulting in "fictions that justify our responses but that we cannot verify" (Asad, 2007, 3). And when social scientists do bother to talk to these actors, it is generally to record narratives of past engagement and violence, which often leads to conflating their justifications with their motivations, while—wrongly—assuming that "violence is easy once the motivation exists"(Collins, 2008, 20). Lastly, this search for causation often leads to equating the factors igniting the conflict with those sustaining it. This is particularly common with processes of social and political polarization: although many analysts see polarization as a prerequisite for conflict, it may in fact be a by-product of the conflict, "its effect rather than its cause" (Kalyvas, 2006, 76). The violent re-socialization of combatants through violence, the effects of state repression on the civilian population, and new power equations arising from the conflict all point to the performative dimension of political violence. In other words, violence is not merely the outcome of social, economic, and political changes predating the conflict; it also takes unanticipated courses and tends to reproduce itself by generating its own causalities. This is as true at the individual as at the collective level: new costs or incentives to participate generated in the course of the conflict may lead individuals to join in or defect at different stages, while social polarization and violence may be endogenous to the conflict (Kalyvas, 2006) and for some belligerents warfare may be a prerequisite for their social reproduction and political survival. This requires us to "put the interaction in the center of the analysis, not the individual, the social background, the culture, or even the motivation"(Collins, 2008, 1). Violence should be treated as a "situational process" (Collins, 2008, 19) and the proper subject of investigation lies in "the sequence of decisions and events that intersect to produce [it]" (Kalyvas, 2006, 22) as well as in those that sustain, contain, or escalate it.

The principal concern here is with the most understudied of these conflict dynamics: violent escalation. What are the mechanisms at play in the shift from one sequence of a conflict to another? What are the technological and organizational contexts in which they operate? How are they related to changes in the social identities of the protagonists and in the maneuvers of the state? These are some of the questions that will be addressed here through an exploration of student violence at the University of Karachi, Pakistan, between 1979 and 1989. During this period there was a spectacular rise in student violence in this university, from fistfights to gunfights (in 1979), to "political" assassinations (from 1981 onwards), and culminating in a massacre (in 1989). On one occasion, this violence spilled over from the campuses and acquired an international dimension (when a PIA airplane was hijacked in March 1981 by a group of student militants). During the second half of the 1980s, it also spread through the city of Karachi, fueling larger social and political conflicts. This case study will therefore consider two different aspects of the dynamics of conflict escalation: that of intensification (which concerns the magnitude of the violence in terms of casualties) and that of expansion (which concerns the amplitude of the violence in spatial terms).

The Prerequisite Conditions for Lethal Violence

Until the late 1970s, skirmishes between leftwing and Islamist student activists at Karachi University (KU) were relatively benign and mainly involved fistfights. A former progressive student leader, who later became the mayor of Karachi, remembers that, "at the end of the 70s, when someone pulled out a knife, it was a really big deal".[4] The escalation of student violence at KU from the late 1970s onwards alienated female student activists, who deserted student politics en masse. Young men were left to their own devices and to their politics of "masculinity" (Chenoy, 2002, 18) in what gradually evolved into a campus war. This escalation of violence at KU was not a sudden, unpredictable development. It was made possible by changes in local warfare technologies, in the manoeuvres of the state, and in dynamics of small groups within student organizations. However, these prerequisite conditions for lethal violence should not be mistaken for causal factors: they facilitated the recourse to lethal violence, but in no way did they trigger it.

Changes in the Technology of Student Warfare

The patterns of student violence started changing with the inflow of firearms to Karachi campuses. Modern weaponry (Sten guns and revolvers, and later Kalashnikovs, locally known as *klashni*s) was introduced onto the campus by the militants of the Islami Jamiat-e-Talaba (IJT)'s "Thunder Squad".[5] They had probably acquired them in the weapons markets of Khyber Agency, and maybe directly from some *mujahidin* factions (such as Gulbuddin Hekmatyar's Hizb-e-Islami, which received a delegation of IJT members in Peshawar as early as 1975).

Leftist and pro-Pakistan People's Party (PPP) student organizations initially had greater difficulty obtaining weapons. In its initial years, the United

Students Movement (USM), a platform of progressive and nationalist student groups,[6] turned to Baloch musclemen to ensure its security and used the Baloch Students Organization's connections to procure its first weapons. Among IJT rivals, the Peoples Students Federation (PSF)[7] was the first organization to acquire fire-power. In 1979 a group of PSF students managed to get hold of a delivery of weapons intended for the IJT. As recalled by one of the participants to this arms raid, PSF leader Akram Qaim Khani:

> We captured all those bags. They were full of pistols, Sten guns, knives… Hundreds of them… That was the day we became rich in Karachi, when we realized that we could conquer all Karachi. Jama'at was vanished from Karachi University for a month. Not a single one of them went outside because they knew that we had guns now. It was the first time that we had seen so many guns. Then the thinkers, the political people [such as himself] realized that something was happening. How come they had that many revolvers and were bringing them into Karachi University? 500 revolvers and Sten guns? What was happening? Everybody realized that things in Karachi were about to change.[8]

As this testimony suggests, changes in student warfare technology, against the backdrop of the Afghan *jihad*, transformed the ontology of the conflict in the eyes of its protagonists. Until then, the power and influence of student organizations were primarily measured by their results in student union elections. But with the militarization of student organizations (by 1982 IJT, PSF, PkSF, BSO, and USM all had a veritable arsenal stash in the hostels under their control, including AK-47s), their actual power became conditional upon their military strength. The stakes of the conflict also became higher, with student organizations now detaining the ambitions of "conquering" the city campuses by "vanishing" their rivals, to use Akram Qaim Khani's words. This representation of the conflict as a fight to the finish, based upon a new way of perceiving the adversary, represented a clear departure from past ways of conceiving of student strife. Until the arrival of weapons and the first gunshot incidents, the distinction between friends and enemies remained blurred by mutual benevolence, if not mutual "respect", as suggested by Akram Qaim Khani:

> We might have had differences but we had respect for each other, like 'I am in politics, he is also in politics'. […] After the NSF broke with Bhutto and I had to go underground, I was given shelter by a local *nazim* of the IJT in my neighbourhood [Shah Faisal Colony]. So we fought but also respected each other.[9]

Although this testimony might be informed by nostalgia for a supposedly "golden age" of student politics ("respect" is a big word indeed for rivals who regularly clashed and denigrated each other with highly derogatory language), it should not be entirely dismissed as an idealized reconstruction of the past. It suggests that, at least at the level of representations, something changed in Karachi student politics at the turn of the 1970s, with the ontology of the conflict taking on a more "Schmittian" dimension in the eyes of its protagonists.[10] In other words, the changes that occurred in the technology and practices of student warfare seem to have transformed its representations, rather than the other way round. Behavioural changes came first, attitudes adjusted later.

State Complicity

This weapons procurement spree was tolerated, if not encouraged, by the regime of General Zia-ul-Haq which sought to reduce the influence of left-wing and pro-PPP forces on the campuses. The participation of the Jama'at-e-Islami in Zia's government also guaranteed Islamist student activists political protection when they flouted the law.

By facilitating the militarization of its IJT protégés, the Zia regime helped "mak[e] violence conceivable; so that it was thinkable and deemed ordinary and inevitable" (Butt, 2009, 15). Yet this state-centric explanation of the increase in student violence on Pakistan's campuses does not provide the full picture. It tends to neglect the forces at play within student organizations, and the new dynamics within student activism arising from internal power shifts. The Zia regime certainly facilitated the militarization of student politics, hoping that the "muscularization" of the IJT would silence left-wing and pro-PPP troublemakers. Yet it is far less clear whether the state played a role in making violence ordinary, at both the practical and the psychological level. Certain Pakistani authors see the Zia regime as the agent to blame not only for the rise of the rightists but also for the brutalization of students by "encroaching upon the cognitive and social constructs of the polity's educated inhabitants". The authors further clarify their stand, by suggesting that "convictions were instilled that made violence possible in the social, political and religious spheres" (Butt, 2009, 15). In other words, the escalation of violence on the country's campuses is said to have been the outcome of a culture of violence patronized by the military regime of Zia-ul-Haq. But cultural or "cognitive" explanations of political violence tend to reify their object, obliterating the social identities of the actors (who are always party to a plurality of social worlds and value systems) and intragroup dynamics (which may be far more effective in constraining individuals than exogenous ideas and vague sentiments).

Changes in the Small Group Dynamics of Student Organizations

The arrival of weapons on the campus was a source of bewilderment for political activists of the time. According to the former General Secretary of the USM, Fahim Khan, "[w]e never decided to become militants, it just happened".[11] This narrative of bewilderment is also one of disempowerment, as it expresses the frustration of these political workers at having gradually lost the initiative to the supposedly more unpredictable militants. Thus whilst political workers such as Fahim Khan claim that "[w]e never wanted violence to replace politics", they nevertheless concede that they had to rely on armed militants for their survival: "[w]hen we came under threat [from the IJT], we needed someone to fire back. Lives were at stake". The relation between activists (*karkun*s) and militants (*jangju*s) was not strictly functional though, and unfolded in a complex emotional context. Militants inspired fear, but also awe, and their impulsivity was not always considered a liability but was also seen as a political virtue infusing the group with energy. This was particularly true as regards the PSF. Under Bhutto's leadership, the PPP had been encouraging the recruitment of party workers from the lower middle class, known for their enthusiasm and loyalty to the Bhutto family. These brave and reckless party workers of low social origins were known as *jiyala*s, and were seen by the party leadership as one of its major assets. Thus the unpredictable and impulsive behavior of militants such as Tipu was as much praised by their comrades as it was feared. When recollecting the role played by Tipu in the aforementioned 1979 arms raid, Akram Qaim Khani does not blame him for having compromised his well thought out plan and having put the lives of his comrades at risk. Tipu's impatience (while his companions were reconnoitring the place, he pulled out a gun and started firing at Jamaati militants present) might have compromised the group's strategy, but it was also the sign of his courage, enthusiasm, and sense of initiative in a tough call. In these troubled times, excess was becoming a political virtue, particularly from the point of view of intellectuals who were as fascinated with violence as they were unfamiliar with it.

These militants were generally petty criminals (*badmash*) recruited from outside the campus to provide muscle to student organizations. The most notorious Thunder Squad militant, Raja Javed, was a Punjabi and the son of a police officer, and he was already involved in petty crime when he joined the IJT. He worked in tandem with another petty criminal, Noshah, and both were later hanged for their involvement in a series of (non-political) murders in the early 80s. Although leftist and pro-PPP student unions were initially hostile to the involvement of outsiders in student conflicts, they promptly emulated this trend. Thus according to Akram Qaim Khani:

> We managed to get these people admitted to the university and colleges, so that we at least had some protection. There was a very famous badmash, Shabir. After that he joined MQM. I got him admitted to Jamia Milia. Then the first day he cut the face of a famous Jama'ati badmash, Mehbub Chishti, who also joined MQM later on. Then we were free to come and go as we liked.[12]

The involvement of these outsiders with a criminal background and familiarity with weapons directly contributed to the escalation of violence on the campus, as shall be seen in detail in the following section. The first viral incident occurred in 1979, at the initiative of the IJT's Thunder Squad. During the swearing-in ceremony of the new members of the student union, notorious Thunder Squad militants Raja Javed and Noshah opened fire with Sten guns on a group of progressive students. One of them, Yunus Shad, was injured and, though he survived this incident, this constituted a major breach in the informal code of conduct of student organizations. Yet the escalation of violence was not a mechanical process, and despite what is suggested by some of the testimonies quoted above, there was nothing "natural" about the increasing number of killings on the campus, which took student conflicts to a whole new level.

The Unfolding of a Critical Event: The First "Political" Murder at KU

At the turn of the 1970s, all was set at KU for a large-scale confrontation between left-wing and Islamist student organizations. The two parties had been acquiring modern weaponry while recruiting petty criminals with firearm expertise, thus making it operational. State authorities, which had the power to stop or at least contain this militarization of student organizations, had not stepped in for political reasons. And lastly, the rise of the militants within student organizations, courtesy of their militarization, played in favor of a more confrontational form of politics. And yet there was nothing mechanical in the spiral of violence that engulfed the university in the early 1980s. The incident which triggered this sudden rise in violence at KU was predictable. But it was also strongly contingent and, as such, was dealt with in an ad hoc and haphazard way. The following section focuses on the dynamics of this "violent situation" in a micro-sociological perspective, which aims to "capture the process of violence as it is actually performed" (Collins, 2008).

Predictable but Contingent: Hafiz Aslam's "Murder"

The unfolding of events which led to the first "political" killing at KU suggests that it was not premeditated and that, however predictable it may have been, it also had a strongly contingent dimension. As shall be seen, the contingency of this critical event was apparent at three distinct levels: it was indeterminate (things could have turned out differently), conditional (founded on the prerequisite conditions set out above), and uncertain (the igniting event had not been anticipated by the protagonists, who had to improvise how to react to it).[13]

On 25 February 1981, a group of NSF students gathering at KU Arts Faculty lobby for a demonstration in downtown Karachi heard that a military jeep was parked in front of the Administration building. An army major had come to help his daughter get admitted to the university and, though he was there for personal reasons, the students were enraged. As the organizer of the demonstration, Akram Qaim Khani, recalls, "it was a surprise. It was a challenge to us. I was a student leader and the army was in my university..." At Khani's instigation, the fifty-odd crowd set off for the administration building, collected petrol from parked cars, filled a Coca-Cola bottle with it and set fire to the jeep. Khani claims that he saved the driver ("he ran away, anyway...") so no one was hurt in the incident, but while the jeep was burning, a group of Thunder Squad militants arrived on the scene and assaulted the agitators. Khani (who contracted polio in his childhood and thus suffered from limited mobility) had been spared from physical assault in the past ("even the big *badmash* thought 'we cannot touch Akram, otherwise his friends will kill us'"), but this time he was roughed up by Thunder Squad militants "Farooq" and Zarar Khan, and he was eventually captured, detained, and delivered to the army which arrested him. As Khani suspected, his powerful friends decided to retaliate and the next day an enraged PSF militant came to the university to exact revenge. Salamullah Tipu, referred to in the account of the 1979 arms raid above, was the PSF's own "big *badmash*". He had returned to Pakistan (from Afghanistan) in January 1981 and was in hiding in Karachi when he heard the news of Akram Qaim Khani's arrest. Despite his mission (Murtaza Bhutto had given him the responsibility of hijacking a PIA plane to protest against the execution of his father, Z.A. Bhutto, by General Zia), he decided to avenge his friend's ill-treatment at the hands of the IJT. When he arrived on the campus, the day after Khani's arrest, he went looking for IJT militants and as soon as he came across a group of them opened fire with a Sten gun and threw a couple of grenades in their direction. When the assault was over a senior IJT activist, Hafiz Aslam, lay dead. Tipu, who was known for his impulsivity, probably fired haphazardly at the IJT group and Aslam might have been killed by a stray bullet. In any case, the use of such firepower by a left-wing militant was unprecedented and baffled the entire student community, including Tipu's comrades ("We were surprised... We did not even know where he had got these grenades from", declares Akram Qain Khani). Khani was brutally tortured over the following weeks, until Tipu managed to obtain his liberation (and that of 53 other political prisoners) by fulfilling his mission to hijack a PIA flight from Karachi to Damascus—via Kabul—the next month (March 1981). In organizing this hijacking, Tipu was also trying to ensure his own survival, since he was facing the wrath of the JI (at the time part of the government) for his involvement in Hafiz Aslam's murder.

The Aftermath of Hafiz Aslam's Murder

A banal incident of arson thus set in motion a chain of events that ended up with a murder, an act of international terrorism[14] and the development of a transnational armed struggle led by the terrorist organization formalized by Murtaza Bhutto shortly after the hijacking, al-Zulfiqar. Incidentally, many early recruits of the group were former student activists, who graduated to international terrorism after joining al-Zulfiqar in Damascus or later on in Kabul. Far from being a smooth process, this evolution was a source of tremendous tensions, which once again were less the outcome of ideological or strategic considerations per se than of small group dynamics within the emerging al-Zulfiqar Organization (AZO). These included factionalization on a linguistic basis (with student activists from Karachi cultivating their difference and limiting their interactions with those from the Punjab, interior Sindh and the Frontier) and, even more importantly for the future of the group, intense power struggles nurturing a climate of suspicion that undermined the group's unity. Thus, soon after regrouping in Damascus with the detainees (most of them PSF activists) freshly freed by Tipu and his two comrades, Murtaza started passing execution orders against "traitors", a move which led some potential recruits to dissociate themselves from al-Zulfiqar. Following these protests, Murtaza denied passing such orders and accused Tipu of trying to discredit him, before adding that the success of the hijacking had gone to this head and that he now thought of himself as a new Yasser Arafat.[15] These power struggles were irreducible to a clash of egos between two unstable personalities, however, and also had to do with the competition over the political and moral leadership of the group between a political leader thinking of himself as a militant and a militant aspiring to become a political leader. In the middle stood former student activists who continued to see themselves as political workers but who gradually drifted towards militancy, under the leadership of their maverick leader but also in conformity and solidarity with their comrades. This was the case, for instance, of PSF activist Asif Butt, who initially refused to get involved in Murtaza's schemes—"I'm not a son of a bitch who [...] will shed blood, only to find myself facing the hangman's noose", he told his comrades shortly after their arrival in Damascus. Despite his abhorrence of violence and his reservations about the Soviets' patronage of AZO, Butt did eventually enroll in the group, under the influence of some of his companions. A few months later, he was arrested in Pakistan while preparing an assassination attempt on General Zia, which indeed led to his being sentenced to death (Butt, 2014, 62). This is not to say that this process of radicalization was not inevitable. Despite the intense dynamics of peer pressure that prevailed among the fifty-four former prisoners set free by the hijackers, only 28 joined Murtaza in Kabul to organize the armed struggle against the Zia regime (Butt, 2014, 71).

The consequences of Hafiz Aslam's death for KU student politics were no less remarkable. Tipu had not only committed a murder: even if it had not been his intention, he had redefined the rules of student strife and elevated it to the level of warfare. Guns had spoken and no one seemed able, or even willing, to silence them. In December 1981, a Punjabi Students Association (PSA) militant, Shaukat Cheema, was shot dead by IJT militants while passing in front of a mosque controlled by the Islamists. A few days later, elections to the students' union were organized and were marked by gunfights between militants of rival organizations, using student hostels as shelter. The following day, a leader of the Thunder Squad, Danish Ghani, was killed by USM militants led by the BSO's strongman, Boro, and by a PSF militant, Shirin Khan. A few months later, on 1 July 1982, it was the turn of a progressive activist, Qadir Abid, to fall to the bullets of the IJT during an attack on a USM stand. Again, it is not clear if this murder was intentional or if, as some of Qadir's friends claim, he was hit by a stray bullet during the gun fight.[16] What was clear was that the patterns of violence had changed in a matter of a few months. Gun battles and targeted killings were now taking place on a regular basis and most student activists had started sporting guns, for security purposes but also to conform to the general trend. Lethal violence was no longer extraordinary. It had become routine due to everyday procedures, language and attitudes, to such an extent that the involvement in violent groups and actions was now seen as a "natural" process occurring independently of agency and as something one was subjected to, as the following quote from a former PSF activist suggests:

> I was with the PSF and I ended up carrying a gun. What was the reason for that? I don't know. The reason given was always security. Otherwise you become an easy target. There was also the politics of numbers [after the ban on students unions in 1984, the power of each student organization was principally measured in terms of military strength]. [...] There was a lot of show as well.[17]

What is striking in this account, apart from the reflexive abilities of the speaker (presently a well-known columnist for a major daily newspaper), is his complete denial of agency in the description of his becoming a "militant". In the same way that Fahim Khan recalls the militarization of his own group, this former student activist suggests that he was acted upon by routines of violence. The striking image of the gun that simply "ended up" in his hands exemplifies the process by which violence—or at least its possibility—may become a routine incorporated into everyday life.

Escalation as a by-product of the Conflict

However contingent it may have been, Hafiz Aslam's murder set in motion a process of violent escalation which was made possible and accelerated by the changes set out above in student warfare technology, in the positioning of the state, and in small group dynamics within student organizations. None of these variables was, in itself, a causal factor for increased violence. Yet after Hafiz Aslam's murder they all worked together to escalate violence, with the militants asserting their authority and conception of politics within student organizations, thanks to their modern weaponry and, at least in the case of the IJT, the covert support of the state.

In the second half of the 1980s, student violence at KU entered a new phase which proved even bloodier than the preceding ones. Once again the role of the state is undeniable: the ban on student politics reinforced its militarization, and the covert support lent by the Zia regime to the Mohajir Qaumi Movement (MQM) radically changed power equations at KU and in Karachi at large. But the MQM was not simply the creature of the military establishment, it also pursued its own agenda and was very much a product of the violent world of student politics which took shape at KU at the turn of the 1970s. In this new phase of the conflict, the escalation of violence was thus largely a by-product of the conflict itself, as it sustained new political polariza-tions, new routines of belligerence, and new thresholds of acceptable violence, where transgression could only lead to capitulation or escalation on the part of the aggrieved party. After Hafiz Aslam's murder, such a transgression of the informal code of conduct of the belligerents occurred for a second time with the 1989 "gymnasium massacre" perpetrated by APMSO activists on their PSF rivals. However by then the impulsion behind such acts of violence no longer came from the student leadership but from party officials. Student violence was now an integral part of a larger conflict, where what was at stake was no longer the control of the campuses but that of the city at large.

The Role of the State

In 1984 General Zia-ul-Haq banned students unions and politics across Pakistan, justifying this on the basis of student violence, even though his motives were probably more political. In the short term this ban contributed to a rapprochement between the IJT and its rivals, with the IJT defying its mother party (which had approved the ban) to take part in protest marches alongside progressive and left-wing students in Karachi. For two months, IJT, PSF, and NSF activists confronted the police across the city and burnt dozens of vehicles. Violence seemed to be spilling out of the campuses and threatened to engulf the city. The situation might have got out of control for the military regime had the IJT not ended up complying with the JI's directive. But after a few months of agitation IJT activists returns to the fold, after having been given assurances that their organization would not be concerned by the ban. This betrayal and the threat of being evicted from KU led progressive and left-wing student activists to retaliate in a big way. They took over the hostels formerly under IJT control and stored weapons in them to deter the Islamists from counterattacking. Fearing an armed uprising, the police launched an operation against these progressive and left-wing militants at the end of the year. But they were met with stiff resistance and a veritable siege ensued, which lasted for more than ten hours. Police fire was returned by well-armed USM students and reinforcements had to be called in to evacuate the buildings where these embattled students had entrenched themselves. Surprisingly, there was no fatality on either side, although dozens were injured in the fighting.

Far from containing violence on the campuses, the ban reinforced the mili-tarization of student politics in the long run: from then on, the relative weight of each student organization was measured exclusively in terms of military capability. Student organizations were thus encouraged to acquire more weapons, and more sophisticated ones. The IJT's main rival, the USM, also built up a veritable arsenal via the same Peshawar-based arms dealers that had provided the IJT with modern weaponry in the early 1980s. Whereas the IJT had benefited from the JI's financial support to acquire arms, the USM had greater difficulty raising funds for the same purpose. PPP leaders were asked to contribute and, out of fear of reprisals, generally obliged. Several Pakhtun and Baloch politicians also contributed to this war effort.[18]

Unlike in the late 1970s and early 1980s, when weapons were stored in safe houses outside the campus, the increasing militarization of the conflict led student activists to store their arsenal in student hostels, either at KU or at the adjacent NED Engineering University. Within these hostels, entire rooms were used to stash guns, ammunition, and drugs. Snipers took position on the roof of these student residences and frequently engaged in gun fights with rivals occupying adjacent buildings. These incidents were particularly frequent between the IJT militants occupying the largest hostel of NED University and the USM militants who controlled the KU hostels, a few hundred metres north. By now student organizations had taken on the attributes of student militias, and the conflict had turned into a war of attrition, which cost the lives of sixty students between 1984 and 1988 (compared to twenty for the period 1981–1983).[19]

Products and Agents of Violence: The Formation of the MQM/APMSO War Machine

The second half of the 1980s was marked by the rise of a new party to the conflict, which aimed to represent and defend the interests of "Mohajirs", i.e. Urdu-speakers whose families migrated from India to Pakistan after Partition. This political force grew out of a student organization to become the city's most powerful—and dreadful—political party. The All Pakistan Mohajir Students Organisation (APMSO) was launched on 11 June 1978. Forcefully expelled from KU by the JI in 1981, its cadres launched a political party in 1984, the Mohajir Qaumi Movement (MQM). With the support of the military authorities, the MQM/APMSO strove to re-establish itself on the campuses. To this end it started requiring its own arsenal from 1984 onwards. After having obtained its first revolvers and Sten guns from progressive students, it started looking for Kalashnikovs. MQM officials had first encountered the *klashni* at Sindh University, in Hyderabad, in January 1986, when

Altaf Hussain, the MQM's supremo, was invited to attend G.M. Syed's birth-day.[20] Jiye Sindh militants (who later on became arch-rivals of the MQM) introduced MQM workers to the handling of modern weaponry, including AK-47s. After their return to Karachi, the participants went looking for their own *klashni* and it was not long before one of Altaf's "bodyguards", Javed Langra, came back with one (Hasnain, 1997, 33). In the following years, the MQM and the APMSO managed to build up a formidable arsenal and they attracted a number of hardened *badmash* previously affiliated with the IJT or with the progressives. These military capabilities were built up with the help of the NSF but also, more surprisingly, of the IJT, whose militants sold weap-ons to the APMSO in the second half of the 1980s (Hanif, 1989, 23). Thus in Karachi IJT and NSF arch rivals who sold weapons to the MQM contributed to its military build-up and ultimately to its military dominance, not only on the campuses but in the city at large.

The Geographical Expansion of "Student" Violence

The military build-up of the MQM, in the second half of the 1980s, coincided with the expansion of student violence across the city. Whereas previously the violence had been confined to the campuses, with the exception of a few cases of rioting (when rival organizations rioted together), the tussle between the APMSO and the IJT brought the conflict to the streets of the city. Rival mili-tants were kidnapped or targeted in their neighborhood and gun fights erupted in the streets. In August 1988, the death of an IJT militant led to armed encounters between IJT and APMSO across the city, in which more than fifty people were injured. The intensity of the violence led the authorities to close down KU, NED University, and Sindh Medical College for several months.[21]

One explanation for this expansion of the geographical scope of student violence resides in the resumption of democratic forms of expression in the last years of the Zia regime. The MQM's rise to power after the 1987 municipal elections was a direct challenge to the political hegemony of the JI, the parent body of the IJT, which had had a strong support base amongst Mohajirs since the 1950s. Thus the conflict was no longer primarily between student organiza-tions defending their local turf but between political parties competing for the control of the city as a whole. With Pakistan's reversion to democracy the stakes of the conflict became higher and the democratic transition, instead of containing it, actually amplified it. Rather than a mere continuity of the cam-pus war, this new sequence of political violence inaugurated a larger and deadlier conflict. This does not mean to say, however, that there was no continuity between these sequences: on the contrary, student activists turned party leaders, such as Altaf Hussain, recycled their experiences of the "campus war" into this new conflict. These former student activists had learnt to think in military terms[22] and had become familiar with modern technologies of warfare on the campuses. For Altaf Hussain and his companions, war was not so much the continuity of politics by other means as a precondition for ensuring their political survival, and for accessing to and remaining at the helm of political power. Had the APMSO been allowed to pursue its activities on the KU campus in the early 1980s, this might never have occurred. But the IJT ban of the APMSO led its officials to expand their activities, holding street-corner meetings given that they no longer had any office space (Athar, 1988, 45). The transformation of student violence, in the second half of the 1980s, was therefore doubly paradoxical, at least from the point of view of the "democratic peace" thesis: it was its shrinking structure of political opportunities that led the APMSO to shift to party politics, whereas the opening of new channels of democratic expression a few years later precipitated its militarization.

If these macro-political explanations, focusing on the changes taking place in the structure of political opportunities, can explain how the nature or more precisely the stakes of the conflict shifted, they are unable to explain the transformations in violent behavior at the individual and micro-group level. Unlike in the late 1970s, when the escalation of violence was largely a by-product of the take-over of student organizations by armed militants, this time it was the activists who took the lead at the expense of the militants. But this is not to say that many militants followed their leaders' directives. At this point it is necessary to examine the inner functioning of these militant micro-groups, which was clearly different from those of the 1970s and early 1980s.

The MQM militant force was built up around Altaf Hussain's "bodyguards", whose role was not limited to providing protection to party leaders but extended to more aggressive practices (kidnappings, torture, targeted killings, etc.). Altaf Hussain, with the firm intention of constituting his own private army, sent a first batch of his "bodyguards" to Afghanistan for military training in 1987.[23] When they returned, Altaf Hussain congratulated the young men and entrusted them with a new mission: imparting military training to others (Khan, 2010).

These militants were regrouped under the MQM's "Security Wing", which initially comprised two cells of seven militants each. Each of these cells corresponded to a "zone" covering half of Karachi. The activities and personalities of one of these two cells (that of "Zone C" based in Liaquatabad and covering Central Karachi) have recently been brought to light by Nichola Khan (Khan, 2010). This ground-breaking work on the inner world of the MQM's killers deserves special attention. Combining ethnographic observation with interview generated life-histories, Khan managed to get close to these elusive characters. Basing her argument on first-hand experience, she suggests that for MQM killers extreme violence provided access to and affirmation of a form of "hyper-masculinity", as well as a source of empowerment and status enhancement. In their testimonies, these militants suggest that the identity of their victims and the way they were killed was left to the initiative of their "leader". In some cases, these "leaders" are even said to have suggested using the most gruesome forms of violence to terrify the "enemies of the MQM". However it is difficult to distinguish between fact and fiction here. These former militants may be tempted to attribute moral responsibility for these atrocities to their "leaders", in order to live in peace with their pangs of memory. In the process, they downplay the role of peer pressure in their acts of extreme violence. Yet, following C. Browning's seminal study of the 101 reserve battalion of the German police during WWII (Browning, 1993), it is hard to believe that the increasing brutality of these killers (involving cases of bone drilling, mutilations, decapitations, etc.) was simply an expression of the ever-more bloody tactics of their leaders. I am more inclined to think that intense dynamics of peer pressure prevailed within these micro-groups, which encouraged each of their members (who often lived together) to emulate if not outsmart his peers by the sheer "creativity" of his macabre designs. "Excesses" would then have occurred at the confluence of party discipline and horizontal interactions which presented affinities with a "professional" competition.[24]

In addition to the formation of this "underground leadership cadre" (Khan, 2010) within the MQM, one last factor must be brought into the picture to explain the expansion of violence in Karachi in the second half of the 1980s. In 1985 and 1986, Karachi experienced a series of bloody "ethnic riots", which erupted in a context of unprecedented demographic, economic, and social changes. There is not sufficient space here to unravel the dynamics of these "rioting" incidents,[25] but suffice it to say, for the purposes of the present argument that the amplification of the violence from the campuses to the city as a whole was not entirely endogenous to student and party politics. It was also a by-product of the transformation of the city, and more particularly of its underground economy, with powerful Pakhtun drug barons trying to diversify their business activities and, in the process, moving into real estate, particularly in the largest slum of the city (and perhaps even in Asia), Orangi, the theatre for the worst cases of "ethnic" violence in 1985 and 1986. Far from triggering Karachi's conflicts, ethnicity only became a resource for mobilization and an interpretative framework for these conflicts after the 1985–86 riots. But once the main fault line in these conflicts shifted from internationalist ideologies to ethnicity, it proved to be more enduring. So much so that ethno-linguistic affinities remain the most powerful means of mobilization in Karachi more than thirty years after the city witnessed its first major "ethnic riot".

By expanding across the city, violence originating in the campuses changed form and intensified to reach an unprecedented level of brutality. This in turn translated into an intensification of student violence, replicating patterns of inter-party violence. Once again, the impact of the democratization process, and in particular the resumption of elections, is evident. In 1989 Prime Minister Benazir Bhutto lifted the ban on students unions, and elections were held the same year. Across the country the IJT paid the price for its collaboration with the Zia regime and was defeated by its rivals. Elections were not held in KU this year but the APMSO, followed by the PSF, defeated the IJT in several colleges of the city. With the IJT withering away, APMSO and PSF activists started flexing their muscles and competing for complete supremacy over the campus. Clashes soon erupted between the two groups at KU as well as in other major academic institutions (NED University, Dow Medical College, Sindh Medical College, etc.).

The most serious of these incidents occurred in late 1989 when a group of PSF militants clashed with their APMSO rivals at NED University. A gunfight ensued and PSF militants managed to push their rivals back into the KU campus. They seemed to be gaining the upper hand when they ran out of ammunition. Although they tried to obtain reinforcements from their comrades at Sindh Medical College (a 30-minute drive from NED University), the PSF boys were soon overpowered by their rivals, who irrupted in the NED hostel where they had taken shelter. The disarmed militants (six of them had been captured, while four others had managed to escape) were taken to the KU gymnasium and rounded up on the basketball court. After a few minutes, APMSO militants released them and ordered them to make a run for it. However, once the PSF militants started running to escape, they were all shot dead by APMSO militants.[26] Even if Karachiites had become accustomed to extreme forms of political violence, this incident sent a shockwave across the city. Violence erupted on all the major campuses, claiming dozens of lives on both sides, including that of the most well-known PSF militant, Najeeb

Ahmad, who was ambushed by a group of APMSO militants. These clashes placed a severe strain on the cooperation between the PPP and the MQM (who were then coalition partners in Islamabad) and precipitated their break up, soon made official by the MQM decision to quit the government and join the opposition. In 1991–92 the conflict between PSF/PPP and APMSO/MQM reached its climax, with Mohajir militants being used by the chief minister of the time, Jam Sadiq Ali, to crush the PPP. By now, the MQM and its student wing were running Karachi as a personal fiefdom, going as far as assaulting outsiders who dared enter their bastions. It was one of these incidents—the kidnapping and torturing of an army major in Landhi, in the south-east of the city—that prompted the army to react. In June 1992 the Chief of Army Staff ordered his troops to enter Karachi to teach the MQM a lesson. This military operation (codenamed "Operation Clean Up"), which ran until 1994, brought the MQM to heel but didn't break it. And when the army finally left the city, the party celebrated its "victory". An uneasy calm prevailed on the campuses, with paramilitary forces deployed at strategic points all across the KU campus. This show of force succeeded in curbing the violence, but did not entirely eradicate it. More importantly, the Rangers' primary concern was with incidents of lethal violence, and they did not interfere in student politics as such. Given the situation, the APMSO has managed to retain its hold over the campus, though the IJT has made a successful comeback in recent years. At present, a precarious balance of power prevails at KU, and although deadly clashes erupted in 2007 and 2008, students and teachers alike consider the situation to be "manageable".[27] In fact, this perception has less to do with any drop in student violence, which is yet to materialize, than with mechanisms developed over the years by teaching staff to contain student conflicts at tolerable levels. Thirty years after the first gunshot incident at the University of Karachi, lethal violence is experienced by its students and personnel as an integral part of student politics, if not of student life.

Conclusion

The escalation of violence at the University of Karachi was not the handiwork of violent entrepreneurs with a political or economic agenda. It was not a deliberate attempt to escalate a conflict which, for two decades, had been relatively benign. Neither was it a matter of ethnicity. Ideological affiliations initially transcended ethno-linguistic identifications, which would only come to play a role at a later stage in the conflict. The intensification of this conflict, at the end of the 1970s, was precipitated by the political strategies of the military elites governing the country at the time, and by a sudden change in student warfare technology. In the wake of the Afghan jihad, student organizations found it easier to obtain weapons which started flooding the campus. In the process new protagonists arrived on the scene of student politics. These outsiders with a background in petty criminality introduced new patterns of violence and upset the internal dynamics of student organizations by challenging the hold political activists had over these organizations. A further outcome of these student conflicts was the rise of the MQM/APMSO in the second half of the 1980s and the subsequent intensification of political violence at KU and beyond. It brought to the fore a new type of political activist, whose militarized way of apprehending and practicing politics traced its roots back to KU's campus wars. Moreover, once it had strengthened its military capabilities, the MQM/APMSO started attracting former Jama'ati and left-wing *badmash*, who gained their expertise in violence at the service of the Mohajir movement.

Rather than seeing the initial motivations of the belligerents as the reason behind the escalation of violence at KU, this escalation is far better explained by changes occurring in the structure of political opportunities for student movements (which, as we have seen, may have paradoxical effects),[28] and even more importantly by the evolving dynamics of the conflict itself. This case study confirms that escalation in violence is largely endogenous to unrestrained conflict, which inevitably transforms "behaviour, beliefs, preferences, and even identities" (Kalyvas, 2008, 403). Violence breeds more violence, not only due to the cycle of assault and retaliation that it sets in motion but more importantly because of the new opportunities and constraints it offers to individuals and groups in the course of the conflict. The preferences of the actors are necessarily affected by these changes, as reflected by the evolving sociology of the belligerents. This is why it is interesting to study conflict in motion, as it transforms its social environment and feeds on these societal changes, rather than in intention, through the hazardous excavation of structural causes and individual motivations. Such motivations may at most figure among the prerequisite conditions for violence and its escalation. But as the conflict intensifies new variables come into play, disrupting initial motivations and opportunities. The performativity of political violence, which is key to its endogenous reproduction and escalation, militates against self-professed "causal explanations" and in favor of more processual approaches that are attentive to its self-generative and yet contingent nature. Psycho-social approaches conducted in terms of "cultures of violence" or "brutalization" rightly point towards this performativity of political violence and of the discourses that justify and sometimes eulogize it. However, these interpretations are severely flawed, relying upon questionable theoretical assumptions (such as the association of political violence with moral breakdown and "primitive" instincts [Mosse, 1991]) and problematic methodological choices (such as aggregating groups and individuals under an all-encompassing national identity, and privileging vague ideas and sentiments spread from the top down to the detriment of the more effective incremental and path-dependent practical logics of violence). The "demotivated" analysis of escalation in violence tested here might seem too materialistic to some, particularly to psychologists and anthropologists attentive to the "fantasies" informing the imagination and actuation of lethal violence. Nevertheless, I believe that this approach offers a robust, empirically grounded account of the chain of events subsumed here within the concept of escalation in violence. And ultimately, debates around the analysis of violence are not—or should not be—ontological but pragmatic: "what works and what doesn't" (Collins, 2008, 34).

12

THE INSTRUMENTALIZATION
OF ETHNIC CONFLICT BY THE STATE

THE AZERI-KURDISH CONFLICT IN IRAN

Chirine Mohséni
Translated by Françoise Gillespie

In 1979 Iran was in turmoil following a popular uprising that had put an end to the Pahlavi regime. The demands of ethnic minorities—Kurds, Arabs, Turkmen, Baluchis—were presented openly because the new regime had broken with the former regime's policies of forced cultural unification. From 1925, the imperial regime had pursued a unification policy promoting "one nation, one language", punishing even the slightest claim of minority cultural or ethnic identity. This repression was all the more severe as the Kurds, Baluchis, Turkmen and Arabs are border-peoples, often seen as a threat to territorial integrity and national sovereignty. Paradoxically, public policy has produced the very outcome it sought to repress, a hierarchy of ethnic groups and identities. Such negation of the identity of minorities for the sake of the building of a nation reminds us of Kemalist Turkey—the two regimes have indeed often collaborated against Kurdish revolts.

After 1979, the new Islamic regime gave new freedom to the expression of ethnic cultures,[1] so long as these did not advocate political transformations beyond the accepted framework. The populist and relatively liberal early months of the revolution rapidly gave way to tensions, and in a few cases, even to violence between ethnic groups. Thus, in April 1979, during the violent clashes between Kurds and Azeris, Naqadeh and surrounding areas in Western Azerbaijan Province experienced several days of fighting and casualties estimated at between 100 and 300, according to sources.[2]

This chapter aims at understanding the effects of a revolutionary situation, i.e. a brutal and unanticipated transformation of the various types of social capital, based on identity capital. Two hypotheses can be put forth. First, the State does not limit itself to guaranteeing the hierarchy between communities by organizing a differentiated access to resources; it also defines which categories are socially relevant in the classification. Accordingly, the Iranian revolution witnesses a relative discredit of ethnic features in favor of religious ones (Shiites against Sunnis). Second, identity related hierarchies are not only national. They are also local and independent of national discourses of public institutions. Lastly, resorting to violence allows for fixed perceptions and expectations of the various communities to develop. This in turn allows for the insertion of repressive institutions, limiting the autonomy of local actors and making it easier for the centralized authorities to infiltrate the periphery. These hypotheses will be verified in the particular case of confrontation between Kurds and Azeris in the context of revolutionary Iran.

How then to identify the processes that originally tipped these people into violence? The Azeris in the region, with the support of the state, held dominant social and political positions in comparison to the Kurds, adding to the tensions between these populations. Yet, as noted by Mark Levene, "ethnic and cultural antipathies can never exist without leading to massacre" (Levene, 1999, 19). The shift to violence is, in fact, the result of several elements: first, the collapse of the old regime brought into question the hitherto legitimate ethnic hierarchy. Being Shi'ite became a key element in the relationship with the state and Sunni Kurds were marginalized. Secondly, Kurdish political demands were a source of concern for the region's Azeri population. Finally, the new government, freshly installed, had yet to establish its authority over Kurdish areas. Ethnic violence among different groups only served to justify government intervention and strengthen state influence. Indeed, under the pretext of protecting ethnic communities, the government recruited Revolutionary Guards (Pasdaran) among the Azeris of Naqadeh, and thus set the stage for the massacre of Kurdish villagers in the region: Qurnah, Qalatan and Inderqash.

Azeri–Kurd Relations Prior to 1979

State and Ethnic Hierarchy

The establishment of an ethnic hierarchy guaranteed and organized by the State in West Azerbaijan brings into play two small communities at the national level. West Azerbaijan is, after Baluchistan, one of the most disadvantaged provinces of Iran. Located in a border area, the territory is home to Kurds, Azeri and Assyrians, who have a long history of living together more or less peacefully. The government plays a key role in ethnic ordering and identity construction, especially using policies of forced resettlement. It is at such times that the privileged position of the Turkic tribes becomes apparent. They are settled more quickly than the Kurds on lands provided by the state and receive preferential treatment for administrative posts within the territory. Turkic tribes were originally resettled to Kurdish areas, especially in West Azerbaijan; this was the case for the Afshar tribes resettled under the Safavids in the sixteenth century, and the Qara Pâpâq resettled under the Qajar in the nineteenth century. The resettlement policy was originally intended as a means of co-opting the military qualities of the Turkic tribes as a defense force for the central government against rebels and foreign enemies, but also to weaken and control them better. This resettlement policy was sometimes imposed by force. Naqadeh is a case in point. In this region, the Pâpâq Qara tribe of Turkic-speaking Shi'ites, were settled by force.

In 1828, Prince Abbas Mirza gave Sulduz[3] in fief to 800 families originally from Qara Pâpâq Qazaqestan as a reward for their support. Although there were in Sulduz at that time between 4000 and 5000 Kurdish and Mukaddam Turkish families, land ownership gradually passed into the hands of the new Shi'ite masters (*Encyclopedia of Islam, Volume IV*, 1934).

Upon arrival, and with support from the Qajars, the Qara Pâpâq attacked the Kurdish tribes who were outside the control of the central power. At that time, the Mamachi, Zarzis and Mangor tribes were rivals in the region of Mahabad, Ushneviyeh and Naqadeh. At first, Naqi Khan, the chief of Qara Pâpâq attacked the Mangor, who were the dominant force in the region, forcing them into the surrounding forests. He then helped the Mamachi overcome their traditional enemy, the Zarzis. As a result, the Qara Pâpâq became large landowners, imposing their hegemony (Qahremanpur, 2006, 112–113). To consolidate power, the king increasingly interfered in inter-tribal affairs, favoring tribes pledging allegiance with land and positions of administrative responsibility, often at the expense of rebel tribes. This situation largely favored the Azeri populations against other ethnicities, including Kurds, whose various tribes in north-western Iran were resettled by the state to other regions.[4] The best-known example is the displacement of 15,000 Kurdish families in Khorassan, in north-eastern Iran by the Safavids in the seventeenth century (Richard, 1991, 55).

One consequence of these historical processes is that several different ethnic and faith groups now reside in the Naqadeh region. The region's fertile, green plains drew populations of Kurds, Turks and Assyrians. Naqadeh is bounded on the south and to east by predominantly Kurdish speaking populations, notably in Mahabad, Piranshahr and Ushnaviye counties, and to the north and west by Miandoab Urumiyeh counties, whose cities have Azeri majorities. While Naqadeh County is majority Kurd, the town itself is predominantly Azeri. A small town of 23,704 inhabitants in 1976, Naqadeh, also counted a few Jewish and Assyrian families.[5] The Azeri population of the city was composed mostly of Turkic-speaking, Shi'ite Qara Pâpâq. Their arrival in the region, as we noted, dates from the nineteenth century. In the 1930s, other Turkic migrants, notably the Shahsavan of Hachtrud, referred to as Hachtrudi, arrived in the region. The immigrant population worked mostly as laborers or in domestic service to the Qara Pâpâq, although their situation has improved through intermarriage with them (Qahremanpur, 2006, 36). Town dwelling Kurds are mostly from the Mâmash and Zarzâ tribes.

Memory and Community Boundaries

Community boundaries are justified and substantiated by reference to history, but history is seldom univocal and its usage refers to the justification of practices above all. In this case, the memory that has been built by the various communities is mostly negative, yet it is largely disconnected from practices that are globally—at least in cities—oriented toward the development of good practices, including marriage. More than the reconstruction of events, it is the chosen reference that marks the instrumental dimension of community memories (see Chapter 5 of this volume). Various discursive strategies, such as euphemizing or resorting to humor, are used to neutralize the negative effects of historical memories that are revived only when relations between communities are radically altered, as a revolution may cause.

As a multiethnic region, West Azerbaijan has a complex history that helps to understand how two opposing narratives have come to be constructed of relations between Sunni Kurds and Shi'ite Azeris.[6] In particular, the city of Naqadeh, located in a border province close to the Ottoman Empire and Russia, has been buffeted by several wars and revolts: the revolt of Sheikh Obeidollah Shamidan in 1880, the occupation of the region in 1904 by Ottoman troops and later Russian troops, and then once again by the Ottomans during the First World War, fighting against the Assyrians (1918), and the revolt of Simko, leader of the Chikak Kurds (1919–1921). The use of stereotypes is often involved, both in marking group boundaries and for the imaginary construction of the Other. Such inter-ethnic relations however, remain complex.

Folk songs and lullabies recount painful moments of armed conflict. Through such songs, the image of the enemy, "the ruthless assassin", a strong notion of the Other is constructed and internalized. Travel accounts of the region often allude to tensions between the Shia Azeris, who are for the most part sedentary, and the Sunni Kurds, whose lifestyle is essentially tribal. Urbanized Kurdish tribes are known for brigandage and rapine (Bouvier, 2001, 141). The *çeteh*,[7] Kurdish clans, or "outlaws", sowed fear among Azeri citizens who considered the Kurds "savage" and "blood thirsty". The Sunnis, surnamed "Omar" owing to their historico-religious affiliation to Omar bin al-Khattab, were labeled the "assassins of Imam Hussein" by the Shi'ites, a reference to the defining schism of the early Islamic world. The Kurds, in turn, referred to the Azeris as *'Ajam*[8] or "descendants of Mongols", as "religious fanatics" and "oppressors". Teymur Zadeh, a Kurdish merchant, tells of his first trip to the Turkic cities in Azerbaijan 1328q/1908:

> When we arrived in Bonâb,[9] the children who saw us fled in terror to their mothers, screaming "the Kurds, the Kurds!" I do not understand the reason for their panic! (...) When we returned to the hamam (public bath), the doorman rushed to meet us and show us to an isolated area reserved for Kurds. He then brought us towels reserved exclusively for Kurds that cost more than others (Teymur Zadeh, 1953, 9–11).

Bouvier, who visited the region in the 1950s, relates with humor, similar facts concerning Kurdish-Azeri relations in Tabriz.[10] But there are also positive memories. In 1945, at the formation of the short-lived republics of Azerbaijan and Mahabad and during the Russian occupation, which followed the Second World War, relations between Kurds and Azeris were friendlier, despite occasional clashes. These conflicts were quickly resolved and brought under control by the leaders of both republics. In fact, the fighting at first seemed inevitable since the two republics claimed the same territory (Kutschera, 1979, 172–173). To avoid conflict both parties agreed to negotiate the boundaries of their autonomous territories. They also agreed to respect the rights of Azeri and Kurdish citizens in their respective territories. Even the Russians played a role in these negotiations. Over this same period, Kurdish elites in their writings frequently praise their union with the "brave Azeris", "the grandchildren of Satar Khan".[11] During this period, and while tracing boundaries for their respective territories, "the Azeri elites were not at all willing to include Urumiyeh within the Republic of Azerbaijan, contrary to what one might think": They wished rather, to remain under the authority of the Republic of Mahabad. The Kurdish Republic proposed a less confrontational policy vis-à-vis the large landowners than did Azerbaijan (Kutschera, 1979, 173).

The use of stereotypes is changing with time and from place to place. In cities where the majority is clearly Kurd or Azeri, behavior with respect to minorities is more restrained and tends towards exclusion (as for example in Bonab which has an Azeri majority). In cities with a history of ethnic diversity, differences and stereotypes disappear or at least remain latent, cultural exchange and inter-marriage become more frequent. This is particularly true in Naqadeh, where relations in the period prior to 1979 were often characterized as good. In fact, according to evidence gathered, the relations between Kurds and Azeris prior to 1979 were excellent. In this small town, Kurdish and Azeri families enjoyed friendly relations. Mixed marriages between Sunnis and Shi'ites were common. "In terms of religion, there were no major problems between us; the Azeris of Naqadeh were less fanatical than Turks in other cities," noted one informant. Most inhabitants of Naqadeh spoke fluent Kurdish and Turkish. Could they not simply have been united by their shared status as minority languages from a Persian point of view? "Even though the language taught in school was Persian, we spoke amongst ourselves in Azeri and Kurdish. I do not know how I learned Azeri but it came naturally just like Kurdish." "I had many Azeri friends, and we would go to each others' homes without thinking of our religious or ethnic differences", said one informant. During religious ceremonies, as for *Molud Xani* or *Ey'd Qorban* for Sunnis or *Moharam* for the Shi'ia, the two communities would gather and support each other. On the days of *Moharam*, in order to show their support, Sunnis would welcome Shi'a into their homes to share a meal (various testimonies gathered in 2009).[12]

Dynamic Identity and Social Mobility

Social and ethnic hierarchies—based on ownership of tangible or cultural property—did not totally disappear. Thus, Teymour-Zadeh, in a narrative of the early 20th century, notes the solidarity and unity between the Azeri and Kurdish merchants, despite the friction that existed between the two ethnic groups in Azerbaijan (Teymour-Zadeh, 1953, 13). The literature on social and economic history of the city of Naqadeh indicates that the socio-economic level of Turks was higher than that of Kurds. The city was divided into two districts. One, located to the north and northeast, was the Turkish quarter. The other located to the south and west was that of the Kurds. In this division of the city, we find that ethnic differentiation correlates with social differentiation. The Turkish quarter of Naqadeh was described as being richer and better maintained than the Kurds. But it was not uncommon to see Turkish or Kurdish families relocating according to social status. Although, even before the advent of the Islamic Republic, a majority of senior administrative positions were held by Azeri Turks, it was apparent that Kurds also had access to senior positions including even election to the Chamber of Deputies. The Friday Imam for the city of Naqadeh was a Sunni cleric, this, despite a Shi'a majority in the city.

> At the time, it shocked no one; Shi'ites in the city had their own clerics and in each neighborhood there was a mosque. If ever you were in another neighborhood there was no personal discomfort in attending the local mosque. In this city, before the Islamic Revolution, the Shi'a, unlike the Sunni, did not attend Friday prayers. All of this started only after the revolution.[13] (Personal interview)

Thus, despite division of the city into Azeri and Kurdish neighborhoods, hierarchical distinctions were more obviously social than either ethnic or religious. Such social divisions however, were not immutable and Kurdish families could succeed socially and move into the more favored Azeri neighborhoods. But the arrival of the Islamic Republic in 1979 changed Kurdish-Azeri relations.

The Opening Gambit

One cannot understand the Naqadeh War and the subsequent massacre of Kurdish villagers without first understanding the revolutionary context. In 1979, the fall of the Pahlavi regime raised new hopes of freedom. The situa-

223

tion encouraged the formulation of multiple identity claims. Here then was a major challenge to the existing ethnic hierarchy along with a greater ability to mobilize. Thus, in West Azerbaijan and in Kurdistan provinces, Kurds aspired openly to "autonomy within the framework of Iran". These claims not only led indirectly to inter-ethnic conflict between Kurds and Azeris, but also to open confrontation with the new regime.

A new framework for differentiation between Azeris and Kurds of Naqadeh first appeared at events in early 1979 when Kurdish religious practices first appeared less fervent than Azeri practices, the Kurds in general being viewed as more secular (evidence collected in Sweden 2009). The revolution thus opened the way for confusing ethnic differentiation (Azeri versus Kurd), with religious differentiation (Sunni versus Shiite, or anti-clerical versus clerical). The government, relying on the traditional Sunni-Shiite rift, which differentiated pious from impious Muslims, placed the two groups in quite different objective situations, each receiving differential treatment. Such treatment was sufficient to revive anti-Sunni sentiment and subsequently, to connect Sunni Kurds to the descendants of "Yazid", the killers of Imam Hussein.[14] Religious distinctions thus took on a new dimension with respect to hierarchical relations between these groups. The Islamization policies introduced by government legislation discriminated primarily against secular and Sunni communities, creating tensions in the region.

Kurdish Demands

Following the departure of the Shah on 16 January 1979, the Kurdish areas, like all of Iran, were booming. Having already experienced autonomy during the short-lived Republic of Mahabad in 1945, Kurds renewed their identity claims. "The presence in most Kurdistan cities of Iranian military garrisons for which the new authorities in Tehran had not yet appointed new commanders" made the situation even more explosive." More or less spontaneous uprisings have occurred in some of these garrisons. Thus, on 1 February 1979, Kurds seized the garrison Sardasht, appropriating for themselves large quantities of food and munitions." (Kutschera, 1997, 164). Throughout Iran, committees of governance (*Chora-ye Shahr*) were created to control and regulate regional affairs. The political tendencies of these committees differed from one city to another. In some cities more than one committee was formed according to the affinities of the constituting authorities. In Mahabad, the *Chora-ye Shahr* was composed of Kurdish autonomists, whereas in Urumiyeh a committee was formed under the influence of Molla Hassani,[15] chief magistrate of the city. In Sanandaj, a committee was formed and chaired by the Kurd, Ahmed Muftizadeh,[16] a Sunni cleric. In Naqadeh, two committees were installed; one composed of Sunni Kurds, the other of Azeri Shi'ites. Despite their differences these committees agreed on a consultative procedure that included regular joint meetings (interviews conducted in Sweden in 2009).

Only a few days following accession to power, on February 5, Khomeini instructed Bazargan to form a provisional government. From the earliest days of his government, Bazargan negotiated with Kurdish nationalists. The KDPI was legalized and offices were opened in various Kurdish cities. 1 March 1979, the KDPI held its first meeting in Mahabad. Despite negotiations with the provisional government of Bazargan, tensions prevailed in the Kurdish region. On March 18, 1979, in Sanandaj, the capital of Kurdistan province, an incident occurred between supporters of Muftizadeh, the Sunni religious leader, and Safdari, the Shi'ite cleric. The latter was sent by the government to take control of the city garrison and armed forces. The clashes lasted until 22 March, when a cease-fire was reached with a government delegation led by Taleghani, a religious leader respected by the Kurds (Kutschera, 1997, 166–167). In West Azerbaijan, the newspapers of the day[17] denounced "peasant revolts against landlords and eviction of villagers by land owners". The newspaper articles went so far as to mention "the presence in the area of agents of the SAVAK and of military refugees who sow disorder". On 1 April, the Kurdish parties (KDPI and Komala)[18] boycotted the Islamic Republic referendum thus differentiating themselves from the Azeris who participated massively.

The KDPI, after a first meeting in Mahabad, decided to organize a rally in Naqadeh on 20 April. Despite legalization of the KDPI and ongoing negotiations, the atmosphere remained tense between the government and Kurdish parties. The Kurdish reputation for insubordination, and the majority's confession of Sunni faith, pushed the Iranian authorities to adopt an attitude of reserve and distrust (Richard, 1991, 55). The incident that took place in February at the Mahabad barracks during autonomy negotiations,[19] further divided government opinion as to the correct attitude to adopt with respect to Kurdish militants. The government was suspicious of Kurdish intentions; recognition as an autonomous region was one thing, but the altogether more troubling prospect of a bid for full independence could not be dismissed. The radical regime represented by Mustafa Tchamran[20] and Molla Hasani Zahir Nejad[21] demanded military intervention to resolve the Kurdish question.

Molla Hasani wrote in his memoirs, that he distributed arms and ammunition to Azeri and Kurdish tribes in the region that supported the government against its opponents. Molla Hasani subsequently played a major part in the clashes between Azeris and Kurds (Abazari, 2005, 163–225).

Community Fears[22]

Kurdish Nationalist claims and the support they received from an enthusiastic population frightened some Azeris, pushing them to support the government. An aura of mistrust overtook the two communities. Only by understanding such divisions can the importance of ethnic and religious identity be appreciated. The state's role in fostering these divisions is not insignificant. On one hand, the State reinforced existing social divisions through discriminatory practices favoring the Azeri community. On the other hand, the State mobilized popular fear and insecurity in preparing public opinion to accept a military presence in the region. In Kurdistan, a war party exacerbated tensions by circulating rumors and lies.[23]

A few months before the "Naqadeh War" (April 1979), with the announcement of the KDPI[24] meeting, rumors circulated about the "intent of Kurdish militants to declare independence, and create a greater Kurdistan, expelling Turks from their territory." At the same time, memories of ethno-religious wars of the nineteenth and early twentieth centuries began to resurface. Kurdish nationalists were compared to "their ancestor [Sheikh Obeidollah or Simko] who sacked the region and massacred Azeri Turks". In this way, the "instrumental or unconscious use of a more or less fantastic and fragmentary past" was used to nurture ethnic fears (Bayart, 1998, 338). The "hardliners", represented by Molla Hassani or Tchamran, spread information about the existence of a conspiracy engineered by "counter-revolutionaries" and their imperialist Kurdish allies whose purpose was to isolate and break away the Kurdish regions of Iran (Abazari, 2005, 176–179 and Tchamran, 1985, 13–16). With respect to the Naqadeh War, Molla Hassani writes "a person familiar to him, warned that an invasion was imminent and that by invading the city of Naqadeh the KDPI intended to seek the independence of Kurdistan with help from strangers." Molla Hossani, upon hearing this threat understood at once "that there was a global conspiracy under foot to help the KDPI secure the independence of Kurdistan. He warned the army while he himself, in the city of Naqadeh, armed his men and formed a committee..." (Abazari, 2005, 176–179). In this way, and by circulating this information, the hardliners evoke "the image of a potential enemy", demonizing the other (Sémelin, 2005, 97). At the same time, the Kurds distanced themselves from their Azeri neighbors, especially those holding government appointments. State efforts to maintain social order only exacerbated the antagonisms.

Clashes in the region (violence in Sanandaj, incidents in Azerbaijan) further implicated Kurdish militants, now fully demonized by regime hardliners.[25] On several occasions, people close to the government spoke of the existence of "a plot to create an independent Kurdistan with the support of foreign forces, endangering national integrity". Using radio announcements, the state mobilized popular sentiment to help "save the Muslims". At the same time, weapons were distributed and rumors circulated about atrocities committed by the enemy against a helpless civilian population even going so far as to mention "rape", the "severed heads of women and children" and "mutilated corpses". In fact, the "counter-revolutionaries" (*Zed-e Enqelab*), "unbelievers" (*kafir*), and "imperialist agents" were capable of anything, even the worst atrocities. In this way, hardliners played on popular fears and insecurity, preparing public opinion for armed intervention and recruiting volunteers.

Confrontations

On 7 April 1979, the newspaper *Etell'aât*[26] announced armed clashes between the Azeri and Kurdish committees of Naqadeh.[27] Following the accidental death of an Azeri (caused by a Kurd), and despite the apology presented by the Kurdish party, differences and mistrust remained high between the two committees. On both sides, there was talk of "conspiracy" and "entrapment". Each camp assumed events were planned and enacted intentionally by the other. As noted by J-F Bayart, "political plotting is a recurring element and universal construct of the political imagination" (Bayart, 1996, 179). Public expression of this political fantasy led, in turn, to the personification of "the enemy" and ultimately, to violence. It is within this context that the meeting of the KDPI at Naqadeh on 20 April 1979, took place.

Kurdish activists gathered at the Naqadeh sports stadium located in the Azeri quarter, to celebrate the opening of the KDPI office. After only five minutes, Abdul Rahman Ghassemlou's[28] speech was interrupted by gunfire. It is not known from where the shots were fired, although armed men were seen on the roofs of neighboring Azeri homes. The Kurds, surrounded on all sides, felt trapped inside the stadium and counterattacked to force their exit from the Azeri quarter. "There was chaos. The killing had begun and it was difficult to stop." With rumors circulating in both the Kurdish and Azeri districts, panic soon overcame good sense. "Kurds in their neighborhoods killed their Azeri neighbors. In retaliation, Kurdish families living in Azeri quarters suffered the same fate." During the confrontations, "it was no longer essential to know whether a particular person was or was not a combatant." Thus, many civilians were massacred. "But there were also a number of incidents where Azeri or Kurdish families helped their neighbors eventually saving them from death."

On the second day of fighting, Molla Hassani, an Azeri cleric and personal representative in Urumiyeh of the Ayatollah Khomeini, arrived in the city at the head of armed force to succor his "fellow Muslims", the Azeris. The city's Kurdish population fled into neighboring towns[29] with the result that the abandoned Kurdish neighborhoods were ransacked. "Only the town's Sunni Imam accompanied by a few Kurdish fighters remained to continue resistance." Fighting in the city stopped after only three days, but continued in nearby villages until 27 April. In all, Kurdish sources reported approximately 350 deaths (Kutschera, 1997, 168). The State intervened after the fourth day, launching negotiations between the parties and preventing any further looting of Kurdish homes. Several Azeri notables engaged with Kurdish residents of Naqadeh to reassure them and to encourage them to return to their homes. Nevertheless, the atmosphere remained tense. Some residents returned to their homes only after a year.

At the Naqadeh political rally and shooting, the Kurds felt "trapped by their Azeri neighbors". By then, Azeris were largely considered "accomplices of an oppressive government", thus conflating the killings with a planned act of oppression. According to eyewitnesses, "All of this was planned in advance. The houses had been boarded-up and shooters had been placed on the roofs." During this period, ethnic and religious identity, whether Kurdish or Azeri, Sunni or Shi'ite, became the basis for mobilization in the region, and the various rumors that circulated regarding the intentions of one or another person only served to inflame ethnic passions. To quote a resident of Naqadeh: "This war was the spark that awakened Azeri-Kurdish differences and ignited the region for some time."

Ethnic Tensions and the Presence of the State

The consequences of violence are visible at three levels: reaffirmation of the city's ethnic geography increased violence between groups, and instrumentalization of the incident to assert state authority and reinforce its presence in the community. Following the war, Azeri families and Kurdish minorities in their villages, fearing reprisals, exchanged their homes and relocated to areas where they found themselves in the majority. Thus, the boundaries of ethnic territories become more visible. At the same time, the relationship between Kurds and government authorities was strained in other ways.[30] Kurdish villagers, notably in Qarna and in Qalatan, were attacked by "unknown persons of Turkish origin". The most prominent of these attacks were the killings in Qurnah. On 2 September 1979, armed Azeris attacked the village, located between Naqadeh and Jaldyan, massacring all villagers who were present at their arrival.[31] These men no doubt wished to avenge slain relatives killed by the KDPI in a clash and the village was suspected of supporting the Kurdish party. Such confrontations spread throughout the province and created great tension between Azeris and Kurds in Western Azerbaijan.

Under the pretext of ethnic tension, the State at last reinforced its presence in the region with an armed force "to prevent the killings." Far from calming spirits, the presence of the army and of the Revolutionary Guards (Pasdaran), essentially recruited from the Azeri population, aggravated the situation so that during the first decade of the Islamic Republic, relations between central government and Kurdish militants oscillated between periods of negotiation and violence. The army and the Revolutionary Guard deployed massive force, with repression lasting through much of 1980. Although there are no official statistics concerning victims of these years of civil war, Kurdish estimates place the cost in lives at 45,000 of whom only 5,000 would have been combatants (Bozarslan, 2009, 65).

The state was, in fact, destabilized for the first few months of the revolution. Different political factions existed within it. The facts suggest these inter-ethnic clashes provided the radical forces the pretext they needed to impose themselves within the government and on the ground in West Azerbaijan and Kurdistan provinces. "It was only after the Naqadeh War that Tehran deployed the Pasdaran to Azerbaijan and to Kurdistan. The media, exaggerated the picture of war in Kurdistan to undermine the provisional government of Bazargan."[32] The spirit of compromise and willingness to negotiate soon yielded to a call to arms and the use of force to settle the Kurdish question. This was the period which gave birth to "the Kurdish Peshmerga Muslim" corps, arming tribes hostile to the Komala and to the KDPI. It was in this climate that the Islamic Constitution of 2 December 1979 was promulgated and voted in. From the outset, certain ambiguities written into the Islamic Constitution aroused the discontent of religious minorities, especially the Sunni.[33] Indeed, it was just such discriminatory policies that led the state to create a few years later the "Great Islamic Centre in Kurdistan" as a center for the dissemination of its policies in the Kurdish regions. More recently, the State has increased its oversight control of Sunni schools across the country. All of this transpired despite the fact that the Islamic Constitution authorized the creation of the Kurdish parties and associations. The government subsequently tried to purge the symbols of Kurdish identity of meaning, such as usage of the word *Peshmerga*, all the while disparaging and downplaying Kurdish personalities. At the same time, the State has sought to co-opt the nationalist movement by creating parallel and pro-government Kurdish movements.

Conclusion: The Impact on National Movements

The Azeri-Kurd conflict in Naqadeh and more generally, in West Azerbaijan, has had an effect on both Kurdish and Azeri nationalist movements. As a result of the incidents reported here, there has occurred a net increase among Azeris of identitary demands. While these clashes do not alone explain the rise of Azeri nationalism in Iran, one might reasonably think they are a major cause. The clashes also strengthened the extremist tendencies of both nationalist movements, even if these trends are marginal within the greater population. For some, the "Naqadeh massacre" marked the beginning of an "anti-Kurdish pogrom". For others, referring to Molla Hassani, the massacre is but another milestone in an "epic struggle" with the Kurdish enemy (Abazari, 2005, 176). Both groups claim the same territory and propose new place names. Azeri nationalists, for example, in their speeches, use the word *Sulduz* to speak of Naqadeh. This traditional name for the Naqadeh city region is also the name of a Mongol tribe, giving symbolic overtones. Kurds on the other hand, speak of Naqadeh as *Sendus*, a traditional name used by the Kurdish people to designate the plains of the region. In 2001, the Kurds of Mahabad, petitioned the Khatami government to establish Mokriyân Province. The petition was not granted, even though such a request necessarily implies an express desire by one people, the Kurds, to distinguish themselves from another, the Azeris. One informant remarked, "The name Azerbaijan implies a region settled by Azeris, whereas in West Azerbaijan Province the majority is Kurdish!"

In recent years, a number of Azeri nationalist events have been repressed by security forces of the Islamic Republic. Changes have also occurred in the

Kurdish nationalist movement. Several Kurdish parties and associations such as the "Kurdish United Front" emerged while reformers governed the Islamic Republic. The disappointment of the Kurds regarding reform policies has guided the younger generation towards a more radical path. Along with the emergence of various peace movements in the form of NGOs, a more radical movement, the PJAK[34] took over the armed struggle.

"We Azeris and Kurds, we must be inspired by the image of Hewraz,[35] the Kurdish-Azeri alpinist from Naqadeh, to rebuild our history together," said a Kurdish Naqahdeyi. According to witnesses, the intermarriage of Shias and Sunnis in the region continues, but not on the same scale as before 1979. As one informant commented, "The War of Naqadeh remained as a large wound in our memories. It can be cured, but unfortunately the scar will remain for a long time in the history of our region. Perhaps with succeeding generations the memories will gradually disappear. We hope so."

NOTES

INTRODUCTION: IDENTITY, HIERARCHY, AND MOBILIZATION

1. This book is based on a research project funded by the French Agence nationale de la recherche (ANR). The project (2007–2010), named "Conflits-TIP" was hosted by the Centre for Ottoman Turkish, Balkan and central-asian studies (Centre d'études turques ottomanes, balkaniques et centrasiatiques—CETOBAC, UMR 8032 EHESS-CNRS-Collège de France). The publication of the book was supported by CERIC, UMR 7318 Aix-Marseille Université-CNRS.

2. A dimension which is developed in part via action, see McAdam, Tilly, and Tarrow, 2000. Gurr adopts a different theoretical point of view and insists on the dual aspect of identity issues as both a cause and a resource within collective action. See Gurr, 1993.

3. For discussion of the use of these categories see de Sardan, 1998.

4. For interpretations of the Kurdish conflict in Turkey, see Loizides, 2009.

5. For an empirical refutation of Huntington's theses, see Fox, 2002. For doomsday predictions (which have not come true), see Robert D. Kaplan, 1994. Kaplan draws a parallel between ethnic conflicts, which he sees as bound to become more widespread, and "urban conflicts" in the United States. The blurring of internal and external perspectives arises here from a political agenda, with the poor and the marginalised classes being explicitly designated as the enemy within.

6. It is rare for violence to erupt, see Brubaker and Laitin, 1998.

7. The differences that exist between these three countries (such as the recognition of Islam as the basis of political society, or the status of ethnic and religious minorities) are sufficient to inform us about the role played by political context. The 2010 ruling by the European Court of Human Rights banning any reference to religious allegiance on identity cards in Turkey is indicative of the Europeanising influence on institutions at that time.

8. Moreover, primordialist approaches are in fact marginal. Geertz for example argues that primordial bonds (of kinship, phenotype, and language) generate stronger

loyalties than those of class or nation, but does not thereby adopt a primordialist stance in that he accepts that these bonds are historical constructs. See Geertz, 1963.

9. For examples of the redefinition of identity so as to mobilise people, see the emergence of a "white" movement in the United States (Alba, 1990) and the failure of the Roma movement in Central Europe, (Vermeersch, 2003).

10. Differences in phenotype are not of uniform significance, which explains for instance why colour defines groups in the United States, but less so in Cuba or Brazil.

11. This is in fact rather rare on the fields we study, since migrations generally lead to people from similar origin moving in to the same neighborhoods.

12. For an example of the complex dynamics at work between religious and ethnic affiliation, see Cuisenier, 2000. Moreover, Hinduism (and sometime Alevism) affords an ideal-type instance of the blurring of the boundary between ethnicity and religion.

13. Insofar as inter-ethnic marriage produces a potentially new identity, or at least an ambiguous one for any children, whereas inter-religious marriage results in a choice with regard to the children.

14. For an overview of the relation between ethnicity and Islam in the Indian subcontinent and the historical rarity of syncretism see Gaborieau, 2007.

15. Translated from the French.

16. See also Akerlof and Cranton, 2000.

17. Fredrik Barth (1956) describes the economic and ecological complementarity of groups in Swat that underpins the hierarchy and inequality between groups.

18. Aghajanian shows how the domination of Persian is a product of centralization, and has influenced industrialisation policies and increased inequalities between the groups.

19. On the lack of proportionality between causes and effects, see Boudon, 1990, p. 270.

20. The massacre of Alevi Kurds by Sunni right-wing extremists in which the police were passively complicit (at the very least).

21. For a demonstration of the role played by collective identities in collective action and of its limits, see Polletta and Rasper, 2001.

22. For discussion of the paradox of the free rider see Olson, 1965, and for discussion of identity social capital, see Portes and Sensenbrenner, 1993.

23. For discussion of the link between transnational movements and ethnic conflict, see Kiyoteru, 2004.

24. The concept of a "cascade" makes it possible to describe the process of horizontal dissemination when an incident in one country triggers a series of movements in different national contexts. See Rosenau, 1991, pp. 298–305.

25. For discussion of the Kurdish case see van Bruinessen, 1994.

26. Which makes it possible to criticise Kalyvas' approach, based on an interpretation

of civil war in which politics is a neutral operator making it possible to link up local instances of violence. His work puts forward an interpretation of violence which significantly underplays the role of ideology, and in which the "historical" and national dimension are superimposed as it were. See Kalyvas, 2006.

27. See "Outraged Communities. Comparative Perspectives on the Politicization of Emotions in South Asia", *South Asia Multidisciplinary Academic Journal*, 2, 2008, URL: http://samaj.revues.org/index1912.html

28. The contexts contributing to the recourse to violence are not necessarily something the actors are aware of, see for a different discussion of context F. M. Beck, 1995.

29. There was nevertheless a change after 1994 when the leaders of movement who did not belong to these communities had recourse to violence precisely because they were not subject to the same constraints. See Bailey (1996).

30. The existence of a strategy does not prevent the forms that the violence takes from drawing on cultural repertoires, which does not mean to say that it is produced by them, for discourses are essentially ambivalent. In a famous study, Geertz, 1973, shows that a cockfight is also a discursive structure denouncing violence and justifying social order, and especially emotional control. Cultural patterns do not lead to undifferentiated violence but to specific forms of violence and to the selection of targets.

31. For an instance of the clearly evolutionist aspect to Elias' thought, see the interview in the afterword to Elias, 1973, p. 437 and the text that follows.

1. "THE NARCISSISM OF THE MINOR DIFFERENCE" AND RELIGIOUS VIOLENCE: THE CASE OF THE ALEVIS AND SUNNIS OF CENTRAL ANATOLIA

1. I wish to thank Marc Aymes, Xavier Bougarel, Marc Darmon and Elise Massicard for their constructive criticism. Christelle Chevallier (CETOBAC, CNRS) accurately and efficiently edited the French-language version of this article, and I offer her my warmest thanks.

2. Turkey is not "secular" in the French sense understood. The state officially oversees matters of religion, primarily through the Office of Religious Affairs.

3. Sıraç are an Alevi group present in Tokat and Yozgat provinces. They are considered by the other Alevi, in central Anatolia, like very "closed" and "conservative" (see Andrews, 1989).

4. On 2 July 1993, the participants in a cultural protest organized by an Alevi organization in Sivas was besieged in a hotel for eight hours, thirty-seven of whom were burned alive by members of the extreme right, among them both Islamists and nationalists. In the Gazi neighborhood of Istanbul on 12 March 1995, armed men in a taxi sprayed four cafés and a pastry shop frequented by Alewites and leftist militants with bullets and fled without being identified, leaving two dead and fifteen

wounded. Rumors accused the police of being accomplices with the authros of the attack, which was attributed to the radical right and triggered a riot against the police station. In the ensuing several days, the protest movement grew and the police opened fire on protesters, causing an estimated thirty or more deaths and hundreds of wounded. Turkey had not experienced urban violence of this intensity since the 1980 coup d'état.

5. Collective memory appears to fail in this instance: few informants "remembered" their grandparents telling them about the rivers of blood, the lynching of a desperately poor Armenian, or the adoption of this brother and sister who sought refuge in a barn.

6. For example, the Ankara-Sivas rail line, built ten years after the revolt, avoids the administrative region by following its border, a detour that no geographical constraint can explain. Initial plans were to connect the three cities of Ankara–Yozgat–Sivas, very logically, with a single line. This was an effective means of strangling the region. It should be recalled, because it is so difficult to believe at present, that Yozgat was one of the richest regions in Central Anatolia at the time of the founding of the Republic. In the nineteenth century, the city of Yozgat, which is awkwardly perched at an altitude of 1300 meters, was depicted by Western travelers as one of the most modern cities in Asia Minor. The Çapanoğlu had in fact invited numerous Armenians artisans and doctors to move to the city to help encourage its growth in prosperity.

7. Ali, the Prophet's brother-in-law and cousin, was assassinated in a mosque.

8. This revolt has been completely reinvented today—the Alevis supposedly fought with Atatürk—whereas there is historical proof that confirms their support for the leaders of the insurrection.

9. "Red head" was the epithet applied to religious heretics and dissidents who supported Shah Ismaël (the "Turcoman") against Selim I (the Ottoman) in the XVIe siècle (Mélikoff, 1975). Today, it is synonymous with "incestuous" and infidel. Calling an Alevi "kızılbaş" is an insult.

10. An identificational object is an object that one identifies with, whereas an identifying object is an object by which one is identified. A soccer team can be an identificational object, while a moustache that signifies membership to a political group can be an identifying object (Fliche, 2000).

11. A doctor of Muslim law responsible for responding to judicial questions using a special formula called "fetva". He is also responsible for maintaining respect of religious law.

12. This argument relates generally to gender separation. Sunnis are ostensibly the oppressors of women who implemented a firm division between men and women, particularly during meetings or in public spaces. On the other hand, the Alevis present themselves as being advocates of equality between men and women, a sign of their "humanity" and "modernity". It goes without saying that even among Alevis there are subjugated women.

2. CULTURAL DIVERSITY AND ETHNIC HIERARCHY: THE USE OF CATEGORIES IN THE KURDISH CONFLICT IN TURKEY

1. The arrest of the PKK leader, Abdullah Öcalan, in 1999 marks the end of the war between the PKK guerrilla and the Turkish army, for a few years. Armed clashes have flared up sporadically, however, since 2003. For critical studies of this "post-conflict" period, see in particular Gambetti (2006) and Biner (2007).

2. In light of work by Bernard Lahire (1999) drawing on sociological analysis of discourse to study the construction of social problems, this article will refer to "discursive pools" ("fonds discursif") and "discursive habits" ("habitudes discursives"): "Shifting the theoretical plane from representations to discursive habits is a way of avoiding apprehending discourse independently of action, practice, and socialisation [...] The collective discursive socialisation explains the existence of a very limited discursive pool that the producers appear to draw on, and thus makes it possible to understand why it is that pronouncements are so incredibly similar, something that even the strongest forms of direct and coercive imposition would not bring about to such a perfect degree." (Lahire, 1999, 37). The formation of French popular colonial culture described by Nicolas Bancel (2003) displays similar phenomena of overlap and interaction between the various forms of media used to propagate colonial representations.

3. Mesut Yeğen made the following observation about this discourse: "The resisters were not Kurds with an ethno-political cause but simply (Kurdish) tribes, bandits, sheikhs—all the evils of Turkey's pre-modern past. The public image of Kurds now became two-fold. They were either proper Turkish citizens or outlaws characterized by tribalism, religious reactionaries or banditry [...] Kurds were considered as prospective Turks and this became the meta-image of Kurds during the Republic" (Yeğen, 2009, 599).

4. The corpus studied here is composed of various TV series set in the south east of Turkey (there are a few exceptions, though most of them were filmed here, at least in part) and whose dominant theme is custom. Whilst the whole production was taken into consideration in a general way, more detailed analysis was carried out of two TV series about the South East (*Sıla*, 2005 for ATV, and *Tek Türkiye*, 2007 for Samanyolu), especially for the second part of this article. They were compared with a series about the Black Sea region (*Tatlı Bela Fadime*, 2007 for Star TV). The three series have similar themes (custom, honor, and vendettas) shaping the way the stories are put together: *Sıla* tells the story of a young woman from Mardin, who has been adopted and brought up by a rich family from Istanbul. Since her natural brother has carried off the sister of the tribal chief, Sıla is forced by her natural family to marry the chief in question so as to stave off the "honor killing" that threatens the runaway couple. She thus returns to Mardin after spending her youth and childhood years in Istanbul. Tarik, the hero of *Tek Türkiye* ("One Turkey") was also handed over to an adoptive family by his natural mother, in the hope of protecting

him from a vendetta and so spare him from death. He returns to his village in the South East (without realising that it is his village) to work as a doctor. *Tatlı Bela Fadime* ("Sweet Calamity Fadime") tells the story of a young woman from the Black Sea seeking to cleanse her honor after a rich man from Istanbul (but of Greek extraction and from Fadime's village) sought to kiss her. However, these TV series differ in terms of their target audiences (*Tek Türkiye* and *Tatlı Bela Fadime* targeting the popular audiences of Star and Samanyolu, whilst *Sıla* targets both a popular audience and a more educated/wealthy audience), and in terms of budget and treatment as well. *Tek Türkiye* and *Sıla* were highly successful (two seasons for *Sıla*, and a new 2010–2011 season for *Tek Türkiye*), whilst *Tatlı Bela Fadime* was a bit less so (one season of thirty-five episodes).

5. Though the first wave of TV series produced in Turkey came out in the second half of the 1980s, it was at the end of the 1990s that the sector started growing significantly, initially for a local market before very rapidly reaching an international one. See in particular the works by Tanrıover.

6. The scene is set in the first episode as follows: "Harran, bilinmeyen bir zaman".

7. He is from Ağrı and also emphasised his tribal origins (from the Zilan tribe). See Can Dündar (2003) "Özcan Deniz, eski defterleri açtı", http://www.candundar.com.tr/index.php?Did=2703. Consulted on 11.05.2010. See also the documentary by Nedim Hazar, *Özcan Deniz Makyajsız*, 2006.

8. It would seem that he moved away from this after *Asmalı Konak*, a series about the life of a "modern Agha" in Cappadocia opening on a clash between two tribes, as the previous series has also done; after his album *Leyla* (2002), including a Turkish translation of the Kurdish song Leyla; and after *Haziran Gecesi* ("June Night", 2004)–a series about love and politics in the Istanbul upper classes in which the two protagonists both have Kurdish first names, Baran and Havîn—the latter being a Kurdish call girl.

9. But she also attracted political criticism (which sometimes resulted in legal proceedings), especially from Büyük Birlik Partisi and the descendants of Esat Oktay Yıldıran, the Diyarbakir prison director during its black years (and referred to in the fourth episode of *Bu Kalp seni unutur mu?*). See "Ünlü diziye soruşturma açıldı", *Bugün*, 17 April 2010.

10. Interview with Gül Oguz, *Sabah*, 18 January 2007.

11. "9 Köyün Çocuğuna Okul", *Milliyet* 25 November 2007.

12. 'Seni gidi anarşist!', *Yeni Şafak*, 15 March 2009.

13. "Baska bir dünya", *Sıla*, Episode 8.

14. 'Gül Oğuz yine bir kadın hikayesiyle karşımızda', http://silatv.blogspot.com/2006/12/gl-ouz-yine-bir-kadn-hikayesiyle.html

15. Specificity of language is no longer a threat. The policewoman in *Pars Narkoterör* meets an imprisoned PKK member. He says to her, in Kurdish: "dijminê kurd!" ("enemy of the Kurds"). She answers: "Dijmin tu yî, û hevalên te ne. Ez jî Kurd

im. Ama senin gibi ne vatanım ne ulusum ihanet ettim ben" ("it is you and your friends who are the enemy. I too am Kurdish"—in Kurdish. Then in Turkish: "but unlike you, I did not betray my Fatherland or nation", Episode 4). The rhetoric in *Kurtlar Vadisi* is similar; for discussion of these other series by Osman Sınav see Yücel, 2008.

16. For instance, Polat Alemdar, the hero of *Kurtlar Vadisi*, was carried off as a boy and entrusted to an adoptive family and brought up to serve his country.

17. This tone is not specific to TV productions. The bestselling author Ayşe Kulin, in his novel *Bir gün* about a meeting between an Istanbul journalist and a woman from the East, an imprisoned activist, refers to the "Middle Ages" (*ortaçağ*) when describing the time in which Kurdish populations and regions live.

18. Phrases such as "don't look for any other solution as there aren't any", "there's no other way", and "powerlessness" come up time and again in *Tek Türkiye* and *Sıla*, underlining how powerful custom is.

19. *Berdel*, a common practice in Kurdish society, consists in marrying two women from different families to two men from these families at the same time. The aim of this practice is to annul the dowry that the groom's family normally gives to the bride's. On the topic of *berdel* see Yücel, 2006.

20. In Turkey the inhabitants of the Black Sea are generally referred to as Lazs, whether or not they actually are so in ethnic and linguistic terms. Meeker compares the Kurdish and Laz categories in relation to this: "Western Anatolians often refer to people who come from areas east of a line roughly through Sivas, Kayseri, and Adana as Kurd regardless of the language they speak or any single characteristic. This category like the category Laz, is based on a regional and cultural classification rather than an unambiguous linguistic criterion" (Meeker, 1971, 322). It is worth noting that, throughout Turkey, the "Laz" are held to be ridiculous.

21. "Gül Oguz, yine bir kadın hikayesiyle karşımızda...", 16 December 2007 http://silatv.blogspot.com, website consulted on 01.06.2008. The chain is materially present when Sıla is chained up in her bedroom after her forced marriage. There is exactly the same image in the series *Bir bulut olsam*.

22. The image of the "missionary" is not new. The superior of Sıdıka Avar, a teacher in the Kurdish regions in the 1930s and 1940s, said to her: "as a Turkish missionary you are now going to go and live among the boarders. It is what Atatürk wanted" (Avar, 1999, 46).

23. "[I]t is the bad character that brings out the worth of the good ones. The more unpleasant he is, the worse I am, the better I can bring out the worth of the good ones," Çetin Azer observed, an actor playing the role of the bad Sabo Ağa in *Tek Türkiye*. 'Seni gidi anarşist!', *Yeni Şafak*, 15 March 2009.

24. "Gül Oğuz, yine bir kadın hikayesiyle karşımızda...", 16 December 2007 http://sılatv.blogspot.com, website consulted on 01. 06.2008.

25. It is interesting to note that the first Turkish film to use entertainment-information techniques was *Berdel* (Atıf Yılmaz, 1990) (See Yaser, 2004).

26. http://www.mostproduction.com/SspSilaAcilis.html, consulted on 8 August 2010. Also see "Nusaybin ilçesinde Sıla ilköğretim okulu törenler Hizmete Açıldı". http://www.mardin.gov.tr/haber/mardinvaliligi.asp?id=2825&kategori=BASINDA %20MARDIN

27. http://www.mostproduction.com/SspSilaAcilis.html, consulted on 8 August 2010.

28. http://haydikizlarokula.meb.gov.tr/pop_.php?p=medya, consulted on 8 August 2010. Generally, it would appear that the state and "civil society organisations" have understood the power of TV series. Thus even though a series might not be devised as an educational tool, state institutions can use it to get across certain messages supported by the director. See *Serpil Yılmaz*, *"Başbakanlık senaryoya sızıyor"*, *Milliyet*, 10 October 2004.

29. http://www.cydd.org.tr/?sayfa=biz, consulted on 8 August 2010.

30. In particular she has expressed her views in *Ebru*, a work calling for a new conception of cultural diversity, for instance: "Yet Turkey is a symphony of colours. A symphony of colours composed of different races, cultures, religions, languages, beliefs, and even personal attitudes. Everyone is different, everyone has as much charm and sense as the others. How could one single colour give life to this wealth, this diversity, and the benefits they bring?" (2010: 51). In summer 2009 she caused waves in the artistic world by openly supporting "the Kurdish opening" of Prime Minister (Nur Çintaya "Sezen Aksu, Hülya Avşar, Kürt açılımı, sanatçı saçılımı...", *Radikal*, 21 August 2009).

31. www.bbog.org, consulted on 9 August 2010.

32. For instance, it would seem that certain Kurdish language authors—thus firmly on the side of protest—take hold of the classical themes of popular Turkish culture such as that of tradition (such as Firat Cewerî in *Ez ê yekî bikujim*, which attributes the reason the woman joins the guerrilla to the domination she underwent as a woman in Kurdish society) or of the love between a Turkish soldier and a Kurdish woman (such as Mehmed Uzun in *Ronî mîna Evînê, Tarî mîna mirînê*).

3. ETHNIC AND REGIONAL FERMENT IN IRAN: THE GILAN EXAMPLE

1. On this opposition between substantial and performative identities, between indicators (differenciating and identification features revealed by a substantive and contrastice study of facts—an *etic* approach, in other words) and markers (those features that are retained and acknowledged by the actors themselves as symbols of identity and alterity, revealed by an approach called *emic*), see a previous article of mine (Bromberger, 1993).

2. This in fact happened to our colleagues Gilles Riaux and Stephane Dudoignon, working on claims in Azerbaijan (see Riaux's contribution in this volume) and on the revival of the Sunni Baloutchestan respectively. "That's what's wrong, not with you! Your subject!", he was told upon his arrest, see Dudoignon, 2009, 176.

3. For an overall presentation of the province, see Bromberger (1989).
4. The information was given to me by PM Jaktaji, director of the great regional review Gilevâ.
5. This is all the more impressive when compared with the regional circulation of French journals of culture and ethnology, noting, in particular, that the population of Gilan is about 2.5 million inhabitants.

4. THE MANAGEMENT OF IDENTITIES IN AND BY TURKEY'S POLITICAL PARTIES

1. This article was written in the context of the ANR under the title 'From cultural friction to armed confrontation. Thresholds, scales, and modalities of conflictuality in Turkey, Iran, and Pakistan.'
2. Here we distinguish between Aleviness, the sociological fact, and Alevism, the mobilization in its name.
3. For an analysis of how the AKP tries to mobilize Kurdish voters in two different districts in Istanbul, see Arıkan-Akdağ (2012).
4. We designate as Alevi the entirety of heterodox and syncretistic groups that constitute between 10 and 25 per cent of Turkey's population.
5. See Turgut (2005) concerning this phenomenon.
6. A case among others: in August 2007, families originally from Sırnak in southeastern Turkey who had been living in tents near Karataş (Adana) since the early 1990s were pressured to leave the site.
7. Another illustration: on 5 October 2008, in the nearby small town of Hadırlı, a young man who was attempting to prevent his motor scooter from being stolen was stabbed; when it became clear that an assailant who was caught by the crowd was of Kurdish origin, there was an outbreak of protests against the PKK.
8. Parties that claim a particular identity (such as Kurdish parties) are not included in the analysis.
9. Law regarding political parties n° 2820 April 22, 1983, art. 78.
10. Law regarding political parties § 12, § 96.
11. This article was modified in 1991 and abolished in 1995. However, a similar prohibition is to be found in Art. 81 of the law regarding parties.
12. This phenomenon is not specific to Turkey and has also marked the history of France, for example.
13. This despite formal denials by organizations. See for example "Aleviler MGK'ya gidiyor", *Hürriyet,* European Edition, 19 January 2001.
14. To this reticence regarding the constraints of legitimization were until recently added judicial restrictions, cooperation between parties on one hand and associations or foundations on the other having been forbidden, as well as the defense by one party, association, or foundation of a part of the population. These constraints were loosened recently by EU harmonization measures.

15. *Sosyaldemokrat Halkçı Partisi*, Social-Democratic Populist Party.
16. *Halkın Emek Partisi*, People's Labor Party.
17. *Partiya Karkeren Kurdistan*, Kurdistan Workers Party.
18. Observation, DYP offices, Adana, April, 2007.
19. Interview, Executive Director, CHP, Adana, 1 April 2009.
20. Interview, Ankara, 6 December 2000.
21. Review of the Parliamentary Proceedings of the Great National Assembly of Turkey, term 19, vol. 24, session 42, 14 December 1992, sitting 2, p. 438.
22. "Alevi kıyımı dursun", *Cumhuriyet*, 29 May 1996.
23. This enables better understanding of certain apparently contradictory voting instructions, such as those of an Alevist foundation that supported the DSP on the national level, but the CHP Alevi candidate in the municipal elections in Istanbul in 1999.
24. "Baykal'ın A takımı", *Hürriyet*, 5 February 1999. In these mixed provinces, because of the denomiationalization of votes, the CHP is often supported by and primarily composed of Alevis. Refusing to project an image of being an Alevi party, the leader, D. Baykal, cancelled internal elections there because they were leading in general to the naming of Alevi candidates.
25. It is interesting to note that the CHP campaigned very little among the Kurds in this district, considering that this was in principle the mayoral candidate's job, whereas the teams that went door-to-door were much more comfortable in the Arab neighborhoods. It should be added that convoys of CHP passing through neighborhoods with strong Kurdish concentrations or where the Kurdish parties were influential were often pelted with stones. Observations, March 2009, Adana.
26. See *Yeni Adana*, 23 December 1997.
27. *Demokratik Sol Partisi*, Party of the Democratic Left.
28. This term describes four schools of jurisprudence that exist in Sunni Islam, only two of which are present in Turkey. In Turkey, the term has taken on the sense of "denominational community" and often describes Alevis on the one hand and Sunnis on the other.
29. "Alevi düşmanlığı yalanı" *Güvercin* [DSP Party Journal] 1, 1 (1988), p. 30.
30. The guitar-Kalachnikov connection having widely been established during the 1970s, it can be considered to draw on a pre-existing stock of associations.
31. *Cumhuriyet Halk Partisi*, People's Republican Party, which is Kemalist.

5. THE TRANSFORMATION OF A CONFLICT IN THE DIASPORA: SIKHS, MUSLIMS AND THE BRITISH STATE

1. Though there are still intellectuals who staunchly defend it, see Modood, 2007.
2. It took place at Corrymeela, a residential center set up in the 1960s in Ireland, working in the field of conflict resolution. It has been particularly active in the Northern Ireland sectarian conflict.

3. On the colonial and indigenous construction of hardened boundaries, see Oberoi, 1994.

4. See among the many recent histories of the period, the reference work of Talbot and Singh, 2009.

5. This ambiguity resides in the fundamental distinction, based on criteria of religious belonging, between spoken and written language. Panjabi can be written using three different alphabets, Persian (*shamukhi*), *devanagari*, and *gurmukhi*. *Gurmukhi*, the holy script of the Sikhs, is the only one of the alphabets to be specific to Panjabi. Traditionally in northern India it was Persian and then Urdu that acted as the language of culture (of the court) and power in the nineteenth century. In colonial Panjab, Urdu and English were taught at school and Panjabi used at home. Only the Sikhs learned how to write Panjabi using the Gurmukhi alphabet, something they were taught at the *gurdwaras*. These linguistic practices followed and reinforced religious boundaries. After partition, the divide between spoken and written language along faith lines was reinforced and "nationalized", with Urdu becoming the national language of Pakistan and Hindi that of India. This linguistic pattern was reproduced in the diaspora, with the Panjabi language being spoken by all Panjabis within the family and home, but only being read, written, and studied by the Sikhs (as an optional subject at secondary school, at University, and in the gurdwaras. On the issue of language in colonial and postcolonial Panjab, see Rahman, 1996, Chapter 11.

6. Among the many publications devoted to the transnationalisation of *bhangra*, see Roy, 2010 and Schreffer, 2013.

7. Released in 2004, *Veer Zaara* (dir. Yash Chopra) narrates the tragic love story between an Indian (East Panjabi) pilot and a Pakistani (West Panjabi) woman, a romance set in the backdrop of the India-Pakistan conflict.

8. The most prominent example of this literature is the work authored by Urvashi Butalia (Butalia, 1998).

9. Interview by phone with the director of the company, Dominic Rai, 17/04/2009.

10. Western converts to Sikhism are called *Gore Sikhs* ('White Sikhs'), and are mostly based in North America. See Dusenbery, 2014.

11. *Community Cohesion: Sikh-Muslim Dialogue. An Alternative Report by Four Sikh Participants*, 1 October 2008, p. 8; Private communication from a Sikh participant.

12. *Talaq* is a unilateral verbal form of divorce, sanctioned in South Asia whereby a man divorces his wife by uttering three times this formula of repudiation.

13. Two Sikh organizations in the Midlands, the Sikh Awareness Society and Shere-Panjab, have even 'specialized' in the issue of grooming and presumed forced conversions of Sikhs girls by Muslim men, sustaining this myth which exerts a particularly mobilizing effect over part of the young British Sikh population.

14. Katy Sian identifies this as a key theme that sustains Sikh-Muslim antagonism in contemporary Britain, see Sian, 2013.

15. Interview with a Sikh activist and social policy consultant, who took part in the week-end of Sikh-Muslim dialogue in Northern Ireland, Ilford, 17 April 2009.

16. Interview with a Sikh activist and social policy consultant, Ilford, 17 April 2009.

17. Interview with a Sikh journalist and participant in the weekend of Sikh-Muslim dialogue, Slough, 22 April 2009. Indian soldiers, among whom 20 per cent were Sikhs, took part in the two World Wars. British Sikhs partly derive their claim to be a model minority with a privileged link to the United Kingdom and their subsequent demand of a differential treatment from the Anglo-Sikh military history.

18. Personal communication by mail with Faith Matters' director, Fiyaz Mughal, 28 May 2010.

19. Interview with a Sikh journalist and participant to the weekend of Sikh-Muslim dialogue, Slough, 22 April 2009.

20. Interview with a Sikh female municipal councilor, which had declined the invitation to attend the Sikh-Muslim dialogue weekend, Ilford, 16 November 2009.

21. Ibid.

22. In March 2009 an arson attack destroyed a Sikh place of worship in East London and in particular eleven copies of the Adi Granth, the Sikhs' sacred book which is especially revered by them. A mobilization campaign based on local committees immediately protested against police inertia.

23. Interview with a Sikh activist, member of an interfaith dialogue forum, Southall, 1 June 2010.

6. THE ORIGINS OF THE PROTEST MOVEMENT AGAINST ETHNIC HIERARCHY: THE AZERBAIJANI CAUSE IN IRAN

1. Article 15 provides that: "the use of regional and tribal languages in the press and mass media, as well as for teaching of their literature in schools, is allowed in addition to Persian."

2. I have chosen not to deal with the period following the Second World War, including the formation of an autonomous government led by Pishevari. For further reading, please see Atabaki (2000).

3. It is not the same being a Turk in Tehran or in Tabriz, nor in a remote village in West Azerbaijan. For further reading on differences in language practices, see the comparison between Tehran and Salma in Bosnali (2003).

4. We should note that women are absent from the group of Azeri identity entrepreneurs active during the revolutionary period.

5. We should emphasize that the autonomist shift is impossible to understand without Soviet support to the *Ferqa-ye Demokrat-e Azerbayjan*.

6. Resistance to Iranian nationalism is the principal explanation provided by the advocates of Azerbaijani cause.

7. This polysemous term can be translated as either presence or existence. It means the presence or existence of Turks in Iranian society despite the denial of the imperial regime.
8. Biographical information collected from sources in Tehran (2004) and in Paris (2006).
9. Similar remarks could be made about the multiple positions of Hamid Notqi (Shafaieh and Notqi, 2003).
10. Some dates are given according to the Iranian calendar for which the first day of the year is 21 March. As a reminder, 21 March 1979 is the first day of the year 1358.
11. Collected from interviews in Tabriz, Tehran and Paris, 2004–2005.
12. Based on interviews with relatives of Hosseyn Sadeq and activists of the 1970s, Tehran, Karaj, Paris, 2004–2007.

7. VIOLENCE AND WAR IN THE MIDDLE EAST IN THE 1980s

1. Departing from a macro scale and assuming the indeterminacy of a region that has grown due to political events towards the East, four cycles in the history of the Middle East in the twentieth century can be identified. The first two, 1919–1948 and 1948–1979, were long, and the two others, 1979–1989/1990 and 1990–2001 lasted only a decade.
2. The United States, whose supremacy at the end of this decade was indisputable, had difficulty imposing itself as master of its "clients". By a cruel historical trick, they became on the contrary a machine for the production of enemies, beginning with their allies. The Afghan Jihad was anti-Soviet out of necessity, but as numerous testimonies show, beginning with certain declarations of al-Zawahiri in the early 1980s, it was also on principle anti-American. Iraq, heavily armed by the United States and France against Iran, became notable beginning in the second half of the 1980s, for its openly anti-American positions.
3. Obviously, the phenomenon of brutalization, that one can observe throughout the twentieth century, was not limited exclusively to the Middle Eastern societies.
4. "The philosophy of the Mujahid is not identical to that of the martyr {…} Martyrdom in the strict sense of the term is a commandment {that comes} after the Jihad. {It} enters into the scene once the Mujahid has failed". Quoted in Khosrokhavar, 2002, 74.

8. SELF-RADICALISATION OF A YOUNG INDIAN JIHADIST IN GREAT BRITAIN: THE QUEST FOR ETHICS AND LONG-DISTANCE SUFFERING

1. Kalyvas underlines that the economic deprivation of the individual might not be a sufficient condition for suicide missions but the severe deprivation of the surrounding can become a motivation (Kalyvas and Sanchez-Cuenca, 2005, 230 & 231).

2. Revenge does not explain Kafeel's action but might be a relevant motive for Bilal (see below).
3. See Asad's critical assessment of the various factors seen as motivations by Strenski, 2003; Jayyusi, 2004; Etienne, 2005; and Pape, 2007.
4. This unusual situation raises epistemological and deontological questions that I will not address here for lack of space.
5. "Long distance suffering" is a phrase from Luc Boltanski (1993). See Blom and Jaoul, 2008.
6. It would have been of course interesting to probe Bilal's trajectory in more depth as a fair amount of Kafeel's action seems to rest on his meeting with Bilal but I have chosen to mainly focus on Kafeel's trajectory because of the exceptional access I had to him.
7. *New York Times*, 16 December 2008, *The Guardian*, 16 December 2008.
8. A state in south India whose capital is Bangalore.
9. This information was available to the press and confirmed by Sabeel.
10. It is worth noting however that Kafeel only spent a short time abroad—a little over four years. The term diaspora is therefore not wholly applicable to him, and he is best thought of as a person in transit, as referred to by Werbner (2004).
11. As described by Benedict Anderson (1998), drawing especially on the example of the Sikhs.
12. A Salafi is a Muslim who emphasizes the example of the Salaf, the earliest Muslims, as model examples of Islamic practice. See Meijer, 2009.
13. It is clear that one interview is insufficient to assess the degree of orthopraxis of an individual. Nevertheless, the declaration which follows is supported by discussions with his family and information found in the press based on interviews with people Kafeel knew.
14. The reference to the hereafter is worth noticing, though it was the only time he referred to it.
15. Since Sunday is a day of rest in India, discussion meetings of the faithful are often held then.
16. "Qadiani" is a reference to the Ahmadiyya, officially declared non-Muslim by Zulfikar Ali Bhutto in 1974, and considered to be non-Muslim by many Muslims around the world, for they elevate the founder of the movement, Mirza Ghulam Ahmad, to the status of prophet, thus bringing into question one of the underpinnings of Islam—the finality of Muhammad's prophecy.
17. *Outlook*, 23 July 2007.
18. In particular he was full of admiration for his mother because in his opinion she combined her family duties with a professional life and pious behaviour.
19. Interview with Sabeel in July 2008.
20. According to Shiraz Maher, a former Hizb-ut Tahrir sympathiser who knew the two young men well.

21. A certain Sheikh Ahmad Al-Qubeisi, according to Bilal's family. Cf. *Sunday Times*, 8 July 2007.
22. http://www.dailymail.co.uk/news/article-1085121/Doctor-suspected-car-bomb-terror-attacks-admits-wanted-Britain-taste-fear.html
23. *The Sunday Times*, 18 December 2008.

9. CONFLICTING EMOTIONS: THE 2006 ANTI-"DANISH CARTOONS" RIOT IN LAHORE (PAKISTAN)

1. Brandishing a sword while two women stand behind him with only frightened eyes uncovered (1); standing on a cloud to stop suicide bombers from getting into heaven because 'our stock of virgins has run out' (2); wearing a turban with a lighted bomb (3).
2. Sunni Islam is divided among three main doctrinal orientations in Pakistan. The Ahl-i-Hadith reject the Hanafi *fiqh* (followed by the two others), rely only on the Quran and *hadith* and claim to 'purge' Islam from 'heterodox' Sufi practices. Deobandis preach a self-consciously reformist faith centred on the mosque and madrasa. Barelwis on the contrary lay special emphasis on Sufi devotional practices and the intercessor power of the Prophet, the great saints of the past and the living *pir*. On the history of Barelwism, see Sanyal (1996).
3. A reformist Islamic sect formed in 1880s-90s in Punjab, accused by its opponents of contradicting the finality of the prophecy. Ahmadis (0.5 per cent of the population according to—unreliable—official figures) were declared a religious minority by the government in 1974.
4. All names have been changed, except for the organizer of the protest.
5. In some popular pictures (especially in Iran), the Prophet can be portrayed with human features (Centlivres and Centlivres-Demont, 2005). In Pakistan the norm is to represent him through his symbolic attributes alone.
6. A local proverb.
7. The TNRM is a vigilant organization formed, in 2002, in reaction to President Musharraf's stated intention to reform the Blasphemy Laws.
8. The resolution stipulating that Ahmadis were a non-Muslim minority was initially presented in the National Assembly by a Barelwi *alim* and JUP leader.
9. Eternally virginal and celestial female beings, mentioned in the Quran and promised to the "good Muslims".
10. As many popular jokes convey it in Pakistan.
11. On the usage of this rhetorical figure in social mobilization's process, see Cefaï, 2007, 505.
12. The JuD (named as such in December 2001 but formerly known as the Markaz Dawa wal-Irshad or by the name of its armed wing, the Lashkar-i-Tayyeba) was formed in 1986 to send Pakistani Ahl-i-Hadith recruits to fight (in marginal number) in Afghanistan and, after 1990, in Indian Kashmir.

13. The shrine of Abu Hasan Ali al-Hujwiri, popularly known as Hazrat Data Ganj Bakhsh ("the giver who bestows treasure"), a Sufi scholar said to have converted the first Hindu to Islam in Lahore, where he died in 1077. His grave is the most popular site of Sufi veneration in the city.

14. Shahrukh Khan is an Indian (Muslim) actor extremely popular in Pakistan and famous for his fits of anger.

15. Being bribed by the police is a very common experience for young middle-class Lahoris using motorbikes.

16. A colloquial expression meaning to pick up a fight, used in the Bollywood movies' slang used by Old City's youngster.

17. In 1978 for instance, the Awqaf Department forbade its employees to say *durud* (request for mercy upon the Prophet and praise) before the *azan* (call for prayer), a decision Barelwi *ulama* eventually fought in court.

18. The ban, enforced in 1984, was lifted in March 2008 only.

19. In 1927, the colonial courts arrested a Hindu man who had published a book (*Rangila Rasul*, "The Merry Messenger of God"), found to be prone to provoke enmity between Hindus and Muslims. After his release from prison two years later, the publisher was stabbed to death by a young Muslim, Ilam Din. The Lahore High Court sentenced Din to be hanged. Huge demonstrations erupted and British officials were eventually forced to return his body to his family. Ilam Din received a hero burial and was given the honorific title of *ghazi* ("victorious") and *shahid* ("martyr") by the Muslim notables of Rang Mahal.

20. Given the lack of academic work, this chronology is tentative. I am very grateful to Professor Tahir Kamran (GCU, Lahore) and to Shohaib Hashmi for helping me with this.

21. After the Sikhs were granted control of the site by the colonial, 2000 people massed at the entrance of Landa Bazaar and put the police station under siege. Twelve of them died. Barelwi *ulama* issued fatwas stating that those who had not joined the agitation could not received Islamic funerals. This dispute over a sacred site (revered by both Muslims and Sikhs) contributed to "dramatize...the emotional power and political importance of Islamic symbols" in Punjabi politics' underlies David Gilmartin (1988, 100).

22. But a much bloodier one as 300 people died (Government of Punjab 1954, 35).

23. Factional infightings within the PML, for instance, also played a crucial role during the 1953 riots.

24. This with the brief exception of the 2007 lawyers movement. Significantly, in the following years, many of its participants allied with Barelwi extremists responsible for assassinating the Governor of Punjab, Salman Taseer (he had called for a revision of the Blasphemy Laws).

25. Blasphemy is defined in Pakistan's Penal Code (a slightly revised version of the 1860 colonial code) as "injuring or defiling place of worship, with intent to insult

the religion of any class of persons" (art. 295) and "the deliberate intention of wounding the religious feelings of any person" by "word", "sound" or "gesture" or any 'object in the sight of that person' (art. 298).

26. Stating that "Whoever by words, either spoken or written, or by visible representation, or by any imputation, innuendo, or insinuation, directly or indirectly, defiles the sacred name of the Holy prophet Muhammad (PBUH) shall be punished with death, or imprisonment for life, and shall also be liable to fine". Accusations of blasphemy had since become a lethal instrument of socio-economical rivalries and personal vengeance.

27. The mention of religion in the passport targeted the Ahmadis to prevent them from going to Mecca. In 1992, Nawaz Sharif decided that the National Identity Card should also mention its holder's religion (a decision cancelled after protests from the civil society). In 2005, the hard-core component of the PML mobilized against the removal of the 'religious column' from the new machine-readable passports. It was restored.

28. This chapter is a revised and updated version of: Amélie Blom, "The 2006 Anti-'Danish Cartoons' Riot in Lahore: Outrage and the Emotional Landscape of Pakistani Politics", *South Asia Multidisciplinary Academic Journal* [Online], 2 | 2008, http://samaj.revues.org/1652.

10. QUETTA CITY AND THE BALUCH GUERRILLA: ISSUES AT STAKE IN POLITICALLY MOTIVATED URBAN VIOLENCE

1. Another set of severe casualties in Quetta is linked to sectarian killings; to take just one example, on 3 September 2010 a suicide bomber exploded in the middle of a Shiite procession on Meezan Chawk, in the heart of Quetta, killing seventy-three people and injuring more than 160 others.

2. For an analysis of the "generative schemes" (terminology explicitly borrowed by the author from Pierre Bourdieu) of violence—that is to say the logical substrate of oppositions, analogies, and homologies on which cultural representations are founded, and which inform or justify violence—see Whitehead, 2004. This work depicts tools that can capture the "cultural forms" giving meaning to "shocking" forms of conflicts and assassinations, while analyzing to what extent the construction of meaning itself contributes to the perpetration of violence. For an anthropological analysis of the "economies of war" and violence, see Stewart and Strathern, 2004. On this topic, see the debate on violence as a sociological concept in Collins, 2009. For a cognitive analysis of violence, see Braud, 2003, 33–47.

3. "Kili", meaning literally "village", is the term used to designate the city quarters of the "rural Quetta". All the names of places and people given in this article have been changed.

4. Scholz distinguishes between two types of urban development in Baluchistan during the colonial period: 1) the "Anglo-Baluch" towns which are characterized by

the development of administrative quarters around an already existing city cen-tre; and 2) the "British colonial" town which were newly built (Scholtz, 2002, 111–119).

5. For an anthropological study on the Hazara networks between Afghanistan, Pakistan, and Iran, see Monsutti, 2004.

6. This tribe owned large portions of land around Quetta, and their main economic occupation was animal husbandry. Most of its members never settled permanently in the area, using it as seasonal grazing grounds (Dur Mohammad Kassi, inter-view, 2 October 2009).

7. Founded in 1967 by students in Karachi, the BSO acted as the cradle for the first Baluch nationalist organizations, whether armed guerrilla groups or political par-ties. It was one of the main initiators of the rebellion against the state of Pakistan from 1973 to 1977. Most of today's nationalist party leaders started their politi-cal career as BSO militants.

8. Interview, 9 October 2009, Quetta.

9. While there are a number of organizations reporting on politically motivated vio-lence and human rights abuses in Pakistan, very few have systematically surveyed and classified such occurrences. The present data has been collected from scruti-nizing local newspapers (mainly *Dawn*, *The News*, *Baluchistan Times* and *Asaap*), reports issued by the Human Rights Commission of Pakistan, and the findings of the South Asian Terrorism Portal (http://www.satp.org/). Discrepancies have been found between all these sources, and only cross-checked information has been retained. The main difficulty has been to identify with certainty acts of vio-lence perpetuated by the Baluch nationalists and those motivated by sectarian con-flicts, many which are not officially claimed by any group. Nonetheless, the nature of the casualties and the identity of the victims often give an indication of what motivated the attack.

10. The BLUF, which was previously unheard of, first came to public attention on 2 February 2009 when it kidnapped the UNHCR director in Quetta. The other nationalist groups were initially sceptical as regards the identity of the group—BLA initially denied having any links with it (*Daily Times*, 7 February 2009). BLUF was asking for "the liberation of 141 women and 6000 men" who are impris-oned or simply disappeared. Solecki was released two months later.

11. The stigmatization of the Punjabis is nothing new. Nationalist rhetoric equates the word "Punjabi" with "the enemy" at least since the 1970s, and this notwith-standing the fact that a charter was voted by the first Baluch provincial govern-ment of 1972 stating, amongst other things, that Punjabis who had lived in the Province for several generations would be respected to the same extent as any other inhabitant.

12. The guerrilla was headed by the tribal chief Nauroz Khan. His main demands were as follows: that the government officially recognize "Baluch customs"; the libera-

tion of the leader of the Kalat state (*Khan*); and the end of the *One Unit* scheme, instituted in 1955, which held Pakistan to be a homogeneous Nation, devoid of any provincial particularities.

13. In Baluchi, the term *parari* is used to describe a person whose grievances are such that they cannot be appeased by words or negotiation.

14. What these spontaneous fronts have in common is that they are based mainly on tribal links. However, both the BPLF and the Parari movement sought to create a para-tribal organization at the service of a Marxist-based revolutionary project (Selig Harrison, 1981, 71–83). For a detailed description of this fourth phase, see: Afzal 2001, 144–6; Breseeg 2004, 227–244, 280–296, & 324–347; Inayatullah Baluch, 1985, 335–373; Janmahmad, *Baluch*,1989, 157–213; Mir Ahmad Yar Khan Baluch, 1975, 180–90; Wayne Ayres Wilcox, 1966, 206; Lawrence Ziring, 1999, 163–214 & 325–335.

15. It covers almost all the Baluch districts in the province, mobilizes thousands of people (10,000 according to the government, 50,000 according to the activists), and attracts sympathy from certain mainstream political groups. Popular support can be gauged from demonstrations in the Quetta streets, the fluttering of nationalist flags on all kinds of vehicles, the sudden emergence of specialized shops in Quetta bazaars exclusively selling posters, CDs, and other propaganda material in favor of the Baluch nationalist struggle, and the treatment of the nationalist theme and armed struggle in local film production, previously known for its comedies (Malik Siraj Akbar, 12 November 2008, http://gmcmissing.wordpress.com/2008/11/12/radicalised-Baluchi-culture-in-the-wake-of-conflict,).

16. This coalition was comprised of the five main Baluch nationalist political parties: the BNP (*Baluch National Party*), the BNM (*Baluch National Movement*), the JWP (*Jamhoori Watan Party*), the BNDP (*Baluchistan National Democratic Party*), and the BSO (*Baluch Student Organisation*). Mohammad Ilyas Khan claims that this coalition had become the political wing of the guerrilla ("Back to the hills", *The Herald*, October 2004, 64–75).

17. Interviews with members of BLA, 2007; according to Akbar, from this period onwards, the rebellion underwent a "change of paradigm" (Malik Siraj Akbar, "Target Killings bring BLA support into new focus", *Daily Times*, 3 June 2008).

18. This is something the policemen openly admit themselves. In September 2007, I interviewed a Chief of Police and asked his opinion about allegations that not more than 100 persons were responsible for conducting attacks in the city, all of them known to the law enforcement agencies, but that no one could arrest them. His answer was that this was absolutely true; the police were unable to arrest these people without the authorization of their superiors, something they would not risk their lives by giving.

19. This short-lived newspaper became one of the leading opposition newspapers in Baluchistan. Its Chief Editor, Jan Mahmad Dashti, who has written several books

on the province and Baluch Nationalism, survived critical injuries after an attempt on his life on 22 February 2009. The attack occurred after *Asaap* had published a list of alleged disappeared Baluch citizens. For details, see Malik Siraj Akbar article, http://gmcmissing.wordpress.com/2009/08/18/bye-bye-asaap/.

20. Interview, 3 October 2009, Quetta.

21. The BRP is one of the most radical Baluch nationalist political parties, and openly supports the armed rebellion.

22. Interview with a Quetta farmer and sympathizer of the armed struggle, but not a political activist (30 September 2009, Quetta).

23. Interview, 29 September 2009, Quetta.

24. The establishment of a mature Baluch and Brahui confederacy is attributed to Mir Ahmad Ahmadzai who, from 1666 onwards, strengthened a fragile political structure and centralized power over scattered tribes. He formed a *diwan* (court) and replicated the Afghan *jirga* principle (a council of elders invested with both judicial and executive powers), in which the different *sardar* (tribal chiefs) were represented; he also consolidated a military system enabling him to extend his authority to the regions of Sibi, Kachhi, Noshki and Jhalawan.

25. The total cost of the lease was of 150,000 rupees per annum. For details, see the letter from Captain R.G. Sandeman, dated 10 April 1872, no. 229, cited by Inayatullah Baluch 1990, 252–253.

26. The author essentially argues that Baluch tribes have been able to increase their territorial domination by developing techniques of absorbing foreign tribes (including former Pashtuns) by including them as a branch of their own Baluch tribes. Observing the reversal of this tendency, Paul Titus invites us to reconsider Barth's article by distinguishing between "tribal and gradual" expansion—which corresponds to the Baluch expansion into Pashtun territory observed by Barth— and the Pashtun "rapid individual entrepreneur[ial]" expansion based on a mechanism of economic competition. In Baluchistan, this expansion is visible not only in the control exerted by Pashtun transporters in Baluch areas, but also in the contractors, traders and farmers working in the same zones. See Paul Titus, "Routes to Ethnicity: Roads, Buses, and Differential Ethnic Relations in Pakistani Baluchistan", in Paul Titus, *Baluch*, 1996, 273–295.

27. A controversy over establishing quotas for admission to schools and universities sparked demonstrations and violent clashes in 2008 and 2009. On 10 February 2009, three buses of the Baluchistan University of Information Technology and Management Science (BUITM, also known as IT University), carrying students daily to the premises, were burned.

28. Interview, 11 September 2009, Quetta.

29. Interview, 2 October 2009, Quetta.

30. Paul Titus, 1996.

31. Interview, 25 September 2009, Quetta.

32. Interview, 6 October 2009, Quetta.
33. Interview, 3 October 2009, Quetta.

11. GRADUATING TO VIOLENCE: THE ESCALATION OF STUDENT STRIFE AT KARACHI UNIVERSITY, 1979–1989

1. Research for this paper was carried out during two field trips to Karachi in June 2008 and July 2009, which were funded by the Conflits Iran, Turquie, Pakistan (Conflits-TIP) research group of the French Agence nationale de la recherche (ANR), under the scientific coordination of Gilles Dorronsoro. I would also like to extend my warmest thanks to Hidayat Hussain and Nadeem F. Paracha for their support in Karachi.
2. In Jalib (2001), 26. This poem became an anthem of the anti-Ayub Khan student movement of 1968–69.
3. As socio-psychologist John Horgan emphasizes, most studies of "terrorism" do not bother to lend an ear to what the so-called "terrorists" have to say about their own actions.
4. Interview with Fahim Khan, Karachi, 2009.
5. The IJT is the student branch of the oldest Islamist organization in the subcontinent, the Jama'at-e-Islami. In the 1960s, the IJT formed a militia at Karachi and Lahore universities to counter left wing student organisations. This militia, known as the Thunder Squad, mainly recruited local petty criminals (*badmash*).
6. The USM included the PSF, the Baloch Students Organisation (BSO), the Pakhtun Students Federation (PkSF), the Punjabi Students Association (PSA), and the newly formed All Pakistan Mohajir Students Organisation (APMSO).
7. The PSF, a student branch of the Pakistan Peoples Party (PPP), was formed in 1972.
8. Interview, London, 2009.
9. Interview, London, 2009.
10. On "Schmittian" *vs*. "Hobbesian" ontologies of conflict, see Kalyvas, 2003, 475–494.
11. Interview, Karachi, 2009.
12. Interview, London, 2009.
13. These three attributes of political contingency are borrowed from Schedler, 2007, 54–78.
14. Although the hijacking was planned earlier in Kabul, it was directly linked to the February 1981 incidents at KU: one of the hijackers (Nasir Jamal) was on the run for his life after having been charged with the murder of Hafiz Aslam, and the first list of political prisoners the hijackers demanded be released were all student activists involved in this incident; see the account of former al-Zulfiqar member Raja Anwar (Anwar, 1997, 99).

15. On this point, see the account of PSF activist Asif Butt in his political memoirs, *Kai Suliyan Sar-e-Rah Thin* (Butt, 2014, 61).

16. Interview with Fahim Khan and Nabu Patel, Karachi, 2008.

17. Interview, Karachi, 2009.

18. Nadeem F. Paracha, "Student Politics in Pakistan: A History, Lament and Celebration", which may be consulted at http://docs.google.com/View?id=dcn65hk2_65ftb4fft

19. "The Campus Mafias", *The Herald* (Karachi), October 1988, 65. This figure is given for all Karachi campuses (which includes the city's numerous colleges).

20. G.M. Syed (1904–1995) was a strong supporter of the movement for Pakistan in Sindh, but became a staunch Sindhi nationalist in the decades that followed the creation of the country. In 1971 he demanded that the province be given the right of self-determination, and the following year he formed the Jiye Sindh Mahaz (Movement for the Protection of Sindh), which advocated the autonomy/independence of Sindh. The first meeting between this protector of the "old Sindhis" and Altaf Hussain, who projected himself as the leader of the "new Sindhis", occurred in 1985.

21. "The Campus Mafias", op.cit.

22. See, for instance, the testimony of "Arshad", in Khan, 2010, chap. 1, where this former MQM militant justifies his killings by the "war situation" which prevailed in Karachi in the late 1980s.

23. I am indebted to Nichola Khan for this information.

24. This hypothesis is freely derived from the testimonies of MQM killers gathered by Khan, whose anthropological perspective focuses on the "political subjectivities", "desires" and "fantasies" of these killers, rather than on their practices *per se*.

25. For further discussion of this topic the reader is referred to Gayer, 2007, 515–544.

26. Nadeem Paracha, "Student Politics in Pakistan: a History, Lament and Celebration", accessible at http://docs.google.com/View?id=dcn65hk2_65ftb4fft. An abridged version of the article is also available at http://www.dawn.com/news/1116782

27. Interviews with students and lecturers, Karachi University, 2008 and 2009.

28. All three elements identified by Hanspeter Kriesi in his definition of the political opportunities structure of social movements were relevant here: the formal structure of the state, the informal procedures and the strategies of political authorities towards political challengers, and internal dynamics within political parties; *cf.* Kriesi, Koopmans, Willem Duyvendak and Giugni, 1995. But since these political opportunities are dynamic, co-produced as they are by dominants and challengers, the use of the term "structure" is problematic here; cf. Fillieule and Mathieu, 2009, 530–540.

12. THE INSTRUMENTALIZATION OF ETHNIC CONFLICT BY THE STATE: THE AZERI-KURDISH CONFLICT IN IRAN

1. Sections 15 and 19 of the Constitution of the Islamic Republic recognize the equality of "all Iranians, regardless of their ethnicity or tribe" and the use of local languages in the press and in schools second to Persian.
2. According to the Kurdish Democratic Party of Iran, the fighting "which still continues on 27 April, in neighboring villages, has caused 350 deaths" (Kutschera, 1997, 168). According to Turkish sources, the fighting in the city lasted three days and caused 210 fatalities among Turks and over 80 among Kurds (Qahremanpur, 2006, 201).
3. Name given to the plain of Naqadeh.
4. The Kurdish regions located in north-western Iran, are spread over several administrative provinces: Kurdistan, West Azerbaijan, Kermanshah and Ilam.
5. In the past there were more Jewish and Christian families. The Jews were probably the oldest among the current populations of the district. In Naqadeh in 1914, there were 80 Christian families and 120 Jewish families (*The Encyclopedia of Islam*, Volume IV, 1934)
6. Among, the Azeris, who are mostly Shi'a, there are also Baha'is, a religious minority which is not recognized by the Islamic Republic. There are also Turkic speaking tribes, the Kuresunni, which have largely dispersed in the region of Urumiyeh, of Salmas and of Khoy. Kurds in the region are predominantly Shafii rite Sunnis, even if their number includes a diverse esoteric community (Ahl-i Haqq, Ali Elahi, etc.) who fall within a general framework of Shi'ite Islam, but present a number of original characteristics.
7. Means bandits.
8. The original use of the "Ajam" dates back to the Safavid era when Shi'ites opposed Sunnis. Coined by the Kurds to speak of Shi'ite authority, the term today is used by Kurds to refer to any person who is not Kurdish. In West Azerbaijan, this word denotes Azeris who are often the central authority. The use of this term takes on both political and ethnic overtones (Naser 'alyar, 2005). The Safavid era seems to be one of the periods that marked the deeper relations between Kurds and Iranians. The Safavids in massacring Sunni Kurds in the name of religion further widened the gap between these two peoples (Abrishamy, 1974, 101–102).
9. A city of northwest Iran located in Eastern Azerbaijan province.
10. "Between mountain dwellers and Sunni shi'ites, there was a perennial gripe nurtured by a thousand incidents. But Kurds are dangerous fighters and feared by the Tabrizi who refuse to attack them while they were yet living, taking revenge mischievously at the hour of death. Kurds found dead in the city ran great risk of being buried face down, instead of being properly installed in the pit, his face turned toward Mecca, as required by custom. Thus, Azrael, the angel of death, wounded by this unseemly posture, denied them access to paradise. It also happens some-

times, that a stricken Kurd, at a hospital in the district, feeling his strength declining, disappears to steal a horse and with slack bridal return home to die in Kurdistan." (Bouvier, 2001, 166).

11. See in particular, Saleh, Rafiq; Saleh, Sedig (in), *Rojnama-ye Kurdistan. Mahabad 1324–1325 hetavi 1946), (The journal of Kurdistan*), Sulaymaniya, ed. Benka-ye Jin, 2007, and the poem by Hemin *"kurd o Azerbaijan"* in Tarik o Run (*Obscurité et Clarté*) collection of poems, (Baqdad, 1974, 93).

12. On relationships between Kurds and Azeris in Western Azerbaijan see Sahfi, 2001, 340–341.

13. Before the 1979 revolution, it was not common to meet every Friday at the mosque in the city. The Islamic Republic will give a political dimension to this prayer by calling the faithful to participate.

14. *Ashura*: the tenth day of Moharam (lunar Islamic calendar). On that day, Shi'ites commemorate the death of Imam Hossein, son of Ali, who was killed with his entire family in Karbala by Yazid son of Mu'awiya.

15. The Azeri cleric from Urumiyeh, Molla Hasani is proclaimed Friday Imam of this city. Controversial of character, he is the "hero of Azerbaijan" to some and "savage anti-Kurd" to others.

16. A Sunni cleric from Sanandaj, Muftizadeh Ahmed founded *Hezb-e mosavat–e Islami* (Islamic Party of Equality) in 1979. He fought for Kurdish autonomy in the early Islamic Republic and opposed the Komala and KDPI, which he considered anti-religious. He reconciled himself to the government position, but shortly after split with the governing party over adoption of the Shi'ite confession as the official religion of the country.

17. See the *'Etell'aât* and *Keyhân* 1979 newspapers.

18. *Komala-ye Shoreshgari-ye Zahmat Keshan-e Kordestan Iran* (Revolutionary Committee of the toiling masses of Iranian Kurdistan) known as Komala was founded in 1969 by some left-wing students in Tehran. Its first congress was held in late 1978.

19. In fact, the day of their meeting in February 1979 with the government delegation, officers of the Mahabad garrison rebelled. The commander was wounded by one of his soldiers. The Peshmerga (Kurdish fighters) intervened and the encircled garrison surrendered.

20. Tchamran, a native of Tehran, left for the United States in 1959 for graduate studies. In the 1970s, he became interested in Middle Eastern Islamic movements. He returned to Iran at the beginning of the revolution. He was sent into Kurdish regions as commanding officer to combat the opponents. He formed the first groups of the Pasdaran. As a reward for his distinguished service in the war, he was promoted Minister of Defense. Tchamran was killed during the Iran-Iraq War (source: http://www.chamran.org/biography).

21. Gen. Zahir Nejad was "appointed" by the authorities in Tehran to command the

64th Division. The Azeri officer, considered by Kurds to be a militant anti-Kurd, himself considered that Kurdish "separatism" is merely the product of "Zionist-imperialist" manipulations (Kutschera, 1997, 170).

22. This section is based on evidence collected in Europe in discussions with people from Naqadeh as well as written sources such as Kutschera, 1997, 168, Qahremanpur, 2006, 199–205 and various websites.

23. Concerning Naghadeh War, see the papers collected in Molla Hasani (Abazari, 2005). Concerning the deployment of armed forces to Sanandaj, Kutschera wrote: "On August 19, Tehran radio interrupted its programming to transmit Khomeiny's call for a general mobilization to "save the garrison at Sanandaj overwhelmed by elements of the KDPI and with city women taken hostage (...) Any delay, even an hour, could have tragic consequences." Even as the call was made, the Kurdistan provincial governor reported that a total calm prevails in Sanadadj and wonders who could have planted such "lies" Khomeini. (Kutschera, 1997, 172). See also the website, www.meisami.com.

24. Democratic Party of Iranian Kurdistan was founded in 1945 by Qazi Mohammad.

25. See Tchamran stories on Kurdistan (1985); Sahifeh-ye Nur, Khomeini's speeches on the events of this period in Kurdistan (www.tebyan.net).

26. Daily Persian official newspaper.

27. In Naqadeh there were two committees: Committee No. 1 was appointed and composed of Shi'ite Azeris and Committee No. 2 composed of Sunni Kurds.

28. The Secretary General of KDPI.

29. According to D. McDowall, following the violence in Naqadeh, 12,000 Kurds sought refuge in neighboring cities (McDowall, 2004, 270).

30. In August 1979, following the incidents in Paveh, a Sunni Kurdish town near Kermanshah, Khomeini delivered a speech outlawing the KDPI and "summoning the army to restore order within twenty-four hours", saying he would take sanctions against any revolutionary officer who refused to execute its instructions (Kutschera, 1997, 172). This statement rather than calming the region contributed to the violence and made it irreversible.

31. The estimated number of deaths varies according to sources. According to the evidence collected from a native inhabitant of this village, forty-two persons, composed of children, women and old men were killed.

32. See Vijeh nâme-ye Kordestan No. 1, 1993 at http://www.meisami.com; also Bluryan, 2005, 368–377.

33. While Articles 15 and 19 of the Constitution guaranties the equality of "all Iranians, regardless of ethnicity or tribe" and authorizes the use of local languages in the press and in schools side-by-side with Persian. Art. 19, Section 115 excludes religious minorities, including Sunni, from any position of responsibility as revolutionary guide, president as well as other position of senior authority (Potocki, 2004, 49 and 91).

34. PJAK (Party of Free Life of Kurdistan) was founded in 2003 by former member of KDPI Haji Ahmadi. This movement is close to the PKK, the Kurdistan Workers' Party, a Marxist nationalist movement originating in Turkish Kurdistan.
35. Mohammad Oraz (Hewraz) was a mountaineer born in 1969 in Naquadeh. His mother is an Azeri Turk and his father a Kurd. In 1998 he climbed to the top of Mount Everest and became a symbol for young people. He died on 6 September 2003 attempting an ascent of Gasherbrum Mountain, Pakistan. His grave is regularly visited by young athletes.

BIBLIOGRAPHY

ABAZARI, Abdolrahim (collected by) (2005), Xâterât-e Hojatoleslâm Hasani, Imam jome-ye Urumiyeh (Memories of Hojatoleslâm Hasani, imam of Urumiyeh Friday), Tehran, Merkaz-e Asnâd-e Enqelâb-islmani.

ABBAS, Hassan (2007), "Transforming Pakistan's Frontier Corps", *Terrorism Monitor*, 5 (6) (http://www.jamestown.org/programs/gta/single/?tx_ttnews[tt_news]=1056&tx_ttnews[backPid]=182&no_cache=1).

ABDOLI, Ali (2007), *Tâlesh, Birthplace of Zoroaster, The Prophet of Ancient Iran*, Tehran, Majmu'e enteshârât-e Tâleshân-e moqim-eTehrân, 1.

ABOU ZAHAB, Mariam (1999), "Le Sipah-e Sahaba dans le Penjab. Islamisation de la société ou conflit de classe?", *Cahiers d'études sur la Méditerranée orientale et le monde turco-iranien*, 27, pp. 143–157.

ABRAHAMIAN, Ervand (1970), "Communism and Communalism in Iran: The Tudah and the Firqah-I Dimukrat", *International Journal of Middle East Studies*, 1 (4), pp. 291–316.

ABRISHAMY, Abdollah (1994), Naqd va baresi-ye Nasionalime (melligarâyi) (A Study of Nationalism), Tehran.

AFSHAR, Mahmoud (1925), *Ayandeh*, 1, quoted by Touraj Atabaki and Erik J. Zürcher (eds), *Men of Order: Authoritarian Modernization under Atatürk and Reza Shah*, London: I. B. Tauris, 2004.

AFZAL, Mohammad Rafique (2001), *Pakistan, History and Politics (1947–1971)*, Karachi: Oxford University Press.

AGHAJANIAN, Akbar (1983), "Ethnic Inequality in Iran: An Overview", *International Journal of Middle East Studies*, 15 (2), pp. 211–224.

AHMAD, Mujeeb (1993) *Jamiyyat Ulama-i-Pakistan*, Islamabad: National Institute of Historical and Cultural Research.

AHMED, Ishtiaq (2004) "Forced Migration and Ethnic Cleansing in Lahore in 1947: Some First Person Accounts", in Ian Talbot & Shinder Thandi (eds.), *People on the Move: Punjabi Colonial and Post-Colonial Migration*, Karachi: Oxford University Press, pp. 96–141.

BIBLIOGRAPHY

AKBAR, Malik Siraj (2008), "Target Killing bring BLA Support into New Focus", *Daily Times*, 3 June.

AKERLOF, George A. and Rachel E. CRANTON (2000), "Economics and Identity", *The Quarterly Journal of Economics*, 115 (3), pp. 715–753.

AKSU, Sezen (2009), "La Turquie en Ebru", in Attila Durak (ed.), *Ebru. Reflets de la diversité culturelle en Turquie*, Arles: Actes Sud.

ALBA, Richard D. (1990), *Ethnic Identity. The Transformation of White America*, New Haven, CT: Yale University Press.

ALEXANDER, Claire (2004), "Imagining the Asian Gang: Ethnicity, Masculinity and Youth after the Riots", *Critical Social Policy*, 24 (4), pp. 526–549.

'ALI FARZANE, Mohammad (1979–1980a), *Kitab-e Dede Korkud*, Tehran: Ferzane.

——— (1979–1980b), *Mabani-ye Dastur-e Zaban-e Azerbayjan*, Tehran: Ferzane.

——— (1981–1982), *Bayatilar*, Tehran: Ferzane.

'ALYAR, Naser (2005), "Gâmi khord dar kashf-e ârmânha-ye Kurd", Chechm-Andaz, Vijeh nameh-ye Kurdistan, 2, (http://www.meisami.com/@oldsite/index.htm/ Cheshm/Special/Kordestan02).

AMENEH, Ali and Hussain ZAHID (1986), "Baluchistan: High-Stake Game", *Herald*, 17 (7), pp. 43–66.

AMINZADE, Ronald and Doug MCADAM (2002), "Introduction: Emotions and Contentious Politics", *Mobilization*, Special Issue "Emotions and Contentious Politics", 7 (2).

AMSELLE, Jean-Loup (2011), *L'ethnicisation de la France*, Paris: Lignes.

AMSELLE, Jean-Loup and Elikia M'BOKOLO (eds.) (1985), *Au coeur de l'ethnie. Ethnie, tribalisme et État en Afrique*, Paris: La Découverte.

ANDERSON, Benedict (1998), *The Spectre of Comparisons: Nationalism, South East Asia and the World*, London: Verso.

ANDREWS, Peter Alford (1989), *Ethnic Groups in the Republic of Turkey*, Wiesbaden, Dr Ludwig Reichert.

ANWAR, Raja (1997), *The Terrorist Prince: The Life and Death of Murtaza Bhutto*, London: Verso.

ARANI, Taqi (1924), "Azerbayjan ya yek Mas'aleh-ye Hayati va Mamati-ye Iran", *Farhangestan*, 1, pp. 247–254.

ARENDT, Hannah (1970), *On Violence*, London: Harvest Books.

ARIKAN-AKDAĞ, Gül, (2012) "AKP's local politics. Perceived discrimination as an obstacle to ethnic mobilization", *Alternatif Politika/Alternative Politics*, 4(2), pp. 147–179.

ASAD, Talal (2007), *On Suicide Bombing*, New York: Columbia University Press.

ATABAKI, Touraj (2000), *Azerbaijan, Ethnicity and The Struggle for Power in Iran*, London: I. B. Tauris.

——— (2005), "Ethnic Diversity and Territorial Integrity of Iran. Domestic Harmony and Religious Challenge", *Iranian Studies*, 38 (1), pp. 23–44.

BIBLIOGRAPHY

ATHAR, Khalid (1988), *Safar-e-Zindagi. MQM ki Kahani, Altaf Hussain ki Zabani Main* (Urdu) (The Journey of Life. The Story of MQM in the Words of Altaf Hussain), Karachi: Jang Publishers.

AXMANN, Martin (2008), "Phoenix from the Ashes? The Baloch National Movement and Its Recent Revival", in Carina Jahani, Agnes Korn and Paul Titus (eds), *The Baloch and Others, Linguistic, Historical and Socio-Political Perspectives on Pluralism in Balotchistan*, Wiesbaden: Reichert Verlag.

AYAR, Sıdıka (1999), *Dağ Çiçeklerim (anılar)*, Ankara: Öğretmen Dünyası.

AYATA, Ayse (1997), "The Emergence of Identity Politics in Turkey", *New Perspectives on Turkey*, 17, pp. 59–73.

AZERBAYJAN ELMLER AKADEMYASI (Azerbayjan Academy of Science) (1980–1981), *Tarikh-i Azerbayjan* (translated by N. Felsefi), Tabriz, ark Yay.

AZEROĞLU, Balash (1985–1986), *Savalan Nağmeleri*, Tabriz: Telash.

BADIE, Bertrand and Marie-Claude SMOUTS (1992), *Le retournement du monde: Sociologie de la scène internationale*, Paris: Dalloz.

BAILEY, Frederick G. (1996), *The Civility of Indifference: On Domesticating Ethnicity*, Ithaca, NY: Cornell University Press.

BALOCH, Inayatullah (1985), "The Baluch Question in Pakistan and the Right of Self-détermination", in Zingel Lallemant (ed.), *Pakistan in the 80s. Ideology, Regionalism, Economy, Foreign Policy*, Lahore: Vanguard Books.

—— (1990), *Baluchistan Newsletter*, 1.

BALUCH, Mir Ahmad Yar Khan (1975), *Inside Baluchistan. Political Autobiography of Khan-e-Azam Mir Ahmed Yar Khan Baluch, ex-Ruler of Kalat State*, Karachi: Royal Book Company.

BANCEL, Nicolas (2003), "Le bain colonial: aux sources de la culture coloniale populaire", in Pascal Blanchard and Sandrine Lemaire (eds.), *Culture coloniale. La France conquise par son empire (1871–1931)*, Paris: Autrement, pp. 179–190.

BARKEY, Karen (2008), *Empire of Difference: The Ottomans in Comparative Perspective*. Cambridge: Cambridge University Press.

BARTH, Fredrick (1956), "Ecologic Relationships of Ethnic Groups in Swat", *North American Anthropologist*, New Series, 58 (6), pp. 1079–1089.

—— (1969), *Ethnic Groups and Boundaries. The Social Organization of Culture Difference*, Boston, MA: Little, Brown.

—— (1981), "Ethnic processes on the Pathan-Bluchi boundary", in *Feature of Person and Society in Swat, Collected Essays on Pathans*, Volume II, London: Routledge/Kegan Paul, pp. 83–102.

BATES, Robert H. (1983), "Modernization, Ethnic Competition, and the Rationality of Politics in Contemporary Africa", in Donald Rothchild and Victor A. Olorunsola (eds), *State Versus Ethnic Claims. African Policy Dilemmas*, Boulder, CO: Westview Press, pp. 152–172.

BAUDRILLARD, Jean (2002), *L'esprit du terrorisme*, Paris: Galilée.

BAUMAN, Gerd (1990), "The Re-invention of Bhangra: Social Change and Aesthetic Shifts in a Punjabi Music in Britain", *The World of Music*, 32 (2).

—— (1996), *Contesting Culture: Discourses of Identity in Multi-ethnic London*, Cambridge: Cambridge University Press.

BAX, Mart (2000), "Planned Policy or Primitive Balkanism? A Local Contribution to the Ethnography of the War in Bosnia-Herzegovina", *Ethnos*, 65 (3), pp. 317–340.

BAYART, Jean-François (2005), *The Illusion of Cultural Identity*, London: Hurst.

—— (1998), "L'imaginaire dans l'affirmation identitaire", in Catherine Halpern and Jean-Claude Ruano-Borballan (eds), *L'Identité. L'individu, le groupe, la société*, Auxerre: Éditions sciences humaines, pp. 337–341.

BAYAT, Asef (2007) "Islamism and the Politics of Fun", *Public Culture*, 19(3) URL: http://www. publicculture.org/articles/volume_19_number_3/islamism_and_politics_fun

BAZIN, Marcel (1980), *Le Tâlech: Une religion ethnique au nord de l'Iran*, Paris: ADPF.

BAZIN, Marcel and Christian BROMBERGER (1982), *Gilân et Azarbâyjân oriental. Cartes et documents ethnographiques*, Paris: Institut français d'iranologie de Téhéran (bibliothèque iranienne no 24), Recherches sur les civilisations.

BECK, E. M. (1995), *A Festival of Violence. An Analysis of Southern Lynchings (1882–1930)*, Urbana, IL: University of Illinois Press.

BENSLAMA, Fethi (2006) "L'outrage global", *Lignes*, 21, pp. 102–13.

BESSIN, Marc, BIDART Claire and Michel GROSSETI (eds.) (2009), *Bifurcations: Les sciences sociales face aux ruptures et à l'événement*, Paris: La Découverte.

BIÇER Birol (2009), "Elveda Rumeli ile Rumeli'ye Merhaba", *Yeni Aktüel*, 200, 17–30 September.

BIGDELI, Hosseyn (1979–1980), *Shahriyarla Gorush*, Tehran.

—— (1980–1981), *Kehliye Salam*, Tabriz: Vahid Mat.

BILA, Fikret (1995), "Millet Türk milletidir", *Milliyet*, 2 January.

BIRIYA, Mohammad (1981–1982), *Urek Sozleri*, Tabriz: Yahya Shayda.

BLOK, Anton (1998), "The Narcissism of Minor Differences", *European Journal of Social Theory*, 1 (1), pp. 33–56.

BLOM, Amélie (1999), "Towards Global Belongings? 'Interpretive Communities', Minorities and Protests Against 'The Satanic Verses'", in Andrew Geddes and Adrian Favell (eds), *The Politics of Belonging*, Avebury: Ashgate, pp. 192–208.

—— (2009) "The 'Re-Islamised' Youth of Pakistan: Intimate and Militant Trajectories", *International Journal of Middle East Studies*.

BLOM, Amélie and Nicolas JAOUL (eds) (2008), "Outraged Communities: Comparative Perspectives on the Politicization of Emotions in South Asia", *South Asia Multidisciplinary Academic Journal*, 2 (http://samaj.revues.org/index1912. html).

BLURYAN, Qani (2005), *Alekok: Les souvenirs de Qani Bluryan* (translated by Réza Keyiri Motlaq), Tehran: Khedemat Farhangi Rasa.

BOIX, Carles (2008), "Civil Wars and Guerrilla Warfare in the Contemporary World: Toward a Joint Theory of Motivations and Opportunities", in Stathis N. KALYVAS, Ian SHAPIRO and Tarek MASOUD (eds.), *Order, Conflict and Violence*, Cambridge: Cambridge University Press.

BOLTANSKI, Luc (1993), *La souffrance à distance. Morale humanitaire, médias et politique*, Paris: Métailié.

BOLTANSKI, Luc and Laurent THÉVENOT (2006), *On Justification: Economies of Worth*, Princeton, NJ: Princeton University Press.

BOLTANSKI, Luc, DARRE, Yan and Marie-Ange SCHILTZ (1984), "La dénonciation", *Actes de la recherche en sciences sociales*, 5, pp. 3–40.

BOSNALI, Sonel (2003), *Patrimoine linguistique et littéraire turcophone de l'Iran (une étude sociolinguistique)*, PhD dissertation, Paris: Inalco.

BOUCHET, Thomas (2005) "Conclusion", in Thomas Bouchet (ed.) *L'Insulte (en) politique*, Dijon: Editions Universitaires de Dijon, pp. 269–73.

BOUDON, Raymond (1990), *L'art de se persuader des idées douteuses, fragiles ou fausses*, Paris: Seuil.

BOURDIEU, Pierre (1987), *Distinction. A Social Critique of the Judgement of Taste*, Cambridge, MA: Harvard University Press.

—— (1990), *The Logic of Practice*, Stanford, CA: Stanford University Press.

—— (2015), *On the State: Lectures at the College de France 1989–1992*, Cambridge: Polity Press.

BOURDIEU, Pierre (with Loïc D. WACQUANT) (1992), *An Invitation to Reflexive Sociology*, Cambridge: Polity Press.

BOUVIER, Nicolas (2001), *L'Usage du monde*, Paris: Payot-Rivages.

BOZARSLAN, Hamit (1999), "Le phénomène milicien: une composante de la violence politique dans la Turquie des années soixante-dix", *Turcica*, 31, pp. 185–244.

—— (2000), "L'alévisme, la méta-histoire et les mythes fondateurs de la recherche", in Isabelle Rigoni (ed.), *Turquie. Les mille visages: Politique, religion, femmes, immigration*, Paris: Syllepse, pp. 77–88.

—— (2004), *Violence in the Middle-East. From Political Struggle to Self-Sacrifice*, Princeton: Markus Wiener Publishers.

—— (2009), *Conflit kurde. Le brasier oublié du Moyen-Orient*, Paris: Autrement.

—— (2014), "The Kurds and Middle Eastern 'state of violence', 1980s and 2010s", *Kurdish Studies* 2, pp. 4–13.

—— (2015), "Arab World and Middle East 2010–2015: From Revolutionary Configurations to the State of Violence" in Jülide Karakoç, (ed.), *Authoritarianism in the Middle East. Before and After the Arab Uprisings*, New York: Palgrave Macmillan, pp. 67–91.

BRASS, Paul R. (2003), *The Production of Hindu-Muslim Violence in Contemporary India*, Seattle, WA: University of Washington Press.

BRAUD, Philippe (2003), "Violence symbolique et mal-être identitaire", *Raisons politiques*, 9, 2003, pp. 33–47.

BRESEEG, Taj Mohammad (2004), *Baloch Nationalism. It's Origins and Development*, Karachi: Royal Book Company.

BROMBERGER, Christian (1986), "Les blagues ethniques dans le nord de l'Iran. Sens et fonction d'un corpus de récits facétieux", *Cahiers de littérature orale*, 20, pp. 73–101.

———— (1988), "Comment peut-on être Rashti? Contenus, perceptions et implications du fait ethnique dans le nord de l'Iran", in Jean-Pierre Digard, *Le Fait ethnique en Iran et en Afghanistan*, Paris: CNRS Éditions, pp. 89–108.

———— (1989), "Changements techniques et transformation des rapports sociaux. La sériciculture au Gilân dans la seconde moitié du XIXe siècle", in Yann Richard (ed.), *Entre l'Iran et l'Occident. Adaptation et assimilation des idées et techniques occidentales*, Paris: Éditions de la Maison des sciences de l'homme, pp. 71–90.

———— (1993), "L'ethnologie de la France et le problème de l'identité", *Civilisations*, 42 (2), pp. 45–64.

———— (2001), "Aux trois sources de l'ethnologie du monde méditerranéen dans la tradition française", in Dionigi Albera, Anton Blok and Christian Bromberger (eds.), *L'Anthropologie de la Méditerranée*, Paris: Maisonneuve et Larose, pp. 65–84.

———— (2007a), "Tâlesh dar hâl-e pres shodan ast" ("Tâlech is sandwiched"), *Tâlesh*, 32, pp. 20–22.

———— (2007b), "D'un musée... l'autre. Réflexions d'un observateur participant", *Etnografica* (Lisbon), 11 (2), pp. 407–420.

———— (2013a), *Un autre Iran, Un ethnologue au Gilân*, Paris: Armand Colin.

———— (2013b), "Ethnic Groups", in Christian Bromberger, *Gilân*, New York: Tehran, Encyclopaedia Iranica-Institut français de recherche en Iran, pp. 43–48.

BROMBERGER, Christian and Alain MOREL (eds.) (2001), *Limites floues, frontières vives*, Paris: Éditions de la Maison des sciences de l'homme.

BROWNING, Christopher (1993), *Ordinary Men: Reserve Battalion Police 101 and the Final Solution in Poland*, London: Harper Collins.

BRUBAKER, Rogers (2001), "Au-delà de l'identité", *Actes de la recherche en sciences sociales*, 139 (4), p. 66–85.

BRUBAKER, Rogers and Frederick COOPER (2000), "Beyond 'Identity'", *Theory and Society*, 29 (1), pp. 1–47.

BRUBAKER, Rogers and David D. LAITIN (1998), "Ethnic and Nationalist Violence", *Annual Review of Sociology*, 24, pp. 423–452.

BRUBAKER, Rogers, LOVEMAN, Mara and Peter STAMATOV (2004), "Ethnicity as Cognition", *Theory and Society*, 33 (1), pp. 31–64.

BRUCE, Richard Isaac (1900), *The Forward Policy and Its Results. Thirty-Five Years'*

Work amongst the Tribes on our North-Western Frontier of India, London-Bombay: Longman, Green and Co.

BRUINESSEN, Martin van (1994), "Nationalisme kurde et ethnicités intrakurdes", *Peuples méditerranéens*, 68–69, pp. 11–37.

—— (2000), *Kurdish Ethno-Nationalism Versus Nation-Building States. Collected Articles*, Istanbul: Isis Press.

BUTALIA Urvashi (1998), *The Other Side of Silence: Voices from the Partition of India*, Delhi: Penguin.

BUTT, Asif (2014), *Kai Suliyan Sar-e-Rah Thin* (Urdu) (Nooses All Around), Lahore: Jahangir Books.

BUTT, Iqbal Haider (2009), *Revisiting Student Politics in Pakistan*, Gujranwala: Bargad. http://www.bargad.org.pk/downloads/Revisiting%20Student%20Politics%20in%2 Pakistan.pdf

ÇALIŞKAN, Nurcan (2007), "Tarihin her sayfasından bir film çıkarıyor", Yeni Şafak, 18 December.

CARLIER, Omar (1995), *Entre Nation et Djihad: Histoire sociale des radicalismes algériens*, Paris: Presses de Sciences Po.

CEFAÏ, Daniel (2007), *Pourquoi se mobilise-t-on? Les théories de l'action collective*, Paris: La Découverte et MAUSS.

CENTLIVRES, Pierre (1980), "Identité et image de l'autre dans l'anthropologie populaire en Afghanistan", *Revue européenne des sciences sociales*, 18 (53), pp. 29–41.

CENTLIVRES Pierre and Micheline CENTLIVRES-DEMONT, (2005) "Une étrange rencontre: la photographie orientaliste de Lehnert et Landrock et l'image iranienne du prophète Mahomet", *Etudes photographiques*, 17, pp. 5–15.

CERTEAU, Michel, de (1993), "La beauté du mort", in Michel de Certeau, *La Culture au pluriel*, Paris: Christian Bourgeois, pp. 45–72.

CHATTERJEE, Partha (1986), *Nationalist Thought and the Colonial World: A Derivative Discourse?*, Oxford: Oxford University Press.

CHEBEL, Malek (1995) *Dictionnaire des symboles musulmans: rites, mystique et civilisation*, Paris: Albin Michel.

CHEHABI, Houchang (1997), "Ardabil Becomes a Province: Center-Periphery Relations in Iran", *International Journal of Middle-East Studies*, 29, pp. 235–253.

CHENOY, Anurada M. (2002), *Militarism and Women in South Asia*, Delhi: Kali for Women.

ÇILLER, Tansu (1995), "Ne mutlu Türkiye'nin vatandaşıyım diyene", *Milliyet*, 1 January.

ÇINTAYA, Nur (2009), "Sezen Aksu, Hülya Avşar, Kürt açılımı, sanatçı saçılımı... ", *Radikal*, 21 August.

CLAVERIE, Élisabeth (2004), "Techniques de la menace", *Terrain*, 43, pp. 15–30.

CLER, Jérôme (2013), "Neden bu ikilik? "Pourquoi cette dualité?". Ethnographie de la division dans un village bektashi du Taurus", in Nathalie Clayer, Benoît Fliche and

Alexandre Papas, *L'Autorité religieuse et ses limites en terres d'islam*, Boston (Mass.)-Leyde: Brill, pp. 209–230.

COLLINS, Randall (2009), *Violence: A Micro-Sociological Theory*, Princeton, NJ: Princeton University Press.

Communities & Local Government, Department of (2008), *Face to Face and Side by Side: A Framework for Partnership in our Multi Faith Society*. Available at: http://webarchive.nationalarchives.gov.uk/20120919132719/www.communities.gov.uk/publications/communities/facetofaceframework

COPEAUX, Étienne (2000), "Le consensus obligatoire", in Isabelle Rigoni (ed.), *Turquie. Les mille visages: Politique, religion, femmes, immigration*, Paris: Syllepse, pp. 89–104.

CRONIN, Stephanie (1997), *The Army and The Creation of The Pahlavi State in Iran (1910–1926)*, London: I. B. Tauris.

—— (2003), "Riza Shah and the Paradoxes of Military Modernization in Iran—1921–1941", in Stephanie Cronin (ed.) *The Making of Modern Iran. State and Society under Riza Shah (1921–1941)*, Abingdon: Routledge, pp. 37–64.

CUISENIER, Jean (2000), "Ethnicité et religion. La tradition du conflit dans les Balkans méditerranéens", in Dionigi Albera, Anton Block and Christian Bromberger (eds), *L'Anthropologie de la Méditerranée*, Paris: Maisonneuve et Larose, pp. 445–465.

DAECHSEL, Markus (2004), "De-Urbanizing the City: Colonial Cognition of the People of Lahore", in Ian Talbot and Shinder Thandi (eds), *People on the Move: Punjabi Colonial and Post-Colonial Migration*, Karachi: Oxford University Press, pp. 21–44.

—— (2006), *The Politics of Self-Expression: The Urdu Middle-Class Milieu in Mid-Twentieth Century India and Pakistan*, London: Routledge.

DELLA PORTA, Donatella (1995), *Social Movement, Political Violence and the State. A Comparative Analysis of Italy and Germany*, Cambridge: Cambridge University Press.

DERRIDA, Jacques (1992), "Force of Law: The 'Mystical Foundation of Authority'" in Drucilla Cornell, Michel Rosenfeld and David Gray Carls (eds), *Deconstruction and the Possibility of* Justice, New York: Routledge, pp. 3–68.

—— (1994), *Force de loi. Le "fondement mystique de l'autorité"*, Paris: Galilée.

DEVJI, Faisal (2009), *The Terrorist in Search of Humanity: Militant Islam and Global Politics*, London: Hurst.

DIECKHOFF, Alain (2000), *La Nation dans tous ses États*, Paris: Flammarion.

DIGARD, Jean-Pierre (ed.) (1988), *Le Fait ethnique en Iran et en Afghanistan*, Paris: CNRS Éditions.

DOGAN, Yalçın (1992), "Londra'da Demirel İdaresi", *Milliyet*, 24 November.

DORRONSORO, Gilles (ed.) (2005), *La Turquie conteste: Mobilisations sociales et régime sécuritaire*, Paris: CNRS Éditions.

DSP (1987), Demokratik Sol Parti Seçim Bildirgesi, Ankara.

DUDOIGNON, Stéphane (2009), *Voyage au pays des Baloutches*, Paris: Cartouche.

DURAK, Attila (2010), *Ebru*, Paris: Actes Sud.

DURGUNOĞLU, Aydın Yücesan and Hilal ÖZUYGUN KUŞCUL (2008), "Providing Access to Basic Literacy Education with Educational TV", *European Journal of Open, Distance and E-Learning* (http://www.eurodl.org/materials/contrib/2008/Durgunoglu_Kuscul.htm).

DUSENBERY, Verne A. (1990), "On the Moral Sensitivities of Sikhs in North America", in Owen Lynch (ed.), *Divine Passions: The Social Construction of Emotion in India*, Berkeley, CA: University of California Press, pp. 239–261.

—— (2014), 'Punjabi Sikhs and Gora Sikhs' in Pashaura Singh and Lou Fenech, *The Oxford Handbook of Sikh Studies*, Oxford: Oxford University Press.

DUZGUN (1979–1980), *Mecmue-ye She'r*, Tehran.

—— (1980–1981), *Kichik Shiirler*, Tehran.

—— (1981–1982), *Bakı Levhaları*, Tehran.

EDELMAN, Murray (1991), *Pièces et règles du jeu politique*, Paris: Seuil, 1991.

ELIAS, Norbert (1973), *La civilisation des mœurs*, Paris: Calman-Lévy.

—— (1982), *The History of Manners (The Civilizing Process, Vol 1)*, London: Pantheon Books.

ELIAS, Norbert and John L. SCOTSON (1994), *The Established and the Outsiders*, London: Sage.

ELSTER, Jon (2005), "Motivations and Beliefs in Suicide Missions", in Diego Gambetta (ed.), *Making Sense of Suicide Missions*, New York: Oxford University Press, pp. 233–258.

EMIROGLU, Kudret (2007), "Adana'da Sanayi ve Sanayiciler Hakkında", in Çelik Behçet (ed.), *Adana'ya Kar Yağmış. Adana üzerinde Yazılar*, Istanbul, İletişim.

ETIENNE, Bruno (2005), *Les combattants suicidaires*, Paris: Éditions de l'aube.

FABIAN, Johannes (1983), *Time and the Other. How Anthropology Makes Its Object*, New York: Columbia University Press.

FAVRET-SAADA, Jeanne (1992) "Rushdie et compagnie: préalables à une anthropologie du blasphème", *Ethnologie Française*, Special issue 'Paroles d'outrage', 22(3).

—— (2007) *Comment produire une crise mondiale avec douze petits dessins*, Paris: Les prairies ordinaires.

FELDMAN, Herbert (1972), *From Crisis to Crisis: Pakistan (1962–1969)*, Oxford: Oxford University Press.

FÉRON, Élise and Michel HASTINGS (eds) (2002), *L'Imaginaire des conflits communautaires*, Paris: L'Harmattan.

FILLIEULE, Olivier (2001), "Propositions pour une analyse processuelle de l'engagement individuel", *Revue française de science politique*, 51(1–2), February–April.

FILLIEULE, Olivier and Lilian MATHIEU (2009), "Structure des opportunités politiques", in Olivier Fillieule, Lilian Mathieu and Cécile Péchu (eds), *Dictionnaires des mouvements sociaux*, Paris, Presses de Sciences Po, pp. 530–540.

FLAM, Helena (2005), "'Emotions' Map: A Research Agenda", in Helena Flam and Debra King (eds), *Emotions and Social Movements*, New York: Routledge, pp. 19–40.

FLAM, Helena and Debra KING (eds) (2005) *Emotions and Social Movements*, New York: Routledge.

FLICHE, Benoît (2000), "Quand cela tient à un cheveu. Pilosité et identité chez les Turcs de Strasbourg", *Terrain*, 35, pp. 155–165.

—— (2005), "The hemşehrilik and the Village: The Stakes of an Association of Former Villagers in Ankara", *European Journal of Turkish Studies*, Thematic Issue 2, "Hometown Organisations in Turkey" (http://www.ejts.org/document385.html).

—— (2007), *Odyssées turques. Les migrations d'un village anatolien*, Paris: CNRS Éditions.

FOUCAULT, Michel (1978), *The History of Sexuality. Volume 1: The Will to Knowledge*, New York: Pantheon Books.

FOX, Jonathan (2002), "Ethnic Minorities and the Clash of Civilizations: A Quantitative Analysis of Huntington's Thesis", *British Journal of Political Science*, 32 (3), pp. 415–434.

FREITAG, Sandra B. (1989), *Collective Action and Community. Public Arenas and the Emergence of Communalism in Northern India*, Berkeley, CA: University of California Press.

FREUD, Sigmund (1962 [1921]), *Psychologie collective et Analyse du moi*, Paris: Payot.

GABORIEAU, Marc (2007), *Un autre islam: Inde, Pakistan, Bangladesh*, Paris: Albin Michel.

GAMBETTA, Diego (2005), "Can we Make Sense of Suicide Missions?", in Diego Gambetta (ed.), *Making Sense of Suicide Missions*, New York: Oxford University Press, pp. 259–299.

GAMBETTI, Zeynep (2006), "The Search for a New Ground. Interview with Zeynep Gambetti", *European Journal of Turkish Studies*, 5 (http://ejts.revues.org/index784.html).

GAMSON, William (1992), *Talking Politics*, Cambridge: Cambridge University Press.

GARBAYE Romain and Pauline SCHNAPPER (2014), *The Politics of Ethnic Diversity in the British Isles*, London: Palgrave Macmillan.

GAYER, Laurent (2007), "Guns, Slums and Yellow Devils: A Genealogy of Urban Conflicts in Karachi", *Modern Asian Studies*, 41 (3), pp. 515–544.

GAZDAR, Haris, KAKER, Sobia Ahmad and Irfan KAN (2010), "Buffer Zone, Colonial Enclave or Urban Hub? Quetta: Between Four Regions and Two Wars", Working Paper 69, London: Crisis State Research Center.

GEERTZ, Clifford (1963), "Integrative Revolution", in Clifford Geertz (ed.) *Old Societies, New States*, New York: Free Press.

—— (1973), *The Interpretation of Cultures*, New York: Basic Books.

GELLNER, Ernest (1981), *Muslim Society*, Cambridge: Cambridge University Press.

GIDDENS, Anthony (1987), *The Nation-State and Violence*, Berkeley, CA: University of California Press.

—— (1991), *The Consequences of Modernity*, Stanford: Stanford University Press.

GILMARTIN, David (1988) *Empire and Islam: Punjab and the Making of Pakistan*, London: I. B. Tauris.

GIL-WHITE, Francisco J. (2001), "Are Ethnic Groups Biological 'Species' to the Human Brain? Essentialism in Our Cognition of Some Social Categories", *Current Anthropology*, 42 (4), pp. 515–553.

GILLEY, Bruce (2004), "Against the Concept of Ethnic Conflict", *Third World Quarterly*, 25 (6), pp. 1155–1166.

GOFFMAN, Erving (1963), *Stigma: Notes on the Management of spoiled Identity*, New York: Simon & Schuster.

—— (1974), *Frame Analysis: An Essay on the Organization of Experience*, New York: Harper & Row.

GÖKDAG, Bilgehan A. and Rıza HEYET (2004), "İran Türklerinde Kimlik Meselesi", *Bilig*, 30, pp. 6–79.

GOODWIN, Jeff, James JASPER and Francesca POLLETTA (2001), "Introduction: Why Emotions Matter", in Jeff Goodwin, James Jasper and Francesca Polletta (eds), *Passionate Politics. Emotions and Social Movements*, Chicago, IL: University of Chicago Press, pp. 1–24.

—— (2004), "Emotional Dimensions of Social Movements", in David A. Snow, Sarah A. Soule and Hanspeter Kriesi (eds), *The Blackwell Companion to Social Movements*, Malden, MA: Blackwell, pp. 413–432.

GOODWIN, Jeff, James JASPER and Francesca POLLETTA (2004) "Emotional Dimensions of Social Movements", in David A. Snow, Sarah A. Soule & Hanspeter Kriesi (eds.), *The Blackwell Companion to Social Movements*, Malden: Blackwell, pp. 413–432.

GOULD, Deborah (2002), "Life During Wartime: Emotions and the Development of Act Up", *Mobilization*, 7 (2), pp. 177–200.

GOURISSE, Benjamin (2010), *L'État en jeu. Captation des ressources et désobjectivation de l'État en Turquie (1975–1980), Thèse de doctorat en science politique*, Université Paris 1-Panthéon-Sorbonne.

GOVERNMENT OF PUNJAB (1954) *Report of the Court of Inquiry Constituted under Punjab Act II of 1954 to Enquire into the Punjab Disturbances of 1953 [Munir Report]*, Lahore: Government Printing.

GROJEAN, Olivier (2005), "Les répertoires du conflit kurde", in Gilles Dorronsoro (ed.), *La Turquie conteste: Mobilisations sociales et régime sécuritaire*, Paris: CNRS Éditions, pp. 167–182.

—— (2008), *La Cause kurde, de la Turquie vers l'Europe. Contribution à une sociologie de la transnationalisation des mobilisations*, Thèse de doctoriat en sociologie politique, Paris, EHESS.

GROS, Frédéric (2005), *États de violence: essai sur la fin de la guerre*, Paris: Gallimard.

GURR, Ted Robert (1993), *Minorities at Risk: A Global View of Ethnopolitical Conflicts*, Washington, DC: United States Institute of Peace Press.

GUSFIELD, Joseph R. (1986) *Symbolic Crusades: Status Politics and the American Temperance Movement*, Chicago: University of Illinois Press, [1963].

HANIF, Mohammed (1989), "The gun-runners of Karachi", *Newsline*, October, p. 23.

HANNAN, Michael T. (1979), "The Dynamics of Ethnic Boundaries in Modern States", in John W. Meyer and Michael T. Hannan (eds), *National Development and the World System*, Chicago, IL: University of Chicago Press, pp. 253–275.

HARRISON, Selig (1981), *In Afghanistan's Shadow. Baluch Nationalism and Soviet Temptations*, New York: Carnegie Endowment for International Peace.

HASAN, Aydın (1995), "Türk Kimliği bir üst kimliktir", *Milliyet*, 8 January.

HASNAIN, Ghulam (1997) "'For us, Altaf Hussain was like a God'. The diary of a former MQM militant...", *Newsline* (Karachi), May, p. 33.

HASSNER, Pierre (2002), "À long terme, la complexité du monde se vengera", *Le Monde*, 28 Septembre.

HEART NEWS (2003), "Iranian Pioneers in Heart Surgery", *Heart News*, 1 (2), pp. 12–18.

HECHTER, Michael (1975), *Internal Colonialism: The Celtic Fringe in British National Development (1536–1966)*, Berkeley, CA: University of California Press.

HEMIN (1974), "kurd o azerbaïdjani", in *Tarik o Run* (a collection of poems), Bagdad.

HEYAT, Javad (1979–1980a), *Azerbayjan Edebiyat Tarikhine Bir Bakish*, Tehran.

—— (1979–1980b), *Tarikhche-ye Torki-ye Azeri*, Tehran: Varliq.

—— (1982–1983), "Regression of Azeri Language and Literature under The Oppressive Period of Pahlavi and Its Renaissance after The Islamic Revolution", unpublished.

—— (1984–1985), *Mukayiset'ol Lugateyn*, Tehran: Varliq.

HM GOVERNMENT (2009), *Pursue, Prevent, Protect, Prepare: The United Kingdom's Strategy for Countering International Terrorism*.

HOBSBAWM, Eric (1993), "Qu'est-ce qu'un conflit ethnique?", *Actes de la recherche en sciences sociales*, 100, pp. 51–57.

HOCHSCHILD, Arlie R. (1979), "Emotion Work, Feeling Rules, and Social Structure", *American Journal of Sociology*, 85, pp. 551–575.

—— (1983), *The Managed Heart: Commercialization of Human Feeling*, Berkeley, CA: University of California Press.

HOLLAND, Henry (1958), *Frontier Doctor*, London: Hodder and Stoughton.

HOLMES, Mary (2004), "The Importance of Being Angry: Anger in Political Life", *European Journal of Social Theory*, 7 (2), pp. 123–132.

HOLSTI, Klevi J. (1996) *The State, War and the State of War*, Cambridge: Cambridge University Press.

HORGAN, John (2009), *Walking Away from Terrorism: Accounts of Disengagement from Radical and Extremist Movements*, London: Routledge.

HOROWITZ, Donald (1989), "Incentives and Behaviour in the Ethnic Politics of Sri Lanka and Malaysia", *Third World Quarterly*, 10 (4), pp. 18–35.

HOURCADE, Bernard (2004), "La recomposition des identités et des territoires en Iran islamique", *Annales de géographie*, 638–639, pp. 511–530.

HOURCADE, Bernard, MAZUREK, Hubert, TALEGHANI, Mahmoud and PAPOLI-YAZDI, Mohammad-Hosseyn, (1998), *Atlas d'Iran*, Montpellier-Paris: Reclus-La Documentation française.

HUGHES, Albert William (1877), *Country of Balochistan: Its Geography, Topography, Ethnology and History*, London: George Bell & Sons.

IBN-E INSHA (Sher Muhammad Khan) (2001) *Urdu: The Final Book* (translated by D. Matthew), Lahore: Alhamra, [1971].

IGNATIEFF, Michael (1998), *The Warrior's Honor. Ethnic War and the Modern Conscience*, New York: Metropolitan Books.

JAFFRELOT, Christophe (1993), "Processions hindoues, stratégies politiques et émeutes entre Hindous et Musulmans", *Purusartha*, 16, pp. 261–287.

JAGGAR, Alison M. (1989) "Love and Knowledge: Emotions in Feminist Epistemology", in Alison M. Jaggar and Susan R. Bordo (eds.), *Gender/Body/Knowledge: Feminist Reconstructions of Being and Knowing*, New Brunswick: Rutgers University Press, pp. 145–71.

JAHANI, Carina, KORN Agnes, and Paul TITUS (eds.) (2008), *The Baloch and Others, Linguistic, Historical and Socio-Political Perspectives on Pluralism in Balochistan*, Wiesbaden: Reichert Verlag.

JALAL, Ayesha (2001) *Self and Sovereignty: Individual and Community in South Asian Islam since 1850*, Lahore: Sang-e-Meel.

JALIB, Halib (2001), *Harf-e-Haq* (Words of Truth, Urdu), Karachi: Danyal.

JANMAHMAD (1989), *Essays on Baloch National Struggle in Pakistan: Emergence, Dimensions, Repercussions*, Quetta: Gosha-e-Adab.

JANOWITZ, Morris (1979), "Collective Racial Violence: A Contemporary History", in Hugh D. Graham and Ted R. Gurr (eds), *Violence in America*, Beverly Hills, CA: Sage, pp. 261–286.

JASPER, James M. (1997), *The Art of Moral Protest: Culture, Biography and Creativity in Social Movements*, Chicago, IL: University of Chicago Press.

JAYYUSI, May (2004), "Subjectivity and Public Witness: An Analysis of Islamic Militance in Palestine," unpublished paper for the SSRC Beirut Conference on the Public Sphere in the Middle East, October.

KALYONCU, Cemal A. (2000), "Sinemanın devrimci kızı", *Aksyon Dergisi*, 267, 15 January.

KALYVAS, Stathis N. (2003), "The Ontology of 'Political Violence': Action and Identity in Civil Wars", *Perspectives on Politics*, 1 (3), pp. 475–494.

—— (2006), *The Logic of Violence in Civil War*, Cambridge: Cambridge University Press.

—— (2008), "Promises and Pitfalls of an Emerging Research Programme: The Microdynamics of Civil War", in Stathis N. Kalyvas, Ian Shapiro and Tarek Masoud (eds.), *Order, Conflict and Violence*, Cambridge: Cambridge University Press.

KALYVAS, Stathis and Ignacio SANCHEZ-CUENCA (2005), "Killing without Dying: The Absence of Suicide Missions", in Diego Gambetta (ed.), *Making Sense of Suicide Missions*, New York: Oxford University Press, pp. 173–208.

KANAFANI-ZAHAR, Aïda (2000), "Une brèche dans le séparatisme confessionnel en Méditerranée: s'adapter aux contraintes rituelles d'une communauté. L'exemple de Hsoun (Liban)", in Dionigi Albera, Anton Block and Christian Bromberger (eds.), *L'Anthropologie de la Méditerranée*, Paris: Maisonneuve et Larose, pp. 423–444.

KANCHAN, Chandra (2005), "Ethnic Parties and Democratic Stability", *Perspectives on Politics*, 3 (2), pp. 235–252.

KAPLAN, Robert D. (1994), "The Coming Anarchy", *The Atlantic Monthly*, 273 (2), pp. 44–76.

KAYA, Ayhan (2003), "Unity in Diversity: Ethnic/Cultural Diversity in Turkey and the European Union", *Cemoti*, 36, pp. 299–220.

KESER, İnan (2008), *Kent Cemaat Etnisite, Adana ve Adana Nusayrileri Örneğinde Kamusallık*, Ankara: Ütopya.

KHAN, Mohammad Ilyas (2004), "Back to the hills", *The Herald*, October.

KHAN, Nichola (2010), *Mohajir Militancy in Pakistan: Violence and Practices of Transformation in the Karachi Conflict*, Abingdon: Routledge.

KHAN, Shahnawaz (2006) "City under Siege", *Daily Times* (Lahore), 16 February.

—— (2008) "Student Politics: Start of a New Violent Chapter", 1 May, http://www.interface.edu.pk/students/May–08

KHOSROKHAVAR, Farhad (1993), *L'Utopie sacrifiée. Sociologie de la révolution iranienne*, Paris: Presses de la Fondation nationale des sciences politiques.

—— (2002) *Les nouveaux martyrs d'Allah*, Paris: Flammarion.

KIAN-THIÉBAUT, Azadeh (1998), *Secularization of Iran, a Doomed Failure? The New Middle Class and the Making of Modern Iran*, Louvain and Paris: Peeters and Institut d'études iraniennes.

KILIÇ Şengül (1992), *Biz ve Onlar. Türkiye'de etnik ayrımcılık*, Istanbul: Metis.

KIYOTERU, Tsutsui (2004), "Global Civil Society and Ethnic Social Movements in the Contemporary World", *Sociological Forum*, 19 (1), pp. 63–87.

KOCAL, Ece (2006), "'En ciddi rakibim Erol Avcı!!!' Tomris Giritlioğlu dizi rekabetini anlattı!", 7 October (http://www.medyafaresi.com/142haber/1395/medya-en-ciddi-rakibim-erol-avci-tomris-giritlioglu-dizirekabetini-anlatti.html).

KOĞACIOĞLU, Dicle (2004), "The Tradition Effect: Framing Honor Crimes in Turkey", *Differences. A Journal of Feminist Cultural Studies*,15 (2), pp. 119–151.

KOLSTØ, Pål (2007), "The Narcissism of Minor Differences'-Theory: Can It Explain Ethnic Conflict?", *Filozofia I Drutvo*, 2 (33).

KRIESI, Hanspeter, KOOPMANS Ruud, DUYVENDAK, Jan Willem and Marco GIUGNI (1995), *New Social Movements in Western Europe*, London: UCL.

KÜÇÜK, Hülya (2002), *The Role of the Bektashis in Turkey's National Struggle*, Leiden: Brill.

KULIN, Ayse (2004), *Kardelenler*, Istanbul: Remzi Kitapevi.

KURIN, Richard (1993) "Islamization in Pakistan: The Sayyid and the Dancer", in Dale F. Eickelman (ed.), *Russia's Muslim Frontier: New Directions in Cross-Cultural Analysis*, Bloomington, IN: Indiana University Press, pp. 175–89.

KUTSCHERA, Chris (1979), *Le Mouvement national kurde*, Paris: Flammarion.

—— (1997), *Le Défi kurde, ou le rêve fou de l'indépendance*, Paris: Bayard.

LACAN, Jacques (1957–1958), *Les Formations de l'inconscient*, Paris: Seuil.

—— (1961–1962), *L'Identification*, Paris: Association lacanienne internationale.

LAGROYE, Jacques (ed.) (2003), *La Politisation*, Paris: Belin.

LAHIRE, Bernard (1999), *L'Invention de l'"illettrisme." Rhétorique publique, éthique et stigmates*, Paris: La Découverte.

LATTÉ, Stéphane (2006) "'Vous ne respectez pas les morts d'AZF': ordonner l'émotion dans les situations commémoratives" (unpublished paper), *Colloque: Mobilisation de victimes*, Centre de Recherches Politiques de la Sorbonne (CRPS), 15–16 Juin.

LEMAIRE, Sandrine (2003), "Propager: l'agence générale des colonies", in Pascal Blanchard and Sandrine Lemaire, *Culture coloniale. La France conquise par son empire (1871–1931)*, Paris: Autrement, pp. 137–147.

LEVENE, Marc and Robert PENNY (eds) (1997), *The Massacre in History*, New York: Berghahn.

LOIZIDES, Neophytos G. (2009), "Elite Framing and Conflict Transformation in Turkey", *Parliamentary Affairs*, 62 (2), pp. 278–297.

LYNCH, Owen (1990), "The Social Construction of Emotions in India", in Owen Lynch (ed.), *Divine Passions: The Social Construction of Emotion in India*, Berkeley, CA: University of California Press, pp. 3–34.

MADANIPOUR, Ali Tehran (1998), *The Making of a Metropolis*, Chichester: John Wiley and Sons.

MAHMOOD, Amjad (2006) "Who are the Protestors?", *Dawn Metropolitan* (Lahore), 18 February.

MAINI, Trividesh Singh, Tahir MALIK, and Ali Farooq MALIK (2008), *Humanity Amid Insanity: Hope During and After the Indo-Pakistan Partition*, New Delhi: UBS Publishers.

MAKAL, Mahmut (2010), *Un village anatolien. Récit d'un instituteur*, Paris: CNRS Éditions.

MALIK, Jamal (1996) *Colonization of Islam: Dissolution of Traditional Institutions in Pakistan*, New Delhi: Manohar.

MARIOT, Nicolas (2003), "Faut-il être motivé pour tuer? Sur quelques explications aux violences de guerre", *Genèses*, 53.

MARX, Anthony W. (1998), *Making Race and Nation: A Comparison of the United States, South Africa, and Brazil*, New York: Cambridge University Press.

MARX, Gary (1970) "Issueless Riots", *The Annals of the American Academy of Political and Social Sciences*, 391(1), pp. 21–33.

MASSICARD, Élise (2002a), "Les alévis et le discours de l'unité en Turquie", in Hans-Lukas Kieser (ed.), *Aspects of the Political Language in Turkey (19th-20th centuries)*, Istanbul: Isis, pp. 117–137.

——— (2002b), "La réforme pénitentiaire en Turquie: du bon usage de la norme européenne", *Critique internationale*, 16, pp. 169–181.

——— (2004), "Entre l'intermédiaire et "l'homme d'honneur". Savoir-faire et dilemmes notabiliaires en Turquie", *Politix*, 17 (67), pp. 101–127.

——— (2005a), "Les mobilisations 'identitaires' en Turquie après 1980: une libéralisation ambiguë", in Gilles Dorronsoro (ed.), *La Turquie conteste. Mobilisations sociales et régime sécuritaire*, Paris: CNRS Éditions, pp. 89–107.

——— (2005b), *L'Autre Turquie. Le mouvement aléviste et ses territoires*, Paris: PUF.

——— (2005c), "Politiser la provenance. Les organisations d'originaires de Sivas à Istanbul et Ankara", *European Journal of Turkish Studies*, 2, "Hometown Organisations in Turkey," (http://www.ejts.org/document362.html).

——— (2006), "Claiming Difference in an Unitarist Frame: the Case of Alevism" in Hans-Lukas Kieser (ed.), *Turkey Beyond Nationalism: Towards Post-Nationalist Identities?*, London: I. B.Tauris, pp. 71–79.

——— (2010), "Le factionnalisme comme mode d'ancrage social. Le Parti républicain du peuple à Adana, Turquie", *Politix*, 92.

——— (2012), *The Alevis in Turkey and Europe. Identity and Managing Territorial Diversity*, London: Routledge.

——— (2013), "The Uses of Team Rivalry: Reconsidering Party Factionalism in Turkey", in Élise Massicard and Nicole F. Watts (eds) *Negotiating Political Power in Turkey: Breaking up the Party*, London: Routledge.

MATHIEU, Lilian (2002), "Rapport au politique, dimensions cognitives et perspectives pragmatiques dans l'analyse des mouvements sociaux", *Revue Française de Science Politique*, 52 (1), pp. 75–100.

MAUSS, Marcel (1969), *Œuvres, 3. Cohésion sociale et divisions de la sociologie*, Paris: Minuit.

MAZARI, Sherbaz Khan (1999), *A Journey to Disillusionment*, Karachi: Oxford University Press.

MCADAM, Doug, Charles TILLY and Sidney TARROW (2000), *Dynamics of Contention. Studies in Contentious Politics*, Cambridge: Cambridge University Press.

MCDOWALL, David (2004), *A Modern History of the Kurds*, London: I. B. Tauris.

MEEKER, Michael (1971), "The Black Sea Turks: Some Aspects of Their Ethnic and Cultural Background", *International Journal of Middle East Studies*, 2, pp. 318–345.

—— (1976), "Meaning and Society in the Near East: Examples from the Black Sea Turks and the Levantine Arabs (I)", *International Journal of Middle-East Studies*, 7 (2), pp. 243–270.

MEIJER, Roel (2009), *Global Salafism: Islam's New Religious Movement*, London: Hurst.

MELIKOFF, Irène (1975), "Le problème kızılbaş", *Turcica*, 6, pp. 49–67.

METCALF, Barbara D. (1982) *Islamic Revival in British India: Deoband 1860–1900*, New Delhi: Oxford University Press.

—— (2004), *Islamic Contestations: Essays on Muslims in India and Pakistan*, New Delhi: Oxford University Press.

MEYER, John W. (1987), "The World Polity and the Authority of the Nation-State", in George M. Thomas, John W. Meyer, Francisco O. Ramirez and John Boli (eds), *Institutional Structure. Constituting State, Society and the Individual*, Beverly Hills, CA: Sage, pp. 41–70.

MODOOD, Tariq (2007), *Multiculturalism: A Civic Idea*, Cambridge: Polity Press.

—— (1988), "Black, racial equality and Asian identity", *Journal of Ethnic and Migration Studies*, 14 (3), pp. 397–404.

MOLINER, Christine (2007), "*Frères ennemis*? Relations between Panjabi Sikhs and Muslims in the Diaspora", *South Asia Multidisciplinary Academic Journal* [Online], 1, http://samaj.revues.org/index135.html

MONOD, Jean-Claude de (2006), *Penser l'ennemi, affronter l'exception. Réflexions critiques sur l'actualité de Carl Schmitt*, Paris: La Découverte.

MONSUTTI, Alessandro (2004), *Guerres et Migration: Réseaux sociaux et stratégies économiques des Hazaras d'Afghanistan*, Neuchâtel-Paris: Institut d'ethnologie-Maison des sciences de l'homme.

MOSSE, George L. (1991), *Fallen Soldiers: Reshaping the Memory of the World Wars*, Oxford: Oxford University Press.

MUHIDINE, Timour (2000), *La Littérature turque à l'aube du millénaire (1999–2000)*, Istanbul: IFEA.

NAGEL, Joane and Susan OLZAK (1982), "Ethnic Mobilization in New and Old States: An Extension of the Competition Model", *Social Problems*, 30 (2), pp. 127–143.

NASSERI, Halil (1981), "Farhang-e Mâ Huiyat-e Mast, Tabriz", Ulker.

NAVARO-YASHIN, Yaël (2002), *Faces of the State. Secularism and Public Life in Turkey*, Princeton, NJ: Princeton University Press.

NCJP (National Commission for Justice and Peace/Pakistan Catholic Bishop's Conference) (2007) *Human Rights Monitor 2007: A Report on the Religious Minorities in Pakistan*, Lahore: Visionaries Publishers.

BIBLIOGRAPHY

NEVEU, Éric (1999), "L'approche constructiviste des 'problèmes publics', un aperçu des travaux anglo-saxons", *Études de communication*, 22, pp. 41–57.

NISSMAN, David (1987), *The Soviet Union and Iranian Azerbaijan: The Use of Nationalism for Political Penetration*, Boulder, CO: Westview Press.

NORDSTROM, Carolyn (2004), *Shadows of War: Violence, Power and International Profiteering in the Twenty-First Century*, Berkeley, CA: University of California Press.

NOTQI, Hamid (1979a), "Sehere geden bir yol var", *Varliq*, 1, pp. 50–51.

—— (1979b), "Jadu", *Varliq*, 2, p. 46.

—— (1979c), "Mesele-ye Farhang-e Akvam-e Mohtalef-e Iran ve Kanoun-e Esasi Joumhouri-ye Islami", *Varliq*, 2, pp. 12–13.

NOZAD, Fereydoun (2000), Târikh-e jarâyed va majalât-e Gilân (az âqâz tâ enqelâb-e eslâmi) ("A History of the press and Gilân journals from their beginning to the Islamic Revolution"), Tehran: Sâzeman-e chap va enteshârât-e vezârat-e farhang va ershâd-e eslâmi.

OBEROI, Harjot (1994), *The Construction of Religious Boundaries: Culture, Identity and Diversity in the Sikh Tradition*, Delhi: Oxford University Press.

OBERSHALL, Anthony (1973), *Social Conflicts and Social Movements*, Englewood Cliffs (N. J.): Prentice Hall.

—— (2007), *Conflict and Peace Building in Divided Societies: Responses to Ethnic Violence*, London: Routledge.

OFFICE OF NATIONAL STATISTICS, *2001 Census*, HMSO.

ÖKTEM, Kerem (2005), "Faces of the City: Poetic, Mediagenic and Traumatic Images of a Multi-Cultural City in Southeast Turkey", *Cities*, 22 (3), pp. 241–253.

OLLIVIER, Bruno (2009), *Les Identités collectives à l'heure de la mondialisation*, Paris: CNRS Éditions.

OLSON, Mancur (1965), *The Logic of Collective Action*, New York: Schocken.

OST, David (2004), "Politics as the Mobilizing of Anger", *European Journal of Social Theory*, 7 (2), pp. 229–244.

PAKISTAN PENAL CODE (2007) (commented by Shahid Hussain Qadri), Lahore: Mansoor Book House.

PAPE, Robert (2005), *Dying to Win: The Strategic Logic of Suicide Terrorism*, New York: Random House.

PIKE, Kenneth (1947), *Phonemics. A Technique for Reducing Languages to Writing*, Ann Arbor, MI: University of Michigan Press.

PLANHOL, Xavier de (1988), "Le fait turc en Iran: quelques jalons", in Jean-Pierre Digard (ed.), *Le Fait ethnique en Iran et en Afghanistan*, Paris: CNRS Éditions, pp. 123–129.

POLETTA, Francesca and Amenta EDWIN (2001), "Second that Emotion? Lessons from Once-Novel Concepts in Social Movement Research", in Jeff Goodwin, James

Jasper and Francesca Polletta (eds), *Passionate Politics. Emotions and Social Movements*, Chicago, IL: University of Chicago Press, pp. 303–316.

POLLETTA, Francesca and James JASPER (2001), "Collective Identity and Social Movements", *Annual Review of Sociology*, 27, pp. 283–305.

PORTES, Alejandro and Julia SENSENBRENNER (1993), "Embeddedness and Immigration: Notes on the Social Determinants of Economic Action", *American Journal of Sociology*, 98, pp. 1320–1550.

POTOCKI, Michel (2004), *Constitution de la République islamique d'Iran*, Paris: L'Harmattan.

POUILLON, François and Jean-Claude VATIN (eds.) (2011), *Après l'orientalisme: L'Orient créé par l'Orient*, Paris: Karthala.

QADEER, Mohammad A. (1983) *Urban Development in the Third World: Internal Dynamics of Lahore, Pakistan*, New York: Praeger.

QAHMREMANPUR, Yusef (2006), Farhang-i 'Ammih-yi Il-e Qara Pâpâq (Culture of Qara Pâpâq tribe), Urumiyeh: Yaz Nashriyani.

RAHMAN, Tariq (1996), *Language and Politics in Pakistan*, Oxford: Oxford University Press.

RAMEZANZADEH, Abdollah (1996), *Internal Conflict and International Dynamics of Ethnic Conflict: The Case of Iran*, Louvain: Université Catholique.

RIAUX, Gilles (2008), "The Formative Years of Azerbaijani Nationalism in Post Revolutionary Iran", *Central Asian Survey*, 27 (1), pp. 45–58.

RICHARD, Yann (ed.) (1989), *Entre l'Iran et l'Occident. Adaptation et assimilation des idées et techniques occidentales*, Paris: Éditions de la Maison des sciences de l'homme.

—— (1991), "Les Kurdes d'Iran: révoltes, idéalisme et silence", in Élisabeth Picard (ed.), *La Question kurde*, Bruxelles: Complexe, pp. 53–78.

ROSALDO, Michelle Z. (1984), "Towards an Anthropology of Self and Feeling", in Richard Shweder & Robert LeVine (eds.), *Culture Theory: Essays on Mind, Self, and Emotions*, Cambridge: Cambridge University Press, pp. 137–57.

ROSENAU, James (1991), *Turbulence in World Politics: A Theory of Change and Continuity*, Princeton, NJ: Princeton University Press.

ROY, Anjali (2010), *Bhangra Moves: From Ludhiana to London and Beyond*, Aldershot: Ashgate.

—— (ed.) (2015), *Imagining Punjab, Punjabi and Punjabiat in the Transnational Era*, London: Routledge.

RUANO-BORBALLAN, Jean-Claude (ed.) (1998), *L'Identité. L'individu, le groupe, la société*, Auxerre: Éditions Sciences Humaines.

SADEQ, Hosseyn (1977–1978), *Govsi Tabrizi*, Tchran.

—— (1978–1979), *Sayalar*, Tehran.

—— (1981–1982), *Guneshli Vatan Yaddashtları*, Tehran.

SAHFI, Seyyed Mohammad (2001), Geopolitik-e farhangi va masale-ye amniyat-e melli (Cultural Geopolitics and the issue of national security), Tehran, Sepehr (with the collaboration of Vezârat-e farhang va ershâd-e Eslami).

SAHLINS, Marshall (2005), "Structural Work, How Microhistories Become Macrohistories and Vice Versa", *Anthropological Theory*, 5 (1), pp. 5–30.

SAÏD, Edward W. (2005), *L'Orientalisme. L'Orient créé par l'Occident*, Paris: Seuil.

SALAMÉ, Ghassan (ed.) (1994), *Democracy Without Democrats? The Renewal of Politics in the Muslim World*, London: I. B. Tauris.

SALEH, Rafiq and Sedig SALEH (2007), Rojnama-ye Kurdistan. Mahabad (1324–1325 hetavi 1946) (The journal of Kurdistan), Sulaymaniyé, Benka-ye Jin.

SAMIN, Abbas Tahira (1987), *Histoire du peuple Baluch et la construction de son royaume*, PhD Dissertation, University Montpellier 3, unpublished.

SANYAL, Usha (1996) *Devotional Islam and Politics in British India: Ahmed Riza Khan Barelwi and His Movement, 1870–1920*, Delhi: Oxford University Press.

SARDAN, Jean-Pierre Olivier, de (1998), "Émique", *L'Homme*, 38 (147), pp. 151–166.

SARTORI, Giovanni (1976), *Parties and Party Systems: A Framework for Analysis*, New York: Cambridge University Press.

SAVALAN (1978–1979), *Apardi Seller Sarani*, Tehran.

SAYEED, Khalid B. (1980) *Politics in Pakistan: The Nature and Direction of Change*, New York: Praeger.

SCHEDLER, Andreas (2007), "Mapping Contingency", in Ian Shapiro and Sonu Bedi (eds), *Political Contingency. Studying the Unexpected, the Accidental and the Unforeseen*, New York: New York University Press, pp. 54–78.

SCHOLTZ, Fred (2002), *Nomadism and Colonialism: A Hundred Years of Baluchsitan (1872–1972)*, Karachi: Oxford University Press.

SCHREFFER, Gibb (2013), "Situating bhangra dance: a critical introduction", *South Asian History and Culture*, 4(3), pp. 384–412.

SCHÜLER, Harald (1998), *Die türkischen Parteien und ihre Mitglieder*, Hamburg: Schriften des Orient-Instituts.

——— (2000), "Secularism and Ethnicity: Alevis and Social-Democrats in Search of an Alliance", in Stefanos Yerasimos, Gunter Seufert and Karin Vorghoff (eds), *Civil Society in the Grip of Nationalism*, Istanbul: Orient-Institut, pp. 197–250.

SCOGNAMILLO, Giovanni (2004), *Bay Sinema Türker İnanoğlu*, Istanbul: Doğan Kitap.

SEMELIN, Jacques (2007), *Purify and Destroy: The Political Uses of Massacre and Genocide*, London: Hurst.

ŞENER Cemal and Miyase ILKNUR (1995), *Alevilik ve Seriat*, Istanbul: Ant.

SEWEL, William H. (1994), "A Theory of Structure: Duality, Agency, and Transformation", *American Journal of Sociology*, 98 (1), pp. 1–29.

SHAFAIEH, Nima and Hamid NOTQI (2003), "('Aytan'): Azerbaijani Iranian Author, Poet, Scholar", paper presented during the 37th Congress of the Middle East

Studies Association (MESA) of North America, 6–9 November 2003, Alaska: Anchorage.

SHAHZAD, Asif (2002), "Over 250 000 Students in Punjab Seminaries", *Dawn*, 22 January.

SHANKLAND, David, *The Alevis in Turkey: The Emergence of a Secular Islamic Tradition*, London: Routledge.

SIAN, Katy (2013), *Unsettling Sikh and Muslim Conflict: Mistaken Identities, Forced Conversions, and Postcolonial Formations*, New York: Lexington Books.

SIDHU G. S. (1998), *A Challenge to Sikhism*, Birmingham: Council of Sikh Gurdwaras in Birmingham.

SIDHU, G. S and Gurmukh SINGH (2001), *Sikh Religion and Islam: A Comparative Study*, London: Gurdwara Dasmesh Darbar.

Sikh Woman's Awareness Network (1998), *Islam and Sikhism: A Comparative View on Women*, Akaal Purkh Ki Fauj UK.

SIMMEL, Georges (1990), *Philosophie de la modernité*, v°2, Paris: Payot.

SINCLAIR-WEBB, Emma (2003), "Sectarian Violence, the Alevi Minority and the Left: Kahramanmaraş 1978", in Joost Jongerden and Paul J. White (eds), *Turkey's Alevi Enigma. A Comprehensive Overview*, Leiden: Brill, pp. 215–235.

SINGH, Gurharpal (2005), "British Multiculturalism and the Sikhs", in *Sikh Formations: Religion, Culture and Theory*, 1(2).

SINGH, Gurharpal and Darshan SINGH TATLA (2006), *Sikhs in Britain: The Making of a Community*, London: Zed Books.

SOLOMON, Robert C. (1984), "Getting Angry: The Jamesian Theory of Emotion in Anthropology", in Richard A. Shweder et Robert A. Levine, (eds), *Culture Theory: Essays on Mind, Self and Emotions*, Cambridge: Cambridge University Press, pp. 238–254.

SONMEZ (1979–1980), *Ağir Iller*, Tabriz.

SONMEZ (1980–1981), *Isa'nın Son Shami*, Tabriz.

SPAIN, James (1962), *The Ways of the Pathans*, Karachi: Indus Publications.

STEWART Pamela J. and Andrew STRATHERN (2002), *Violence and Ethnography*, New York: Continuum.

STRENSKI, Ivan (2003) "Sacrifice, Gift and the Social Logic of Muslim Human Bombers", *Terrorism and Political Violence*, 15(3), p. 8.

TAGYEVA, S. A. (1991), "1978–1979. Iller Iran Enqelabendan Sonra Jenoubi Azerbayjan'da Milli Hukuklar Ugruna Mubarize", Jenubi Azerbayjan Tarikhi Meseleleri, Elm yay, Bakou, pp. 143–175.

TAJFEL, Henri and John C. TURNER (1985), "The Social Identity Theory of Intergroup Behavior", in Henri Tajfel and John C. Turner, *Psychology of Intergroup Relations*, Chicago, IL: Nelson Hal, pp. 7–24.

TALBOT, Ian (2005) "Understanding Religious Violence in Contemporary Pakistan: Themes and Theories", in Ravinder Kaur (ed.), *Religion, Violence and Political Mobilisation in South Asia*, New Delhi: Sage, pp. 145–64.

—— (2006) *Divided Cities: Partition and its Aftermath in Lahore and Amritsar, 1947–57*, Karachi: Oxford University Press.

TALBOT, Ian and Gurharpal SINGH (2009), *The Partition of India*, Cambridge: Cambridge University Press.

TAMBIAH, Stanley J. (1996), *Leveling Crowds: Ethnonationalist Conflicts and Collective Violence in South Asia*, Berkeley, CA: University of California Press.

TANRIÖVER, Hülya Tufan (2004), "La famille, le quartier et la vie communautaire dans les feuilletons télévisés turcs", *Anatolia Moderna*, 10, pp. 225–234.

TAPIA, Stéphane, de (1996), *L'Impact régional en Turquie des investissements industriels des travailleurs émigrés*, Paris: L'Harmattan, Varia Turcica XIX.

TARROW, Sidney (1989), *Democracy and Disorder. Protest and Politics in Italy (1965–1975)*, Oxford: Oxford University Press.

TAYLOR, Charles (1992), *Multiculturalism and the Politics of Recognition*, Princeton, NJ: Princeton University Press.

TCHAMRAN, Mustafa (1985), Khâterât va soxanrâni-haye Chahid Tchamran pirâmun-e Qâ'yele-e Kordestan (Memories and Discourse of the martyr Tchamran about Kurdistan), Tehran: Boniad Chahid Tchamran.

TEYMUR-ZADEH (Mostafa) (1953), Târikh-e zendegi-ye marz yâ vahshat-e Saqez (The story of Life at the Border of Terror at Saqez), Tehran: Musavi.

THÉVENOT, Laurent (1995) "Emotions et évaluations dans les coordinations publiques", in Patricia Paperman & Ruwen Ogien (eds.), *La couleur des pensées: émotions, sentiments, intentions* (Raisons pratiques n°6), Paris: Editions de l'EHESS, pp. 145–74.

THIESSE, Anne-Marie (2005), "National Identities. A Translational Paradigm", in Christophe Jaffrelot and Alain Dieckhoff, *Revisiting Nationalism*, London: Hurst, pp. 122–143.

THORNTON, Thomas Henry (1888), "Baluchistan and the New Indian Province", *Asiatic Quarterly Review*, 1, pp. 54–83.

TITUS, Paul (1996), "Routes to Ethnicity: Roads, Buses, and Differential Ethnic Relations in Pakistani Balochistan", in Paul Titus (ed.) *Marginality and Modernity. Ethnicity and Change in Post-Colonial Balochistan*, Oxford: Oxford University Press, pp. 273–295.

TODD, Jennifer (2005), "Social Transformation, Collective Categories, and Identity Change", *Theory and Society*, 34 (4), pp. 429–463.

TURGUT, Mirza (2005), *Göçler ve Mersin tarihi*, Istanbul: Etik.

TURNER, Victor (1974), *Dramas, Fields, and Metaphors: Symbolic Action in Human Society*, Ithaca, NY: Cornell University Press.

VANER, Sémih (1984), "Violence politique et terrorisme en Turquie", *Esprit*, 94–95, pp. 79–104.

VAZIRI, Mostafa (1993), *Iran as Imagined Nation: The Construction of National Identity*, New York: Paragon House.

VERKAAIK, Oskar (2004), *Migrants and Militants: Fun and Urban Violence in Pakistan*, Princeton, NJ: Princeton University Press.

VERMEERSCH, Peter (2003), "Ethnic Minority Identity and Movement Politics: The Case of the Roma in the Czech Republic and Slovakia", *Ethnic and Racial Studies*, 26 (5), pp. 879–901.

VIRINDER, Kalra (2002), "Extended View: Riots, Race and Reports: Denham, Cantle, Oldham and Burnley Inquiries", *Race Relations Abstracts*, 4 (27).

VOVOU, Ioanna and Angeliki KOUKOUTSAKI-MONNIER (2007), "La redécouverte de l'Autre par écrans interposés: fiction télévisuelle et redefinition des relations gréco-turques", *Communications*, 26 (1), pp. 48–78.

WASEEM, Muhammad (2007) "Political Source of Islamic Militancy in Pakistan", in Ian Talbot (ed.), *The Deadly Embrace: Religion, Politics and Violence in India and Pakistan 1947–2002*, Karachi: Oxford University Press, pp. 145–63.

WEBER, Max (1978) *Economy and Society: An Outline of Interpretive Sociology* (ed. by G. Roth and C. Wittich), Berkeley, CA: University of California Press, [1922].

WEDEL, Heidi (1999), *Lokale Politik und Geschlechterrollen. Stadtmigrantinnen in türkischen Metropolen*, Hamburg: Schriften des Deutschen Orient-Instituts.

WEISBROD, Bernd (2002) "La violence fondamentaliste: violence politique et religion politique dans le conflit moderne", *Erès. Revue Internationale des Sciences Sociales*, 4(174), pp. 551–60.

WERBNER, Pnina (2004), "The Predicament of Diaspora and Millennium Islam: Reflections on September 11, 2001", *Ethnicities*, 4(4).

WESTWOOD, Sallie (1995), "Gendering Diaspora: Space, Politics and South Asian Masculinities in Britain", in Peter Van der Veer (ed.) (1995), *Nation and Migration: The Politics of Space in the South Asian Diaspora*, Philadelphia, PA: University of Pennsylvania Press, pp. 197–219.

WHITE, Jenny (1999), "Amplifying Trust: Community and Communication in Turkey", in Dale F. Eickelman and Jon W. Anderson (eds) (2003), *New Media and the Muslim World: The Emerging Public Sphere*, Bloomington, IN: Indiana University Press, pp. 162–179.

WHITEHEAD, Neil L. (2004), *Violence*, Santa Fe, NM: School of American Research.

WIEVIORKA, Michel (1995), *Face au terrorisme*, Paris: Liana Levi.

WIKTOROWICZ, Quitan (ed.) (2004) *Islamic Activism: A Social Movement Theory Approach*, Bloomington, IN: Indiana University Press.

WILCOX, Wayne Ayres (1966), *Pakistan: The Consolidation of a Nation*, New York: Columbia University Press.

WILLIAM SAMII, Abbas (2000), "The Nation and its Minorities: Ethnicity, Unity and State Policy in Iran", *Comparative Studies of South Asia, Africa and the Middle-East*, 20 (1–2), pp. 128–142.

WUCHERPFENNIG, Julian, Niels W. METTERNICH, Lars-Erik CEDERMAN and Kristian S. GLEDITSCH (2012), "Ethnicity, the State, and the Duration of Civil War", *World Politics*, 64 (1), pp. 79–115.

XANTHAXOU, Margarita (1999), "Violence en trois temps. Vendetta, guerre civile et désordre nouveau dans une région grecque", in Françoise Héritier, *De la violence II*, Paris: Odile Jacob, pp. 171–189.

YASER, Yasar (2004), "The Turkish Family Health and Planning Foundation's Entertainment-Education Campaign", in Arvind Singhal, Michael J. Cody, Everett M. Rogers and Miguel Sabido, *Entertainment-Education and Social Change. History, Research, and Practice*, London: Lawrence Erlbaum Associates, pp. 321–329.

YEĞEN, Mesut (2009), "'Prospective-Turks' or 'Pseudo-Citizens': Kurds in Turkey", *Middle East Journal*, 63 (4), pp. 597–615.

YÖRÜK, Zafer F. (1997), "Turkish Identity from Genesis to the Day of Judgement", in Kathryn Dean (ed.), *Politics and the Ends of Identity*, Aldershot: Ashgate, pp. 103–134.

YÜCEL, Müslüm (2006), *Berdel Evlilik İttifakı*, Istanbul: Kesit.

—— (2008), "Evdeki 'Derin' Okul, Mafya Dizileri", *Birikim* (http://www.birikim-dergisi.com/birikim/makale.aspx?mid=437&makale=Evdeki%20%22Derin%22%20Okul,%20Mafya%20Dizileri).

ZEHTABI, Mohammad (1979–1980), *Iran Turkchesinin Sarfi*, Tehran: Aramağan.

—— (1980–1981), *Vayganlı Adem*, Tabriz: Shabistar.

—— (1981–1982), *Ana Dilimizi Nece Yazak?*, Tehran.

ZEMON DAVIS, Natalie (1973), "The Rites of Violence: Religious Riots in Sixteenth century France", *Past and Present*, 59, pp. 51–91.

ZIRING, Lawrence (1999), *Pakistan in the Twentieth Century: A Political History*, Karachi: Oxford University Press.